THE LAST ENGLISHMEN

Also by Deborah Baker

The Convert: A Tale of Exile and Extremism

A Blue Hand: The Beats in India

In Extremis: The Life of Laura Riding

Making a Farm: The Life of Robert Bly

THE
LAST
ENGLISHMEN

LOVE, WAR, AND THE END OF EMPIRE

DEBORAH BAKER

Graywolf Press

Poetry excerpts from "Mountains," "Letter to William Coldstream, Esq.," "Tell Me the Truth About Love," "Memorial for the City," "Palais des Beaux-Artes," and "Everest" © copyright 1930, 1937, 1940, 1952, 1994 by W. H. Auden, renewed. Reprinted by permission of Curtis Brown, Ltd. and Penguin Random House. Unpublished excerpts from the letters and expedition journals of Michael Spender are quoted with the permission of the Estate of Michael Spender; unpublished excerpts from the letters and journals of J. B. Auden are quoted with the permission of Anita Money; quotations from W. H. Auden's letters and his unpublished "Berlin Diary" are quoted with the permission of his executor, Edward Mendelson. Excerpts from "Autumn Journal" first published by Faber and Faber and the unpublished "India Diary" by Louis MacNeice, parts of which appear in *Selected Prose of Louis MacNeice* first published by the Clarendon Press, are quoted with the permission of the Louis MacNeice Estate and the David Higham Agency, Ltd.

This publication is made possible, in part, by the voters of Minnesota through a Minnesota State Arts Board Operating Support grant, thanks to a legislative appropriation from the arts and cultural heritage fund, and a grant from the Wells Fargo Foundation. Significant support has also been provided by Target, the McKnight Foundation, the Lannan Foundation, the Amazon Literary Partnership, and other generous contributions from foundations, corporations, and individuals. To these organizations and individuals we offer our heartfelt thanks.

Published by Graywolf Press
250 Third Avenue North, Suite 600
Minneapolis, Minnesota 55401

www.graywolfpress.org

Published in the United States of America
Printed in Canada

ISBN 978-1-55597-804-4

2 4 6 8 9 7 5 3 1
First Graywolf Printing, 2018

Library of Congress Control Number: 2017953357

Jacket design: Kimberly Glyder

Jacket art: Photograph of John Auden in Karakoram courtesy of Philip Spender

For Lila

I am the last Englishman to rule in India.

JAWAHARLAL NEHRU

CONTENTS

PART III – The Fall of the Gods

CAST OF CHARACTERS

Explorers and the Royal Geographical Society

John Auden, geologist of the Geological Survey of India

Michael Spender, surveyor and mapmaker

Arthur L. Hinks, secretary of RGS and Mount Everest Committee

Eric Shipton, explorer, leader of the 1935 reconnaissance of Everest

Bill Tilman, mountaineer and leader of the 1938 Everest expedition

Bill Wager, Greenland geologist and Everester

Frank Smythe, leader of the 1931 climb of Kamet, Everester

Hugh Ruttledge, leader of the 1933, 1936 Everest expeditions

Sir Francis Younghusband, first president of Mount Everest
Committee, explorer, soldier

English Writers

W. H. Auden, Stephen Spender, Christopher Isherwood,
Louis MacNeice, and George Orwell

London Art Crowd

Nancy Sharp, William Coldstream, and Sonia Brownell,
the "Euston Road Venus"

Calcutta Parichay Adda

Sudhindranath Datta, poet, intellectual, founding editor of
Parichay

Apurba Chanda, school friend of Sudhin's, secretary to Tagore,
civil servant and later secretary to Shaheed Suhrawardy

Rabindranath Tagore, Nobel laureate, patron of *Parichay*

Basanta Kumar Mallik, Oxford flaneur, philosopher, author of the theory of conflict

Hassan Shahid Suhrawardy, professor of art history, Russophile and anti-Bolshevist

Huseyn Shaheed Suhrawardy, rogue brother of Shahid, Muslim League politician

Susobhan Sarkar, professor of art history, Calcutta University

Hirendranath Mukherjee, lecturer in history and political philosophy, Calcutta University

Humphry House, Oxford friend of Susobhan Sarkar, lapsed cleric, professor of literature, Calcutta University

Michael John Carritt, Indian Civil Service officer

Reverend Michael Scott, vicar

Mulk Raj Anand, novelist, Indian nationalist

Protap, Bharat, Minnie, Anila, and Sheila Bonnerjee, grandchildren of W. C. Bonnerjee, first Indian president of Indian National Congress

Lindsay Emmerson, editor of the *Statesman*

Sinbad Sinclair, Burmah Shell executive and husband of Elinor

Jamini Roy, painter

Sarojini Naidu, poet and Congress leader

Secret diarist

Relatives

George Augustus and Constance Rosalie Auden, parents of Bernard, John, and Wystan

Harold and Violet Spender, parents of Michael, Christine, Stephen, and Humphrey

Uncle John Alfred Spender (Aunt May), editor of *Westminster Gazette*, writer on India, uncle to Spender children

Uncle George Ernest Schuster, finance minister of India, uncle to Spender children

Granny Schuster, guardian of Spender children

Erika Haarmann, Michael Spender's German first wife

Margaret Marshall, John Auden's analyst and first wife

Nationalists and Communists, Die Hards and Conservatives

Mohandas Gandhi, leader of the Civil Disobedience campaigns of 1920–22, the 1930 Salt March, the 1942 Quit India Uprising, and the Indian National Congress

Motilal Nehru, leader of the Indian National Congress, father of Jawaharlal

Jawaharlal Nehru, leader of the Indian National Congress

Subhas Chandra Bose, Bengali revolutionary, wayward member of Congress

Muhammad Ali Jinnah, leader of the All India Muslim League

P. C. Joshi, first general secretary of the Communist Party of India

M. N. Roy, founder of the Mexican Communist Party, the Communist Party of India, member of the Comintern

Ben Bradley, secretary, League Against Imperialism, leader of the Communist Party of Great Britain, convicted in Meerut Conspiracy Case

S. S. Mirajkar, member of the Communist Party of India, convicted in Meerut Conspiracy Case

Winston Churchill, former subaltern, Die Hard, prime minister of wartime Britain

Lady Poppy Houston, Die Hard, aviation patroness

Sir John Anderson, governor of Bengal, minister of civil defense of London, member of War Cabinet

Victor Alexander John Hope, 2nd Marquess of Linlithgow, longest-serving viceroy of India, 1936–43

Leo Amery, Secretary of State for India during the war

ACKNOWLEDGMENTS

I first came across the papers of John Bicknell Auden while looking for a way to write about India during World War II. Very few books had looked at the war and the decade that preceded it from the point of view of those for whom the Second World War meant finally getting out from under British rule. From 1926 until 1953 John Auden was a geologist with the Geological Survey of India. Among his papers I found a number of letters from his circle of Bengali friends in Calcutta, as well as from his fellow Himalayan explorers. There were also decades of letters from his younger brother, Wystan. W. H. Auden is so closely identified with the English writers who came of age between the wars that they have come to be known as the "Auden generation."

I had always been curious about W. H. Auden's reasons for staying on in the United States after England declared war on Germany. Auden had firsthand experience of the rise of Hitler and Nazism. He gave speeches and wrote poems and essays about the dangers posed by fascism and what was required to fight it. Inevitably, his failure to return to England when war was declared on September 3, 1939, did not sit well with many of his friends and contemporaries. From Auden's letters to his brother John, I gained a fresh understanding of why he left and why he didn't come back. And though John Auden's Calcutta circle struggled with some of the same questions of political allegiance, manliness, and Englishness as their London-based cohort, as colonial subjects they had a different take on the politics that roiled the 1930s, views that framed how they experienced the war when it finally arrived in Calcutta. So I am deeply indebted to the Berg Collection at the New York Public Library, and the library's archivists, librarians, and support staff. It was Isaac Gewirtz, the Berg's director, who first suggested I take a look at John Auden's papers.

In the course of writing and researching this book a number of titles on India's wartime role appeared; most helpful among them was Yasmin Khan's *The Raj at War* and Srinath Raghavan's *India's War*. Madhusree Mukerjee's earlier *Churchill's Secret War* was also an important source. I am also personally grateful to those who saw to my Indian education with patience. Any list would have to begin with my mother-in-law, Anjali Ghosh, and my late father-in-law, Shailendra Chandra Ghosh. I will always be thankful, too, to my sister-in-law Chaitali Basu and my brilliant niece Malini who read my Parichay adda sections and added page citations from the Bengali sources. Sukanta Chaudhuri, founder of the School of Cultural Texts and Records at Jadavpur University, and editor of Sudhin Datta's unpublished works, was extremely helpful. Supriya Chaudhuri introduced me to Sajni Mukherjee, who, in turn, passed along Humphry House's quirky *I Spy with My Little Eye* and an equally rare copy of *Parichayer-Adda*, translated for me by Gouri Chatterjee. I am grateful to Sunanda K. Datta-Ray for his memories of the Bonnerjee family and to Prasad Ranjan Ray, former home secretary of West Bengal, who helped me access the archives at the Police Museum.

A list of those who helped me with the sections on geology, all eminent geologists of the Himalaya, includes K. S. Valdiya, Shekar Pathak, Rasoul Sorkhabi, and most of all Djordje Grujic, who answered a long list of questions and was subjected to various drafts of my geological sections. Darya Oreshkina made tactful corrections to my chapter on surveying. Finally, the writer and naturalist Emmanuel Theophilus was a superb guide on a trek in the Gangotri region of the Garhwal Himalaya. Raju Koranga, our cook, kept me from losing my footing, and the dour triad, Moni Prasa Joshi, Moni Krishna Kafle, and Tularam, carried inconceivable loads up the steepest, most slippery slopes. One can read a lot about expeditions, but it helps to have a small taste of one.

Foremost among the archivists whose skill, expertise, and knowledge I drew on was Christine Halsall of the Medmenham Collection. She saved me from the sort of errors a nonmilitary person might make. Sue Hodson at the Huntington Library, Rachael Dreyer at the American Heritage Center University of Wyoming, Natalie Zelt at the Harry Ransom Humanities Research Center, Samir Paik at Kolkata's National Library, Dan Mitchell and Mandy Wise at University College London, Colin Harris and Charlotte McKillop-Mash of the Bodleian, Hannah Griffiths at the National Archives at Kew, Julie Parry at the People's History Museum and Antonia Moon of the Indian Office Records at the British Library all answered endless questions or photocopied relevant material. I am also grateful to Julia Wagner, who translated a selection of Erika Haarmann's journals from German.

Anita Money, Philip, Jason, and Jane Spender, and Miranda and Juliet Coldstream allowed me access to their parents' letters, photographs, and writings. Nearly as important but equally impossible to footnote or convey is all that I internalized from Amiya Dev on Sudhindranath Datta, the late Jon Stallworthy on Louis MacNeice, John Sutherland on Stephen Spender, Peter Parker on Christopher Isherwood, and Humphrey Carpenter on W. H. Auden. Richard Davenport-Hines's book *Auden* is a particularly sensitive and lucid look at that poet's protean imagination. I am grateful to Edward Mendelson, Auden's executor and editor of his collected poems, for slogging through the first monumentally long draft.

Sarah Chalfant, my agent, was the first person to say yes. Fiona McCrae at Graywolf Press quickly followed. Between my editors in America, England, and India, I had my own triangulating to do. My tactful and tireless editor Ethan Nosowsky saw me through the briar patch of several drafts with unflappable grace. Mary Byers brought a keen eye to the copy-editing. Juliet Brooke at Chatto & Windus brought another fresh and bracingly sharp set of eyes. Meru Gokhale and Manasi Subramaniam at Penguin Random House in Delhi helped me clarify my more inchoate thoughts. I also had the generous financial support of both the Guggenheim and Whiting Foundations, about which enough can't be said and frankly without which this book wouldn't have been written. To my earliest readers, Adina Hoffman and Deborah Cohen, apologies and thanks for your struggle to see your way to what I was trying and often failing to do.

And for the leg ups, conversations, guest beds, and meals along the way, thank you (in alphabetical order now), Ravi Agrawal, Marisa Atkinson, Partha Chatterjee, Christopher Clark, Nicole Yoko D'Alessandro, Amlan Dasgupta, Rosie Dastgir, Kiran Desai, Katie Dublinski, John Gapper, D. W. Gibson, Lyndall Gordon, Christopher Harper, Edward Hirsch, Courtney Hodell, Pico Iyer, Mukul Kesavan, Melanie Locay, Yana Makuwa, Laura McPhee, Pankaj Mishra, Mary Mount, Prasun Mukherjee, Nandita Palchoudhuri, Cecil Pinto, Elizabeth Rubin, Madhumina Sen, Subrata Sinha, Rahul Srivastava, Michele Stephenson, Jean Strouse, Stella Tillyard, Jeannie, Peter, and Emma Vaughn, Jonathan Westaway, and Steve Woodward.

Finally, I am deeply indebted to my husband, Amitav. I can't imagine my life or my work without him and the books he has written, the meals he has cooked, and the people he has drawn into our lives. As for Lila and Nayan, I am wildly thankful to them for keeping me on my toes.

PROLOGUE

Lahore Refugee Camp,
  Wednesday, September 3, 1947

The end of the Raj would doubtless be accompanied by the pomp and pageantry by which the British Empire had always set great store. Fireworks, marching bands, military parades in full regalia. Vast jostling crowds lining Delhi's Kingsway from Government House to Memorial Arch. No elephants caparisoned in brocade and gold, but solemn oaths administered and new flags raised. All in all it would amount to the biggest story since the signing of the armistice two years before, and far more showy. With that in mind the BBC was sending a film crew to cover the festivities and wanted their man Louis MacNeice to accompany them with an eye to writing a series of radio plays.

But apart from what he'd read of Kipling and Tagore at school, Louis MacNeice knew next to nothing about India. He vaguely remembered a debate about India at the Oxford Union from his student days twenty-some years before, but that was about it. What does India have to do with me, he had asked himself, alarmed at the prospect of traveling all that way. There were other reasons for his reluctance. He didn't really like Indians, for one. And the whole business of swamis really set his teeth on edge. His one Indian friend, a fine-featured writer who favored colorful shirts, had tried to convince him it was the English who concocted this notion of a spiritual India. The great Rabindranath Tagore, an otherwise fine poet, got his mystical cues from them, the man said.

Even so, Louis thought, what was the point of looking at India through Western eyes? He was a poet from Northern Ireland. Who was he to mediate India and England's everlasting quarrel? Destroyed our country and our culture, the Indians said. Developed your country and brought you education, the apologists replied. Divided and ruled, the Indians said. Brought law and order, the English replied. Tyranny. Trusteeship. Our foe. Your friend. On and on it went.

Lastly, what did he know of India's struggle for freedom?

Seven years before, during that first awful winter of the war, Louis had given the idea of freedom some thought. Snowbound and broken-hearted in Ithaca, New York, he'd been torn between sitting the war out in disgust and returning to England to join up.

Was this war, as some said, really being fought for freedom? It certainly hadn't been about freedom for the Republicans in Spain in 1937. And England hadn't come to the defense of the sovereignty of Austrians or the Czechs in 1938. So it had been hard for him to believe that the war was suddenly about the attack on Poland in 1939. For his Cornell University students, India alone justified America's sitting it out. They'd been suckered into enabling the British Empire to see another day during the last war, they said. It wouldn't happen again. Louis found them surprisingly well informed. Though he'd never given India much thought, he had known immediately they were right. The war would not be fought on behalf of freedom for India.

And what did freedom even mean? Freedom for the woman who'd broken his heart meant getting out of a bad marriage without becoming trapped in another one. Was freedom for India like getting out of a bad marriage? Was independence incompatible with love? Or was freedom simply another word for power, including the power of the powerful to decide what a war was being fought for and who would fight it. And yet wasn't he himself part of this elite; hadn't he aspired to a spot at the top? And then there was his suspicion that his worth came at the cost of the less fortunate and his habit of assuming their freedom spelled his own defeat.

In the end Louis concluded that Chamberlain's England was the lesser of two evils. He would return to London and join the Navy. "If one's going to be defiled," he had written a friend, "one may as well keep one's mind out of it."

But he had failed his medical. He'd spent the war writing radio plays for the BBC.

Finally, Louis tried to justify his reluctance to travel to India by telling himself that the world he already knew was confusing enough. Why take on another? Just thinking about India, about freedom, was exhausting. He was *tired* of thinking.

Yet a small voice in his head hadn't let him alone. The earth isn't the moon, the voice said. There is no dark side. One can easily travel to see how the other half lives.

Perhaps, he thought, real freedom wasn't a matter of getting out of things but of getting into them. Perhaps if he stuck a little bit of himself into India, India would stick him back. So he had started reading. He read translations of the Gita and the Vedas. He read Babur on the history of Hindustan and Hume on the Upanishads. He read about the 1905 partition of Bengal, about mass civil disobedience and mass arrests, about viceroys and Government of India acts. He jotted down lines from Tagore, Iqbal, and Kabir in his notebook as well as quotes from Gandhi, Nehru, and Muhammad Ali Jinnah.

He began to think that if Indians had a chance to live freely and independently, perhaps something of value might be learned from them. And maybe a look into their lives would throw some light on his own.

In this way, Louis talked himself into going to India. Then he packed a dinner jacket and rumpled summer suit and caught a flight.

It was only on his arrival at the reception center in Pakistan that Louis MacNeice understood just how little he really knew, not just about India, but about anything. He had never expected *this*. *This* was the kind of thing one read about in newspapers. If *this* was freedom, then perhaps it was possible to have too much of it.

The reception center was west of the Indian border, just outside Lahore in the freshly divided Punjab province. Two weeks after the Independence Day celebrations had ended, Muslim families were still coming through the center's gates, joining the thirty thousand already there. Fearful of what would happen if they stayed in India, these families had run the blood-soaked gauntlet on the road to the border, a biblical-size exodus that stretched to the horizon. For seven years Muhammad

Ali Jinnah, the leader of the Muslim League, had held out for a dream of a Muslim homeland, a new nation he called Pakistan. That dream had ended for many in the nightmare that greeted Louis now.

The first woman he saw had a fixed expression on her face. Someone told him she was looking for her son and by then Louis knew she wouldn't find him. The second woman was holding her child the way a little girl might hold a doll cut open with a penknife. Twenty miles away, in Sheikhupura, the victims were largely Sikhs. Before they could make their escape in the other direction, across the border to India, about fifteen hundred of them had been set upon by Muslims. A good number had been shot, stabbed, speared, clubbed, or set on fire. They lay in a field hospital with eighty beds and one doctor with no medical equipment. Their faces, too, wore a look of puzzled abstraction.

He found the third woman outside the compound walls. She was lying on her back in a gutter with her legs splayed out. Her skirt was covered with blood the color of rust, and an iridescent spiral of flies moved over the spear wound in her side. The scene struck him as something for which the word *tragic* was both too precious and miserably insufficient.

But what other word was there?

The BBC cameraman, used to Louis MacNeice's air of icy indifference, was astonished to see him suddenly come to life, loading a family of Sikhs into a lorry and barking at the Punjab Boundary Force to get them out of there.

From Lahore Louis went to Peshawar in the North-West Frontier Province to meet the eagle-eyed "Frontier Gandhi," Khan Abdul Ghaffer Khan. Imprisoned during the war for his support of Mahatma Gandhi's "Quit India" uprising, Khan had lost control over the frontier tribal areas to Jinnah's Muslim League. Khan told Louis that if Jinnah didn't accede to his demands for an independent Pashtun state, "We will do what we have to do."

As if Pakistan, a nation barely two weeks old, needed a civil war now, too.

Khan was undeniably a personality, Louis noted, and on the frontier personalities appeared to matter. And weapons. A dozen bearded
tribal chiefs from Waziristan had traveled down from the hills to seek
Khan's permission to march on India.

The situation was akin to another era's warring Scots, Louis
supposed, or the blood feuds between Catholics and Protestants in
Ireland. Still, every historical parallel he grasped at felt inadequate.
The dead were now said to be in the hundreds of thousands and the
bloodshed wasn't near over. An ox of a man with a black mustache
and a chest crisscrossed with bandoliers had stood plumb in front of
him and, in compelling and incantatory Pashto, made a cutting gesture across the neck to indicate his plans for the Sikhs and, again with
the cutting gesture, the Hindus, and one last cutting gesture, anyone
who tried to stop him.

On his arrival in Delhi a month earlier, Louis had been astonished
to find the BBC van cheered wherever it went. Even the viceroy of
India was hailed: *Pandit Mountbattenji ki Jai!* A few months before, he
was told, it had been a different story, but on the eve of Independence
he'd seen little evidence of the acrimony he'd been led to expect. It
was hard not to conclude that Indians had been united only in their
hatred of the English and once the English had left they could at last
turn on each other. Nancy might have said that India had been freed
from one bad marriage only to get trapped in another.

The London papers were already gloating; the carnage on both sides
of the Punjab border was proof Indians were unfit for self-government.
But who were we to feel superior? he asked himself. One had only to reflect on the genocides of Europe to be chastened. Was everyone really
so certain that the British bore no responsibility for this? Traveling
to Srinagar, the capital of the princely state of Kashmir, Louis had a
long conversation with the former editor of the Calcutta *Statesman*.
The editor, a liberal soul with a Colonel Blimp's face, promised that if
the violence didn't abate, blame would fall on the British. Britain's sole
justification for two centuries of rule, he said, was that through lofty,
selfless, and balanced administration Britain had unified India. That
had been their mantra.

Gandhi's contribution was far greater, the editor said. Gandhi had made India a nation and given it a spine.

A fortune-teller once told Louis he would never get the thing he most wanted. Back then what he wanted more than anything was Nancy Coldstream. After she refused him, a velvet-like sadness settled over his life. It was Nancy who had once suggested he write a poem about Gandhi. Was she the reason he had come? Was she the small voice in his head? And was he now destined to spend the time he had left as a competent writer of radio plays? Was that all life now held out for him?

After watching Gandhi address the crowds at Birla House, Louis MacNeice would have a small epiphany. If nothing else, he would return from India with an awareness of the vanity of such questions, vanity in the Ecclesiastes "vanity of vanities" sense.

From Srinagar, Louis rode ponies 14,000 feet up into the mountains, an expedition he referred to, in a private joke with the BBC man accompanying him, as "The Ascent of C3." Looking out over the undulating ranges of the Himalaya he could just make out Nanga Parbat. Once upon a time Nanga Parbat had been Nazi Germany's Schicksalsberg, its mountain of destiny, just as Mount Everest had once been England's. A vanity if there ever was one. With its white mane of snow, the mountain looked like the tiny head of a lion, one that seemed to float between the clouds and the horizon, like a spirit eternally trapped between heaven and earth.

PART I

To Live as on a Mountain

I wanted to be as great as Caesar
Great
As great as Caesar
I wanted love
Nothing without trying you know
To fly the equator
Control a Blenheim bomber
And floundering
I wanted admiring eyes in a restaurant

JOHN AUDEN, "1938–1939 JOURNAL"

Hunt the lion, climb the peak
No one guesses you are weak.

W. H. AUDEN, "1929 BERLIN JOURNAL"

– CHAPTER 1 –

The Lakes

Skelgill Farm below Cat Bells, Newlands Valley,
Cumberland, August–September 1917

The path from the farmhouse door led past a clump of blue willow herb, through a green wicket gate, and down a slope that fell away into the valley. Seen from the children's bedroom window, Skiddaw's broad shoulders presided over Newlands Valley like a benevolent pater-familias. Cat Bells, rising directly behind the house, was more suit-able for small legs. On their arrival on August 2, 1917, the children left their mother behind to race each other to the top. Michael, the eldest, passed by his father and Miss Cox, their nanny, on the way up. Arms raised in victory, he gave a shout of triumph as he reached the summit while Stephen, his younger brother, straggled up behind him. This was the first of many mountains Michael Spender would climb.

"Daddy! What's that noise like a motor bike in the bracken?" Humphrey had called out three days later, more accustomed to the sounds made by soldiers than the sound of crickets. Humphrey was the baby of the family; his nickname was "Little Mouse."

"Look how ripe my hands are getting!" Stephen shouted, extending his berry-stained fingers toward his mother, Violet.

With war rationing, berry picking was considered a patriotic duty and the three Spender boys approached the task like little soldiers. Stephen wanted to become a naturalist; he kept a collection of yellow-striped caterpillars in matchboxes. When not picking bilberries, he was weaving back and forth over the footpath trying to catch butterflies with the net his father had bought him in Keswick the day before. His sister, Christine, had surprised everyone by hooking a large pike in Derwentwater. She screamed and dropped the rod, but her father had jumped up and landed it for lunch. It had been ages since they'd had fish.

With his golden locks and bright blue eyes, Michael was his mother's favorite. After a year of piano lessons his music teacher told Violet she had nothing left to teach him. His first year at Gresham's had been a brilliant success. Yet since his return from boarding school, Violet had become concerned about a change in his manner. He had taken to a rather slangy way of talking, setting himself apart from his siblings with a schoolboy swagger.

Even so, she couldn't help but admire his remarkable appreciation of nature.

Michael directed everyone to stop, turn around, and take in the way a beam of sunlight was breaking through a bank of clouds. It brushed the flank of the facing mountain and traveled down the valley, striking a clutch of farm buildings among the trees and lighting them up with an irrepressible whiteness.

On such a day, it was hard for Violet to believe there was a war on.

Not long after Violet's death four years later, Christine and Stephen would vie to see who could recall the most about that summer of 1917. Humphrey had been too young to remember much. And Michael, well, he was something of a mystery to them. But for Christine and Stephen the holiday not only marked the early end of their childhood innocence but also represented England, at its dearest and most glorious. Christine remembered how the rain had left the raspberries in a copse of larch looking like tiny ruby-encrusted cushions. Stephen would describe how slugs, sliding through tiny rivulets of water, looked like barges on the Thames and how the sound of his father reading poetry came in through their bedroom window, as if Skiddaw itself were reciting. But at the center of those fairytale days was their mother, Violet, then twenty-seven years old. Stephen was tireless in trying to unravel the tiny knots of feelings his scattered memories of her evoked.

Once celebrated for her flushed Pre-Raphaelite beauty, Violet Schuster had been sheltered by family wealth. While her brothers followed their father, a King's Counsel, into the sober field of banking, she nurtured a love of poetry. But after four children in four years— Michael was then ten, Christine nine, Stephen eight, and Humphrey seven—Violet in 1917 was no longer the ingénue she'd once been. Poetry hadn't prepared her for the household chaos brought about by four young children and a husband often called away on business.

Before Violet had time to reckon what the war might mean, her youngest brother had been killed at the first battle at Ypres. From that moment the battlefield was never far from her thoughts and each week it came closer. The back garden of their house in Norfolk received the first of the German bombs to fall on English soil. A dud. Soldiers had invaded her home, carrying her children to dugouts below the cliffs while it was safely detonated. A Zeppelin came so close to the roof, she feared it might be scraped off. The fields between the house and the bluff filled up with the tents of billeted troops. Cavalry officers in bright uniforms thundered around on horseback. There were cease-less drills: "Present arms! Form fours! Eyes front! Eyes right!" The sound of guns reverberated in her small chest, sending her to the edge of collapse. Her black eyes acquired a hunted look.

In the summer of 1917 it had taken several days in the Lake District before Violet realized that lowing cattle and the drone of haymowing machines had replaced the sound of guns. Yet watching families with picnic baskets filled with sandwiches, she could think only of the insufficiency of the wall that lay between them and the terror overwhelming Europe. Everyone else might pretend all was well, she fretted, but few really dared think of all those boys going off to die in France. No one, not even her husband, Harold, could say why. Being part German, Violet didn't recognize the enemy the newspapers de-scribed with such shocking venom. She knew only that something had gone terribly wrong. "Our laughing children, all too young as yet / to know French fields with English blood are wet," she wrote.

On clear evenings Violet and Harold would sit out in deck chairs reading the Romantic poets and admiring Dame Nature, wearing all her jewels, as Harold liked to say. Harold's engagement with his off-spring involved piggyback rides, roaring like a lion, and a daily in-quiry as to whether they had done their little duty. But after ten days of steady rain he became eager to catch up with the progress of the war at his London club. One day before he left, the sun broke through the clouds. Violet got up early, leaving Harold snoring in bed.

Miss Cox was already in the kitchen making sardine and egg sandwiches. After breakfast, Violet hustled the family down to Derwentwater, directing the procession of children, baskets, and thermoses of tea, into the rowboat. Settling in a lakeside cove Violet was a blur of high spirits, flirting shamelessly with Harold, calling him her darling Buffalo, hanging on his neck and covering him with kisses.

For Christine looking back on that day there was something desperate in her mother's behavior. She believed the lakeside picnic marked the beginning of the end.

"But she seemed so well on the day of the picnic!" Stephen protested.

"That's what she pretended," Christine said. "Pretended to him, pretended to us, pretended to herself: *Because she didn't want the operation.*" Violet's death was attributed to a botched hysterectomy.

"You worked this all out yourself?" Stephen asked.

In the summer of 1917 Michael was still Harold's "little man," the one he chose to accompany him to Keswick to mail important letters. To his siblings, Michael was a demigod. They never questioned his right to pronounce upon their shortcomings or his instruction on the most efficient way to row a boat. In Harold's absence, Michael took over the drills. When the sun returned, he marched his brothers and sister off to collect butterflies while he and his mother walked to the end of Newlands Valley to climb the ridge.

Michael had been impatient to reach the saddle that day, eager for a sight of Borrowdale Valley on the other side. Violet, finding the sodden slopes slippery without hobnailed boots, fell farther and farther behind. At five o'clock she had insisted they stop for tea, though the pass was at most fifteen minutes away. Michael ate his bread and jam while studying the map, loudly insistent that he was not giving up hope of a view. Violet poured a mother's worries into her holiday journal.

When Stephen asked why Wordsworth had become a poet, she knew how to answer him. But Michael's questions were those of a stranger. How many tons of water come over the weir by the Penrith pencil factory in one minute? She hadn't the faintest idea. If the earth were flat instead of round would there be a horizon? She'd never wondered. Is it possible to determine the weight of Skiddaw? Whatever for?

A passage from a memoir by a poet all of London had been talking about seemed to directly address Violet's concerns about Michael. She wrote it down.

"I now clearly see that the mistake is to judge boys by the standard of grown-ups," Rabindranath Tagore had written. As a young man Tagore had been plagued by a nameless melancholy. Yet he had gone on to great fame and was now considered a font of Eastern wisdom. In his memoirs he drew on his own example and cautioned anxious parents not to "forget that a child is quick and mobile like a running stream; and . . . any touch of imperfection need cause no harm, for the speed of the flow is itself the best corrective." Violet's worries quieted.

But a few days later a sleepless night found her staring out her window at the moon. A letter from Harold said the earliest he could get away was the coming Saturday. Violet's thoughts, like the waterwheel at the pencil factory, tumbled fast and furious. After the boys left to go fishing, she'd unburdened herself to Miss Cox.

She'd ruined her husband's life. Marriage had held Harold hostage to her fears, her headaches and spells of weakness. Harold had once been a great climber. He climbed monuments, statues, chimneys, and mountains. But his love for her was destroying him. He would be better off alone. If she died he would be free. What should she do?

Miss Cox, a sensible woman, had pointed out that there were plenty of opportunities for climbing in the Lake District.

"You have missed my point *entirely*," Violet cried. "I was speaking *metaphorically*."

Christine, listening on the other side of the door, hadn't entirely understood what her mother meant by "metaphorically" but she'd known even then it was important. After Violet's death she tried to explain this to Stephen.

"Mummy was saying that she'd lost Daddy and poor Coxie was trying to reassure her."

"How could she lose him?" Stephen asked, still not getting the metaphor business.

"She said that he was a man of action, who needed excitement and adventure."

"She told Coxie all this?"

"Yes but Coxie made the great mistake of taking Mummy seriously. She said, very sweetly and humbly: 'But if Mr. Spender wants action and adventure, might he not go fight in the war?'"

"And what did Mummy say to that?"

"She was absolutely furious. She shouted at Coxie: 'How dare you have the impertinence to answer me like that.' And then Mummy got out of bed, flew across the room and shook the old woman so hard her spectacles flew off and false teeth popped out. I had to run into the room to stop her."

"You never told me all this," Stephen said.

If the act of pitting the steel of an ice ax into the icy white rump of Dame Nature was a metaphor, Harold missed it. Coming upon his wife writing a poem, in a sea of papers and cross-outs, he saw a woman possessed. It worried him. He believed poetry, like music and art, had to be rationed. He made a point of leaving concerts at intervals, and never spent more than half an hour looking at pictures in the National Gallery. When he returned to the Lakes from London he took the children on a long hike, leaving Violet under a nurse's care.

The mist made it easier to believe they were so high up, the clouds were below them. The path became a knife-edge arête high in the Swiss Alps. Unless they were roped together, Harold told them, one careless step might send them plummeting to their deaths. Stephen, who suffered from nosebleeds and had a fear of heights, distracted himself by noticing how the scraggy lines of his father's neck collected at his collar like sedimentary layers of rock. With his snowy hair capping the summit of his head, his father seemed more mountain than man.

Why climb mountains? Harold asked them. Why seek to scale impossible heights, reflect on the Great Questions? Whence the spirit of adventure? After thirty years of public life, Harold had a parliamentarian's love of rhetorical questions and a Victorian notion of what constituted a manly pursuit. Climbing mountains was paramount among them.

That is what all must ponder, he would say, looking at their up-turned faces before turning to narrow his gaze on some distant prospect. One's entire life can be spent asking why, he continued, as if speaking to himself, while pretending to whack ice steps at his feet and tighten the rope at his waist. As a man of action, Harold wasn't truly interested in *why*.

After Oxford, Harold had written for a string of Liberal newspapers and was a much-sought-after dinner party guest. He saw himself as a Liberal crusader. Good-humored rants against vested interests were a staple. He often found himself resigning his position on principle, before embarking on a Continental climbing holiday. Unusual for Fleet Street, Harold had a great many principles.

When war was declared Harold had just turned fifty. He took on the self-appointed duty of preparing the Sheringham Home Guard for a possible invasion, mustering a force of five thousand. He spent nights tramping up and down the bluff until he was nearly bayoneted by British soldiers on patrol. Still, it was hard for Harold not to compare his war with that of his elder brother, Alfred. In weekly Downing Street meetings with Prime Minister H. H. Asquith, Alfred, the editor of the *Westminster Gazette*, was kept abreast of the true conditions on the Western Front and prevailed upon not to publish any of it. Yet when Harold's idol, David Lloyd George, supplanted Asquith as prime minister, Harold had been left to sit in the lounge of the National Liberal Club waiting for a call that never came. The envelopes from his clipping service thinned. He would not have a good war.

That fall every day would bring news of another raid, and when they were over Violet would be hollowed out with terror. In October a package from Harrods arrived—three sets of matching brown corduroy knickerbockers, brown stockings, and brown mercerized cotton jerseys with blue cuffs and collars. Violet liked to dress her children like dolls, forcing her boys into stiff Eton collars, patent leather dancing pumps, and gaiters that cut into the backs of their knees.

But Michael now refused to wear such outfits and hated being kissed. Soon Stephen, too, would go to Gresham's and have his hair close cropped. Were the trenches going to swallow all her boys before the war ended? In the years that remained to her, Violet left it to Harold to deal with the war and the doctor to handle her health. She fussed over velveteen jackets or took to her bed, consumed by fears of going mad.

Harold's London of gas lamps and hansom cabs, frock coats, five-course meals, and the two-party system would not survive the war. After Violet's death, he became the one having to appear, hat in hand, before Granny Schuster, begging her to cover his overdrafts. He would travel and give dinner speeches on the prime ministers he had known, but it was his brother Alfred who was appointed to the Milner Mission in 1919, Alfred who would cover the Paris Peace Conference the same year. And it was Violet's brother George who would receive the Military Cross and the Commander of the Order of the British Empire, George Ernest Schuster who would oversee the family fortune that sustained them all.

Sometime between the summer of 1917 and his mother's death in 1921, Michael realized that both his parents were irrational. They'd had too many children. They couldn't keep servants or run an efficient household. Once he understood this, he began to sit out his father's speeches in stony silence. He walked glumly ahead during Harold's climbing performances on Hampstead Heath while Stephen, angling for the newly open seat of favorite son, egged Harold on. No longer his father's "little man," Michael became "the bear with the sore head." He had his own latchkey, coming and going as he pleased, not answering to anyone. To keep himself free of his family's entanglements, he used the language of scientific expertise, exaggerated for effect, to build a wall around himself.

Michael shared this detachment with his lab partner at Gresham's, an ungainly and freakishly pale boy named Wystan Auden. Wystan and Michael were the school scientists; their names were posted on the honors board side by side. In 1925 both would win science scholarships to Oxford. Michael's arrogance didn't put Wystan off; his knowledge of steam power engines sat nicely with Wystan's fascination with the beam engines, pithead gear, and water turbines used in mining ventures. Indeed, Wystan's friendship with Michael was not unlike his alliance with his elder brother, John, who left Cambridge the year

Wystan and Michael began at Oxford. Where Michael and his brother Stephen would become perfect foils, apt to exaggerate their differences or use the existence of the other to define their own, Wystan and John, though nearly three years apart in age, had more in common.

Fatherless for the five war years and living with a succession of aunts, they discussed pyrite, smectite, ammonite, and coprolite, marlstone, carstone, *Carbonicola*, and igneous with the singleminded passion of adolescent boys eager to escape a home life ruled by a high-strung mother. They made boyhood expeditions to exhausted limestone quarries, walking down narrow gauge rail beds overgrown with melancholy thistle. They explored the Blue-John Cavern near Bradwell in Derbyshire and derelict mines of lead and gold. Such places seemed to promise an underground passage to a time when England was not the ponderous imperial power they were taught about in school but a vast swamp, a rain forest teeming with exotic ferns and horsetails.

Though the bond between John and Wystan was not without rivalry, it was steadfast. They kept no secrets from each other. They shared everything, including a dimly grasped sense that something formidable was expected of them, a task that might redeem the great blood sacrifice of the war. So how might they prove themselves worthy? By John's final year at Cambridge, his oldest brother, Bernard, had already left for Canada. Had there been money for a stake, John might have chosen Africa. Had he had business connections, a stomach for trade, and a readiness to start at the bottom he might have tried that, but here too he was lacking. Those were the options for young men with impeccable educations and fertile imaginations, but few practical notions and no independent means.

And then there was India.

CHAPTER 2

The Steamship and the Spinning Wheel

SS City of Venice, *at Sea,*
October–November 1926

In October 1926 John Bicknell Auden arrived at the landing stage at Birkenhead, near Liverpool, a trunk by his side and a steamship ticket for Bombay in his pocket. Having left university with a first in geology, he was en route to Calcutta to take a post at the Geological Survey of India. Before he knew what was happening, a slight figure stepped out smartly from a long line of Indian porters, his feet bare in black slippers and talking excitedly in a way an English sailor never would. Suddenly, his trunk was atop this man's embroidered red cap and he was left to watch it sail away, as if his belongings had acquired a life of their own and had no further need of him.

The scene in the hallways of the *City of Venice* just then was pure chaos. Mailbags filled with Christmas presents bound for Australia were being crammed haphazardly in storage rooms on the lower decks, while innumerable public school boys crowded in to the first-class cabins, heading off to join business concerns in eastern ports they would be hard pressed to find on a map. When the ship got under way they would be needlessly fussed over by young wives going out to join husbands in Siam, Ceylon, and Singapore. Eyeing the goings-on, older Empire hands were reminded of their own maiden voyages.

At the Marseilles dock fine-featured men in silk waistcoats with matching turbans followed a procession of enormous trunks up the gangway. There was always a royal entourage or two on steamships bound for Bombay. Nizams or rajas returning to their palaces and princely states, flush with Paris purchases, were often accompanied by trunks heavy with pearls, gold, and brocades, with perhaps a sparkling new Daimler in the hold. In the lounge they spoke of politics with the knowingness of Westminster wags, but it was their changes of costume that were most remarked upon at dinner.

A scrum of high-spirited English ICS officers, returning from their first furloughs home, also drew the attention of the diners. In the aftermath of the 1914–18 war, recruitment to the Indian Civil Service had practically halted. The Secretary of State for India had devised a new pitch, urging idealistic young Englishmen to go to India to witness the final triumph of England's great mission. Though no one would ever have said so, it was as if the deadliest war in human history required an absolution of equal scale in India. Unlike the war their fathers fought, India was an adventure to feel good about. Enlistment surged.

At Port Said, as if by prearranged signal, everyone hauled out enormous pith helmets, freshly whitened with pipe clay, to protect their eyes from the glare of the starboard sun in the Gulf of Suez. All at once, a hundred singing Egyptians emerged from a fleet of lateen-rigged sailing boats to pour baskets of coal into the ship's side. While Gali-Gali men boarded to perform magic tricks for baksheesh, packages bound for the African interior were offloaded and passengers disembarked for a brief tour. Touts would have seen in John Auden's large, pale presence a beacon of wealth. Men in long white dresses would have surrounded him, hawking pornographic postcards, belly dancing venues, and boxes of Turkish delight.

The ship entered the canal at nightfall. The bronze statue of Dr. Ferdinand de Lesseps, right hand hailing welcome, left hand holding a map, glowed as the sun set. For reasons no one recalled, it was considered bad form to dress for dinner once the canal had been reached. That night the groaning steam whistles and chugging of trains along the canal likely kept John awake and tossing restlessly in his cabin. The next morning khaki shorts replaced trousers and the matrons on board became slightly more la-di-dah, exclaiming over the deep indigo green of the Red Sea, or the distant blue moors of Somaliland's coast. Their husbands had also come to life, given to summoning stewards with a stentorian cry of "Boy!" By the time the ship reached Aden, the desert air smelling of incense and camel, newly minted Indian officers of the Indian Civil Service had noted the change in manner.

But John Auden hadn't changed. He was more at ease watching lascars swab the deck with Dettol than raising toasts in the smoking lounge with strangers. Extremely conscious of his newly exposed knock-knees, he remained his unalterably awkward twenty-two-year-old self. John was nicknamed "Dodo" at school, a name that captured a handsome but ungainly appearance, a sepulchral air of gloom, and the unerring cruelty of schoolboys. He cultivated a casual air to camouflage his shyness, but he was trapped by the paleness of his skin. If teased or scolded he would flush to the roots of his white-blond hair, pleasing his tormentors no end.

As a child his sensitivity was such that there had been no escaping Wystan was their mother's favorite, chewed fingernails, appalling table manners, and untied shoes notwithstanding. Bernard, the eldest, was a peaceable fellow and didn't seem to mind, but with John it hurt. Plump and cheeky, Wystan treated his brothers' disfavor as his good luck. He always got to ride pillion. He sang church hymns in the bath at the top of his voice. He reveled in the scatological. John could not fathom how Wystan managed to be so coddled and adored, though he never ever ceased trying. He lacked his younger brother's cherubic command, his easy way with words. On a holiday in Wales just before the war Wystan, six years old to John's disbelieving nine, was carried most of the way up Cader Idris.

It was on another Welsh holiday that John first became interested in geology. His father, a medical man of wide and varied interests, would have explained to him how the earliest geologists delineated the Cambrian, Ordovician, and Silurian epochs from the fossils they found in the stone of the Welsh hills. John became an avid collector. He was ten when his father left for the war, Bernard fourteen, and Wystan only seven. Though the credo "Live as on a mountain" was carved in Greek on a plaque outside his study, George Augustus Auden's service as a medic had soon quenched his appetite for adventure. For all the family's scrambles in bracken and gorse, Dr. Auden was more at home among books.

The Audens had wrapped themselves in a weave of ideas set permanently at cross-purposes: a belief in science and rationality as well as a deep and sustaining piety, liberal views tempered by donnish restraint. Egalitarian, they nonetheless kept a coachman, a Swiss nanny, two maids, and a cook. By the time John left for India, the upper-middle professional class to which his family belonged had begun to unravel. The trickle of revelations that followed the end of the war, the accounts of secret treaties and false propaganda undid it further. Those like Dr. Auden who survived the war unscathed were too benumbed to fully acknowledge the scale of the disaster.

In this stunned silence a generation of young Indians found their voice. The news, still only half grasped, of Lenin's revolution in Russia riveted them. And though they weren't entirely sure what to make of Gandhi, his Non-Cooperation campaigns of 1919–22 awakened them further. Their parents had left their positions as civil servants, solicitors, doctors, and educators in service to the Raj to protest the imposition of laws enabling the viceroy to convict political cases without juries and imprison without trials. Invisible to their peers at Oxford and Cambridge, these young men began to ask themselves: did Western civilization entail anything beyond these perpetual bloody wars over colonies? England needed an empire to entice its young men to leave, goading them into ruling over others by tarting it up as the stamp of honor, duty, and good intentions.

They knew better.

Stowed in a trunk in John's second-class stateroom was a pamphlet, *The Cinematograph Record of the Mount Everest Expedition of 1922*. He'd picked it up at a school lecture given by a dashing young mountaineer named George Mallory. Mallory's 1922 expedition was the first ever undertaken to reach the top of the highest mountain in the world. The lecture was accompanied by a screening of footage taken on Everest and the daunting mountainscape surrounding it. Accustomed to the rounded hills of the Lakes and the rocky fells of the northern Pennines where no peak reached 1,000 meters, John had been deeply impressed by the idea of mountains seven or eight times higher. What accounted for such phenomenal heights? When did they arise? Two years later, during the summer following John's first year at Cambridge, Mallory and his climbing partner, Sandy Irvine, made another attempt on Everest only to suddenly disappear 800 vertical feet from the summit. Their bodies had never been found.

The 1922 and 1924 expeditions had come in the long aftermath of the war. The hope then was that by reaching the summit a traumatized nation would find the perfect Englishman, and through him the perfect means, to memorialize all the lives lost. Instead, in George Mallory England was landed with yet another martyr to exalt in the florid language that now came all too easily from the pulpits (Irvine's death didn't seem to count as much). So alongside a trunkful of books and belongings, John Auden was traveling to India with a secret ambition. He wanted to succeed where Mallory had failed.

But here, too, was the question of money.

Launches flying the Union Jack greeted the SS *City of Venice* in Bombay harbor, reminding those venturing east for the first time that there really was such a thing as the British Empire. If the ICS officers on board burst out singing the verse chorus of "Rule, Britannia!" John's voice wasn't among them. He regarded the empire much like some family heirloom that has outlasted its usefulness, as relevant to him as his family's descent from John of Gaunt (a point of maternal pride). As a scientist, he imagined himself aloof from the fusty paperwork of British rule, the petty snobberies of bungalow life.

But then here it was: Malabar Hill catching the first light, the Gateway to India on its narrow jetty. Only the viceroy and a handful of extremely important officials were allowed to pass through it. All else scurried around, trunks once again leading the way. What residential buildings John saw were in the style of Kensington, only shabbier. The air was suffused with an unidentifiable but not unpleasant smell.

It is at this point that a newcomer's impressions will outrun any ability to keep track of them, and John would have been no exception. He let himself be hurried along to the oriental-looking Taj Mahal Hotel where waiters in turbans swanned between tables serving tea on the veranda.

There were few words to describe the circus before him. The infernal hubbub sounded as if a riot were under way. There were men in loincloths and men in frock coats. There were dozens of children, some handsomely decked out, others stark naked. An eye might light on the unexpected beauty of an apricot saree against nearly black skin or on the line of motorcars and shuttered horse-drawn carriages competing to make their way through the streets. Every veranda held a crowd, every window a curious face. Then there was the wretchedness: a one-legged beggar, a half-dressed old woman with a flyblown baby, a fingerless leper, hands trailing bandages, all of them trying, winningly or soulfully, to catch his eye. At the next table a young woman might titter nervously while a matron looked on in frozen alarm. Perhaps John dropped his gaze in embarrassment, his journal open but empty.

Two days hence the director of the Geological Survey of India will welcome John Auden at Calcutta's Howrah station. The instructions John will receive will be the same as those meted out to other new arrivals, at other rail termini across the country. Between dawn and dusk he must never venture outside without a solar topee on his head. And he must never befriend an Indian, give way to an Indian, or let any Indian imagine that he knows something about India, indeed about anything at all, that he doesn't. By the end of his first day John will be outfitted for camp life and put up in the United Services Club until he leaves for the field. After a week upcountry, he will abandon the preposterous topee. He will realize that most of what he has been told, like most of what he has purchased, is useless or absurd, like the lines and props for a play whose run is long over. And before his first month is out he will ask himself for the first time if India is the right place for him.

But for now his train trundles slowly east, toward the shimmering Deccan Plateau.

Satyagraha Ashram, Banks of the Sabarmati River,
*　　outside Ahmedabad, March 1926*

Earlier that year Michael Spender's uncle had made the same sea journey to India. Alfred Spender had attended the 1911 Imperial Durbar in Delhi marking the coronation of George V as king and emperor fifteen years before. The ruling viceroy, Lord Curzon, had praised the book on India he had written on his return. Alfred now had it in mind to write another, monitoring how far India had progressed in the fifteen years since. His wife accompanied him. Aunt May prided herself on her deep understanding of India. It took her no more than a glance to assess any "Oriental" she came across. Every morning over breakfast, she shared her Night Thoughts with her husband. Long married by then, he only half listened.

For Alfred the British Raj was rooted in a steadfast Liberal doctrine: once India had imbibed the great ideas of liberal democracy and scientific enlightenment, once it had risen above its backwardness and superstition, it would be welcomed into the family of the British Commonwealth, taking its place as a dominion alongside Canada, Australia, and the like. This lofty prospect never failed to inspire him.

But Gandhi's Non-Cooperation Movement had taken place since his last visit. Hundreds of thousands of Indians had foresworn British goods and taken up—of all things—spinning. In less than a year the imperium was brought to the brink of collapse. It was only after some hotheads set fire to a police station that Gandhi finally called a stop to what, in Alfred's view, he had so calamitously begun.

The Government of India Act of 1919 had also been ratified since Alfred's last visit. A new constitution had been drawn up mandating that certain ministries in the provincial assemblies be entrusted to Indian ministers. Anything touching on finance or security would, however, be off limits. And any British governor could veto any legislation emerging from the assemblies he deemed troubling. The 1919 act also established the Central Legislative Assembly in Delhi where elected and appointed Indian officials might work hand in glove with the viceroy to learn the craft of ruling India.

To Alfred's mind this elaborate power-sharing arrangement between British officials and Indian ministers, called a dyarchy, was the real news and constituted a monumental step forward on India's path toward dominion status. But the Indian members in Delhi had recently staged a walkout—a dismaying setback. How would Indians ever learn to rule themselves if they refused to partner with the viceroy?

Gandhi, Alfred knew, had wanted no part of the 1919 act. Released in 1924 after serving two years in prison for sedition, Gandhi had retired to his ashram and washed his hands of politics. Only now could

Delhi high officials admit to Alfred that while the Non-Cooperation Movement was under way, Gandhi had wielded more power than any man since the Buddha. Yet while in Delhi Alfred had heard rumors that Gandhi had objected to the walkout of the assembly. Had Gandhi changed his mind? Did he now understand that England only wanted what was best for India? This was the question that had brought Alfred and May to Gandhi's ashram. While the departing viceroy considered Gandhi a spent force, Alfred had noted that none of India's other nationalist leaders dared make a move without consulting him. Indeed, the incoming viceroy would soon discover Gandhi remained a man to be reckoned with.

When Alfred and May arrived, Gandhi was in the middle of being weighed. To repair a rift between ashram factions, Alfred's fixer told him, the Mahatma had pursued one of his fasts a bit too zealously. This news was imparted in a matter-of-fact manner, leaving him no opportunity to inquire further. Alfred supposed Gandhi undertook fasts when things went wrong in an effort to put them right again. He tried to imagine the present British prime minister, the patrician Stanley Baldwin, refusing his food and turning his face to the wall in response to a threatened strike.

Alfred's thoughts were interrupted by the arrival of the man himself, cutting a hunched but sprightly path to a low wooden desk covered with books. He had hoped for an intimate tête-à-tête, but a half circle of adoring devotees settled cross-legged around him. Alfred got straight to the point.

Was it true that he considered the withdrawal of Indian members a mistake?

A mistake? Gandhi repeated. Perhaps.

Many in Congress felt that Gandhi's calling off of his Non-Cooperation Movement had been a mistake. Motilal Nehru, a prosperous Kashmiri barrister and Congress leader, was one. His Harrow- and Cambridge-educated son, Jawaharlal, along with Subhas Chandra Bose, a young firebrand of the All India Youth Congress, agreed. Though Motilal had initially embraced participation in the legislative councils mandated by the 1919 act, it was he who had orchestrated the walkout, calling for a new constitutional convention. His son wanted to go further.

Jawaharlal Nehru and Subhas Bose called for immediate *Purna Swaraj*—
complete independence.

Wasn't politics made up of mistakes? Gandhi continued, as if defending his own decision to suspend his Non-Cooperation Movement.
If they are honest mistakes, then there is something to be learned
from them. Motilal Nehru has sacrificed a great deal in service to his
country; he has given up his expensive cars and let his magnificent
gardens go to seed. If Motilal is wrong about the walkout, and I am by
no means saying Motilal is, he has earned the right to be.

It was answers like these that tied British officialdom in knots.
Alfred was undaunted. Why was every British proposal to move forward on constitutional reform greeted with suspicion? Was not the
1919 act tangible proof of His Majesty's Government's good intentions?
Alfred assured Gandhi that the king regarded the prospect of India's
reaching full political maturity with cheerful resignation. Yet every proposal was met with hostility and fantastic notions of English duplicity.

I can very well understand why it might seem so to you, Gandhi
replied.

During the Great War India had suffered more fatalities than any
of the dominions. In recognition of the one million Indians who had
fought and the tens of thousands killed, Britain had pledged India
would be rewarded with self-government. Instead, there had been a
crackdown on seditionists (Gandhi foremost).

As for the Government of India Act of 1919, it hadn't taken Motilal
Nehru very long to realize that the bureaucracy could be finessed
so that anything sensitive was withheld from Indian members.
Proposed policies were left unfunded or quietly blocked without the
viceroy or the British governors even having to exercise a veto. Apart
from an increase in the number of files labeled secret, the exercise of
power remained where it had always been, in the hands of the eleven
British governors of the eleven Indian provinces, the viceroy, and the
Secretary of State for India in London. By demanding a new constitutional conference, Motilal had simply drawn back the curtain to
reveal the puppetry.

Gandhi turned Alfred's query on its head. Weren't the British just as
quick to cast aspersions, to impute equally impure motives to Indians?

Alfred bore down, zeroing in instead on the true obstacle to progress: the inability of Hindus and Muslims to see eye to eye on anything.

This was a ritual invocation. Indeed, even Alfred despaired when he heard it coming. He wrote of sitting for nearly an hour while a British high official insisted that no concessions could possibly be made to the "Hindu dominated" Congress Party without alienating the nascent All India Muslim League, the organization founded to protect the rights and advance the interests of India's minority Muslim community.

Yet here Alfred was, sitting in a room with Gandhi, making precisely the same argument. He was astute enough to realize that Gandhi sat through it with more patience than he had.

Tensions between the Hindu and Muslim communities were greatly exaggerated, Gandhi replied calmly. He went on to suggest that England had a hand in stirring the pot.

Alfred vociferously objected.

Yet Gandhi never seemed to lose his easy and friendly manner. With the sounds of spinning continuing without ebb, he pivoted neatly back to his main line of argument.

I personally do not hold any unfriendly feelings toward Englishmen. Just as with Indians, there are good ones and bad ones. But as an Indian I can think only of India and her suffering. Had British rule brought happiness I would not complain. But, foreign rule has put a stake in the heart of India's rural economy. With the flood of textiles from Lancashire mills, Indian weavers in the millions have become landless peasants. Where the peasant was once self-sufficient, he is now dependent, poor, and unhappy.

Even the Great War had failed to puncture Alfred's passionate belief in the inevitability of progress. His conviction that India's present was an improvement on a far darker past was sharpened by a near desperate certainty that her future was destined to be even rosier. Alfred spent the rest of the interview struggling to propose an English remedy for India's afflictions. His new book would require just this sort of ennobling vision of India's bright prospects and England's guiding hand in them. He had yet to settle on a title.

Gandhi brushed his suggestions aside.

To appeal to the masses, I must think of something simple. Like spinning. Every member of my ashram, no matter how accomplished, is directed to spend part of every day at the wheel. Village-based industry will secure India's economic independence—*swadeshi*, self-sufficiency through locally produced goods—not mass manufacturing.

Alfred was only half listening.

Ranigunj Coalfields, Burdwan District,
*   outside Asansol, Bengal, 1927–1928*

John Auden's first assignment took him to the coalfields of Ranigunj, one hundred miles northeast of Calcutta. A successor to the "Coal Committee" of the British East India Company, the Geological Survey of India's mission on its 1851 founding was to field-map the Bengal coalfields, the Black Country of India. This remit was soon expanded when an ambitious director argued it was not possible to find further coal reserves without first mapping the underlying geographical structures of the entire subcontinent. This epic undertaking was duly approved. New recruits, however, began with six months of fieldwork at Ranigunj with a month off in a hill station to write their report.

Once a scrub forest infested with bandits, Ranigunj was then a landscape of smoking chimneys, winding towers, and wheels silhouetted against the sky. In the course of mapping a thirty-meter coal seam John hired porters and shot jungle fowl. Bullock carts carried him, his kit, and equipment from place to place. Pit mines worked by tribal colliers with blackened faces surrounded him. Santhals, Mundas, and Kols lived among the slagheaps. Kaurias had worked the mines for so many generations that they believed the work to be an ancient function of their caste.

As John sweated through fevers and shirts, drawing up maps detailing the dimensions of the seam and quality of the coal within it, memories of curlews, lapwings, and golden plover swooping over meadows reminded him of how far he had come and how homesick he was. In England no leeches insinuated themselves into his boots, soaking his socks with blood. When illness or exhaustion overcame him, he was ready to surrender the Ganges for a cool day's walk along

the Roman Wall. Unlike the life of an ICS officer, comfortably ensconced in well-appointed offices with evenings at the club, this was
a dog's life.

Long letters of complaint went off to Wystan.

When John confessed that a pounding concupiscence had driven
him to seek relief in a brothel, Wystan ragged him about risking fel-
latio with women who bite. As for John's account of the rank philis-
tinism of a certain memsahib, Wystan replied that he would gladly
leap into her lap to escape home life with dear Mother. Similarly,
John's complaints about his work met with no sympathy. If hunting for coal was so dire, if he was sincere about wanting to write, he
should simply chuck India and start writing. What purpose did weeping over hardships serve? To offset the sting, books began to arrive in
the Calcutta post, accompanied by lists of titles to find in the library.
As for John's fears of turning into a sahib, Wystan told him the same
thing he told himself when fears of turning into a bugger waylaid him:
consciousness of his own superiority would save him.

A year in, John and a few colleagues with a shared interest in the
Himalaya had launched the Mountain Club of India. No sooner was
this club launched in Calcutta than it was upstaged by the Himalayan
Club in Delhi, its founder a high-ranking ICS officer and big-game
hunter, and its members a powerful mix of brigadiers, major generals, a commander in chief, and a former viceroy. When the two clubs
merged John suddenly had an entrée to the high tables of the Royal
Geographical Society and the London deliberations of the Mount
Everest Committee, the body that in 1922 and 1924 had tried and failed
to put an Englishman on top.

When the Dalai Lama asked a British consul why the English were
so keen to climb Everest, he was told that a successful ascent would
benefit all humanity. Yet as the expeditions had instead exacted a
great human cost, it stood to reason His Holiness might think the man
wasn't being entirely candid. In 1922 George Mallory had watched in
horror as seven porters were swept away by an avalanche. Another fell
to his death in a crevasse. After the tragic outcome of the 1924 attempt
when Mallory and Irvine were lost, the ministers of Tibet had written
a strongly worded letter to the British undersecretary in Gangtok,

Sikkim, the kingdom in northeast India through which Everest expeditions had to pass. Permission to access Everest via Tibet would never be granted again, they wrote. Should His Excellency hear that members of the Everest Committee were preparing a new petition, he should "please, kindly stop them." The Committee had been moribund ever since.

The founding of the Himalayan Club changed nothing as far as Everest was concerned. One of its initiatives, however, was to publish a quarterly. Modeled on the *Alpine Journal*, which celebrated the adventures and scientific pursuits of European mountaineers, the mission of the *Himalayan Journal* was to "encourage and assist Himalayan travel and exploration and to extend knowledge of the Himalaya and adjoining mountain ranges through science, art, literature, and sport." John's GSI supervisors were not persuaded that his study of the high ranges would produce any material results. But what better way to bring himself to the attention of the Everest Committee than to document the underlying geological structures of the Himalaya? During his first hot season in the hill station of Simla, when he might have been casting about for female company at the Gaiety Theatre, John's eye lit upon a limestone outcrop known as Krol Hill.

Limestone is made up of skeletal fragments of marine animals such as coral and mollusks. Though a hard, sedimentary rock, it can be dissolved by the slight acidity of rainwater. The limestone moors of the North Pennines were a day's walk from the Auden family's holiday cottage in the Lake District. Though only four miles east of Keswick, the open heather moors of the Pennines were an entirely different landscape from the Lakes. The area was riddled with crannies, bogs, caves, and sinkholes, and the gurgle and drip of water could sometimes be heard working its way through tiny catacombs beneath the ground like a telltale heart.

Krol Hill was nothing like the Pennines. The highest point on a sixty-mile strip of limestone just south of Simla, in the Lesser Himalaya, it was the culminating point in a chain of five limestone basins, all strung out along a break in the earth's crust, or thrust fault. A thrust fault is where older rocks from far beneath the earth's surface are pushed up and over rocks of a more recently established stratum, like an ancient history reasserting itself in the present. Auden christened this limestone chain the Krol Belt.

John would spend the better part of four hot seasons and one cold season working his way back and forth and up and down the Krol Belt. During periods of leave and outfitted at his own expense, he would return again and again, bothered by the questions that first occurred to him during Mallory's screening of the 1922 Everest footage. How and when did the Himalaya first arise? Clearly the underlying structures of the region held the answer as to how and perhaps even the problem of when, or over what period of time, the Himalaya were upthrust.

As sedimentary rocks of the same age can look completely different because of the conditions under which they were laid down, the only way to date them is through index fossils. The general absence of fossils in the Himalaya made it difficult to assign precise time periods to individual thrust blocks. The mountains were like a work of history without dates. In the Krol Belt, however, there were great caches of fossils. The Garhwal district had the added advantage of being in easy reach of railheads, in case GSI duty called.

John drew cross sections so the thrust could be visualized, the fault lines made apparent, the bands of rock identified, and their folding, slips, synclines, and orientation shown. He took photographs of unusual formations and brought samples of microcrystalline rock back to his office to study under a microscope. He did a multicolor map in which the sixty-mile arc of the Krol Belt overlay sheet number 53 of the Survey of India map, showing the patches and pools of limestone, slates, red shales, and dolerite. In the Krol Belt, there were rocks bearing evidence of exposure to the heat and compression of the deep crust mixed haphazardly with sedimentary rocks of the upper crust.

There were other puzzling aspects. Whether from a distance or face-to-face the rock formations were amazingly complex. Apart from the limestone, there were varieties of slate, shales, schists, sandstone, quartzite, grits, dolorite, and conglomerates. Sometimes they came in the form of huge boulders, sometimes intricately colored pebbles. While the limestone was generally dark in color John also found instances where it had been transformed into a fine-grained white marble or deformed by some kind of extreme stress.

The area was also distinctive for the ways in which rocks abutted one another. There were immensely intricate folds and twists of shales and limestone; there were layers of two-inch slabs of alternating limestone and shale oriented entirely vertically. Unlike the workaday field mapping he'd done in Ranigunj, here there were signs of a cataclysm. It was hard to account for the chaos. A volcanic eruption or earthquake? The map he drew didn't try to answer the question of how the Himalaya first arose, nor did the paper that accompanied it. Instead it posed a challenge and a question: Explain this. How did this happen?

– CHAPTER 3 –

Bengali Baboo

Hatibagan, 139 Cornwallis Street, Calcutta,
 Early Twentieth Century

Calcutta, the capital of the province of Bengal, was once known as the Second City of Empire. Like London, the First City of Empire, it sat astride a river, the Hooghly, that carried traffic rivaling the Thames. For most up-and-coming Bengali youth of the city, and the handsome and quick-witted Sudhindranath Datta most certainly was one, attendance at Oxford or Cambridge, combined with access to unlimited credit, entitled them on their return to full membership in the high echelons of the Anglo-Bengali elite, otherwise known as the Set. Perhaps because the First World War had prevented Sudhin from attending Oxford, he tended to cast a gimlet eye on his milieu.

Following British traders with imperial pretensions, members of the Set built homes that mixed classical motifs with abandon. Whimsical palaces and stately homes were crowded with Empire sofas, gilded clocks, and candelabras. The walls displayed copies of sentimental paintings by Landseer and Leighton. In Sudhin's maternal grandfather's home, after-dinner music recitals were held in a Paris-style salon, accessorized with nymphs made of alabaster, porcelain from Sèvres and Dresden, and a billiard table. Family libraries of the Set boasted calf-bound copies of Tennyson, Wordsworth, Coleridge, Shelley, illustrated folios of Shakespeare, and the entire run of Sir Walter Scott's Waverley novels, reflecting the Set's boundless respect for the worthies of English literature. Many also acquired a taste for

English mustard, marmalade, cheese, and roast beef. They kept exotic birds, bred dogs and racehorses, and dressed their bearers in whiter liveries and larger turbans than the English had theirs wear. Prodigal sons returning to Calcutta after a ruinous fling at Oxford introduced themselves loftily as "England returned." Deprived of cutlery, they ate their rice with ladles in run-down mansions mortgaged to pay for their English airs.

Though Bengalis relished their halcyon days at Cambridge or Oxford as much as anyone, they were destined to always fall short of that exemplar, the English gentleman himself. For Calcutta's English residents, the Bengalis' cultivation of English habits was more evidence, should more be needed, that their rule was the destined natural order. They granted Bengalis a kind of imitative intelligence as well as a capacity for breeding more and more Bengalis. But unlike the manly warrior races of the North-West Frontier, the Bengali was believed to lack the spirit, physique, and sense of honor required of a ruling race. Consequently, the Anglicized Bengali was reviled and ridiculed.

"By his legs you should know the Bengali," Winston Churchill's favorite globe-trotting journalist wrote. Whereas an Englishman's legs were straight with a tapered calf and a flat thigh, the Bengali had the skin-and-bone leg of a slave. "Except by grace of his natural masters," this writer concluded, "a slave he always has been and always must be." Lord Thomas Babington Macaulay, another author whose violent prose style Churchill did his best to emulate, agreed. The Bengali was "thoroughly fitted by nature and by habit for a foreign yoke." A British Resident once pointed out the perfidy of hymning the praises of liberty and democracy to Bengalis when everyone knew their realization was unlikely. Think of the bitterness, hatred, and resentment that will eventually arise, he warned. "If the baboo had a soul, it might well demand a reckoning."

Bengalis had met the arriving waves of eighteenth-century Englishmen with little of the hostility or indifference the East India Company would encounter elsewhere. Initially, *baboo* or *babu* simply referred to an English-speaking Bengali clerk. Yet while Bengalis may have begun as clerks, they quickly progressed to revenue agents, solicitors, and High Court judges. As Bengalis ascended these rungs, English mockery of the baboo facility with the English language became as unrelenting as the contempt for the figure he cut. "What milk was to the cocoa-nut," Lord Macaulay quipped, "Dr. Johnson's *Dictionary* is to the polysyllabic baboo." Similarly, Bengalis were "quick to discern the fire of ideas behind the smoke of guns," whether that was Darwin's theory of evolution or the rights of widows to remarry. That the conquered should so quickly embrace the language and notions of the conqueror was curious, but that is what happened and Bengalis could argue all night as to why this was. The simplest answer was the most obvious. They were poets and philosophers. They had minds that liked to roam where their lives could not.

Sudhin believed that Viceroy Curzon's 1905 decision to partition Bengal was the result of confusing this Bengali embrace of English fashions, language, and ideas with an abandonment of Bengali ones. As the line Curzon drew divided the largely Muslim eastern half from its largely Hindu western half, Sudhin also understood that the viceroy wanted to empower Bengali Muslims, encourage their loyalty to and identification with the Raj, while sowing suspicion of their Hindu brethren. In this way the babu, with his English pretensions and the mounting political aspirations that accompanied them, might be isolated. It was also true that the viceroy partitioned Bengal simply because he could.

It was a fantastic miscalculation. A boycott was called; bonfires of Manchester cotton and English goods burned at crossroads throughout Bengal. *Swadeshi*—self-sufficiency—was proclaimed. Prefiguring Gandhi's later call for noncooperation, the well-heeled and powerful *bhadralok* class left government service, withdrew their children from educational institutions, and deprived the courts of solicitors. The Raj was paralyzed. Lastly, someone tried to assassinate the British governor of the new state of West Bengal. That and other acts of terrorism gave Bengalis a means to prove they could be fearless; they, too, had a sense of honor. In this way "baboo" ceased to denote a figure of ridicule and came instead to refer to an out-and-out traitor, soon encompassing any educated Indian with nationalist leanings.

The partition of Bengal proved the undoing of one of Sudhin Datta's many uncles. In 1901, this uncle had led a ten-mile-long barefoot cortege mourning the death of Queen Victoria. He worshipped the liberal philosophies of John Locke and John Stuart Mill. For this uncle, however, the presumption that an attachment to things British trumped his love for Bengal was intolerable. His outrage over partition was such that he impetuously forked out twenty thousand rupees to an unlicensed barrister who promised to shoot the viceroy on his behalf. Of course the fellow disappeared with the money and Curzon returned to England unharmed.

It took a further six years of unceasing unrest before partition was reversed and Bengal was again made whole. To spite the triumphant baboos, the capital of British India was wrested from Calcutta and planted in more expansive style in Delhi. A surprise announcement was made at the 1911 durbar marking the coronation of George V. With the departure of the viceroy and thousands of his minions, Bengal lost its largest source of patronage. Calcutta remained an important center of British trade with an unsurpassed nightlife, but its metropolitan glow began to dim. The statues of long-forgotten British officials on horseback still held court on the Maidan—a flat open green that hosted a racecourse, a promenade for Calcutta society, and a memorial to Queen Victoria—but the park itself looked less and less like the Hyde Park it aspired to be.

The twilight of the Set had begun.

The knowledge that the Datta family fortune derived from an alliance with India's occupiers was part of the complicated legacy Sudhin Datta's grandfather, Dwarkanath, shared with Rabindranath Tagore's grandfather, also named Dwarkanath. Dwarkanath Tagore's vast fortune had been made in Ranigunj. When he sailed to England in 1842 he traveled on his own steamship, the *India*, powered by his own coal. Tagore coal also powered jute mills, sawmills, and brick factories on the outskirts of Calcutta. It filled the tinderboxes of trains, tugboats, and steamships on eastern trade routes. In England Dwarkanath was graciously received by Queen Victoria and the Duke of Wellington, but he was astonished to discover that while his English friends might decry the starving coolies of India, he found equal distress in the coal mines of Newcastle. He watched legions of unemployed in Glasgow be violently set upon by British troops.

Dwarkanath Tagore was a pillar of the Bengal Renaissance, a golden age born of the young marriage of England and Bengal. His fortune underwrote colleges and newspapers. His sons founded a Calcutta dynasty of poets, painters, dramatists, and composers. Dwarkanath Datta, too, spawned a dynasty of gifted offspring. The Dattas, too, could trace their ancestry to one of the three fishing villages that formed the backbone of the settlement and trading post that became Calcutta. When plans for the new Fort William encroached upon family land, the East India Company deeded the family property in the city center. The two-hundred-year-old parchment deed might have been an ancient Vedic text, for all the family reverence bestowed upon it.

A mansion was soon built, one that would grow to over one hundred rooms, seven courtyards, and two acres of private orchards. As guarantor of one of the city's largest commercial houses, Dwarkanath became the family's financial mainstay. But after a feud with his brothers over his allotment of rooms, he left to set up a less encumbered household in North Calcutta called Hatibagan. His grandson Sudhindranath was born there in 1901.

Sudhin's childhood visits to the ancestral haunt took place during the annual holiday of Durga Puja. He and his brothers would be ushered into a great hall decorated with mottled Belgium mirrors and Venetian chandeliers wrapped in dusty sheets. Slowly, in ever increasing numbers, distant relations emerged from darkened cubbyholes to inspect his family. A goat was sacrificed, adding to the luridness of the memory.

The shabbier and more quarrelsome these relations grew, Sudhin noted ruefully, the more tightly they clung to the venerated parchment, the more fiercely they upheld their social pretensions. Such affectations were as unseemly to Sudhin as the profligacy of his contemporaries. After witnessing a debauched cousin charge down the street in a charabanc loaded with half-naked women, Sudhin concluded it was an obligation of wealth to behave like an idiot. One scion he knew boasted that he had spent fifty thousand rupees on the wedding of a cat belonging to his mistress, only to be reminded by his wife that her father had spent twice that on her marriage to a monkey. Yet Sudhin was as much a product of the marriage of England and Bengal as his more dissolute cousins.

At Hatibagan Sudhin and his brothers grew up in the company of aunts, uncles, and cousins. While his uncles ran wild, his aunts were ruled by his querulous grandmother, a woman who worked her networks of spies to maintain family propriety. His mother could only leave the house in a shuttered palanquin. The women of the household spent long afternoons in toilettes with a hairdresser who carried gossip from house to house. Every evening was taken up with the worship of the household deities ensconced in Hatibagan's central courtyard. Ghee lamps, bells, conch blowing, and gongs accompanied ceremonies that, on fast days, might last from sunrise to sunset.

After Sudhin came of age, he refused to attend the daily pujas and only reluctantly agreed to marry. Like his aunts, his wife had no formal education and spoke only Bengali. And when, a year into their marriage Chhabi delivered a stillborn child, neither knew how to speak of the loss. After that Sudhin rarely saw her outside their bedroom. For Chhabi there was no escaping Hatibagan's rigid caste prohibitions and its sequestered, nattering women, but when Sudhin was offered an opportunity to travel to the West, he abandoned his law studies without a second thought to accompany the sixty-eight-year-old Rabindranath Tagore as his traveling companion on yet another of his world tours.

Sudhin went with the blessings of his father, a sober and upright High Court solicitor, renowned author, and contemporary of Rabindranath. His father shared the poet's belief that European civilization had enriched Bengal and challenged the more backward notions of Hindu society. Though Sudhin differed with his father on many questions, on this he was inclined to agree, particularly in regard to English laws and English literature. Sudhin's school friend Apurba Chanda accompanied them as the great poet's secretary. The three men embarked in February 1929; Sudhin was just shy of thirty.

By 1929 Tagore's fame had obscured his genius. Always something of a dandy, he dressed in flowing robes, wore his hair long, and sported a sage-like beard. Was it surprising, Sudhin began to wonder, that the West projected an oriental mysticism onto his work, one that existed only in their own woolly minds? With the impatience of youth, he blamed Tagore for doing little to discourage the admirers who mobbed him wherever they went. Then, a few days after they arrived in Los Angeles, Tagore abruptly returned to India with Apurba. An immigration official had asked the 1913 Nobel laureate in Literature if he could read. The insult was too grievous to overcome.

Sudhin continued on alone, disillusioned. After Chicago and New York, he spent six months in London. In Germany he disarmed a band of young Hitlerites by courteously insisting in excellent German that as a true Aryan he was not required to return their *Heil*s. He arrived back in late 1929, his education completed by a love affair with a German woman. Leaving behind the woman he loved for the one sitting in wait behind the curtains of his marital home filled him with a furious distress. The love poems he wrote on his return expressed this anguish, not with the sweet serenity of Tagore, but with bitterly controlled wrath. "The fury of the storm as it pressed upon the shutters," he wrote, "echoed the useless rage of my ruined heart." He would never see the German woman again.

Sudhin's feelings about Calcutta had also undergone a sea change. "A more ill-assorted metropolis you cannot imagine," he wrote despairingly. Unlike the great European capitals he had seen, he now saw all that Calcutta lacked. There were no buildings of grandeur or distinction or archaeological interest, though its climate was such, he noted acidly, that it generated its own ruins in record time. The city was not laid out with radiating avenues but had grown in an ungainly, higgledy-piggledy manner. Factories, godowns, and shipyards had gobbled up fishing villages as the city spread out along the Hooghly River. Tiny, smoke-black workshops were everywhere. Grocers slept among vegetables in elevated bamboo huts along crowded roadways. The turreted mansions of Alipore stood cheek by jowl with overcrowded shanties and desolate tenements whose windows rained garbage on the streets below. For every grand avenue like Chowringhee or Park Street, there were hundreds of dead-end lanes so narrow and twisted one had to walk sideways to get through their dark passages. Finally, because Calcutta was built upon a swamp, when the monsoons arrived its streets turned into fast-flowing rivers. As a child Sudhin would sit on the veranda and wait eagerly for unwary pedestrians gingerly navigating waterlogged streets to be swallowed by potholes. It had been one of his greatest delights. Now such sights filled him with anguish.

Sudhin soon embarked on two projects. *Parichay*, a literary journal modeled on T. S. Eliot's *Criterion*, first appeared in 1931. *Parichay*'s essays, translations, and reviews quickly became required reading for Bengali men of letters, each issue showcasing a sampling of that expensive hobby of intellectuals, critical discernment. What gunfighters were to the Wild West, it was often said, the intellectual was to Calcutta. Among the subjects covered were the fine arts, science, philology, history, philosophy, and, of course, Bengali and European literature. Sudhin's second undertaking grew naturally out of the Friday night meetings of *Parichay*'s editorial board. This gathering became known as the Parichay adda.

The adda was a Calcutta institution. It generally took place at a settled rendezvous at a fixed time. This might be a veranda, a rooftop, an office, or a street corner tea stall. Adda participants could be unemployed graduates or middle-class men with bookish interests. Women and children were scarce. In its purest sense, the adda was an ongoing conversation among strong and sparring personalities. Bengalis were less apt to converse than declaim, even on such abstruse subjects as the best bus to take to Beliaghata. "Ask a Bengali a question and you will get an oration," one Calcutta denizen noted. "He sees all the world as a stage on which he has the star role and even an audience of one is a full house for him. As he gets into his stride you can see him becoming mesmerized by the stirring cadences of his own eloquence." At the center of an adda was the addadhari, the sun around which all members orbited. For the Parichay adda, Sudhindranath Datta was that sun.

In its first year the adda was held in the Light of Asia Insurance Company, where Sudhin worked as a clerk. In its second, it moved to Sudhin's study. On the upper floors of Hatibagan one sat on mattresses covered with sheets. By the time the adda arrived in the large reception hall on Hatibagan's ground floor, the hall was furnished in the manner of a London or Paris salon.

Two enormous bookshelves that went all the way to the ceiling faced off at each end. Eliot, Joyce, and Pound were shelved alongside the Romantics, Victorian doorstoppers, French, German, and Russian writers and philosophers, Sigmund Freud and Karl Jung, but also Bankim Chatterjee, Michael Madhusudan Dutt, Ram Mohan Roy, and, of course, Tagore. A lamp of frosted glass hung in the ceiling's center, reflecting light off the speckled green marble floors. Waist-high wainscoting added to the atmosphere of intellectual gravity. When the adda was in session, Sudhin's nieces and nephews were under strict instruction to be quiet, with the reward of leftover sweets if they were good.

Anyone was welcome to attend adda. Even an Englishman whom Sudhin suspected was a Special Branch police informant was admitted, though he rarely contributed anything as he was too busy trying to keep track of who was saying what. Behind his back he was mocked as "De Sahib." Though Sudhin secretly thought the man a jackass, he treated him with unfailing courtesy. Equally, no subject was off limits. At ease on any number of topics, Sudhin tended to progress dialectically from an "alternately" to a "therefore" and then, on the cusp of a conclusion, swerve to a "yet." He would consider each question carefully, holding it up to the light, so that he might look at it from every possible angle. He then presented his conclusions with unassailable confidence.

The more aggressive nationalists of the adda grumbled that Sudhin's spoken English made him more sahib than babu. That lasted until they read his Bengali. Then they had to admit he wrote like a man who had studied nothing but Sanskrit. Though fluent in French and German as well as Sanskrit and Bengali, Sudhin was well aware that Bengalis delighted in a vocabulary and syntax drawn from the more voluble Victorians. In reaction, he chose his words with a poet's caution.

He took equally fastidious care of his clothes, which included as many beautifully tailored suits of English cut as blindingly white dhotis. Gandhi's enthusiasm for handloom was alien to Sudhin's more sybaritic sensibilities. And the Mahatma's constant resort to a language of Christian repentance, or the way he would lead his followers in a cracked version of "Lead Kindly Light," struck Sudhin as unutterably foolish. At the same time, Sudhin couldn't help but be fascinated.

Gandhi was the first to point out that in their willingness to cooperate with English rule, families like the Dattas had made a devil's bar-
gain and the rest of India had paid the price. However gently said, this
truth, in tandem with Gandhi's near nakedness, unsettled Sudhin the
most. When he encountered khadi-clad Congressites on the tram, out
of a sense of delicacy he would disembark before they could call him
out on his tweeds.

In its early years Parichay adda often began with local political
gossip. Any mention of Calcutta's proud son, the radical Congress
youth Subhas Chandra Bose, always provoked debate. The waxing
and waning of the Congress Party's political fortunes were followed
more dispassionately. And adda members generally paid about as
much attention to European affairs as those in London or Paris literary salons paid to India's, which is to say, not much. All assumed
the silence of English writers on the subject of India's subjugation
merely illustrated how easily the ruling classes had kept the English
intellect from meddling in English business interests. At adda, it was
the Soviet five-year plans that were the most hotly debated. Indeed,
everything about Soviet Russia fascinated those who hoped India too
might free itself from feudalism and foreign rule to become a force to
be reckoned with.

Hassan Shahid Suhrawardy, one of Sudhin's closest and most cosmopolitan friends, was both the adda's resident Russophile and a
ferocious anti-Bolshevist. After Oxford, Shahid taught English at the
Imperial University of St. Petersburg: Alexander Kerensky had been
his student. He took shelter from the revolution in Moscow, working
at Stanislavski's Moscow Art Theatre alongside Maxim Gorky and
the young Igor Stravinsky. Living for years in a ménage à trois with a
Russian actress and her husband, he ignored family letters pleading
with him to come home. On his reluctant return to Calcutta, he wrote
on theater for *Parichay*, styling himself as a long-haired libertine and
waxing volubly on French women, wine, and food. Both Scotland Yard
and the Special Branch of Police followed Shahid closely, finding it
impossible to believe that a man with such a villainous appearance
was not a Bolshevik.

Shahid could never be confused with his younger brother, Huseyn

Shaheed Suhrawardy, though he, too, was a beautifully tailored Oxonian. A former deputy mayor of Calcutta with a gift for demagoguery, Shaheed was a rogue and a scoundrel, a "natural gangster, ready to dabble in strike politics and to make money and political capital out of the most exciting and disgraceful situations." Political intrigue, often involving sexual blackmail, was the air he breathed. He had acquaintances from all walks of life and made good use of them. No sooner had he secured one political post than he schemed to find a better one. He once managed the feat of being vice-chancellor of Calcutta University and chief medical officer of the East Indian Railway at the same time. On his rare visits to Parichay adda, Shaheed was far less expansive than his brother Shahid, limiting himself to local politics. The Suhrawardy brothers agreed on only one thing: England had nothing to offer India. Nothing.

Sudhin liked to mix seriousness with silliness, the parochial with the urbane. A monologue on classical metaphysics might segue into one on the significance of the moustache in Indian politics. A debate over the genius of Charlie Chaplin might devolve into a meditation on empire. But Sudhin had no patience for the suggestion that the Indian mystic Nagarjuna had anticipated Einstein's theory of relativity. And he cut off in midsentence the proposition that the leader of the 1857 Sepoy Rebellion was hiding in the Himalayan foothills. While his interlocutor sat across the room puffing out clouds of smoke, a fixed expression on his face and a long silk chadder wound a bit too tightly round his neck, Sudhin would coolly take him apart, his long fingers tracing circles in the air, one eye closed, the other slightly open. Only the dreadful puns of a scholar of the swastika or the inanities of the adda's resident Naziphile evoked Sudhin's wide-eyed exasperation.

Basanta Kumar Mallik took the same spot every Friday, his beautifully tailored but squat form rooted to a sofa in close reach of a plate of samosas or a selection of sweets from Dwarik's, a legendary North Calcutta confectionery. A Sphinx-like smile hovered around his lips, as if he was ready to pounce on the first appearance of cant. After his father lost the family fortune and died of drink, Mallik had been sent to Oxford by the maharaja of Nepal to be trained in law. When the Great War broke out, he was stranded there, taking further degrees in

philosophy and anthropology and running his own adda out of Robert
Graves's house in Boars Hill. In Calcutta he had vowed never to work
on behalf of empire and was thus marking time until he could return
to his beloved Oxford. Mallik-da had an elegant way of elaborating his
theory of conflict. This theory had a near-universal application when
it came to resolving differences. He never tired of using the adda to
test its efficacy on warring intellects. Sudhin indulged him like a fond
nephew.

Finally, there was the secret diarist, a clerk at an English firm that
exported manganese and iron to Japan. The diarist regarded Sudhin
with unfiltered respect. He rarely volunteered anything himself, and
when he did it was merely to echo the general tenor of the conversation in progress. Otherwise, he made a great effort to follow its
every twist and turn, both to avail himself of an opportunity for enlightenment and to immortalize Sudhin, the Suhrawardy brothers,
the philosopher Mallik-da, and other luminaries in the pages of his
diary when he returned home. Cartoons often accompanied his character sketches, with his subjects' most distinctive features slightly
exaggerated.

Between *Parichay*, the adda, and his poetry, Sudhin lived the life of
a man of letters. To some Sudhin was an *anekantavad*, a believer in the
many-faced nature of truth and reality. Yet whatever face he turned
to his benighted city, he knew that though he was born in Calcutta,
were he to appear on Park Street without some menial occupation
to justify his presence, he risked being slapped or kicked. Though he
could trace his lineage to a time before the arrival of the British, he
was unable to enter a Calcutta club except through the door reserved
for servants. And should a white traveler require a railway berth in the
middle of the night, he would be obliged to give up his own.

This was another kind of nakedness, one that no beautifully tailored suit could completely hide. However well versed in European
manners, literature, and laws, Sudhindranath Datta was forever marked
by a melancholy truth: to the most philistine of Englishmen, he was
yet another Bengali baboo.

– CHAPTER 4 –

The Thrust Fault

GSI Camp, Son River Valley, Mirzapur District,
October–November 1929

During his six-month furlough John Auden had been so consumed with the task of finding a wife that he had given India little thought. While he engaged in a number of flirtations in various European capitals, he had been unable to settle on anyone. Only when darkness fell at the end of his first day back in the field did the familiar sensations of camp life return. There was the same sound of crickets in the stillness, the same play of lamplight in the dak bungalow. Each evening Auden set aside his geological field notes and turned to the journal he'd begun during his stay with Wystan in Berlin.

The most satisfying sound in the world, he began, was the sound of an unseen woodcutter in the forest at dusk. How different the Son River Valley of Mirzapur District was from the rounded sandstone uplands and Silurian slates of Howgill Fells. The Alps were as unlike the karst limestone bogs of the Yorkshire dales as the dales were from the vertical strata of Germany's Harz Mountains. John wrapped himself in the memory of his furlough, not to ward off the loneliness, but to find the thread of his story.

He reassured himself that Calcutta was not entirely without marital prospects. The "fishing fleets" would soon be arriving, bearing young women who had weighed the prospect of a life spent looking after aging parents against the chance to land an ICS officer worth a thousand pounds a year. They spent the winter months in a flurry of phaeton rides and picnics by the Hooghly, ending with the Christmas costume ball hosted by the vicereine. There were Sunday breakfasts at the Tollygunj, teas at the Bengal, and ballroom dances at the Saturday, Calcutta clubs commonly known as the Tolly, the Bally, and the Slap. Such women might at first appear to accommodate walls of taxidermied heads and tiger skin rugs, but once firmly enthroned, bachelor hunting parties gave way to white-gloved teas.

Yet these women were pale imitations of the more glamorous ones John had seen in the society pages of the *Tatler*, expensive-looking women posing with expensive cars. Perhaps such women were a fantasy, he thought, but the mere possibility of them made him rue his station in an almost-but-not-quite upper class. After one too many teas overseen by Calcutta's clutch of socially powerful memsahibs, John invariably returned to the sumptuously decorated bungalows on Karaya Road. These establishments, too, were overseen by superior mesdames, but when it came to hospitality, offered a more cosmopolitan mix. There were White Russians, Anglo-Indians, girls from Europe, Singapore, Hong Kong, and French Indochina. Dinner under the chandeliers, including a round of drink, was ten rupees. Girls were extra.

In the midst of his reverie on his romantic prospects, John suddenly recalled the question his analyst had asked him at the close of their final session that past June.

"You are not giving up analysis simply because you think you are doing the right thing, are you?" Margaret Marshall had asked him. "Not just because of an *idea*?"

And with that, the sense of peace conveyed by the sound of woodcutters deserted him and doubt once again tightened its reins.

If the nineteenth century had been all about piling up one scarcely credible heroic exploit after another and never stopping to ask why, the twentieth century thus far seemed to be all about sitting down and taking apart one's motives. Instead of thrashing through the jungle, battling fevers and hostile tribes in search of the source of the Nile, these new adventurers searched for themselves. This was a different sort of wilderness and required a different set of tools. In Paris, Margaret Marshall had ended John Auden's first formal session of analysis by saying that his candor posed a great difficulty. Honest patients were hard to treat. This was partly because honesty obscured the most important truths and partly because such patients usurped her role by trying to analyze their own behavior. Margaret insisted that she alone could determine his motives.

Why did he want to climb Everest?

"It is a mythical future admiration that you want," she pronounced. "The present and the analytical work required for this result you ignore. Without regard for the present you will be unable to achieve anything." She then compared his two attitudes.

"You expressed dislike of being loved simply for having a handsome face. But you court worldly admiration for some hypothetical achievement. Isn't there a contradiction here? You should wish to be liked simply for yourself."

"Of course I would wish to be liked simply for myself," John replied impatiently. "But what exactly is this self if it is not connected with some action? Should I just sit around all day in Paris cafés?"

Their sessions took place in Paris cafés.

"That is taking it too far. You would not be yourself if you sat all day in a café."

When they were back on the street, Margaret asked him if he was enjoying his analysis.

"Very much."

"Wystan answered in just the same resentful manner," she said, sounding pleased.

It was Wystan who recommended that John see Margaret Marshall. Margaret had pronounced Wystan's libido perfectly normal and so he imagined she might fix John, too.

"What is it that draws you to the mountains?"

"I feel safe when I am isolated and unobserved. I feel most alive and most sane when I overcome my terror and conquer what at first seem to be insuperable difficulties."

"You must project this feeling of safety and sanity into the long moment of your existence," she said. "You must avoid relying on others to prop up your idea of yourself. Only when you have achieved such independence will you discover a capacity to love others.

"Think out the importance of George Mallory to you," she had said in parting.

It hadn't taken long before the question of whether he would return to India at the end of his furlough or commit to a serious and extended treatment took over. The faint hope that the Dalai Lama might allow passage of a new Everest expedition argued for his return. Against this there had been the question of his health and personal happiness. After several days of discussion John decided he would give up India.

To celebrate the laying to rest of his Mallory fantasy and the real beginning of his analysis, they had spent an evening in a mad round of Paris nightclubs. They hit Le Felice first then another club on the rue Sorbonne. There, Margaret had turned to face him as they danced and asked him if he felt he had made the right decision.

"Of course, yes," he said.

But once again John had been annoyed. Thinking back on it three months later, it struck him as an unnecessary question; on the order of, do you love me? He had turned away to watch Margaret's husband dance with another man. By three in the morning he'd been ready to turn in. As often happened when he was tired, a reaction set in.

It had been partly a reaction against the entire world of Paris nightclubs and the louche people in them. But it had also been brought on by the vision of an utterly marvelous girl in pajamas heading to the lavatory in the hotel hallway.

Others have what they want, he thought, why shouldn't I? Though Margaret had been kind, her constant harping on their growing intimacy had irked him. She was twelve years older and he wasn't at all sexually attracted to her. He'd been so thoroughly miserable the next day, a Sunday, that he went to the Marshalls' flat to tell Margaret he had decided to return to India.

That was the thing, he now realized, as he sat at dusk in his dak bungalow in the Son Valley. Margaret had said he shouldn't think he was doing the brave thing by returning to India. But it had never been a question of courage. The effort to break away had simply been too great. Yet given the prospect of an imminent renewal of Gandhi's Non-

Cooperation Movement, the security of his job might prove an equal illusion, he thought.

It was useless to belabor the pleasures of camp life or imagine he'd find a wife in Calcutta. He could no more apply Margaret's theoretical directions to change his ingrained responses than he could speak German. How could talk convert weaknesses into strengths? And if he had truly wanted to climb Everest, why had he limited his furlough to easy rambles in the English countryside and picnics with Wystan in the Harz Mountains? Why had he left the Alps a day after he arrived?

He knew Wystan wanted to be a great poet and had bent his entire being to that. John could never bring himself to read his brother's poems too closely as he tended to see himself in all of them, as if his brother knew him better than he knew himself. He also dreaded seeing his own thoughts more fully expressed. Recalling the wild disorder of his brother's ugly fourth-floor lodgings in Berlin, John wondered how much strength of mind was required to persevere in such a place. He would doubtless have whiled away the time cleaning his nails, pausing every so often to glance at his watch to see how much longer until tea. Also, evenings with Wystan were always lively. His own social life in India was meager. He was tortured by contradictory impulses: either to cling to people or reject them altogether. Though in some ways he was quite vain, when he compared himself with other men, he harbored intense feelings of inferiority. He was always surprised when others sought him out. Feeling himself a fraud, he treated such overtures with skepticism.

As for love, he really only loved himself.

One afternoon in Berlin after his brother had gone out, John went through his papers in search of a clue as to what he did in his room alone all morning. On Wystan's return to the flat, he'd blurted out a question.

"I suppose you think a lot, don't you?" As soon as he said it he realized how ridiculous he sounded.

Wystan had him convinced that finding the right woman was the key to their cure. Toward the end of their stay in the Harz Mountains Wystan had told him that the Viennese Jew whom John had met in

Berlin four months before was almost certainly in love with him. Feeling time was running out and recalling how attractive she was, John had sent her a letter proposing marriage. Her reply arrived while he was out. Wystan had seen it, smiling when he did, John supposed, and doubtless thinking him foolish to act so precipitously. On the cusp of returning to Berlin to marry her, he changed his mind.

So what was the idea to which he could commit himself? This had been Margaret's parting question at the Gare du Nord, the question that now kept him awake and staring into the dark. Was it Everest? A wife? A life in India? Perhaps Margaret was right about his hypochondria, but that didn't alter the fact that he often felt as if he were under a strain so unbearable he felt he'd crack wide open. And what of his anemia, his arrhythmia, and the pain in his back? These were not figments of his imagination. Even his hands looked unnaturally drawn. He performed his daily routines mechanically, bone tired. Cause and effect, symptom and anxious response, can of course be self-perpetuating. But what was the *original* cause?

Margaret had told him of a cousin she'd once been fond of who had married a man in the Indian Army. This cousin had been put out when the Paris railway porters didn't appear to recognize the better class of people when they saw them, that is, herself.

"If that is what passes for society in India it must be pretty lonely. I don't suppose there's any danger of your getting like that," Margaret had said.

But there was a danger. He had often wondered if Englishmen were truly superior to Indians. Had the Indian been provided with a proper education, he might well go higher than the average Englishman. Perhaps the men of the East India Company had been exceptional, but those in India now, to a man, were second rate. Living on capital.

Simla, Viceroy's Summer Residence,
    August 1929

If John meant "living on capital" as a metaphor, the finance member of the Viceroy's Executive Council had a more literal understanding. Sir George Ernest Schuster was, with Alfred Spender, uncle to the Spender children. He also oversaw the Schuster fortune that sustained them all. Whether in his London club, his spread of offices in Delhi, or his A Class Simla bungalow, he cut a splendid figure. Petitioners found him exceedingly gracious.

But he gave up *nothing*.

Sir George did not opine that one petitioner's request—that Bengal be exempted from duties on salt—was impossible. He was as indifferent to the impact of the price of salt on the Bengali peasant as he was to the political cost of refusing to budge.

Ostriches must be equally composed when their heads are planted in the ground, his petitioner, a subdivisional district officer, reflected bitterly. Before departing Calcutta he had had an injection to ward off a plague running rampant in his district, leaving him with a low-grade fever. This fever, combined with his fear of being shown up for the unkempt, malaria-ridden, district hack that he was, might well have blinded him to the overarching reality Uncle George kept foremost in his mind: Capital.

In his former life, Uncle George had been a banker. It was through banking investments and currency regulation that England maintained her hold on the resources and business enterprises of India. Nearing the end of 1929, that investment came to seven hundred million pounds sterling. No one needed to tell George Schuster that English interests could direct the Government of India's financial and exchange policies only if peace was preserved.

One year previously, after learning that the commission set up to determine whether India was ready for further measures of self-government did not include even one Indian, Gandhi had returned to the political field. He gave His Majesty's Government one year to grant India dominion status. If this did not happen, he would once again call for a boycott of British goods. With no movement toward an agreement, unrest had increased. The deadline was only months away.

Uncle George understood better than anyone the inextricable ties between the Indian market for British manufactured goods, the fortunes of his Liberal Party, and Britain's industrial health. And, frankly speaking, the imposition of tariff walls at the end of the last war had put British industry in a death spiral. He didn't care to speculate on what would happen if extremists, and by that he meant the Indian National Congress, prevailed. Uncle George had had a close encounter with one such extremist, sustaining injuries when two bombs were thrown into the Central Legislative Assembly chamber in Delhi.

If Gandhi followed through on his threat to renew mass civil disobedience, India's prospects for financial autonomy would be finished, he announced. But this was disingenuous; Uncle George knew full well that no autonomy was possible while London banks maintained a monopoly on capital. He also knew that if peace was bought with an offer of dominion status, a clash between Lancashire and India was inevitable. It will be a test of our sincerity, Sir George liked to say, for England to consider the national aspirations of India before the immediate welfare of the English mill worker.

By then the collapse of the stock market had taken the possibility of sincerity down with it. In January 1930 the Under-Secretary of State for India said that if India was granted commonwealth status, it wouldn't be a dominion on par with Canada, Australia, and New Zealand. In reply, the Indian National Congress officially stopped pressing for dominion status. In concert with his mentor Gandhi, Jawaharlal Nehru, the new Congress president, turned Congress decisively to the left.

"The British Government in India has not only deprived the Indian people of their freedom but has based itself on the exploitation of the masses and has ruined India economically, politically, culturally, and spiritually." *Purna Swaraj*—full and complete independence for India—was declared and a new campaign of civil disobedience was launched.

On March 12, 1930, at 6:30 a.m., Gandhi and seventy-eight handpicked volunteers began their march to the sea from Sabarmati ashram. Twenty-two days later Gandhi, swaddled in a shawl and grasping a walking stick, reached the Arabian Sea at Dandi, where he picked up a handful of salt. This act was deemed illegal because collecting salt subverted the excise duty Britain imposed on it. The photograph was seen around the world. Jawaharlal Nehru, president of Congress, was arrested that day. Gandhi was arrested a month later. Motilal Nehru, made acting president of Congress to replace his son, was arrested in June. All would be released on January 26, 1931, on the first anniversary of their announcement of India's independence. Motilal died a week later.

Son River Valley, Mirzapur District,
  December 2, 1929

After impotence John Auden's biggest fear was insanity. When the molten heat of the jungle bore down on him like an immense weight, what began as irritation and impatience grew into something uglier. With great effort, he would rein himself back from a venomous rage with the discipline of fieldwork. If he failed to do this, the familiar crescendo would begin in his head. First came self-pity.

He would never be loved or understood.

Then came his fears. The bazaar. The coolie at the train station with his thin, quivering, betel-stained lips. The religious fanatic. The jungle. Worst of all was the sniggering outside his tent. Were his men laughing at him? His fears grew larger, riding on the perpetual pain in his gut. He was being poisoned. A few drops from the bottle of hydrochloric acid from his kit in the supper pot would be sufficient.

Finally, the rupture: a terrifying vision of himself screaming, tearing up maps and notebooks, putting gun to forehead, and pulling the trigger.

Writing all this down one evening eased some of the pressure. The compulsions of his inner life remained as mysterious to him as the subterranean forces that raised the Himalaya. In these moments of rage and despair, he was overcome with longing for someone who would not condemn him as harshly as he condemned himself, someone to free him from loneliness, someone in whom to dissolve those unremitting carnal desires that tortured his every waking thought. Would he ever find the right woman?

Stopped once more at the familiar impasse, he turned his attention to the men with whom he shared his days, men without whom he would truly be lost. He recalled how they had led him back through the forest to the camp they had prepared, stepping aside so he could enter first. The Ranigunj tribals had had a similar delicacy. They took care not to stare at him, freeing him from the self-consciousness he felt in the company of his countrymen. He was grateful. He wanted to be some sort of father to them. It would be painful to let them down. With such thoughts in his head, he was finally able to sleep.

As John Auden waited for tea in the shadow of the Kaimur escarpment the next morning, it occurred to him that the demarcation of the Upper and Lower Vindhyas was too simple. A fourfold classification, comprising the largely marine rock formation of the Semri and the riverine rock of the Kaimur, Rewa, and Bhander, would be more accurate.

Like the questions arising from the Krol Belt, it was an academic distinction. Still, he liked the way his work dovetailed with the work of other Englishmen, men who once sat in the same wilderness and asked the same questions. At some point he would posit a framework that would stand until another man came along and, noticing a new outcrop, shifted the frame to accommodate the questions it raised. This would hold only until a new anomaly was noticed or a new tool was devised that would enable some future geologist to peer more closely, more deeply into the earth beneath his feet.

"*Arre chalo!*" he called out.

"*Chalo aage,*" his bearer replied.

"*Chalo aage,*" echoed his chaprasi. And they were off.

– CHAPTER 5 –
Triangles

Oxford University, Oxford,
  May 3, 1926

While Alfred Spender was arguing with Gandhi at Sabarmati ashram, the Secretary of State for India in London was directing the vice-chancellor of Oxford University to extract a written promise from the two students who had presumed to debate the question of India's freedom with Indians to cease all such talk or be sent down forthwith. The Oxford Union passed a vote of condemnation. The English students' right to express their political views had been violated. After much canvassing, the vote was reversed. As the Indian students in question were Bengalis, both debates received wide coverage in the Calcutta papers. But the hullabaloo at Oxford was soon quickly forgotten once the general strike of 1926 got under way.

At the war's end Great Britain's coal miners, forced to work eleven shifts a fortnight in crumbling shafts with terrible ventilation, had seen their wages cut drastically. When it seemed that further cuts were in the works, they had nothing more to lose; their families were starving. Coal was their leverage. Though the British Navy had by then transitioned to oil, for over a century English coal had powered the empire. Steamships required coal. Industry required coal. Locomotives required coal. Backed by the prime minister, the mine owners refused to parley, so the Trades Union Congress called for a nationwide strike.

Though Michael Spender had nearly come to "intellectual blows" with Stephen over becoming a strikebreaker, there was never a doubt in his mind that he would answer the government's call for engine drivers. Driving a locomotive wasn't in the least like driving a mail truck or double-decker, he explained to a friend from university. At full throttle, the boiler pressure of the Pendennis Castle engine reached two hundred and twenty pounds to the square inch. Michael's only concern was that he might be unable to stop the train when it arrived at the station.

By the second day of the strike there were riots near the East London docks of West Ham and Canning Town. The next day warships began patrolling the Mersey, Tyne, and Plymouth Rivers. By then Michael had his train. "Am not I a man of crisis?" he trumpeted. Approaching Nottingham, he'd had to increase his speed to fifty miles per hour, only to slow again on the climb up through Harrow. Fifty bogies rattled and jostled behind him all the way. He ran one twenty-seven-hour watch, arriving twelve hours late into Marylebone, exhausted but relieved, with dripping crates of fish in the hold. The tense atmosphere up north, the possibility of violent reprisals, underscored the gravity of the moment.

By the fifth day steelworks and factories began to close for lack of coal and the chancellor of the exchequer, Winston Churchill, published the first issue of the *British Gazette*. England would starve, he thundered. By day eight the military had cordoned off the entire docks complex, cavalrymen and foot battalions joining convoys of armored cars escorting food shipments. Oxbridge undergraduates offloaded vessels before sullen dockworkers. Others, like Wystan Auden and his friend Louis MacNeice, supported the miners.

Then, after only nine days, the general strike was abruptly called off.

Still dazed by the glow cast by the firebox and the motion of a train jogging through the dark, Michael returned to Oxford, imagining he now knew the workingman's daily grind. It was only then that he realized that none of the mayhem the *Gazette* had foretold ever materialized. Churchill's threat of a military crackdown, his statement that trade unions had no right to air their grievances was, he now saw, outrageous. Even the Conservative baronet who'd long sparred with his father admitted to Michael that perhaps the danger to the nation had been overdone. Researching an article for *Cherwell*, the Oxford student paper, Michael learned that during the strike's final days the government had commandeered the BBC's nightly programming. His father would have said the *Gazette* was peddling propaganda, but by the time the strike began, Harold Spender had been in his grave a fortnight.

Harold's death on Alfred Spender's return from India had briefly delayed him from resolving his argument with Gandhi to his own satisfaction. His brother's will had left the orphaned Spender children in the hands of their grandmother, the tightfisted but softhearted Hilda Schuster. But Granny never made a move without consulting Alfred. As the eldest, Michael was expected to shoulder some responsibility when he reached the age of majority. Until then, Alfred undertook to provide guidance, not being blessed with children of his own.

When Alfred finally sat down to write his India book, he found instructive parallels between the clash of labor and capital in England and the standoff in India. Gandhi's Non-Cooperation Movement had been something like a general strike, he noted, though of course it went on not for nine days but two years and wreaked a great deal more havoc. And just as the workingman complained of the "Oxford manner" of the gentleman members of Parliament, so did Indians resent the ridicule and contempt heaped on them by the officials of the Indian Civil Service. Alfred was going to sort all this out.

Like the color bar in South Africa, he began, the notion of *swadeshi* was conceived in a spirit of racial hatred. Gandhi believed Europeans and natives could not intermingle without destroying each other's way of life. However earnestly Gandhi might renounce violence and express religious tolerance, an outright fanaticism underlay his perpetual talk of spinning and self-sufficiency. Once every single product of English manufacture was outlawed, Gandhi would surely cast every last Englishman out of India. And just as the general strike intended to overthrow the government, so a renewal of the Non-Cooperation Movement would lead to the unthinkable: the end of the British Raj.

The Changing East laid out Alfred's solution. The nineteenth-century officials who once ruled India were able guardians for the simple inhabitants of an unchanging East. But once the natives became fond of modern conveniences, their needs changed. Progress depended not on a return to preindustrial economies based on human labor, such as those that had once existed in late eighteenth-century England, but on a passionate embrace of enlightened, science-assisted, coal-driven development. Men of science were the remedy.

Uncle Alfred might have hoped his eldest nephew would answer India's need for men of science. But as soon as Michael read of a forth-coming expedition to the Great Barrier Reef in the March 1928 issue of *Nature*, he wanted in. To live for a year on a tiny sunlit coral island, in waters first explored by Captain Cook, on reef islands once studied by Darwin . . . how could a salaried job not seem sordid by comparison? Without telling anyone, Michael wrote a letter to the Royal Geographical Society, volunteering his services for the job of chief bottle washer.

There was no funding for a bottle washer, Arthur L. Hinks, the secretary of the Royal Geographical Society, replied. The RGS was underwriting the posts of geographer and surveyor, and the former position had already been filled. On the eve of his interview, Michael's nerve failed. How could he possibly calculate latitude or longitude without a book to look it up in? If he tried "I am absolutely the man you are looking for" on Hinks he would be cut to pieces and forever snubbed by the class lists. He saw himself stammering, being forced to admit that Hinks had better choose someone else.

Michael Spender was an unduly conceited young man, the head of engineering at Oxford wrote by way of a recommendation, but he was terribly keen. Others at the RGS took issue with Michael's "Oxford manner," but Hinks overruled them, seeing something of himself in the young man's unapologetic arrogance.

On hearing the news that Michael was off to Australia, Alfred Spender decided his nephew was as flighty as his brother Harold had been.

Whatever Granny thought, she let Michael go.

Midnapore Collegiate School, Handicraft Exhibition,
Kharagpur, Bengal, 6:40 p.m., April 7, 1931

The four rugby-playing Carritt brothers were known around Oxford as the Golden Boys. Soon after the eldest of them arrived in India, he began to wonder: did queers rule India just as they had university? The

first two high British officials he met did little to hide their proclivi-
ties. He tried to imagine Wystan Auden, who'd been smitten with his
younger brother Gabriel, ruling a district the size of Sussex County.
During his frequent stays at their family house at Boars Hill, Oxford,
Wystan had made himself at home. Then again perhaps Wystan wouldn't
have made the grade. He'd spent his final term writing poems about
the Golden Boys and left Oxford with a third.

Michael John Carritt's father had long told him that even a second-
class honors degree would mean a short wait for the best jobs going.
Having spent more time in pubs than in the library, Carritt had left
university with a respectable second only to discover that the jobs
he'd counted on were no longer there. That left the colonial services.
He chose the Indian Civil Service because it carried the most prestige. And as it was generally accepted that ICS officers assigned to
the frontier were of the best caliber, Carritt had put the North-West
Frontier Province as his top choice for a posting. He foresaw sharing pegs under staring trophy heads with the Twenty-Fifth Infantry
Punjab at the regimental mess bar and squaring off against Rajput
princes in chukkers of polo. This was the Raj Winston Churchill had
written of in letters to his mother and retired ICS officers revisited in
their memoirs. But to Carritt's bitter disappointment he was posted
instead to the backwaters of Bengal.

Bengal's dismal climate and its perpetually disgruntled populace
accounted for its unpopularity. Bookish nationalists, sneaky terrorists, and vegetarian Gandhians were considered unworthy adversar-
ies for the Indian Army, so those malcontents were left to the local
police and district officers to handle. In Bengal, too, a junior officer
would be lucky to scare up sufficient company for billiards, let alone
polo or pig sticking. This would allow Carritt plenty of time to reflect
that because he had not got a first in Greats he would always be at
the bottom of the ICS deck. As the new assistant district officer of
Midnapore District, he was to appear for duty in the fall of 1930. On his
arrival he learned that a flamboyant Oxford acquaintance, now a district magistrate, had pulled strings to get him assigned to Midnapore.

Raw recruits weren't generally given postings in troubled districts,
he was told by another extravagantly outfitted and queenly toff living

in what had once been the summer residence of Warren Hastings, the first, de facto, viceroy of India. During Gandhi's Salt March that past April, satyagrahis had descended on the Bay of Bengal. Gandhi's volunteers had offered only passive resistance to the lathi charges and dogs set upon them by the superintendent of police. A local leader watched without emotion as the district officer burned his house and food stocks to the ground. When the jails were full, volunteers were hauled off in trucks and dumped by the wayside. Before the rains put an end to it, three satyagrahis were shot and killed. Gandhi wrote the organizers a letter of congratulation from prison. When Carritt arrived in India six months later, Gandhi was still there.

If Carritt distinguished himself in Midnapore, the toff had said, there was the possibility of a transfer to Calcutta. Special officer appointments were proliferating in the new but highly competitive Political and Home Department, reflecting measures taken to combat the increase in terrorism throughout Bengal. The same month the Salt March was completed, a raid on the Chittagong armory resulted in the deaths of seven Europeans. After that dak bungalows were put under police guard and verandas were draped with wire mesh so bombs could not be thrown onto them. Watchers, informers, and spies began popping up everywhere. Letters were intercepted and translated. Reports were sent up the chain of command of the Special Branch of Police, ending up on the desk of the British governor of Bengal and sometimes the viceroy's.

The district officer to whom Carritt eventually reported was neither a toff nor a queer but a battle-hardened Scot. It was he who led the attack on the satyagraha volunteers. James Peddie had received a Military Cross during the last war, when he had been shot in the face. His thickset, muscle-bound body was furred and covered with freckles. One week out of every month Carritt and Peddie heard cases in Kharagpur. The rest of the time they shared a tent or dak bungalow, traveling all over the district inspecting schools, police stations, and village dispensaries. They scanned marriage registries for underage brides. They heard petitions for funding a village improvement or complaints about rapacious zamindars. They filed reports on road conditions and how much progress had been made clearing hyacinth from waterways. If wells they'd approved had yet to be dug or if someone's servant had signed off on an extortionate price, inquiries were threatened.

Yet Carritt did admit that about half their time on tour was spent in near-fanatical pursuit of game. Lying before dawn in a dugout canoe, listening to birds call out to each other and watching the low-lying mist over the marshes be burned off by the sun, felt like a dream. But eight months into his posting, having just returned from duck hunting in a remote corner of the district, Carritt was awakened.

He and Peddie had been met at dusk by a delegation eager to escort them to an opening-day ceremony of a handicraft exhibition. They wandered through four or five shabby classrooms before the lights went. At the sound of gunfire there was a stampede to the veranda, where Carritt discovered Peddie was missing. Using a hurricane lamp he retraced his steps and found the DO leaning against a classroom wall. Peddie's last words before collapsing were "They have got me."

Peddie had been shot three times, twice in his left arm and once in the back. The hospital had no morphine, no operating theater, and no doctor. He died the next morning. In the subsequent investigation Carritt gave a description of the two assailants. Both were members of the Bengal Volunteers, a terrorist group that vowed the office of Midnapore DO would henceforth remain empty. The next district officer barely lasted a year. The man who followed him was also shot and killed. In this way Parliament learned that all was not well in Midnapore, in Bengal, in India. Peddie's assassins were arrested and executed but not before the police organized raids on local villages and mass arrests of young men.

Within days of Peddie's death, a new viceroy arrived. The Marquess of Willingdon soon found India ridiculously easy to govern. All it required, he told a reporter for the Calcutta *Statesman*, was kindness. When another campaign of civil disobedience was launched in 1932, kindness would involve outlawing the Congress Party, and arresting and imprisoning every member of its working committee as well as tens of thousands of their followers. During Willingdon's five-year tenure, both Gandhi and Jawaharlal Nehru would spend more than a year in prison. Muhammad Ali Jinnah, the leader of the All India Muslim League, returned to his London law practice in disgust.

Finally, Willingdon placed Bengal under martial law. Once the Indian Army was called in, Carritt noted, the only function of district officers in Midnapore was to provide terrorists with sitting targets.

Dr. Auden's credo, "Live as if on a mountain," had left off Marcus Aurelius's next words, a wisdom ideally tailored for district officers, rebel insurgents, and bugger poets.

"Let them see, let them know that a real man lives according to his nature. If they cannot endure this, let them kill him. For that is better than to live thus."

Classroom, Zurich Polytechnic University,
       Switzerland, January–August 1931

Michael Spender had spent a year surveying and drawing up a lovingly detailed map of two tiny and remote islands off the Great Barrier Reef whose terrain consisted largely of mangrove swamp and broken bits of coral. On his return he accepted a job at His Master's Voice Gramophone Company where he invented a way to record music that would yield better sound than their scratchy disc reproductions. When told his invention would be too expensive to engineer, he would have resigned on principle but they let him go to Paris for a month. Then he resigned. To Arthur Hinks, the secretary of the Royal Geographical Society, Michael explained that fetching and carrying for a firm quickly progressing toward Queer Street felt futile.

But what could be more futile than mapping a place with no inhabitants and no extractable resources? Unlike the GSI project of mapping the underlying geological structure of the subcontinent in pursuit of minerals and coal, Michael's mapping of the Barrier Reef islands, like the ongoing effort to survey and map the fifteen-hundred-mile-long chain of the Himalaya, was largely an academic exercise, though with the Himalaya there was at least the possible question of border security. It is hard to escape the feeling that the English were apt to mistake the map for the place itself. And the magical belief that maps consolidated sovereignty, accuracy equaled impartiality, and heavenly perspective mimed the eye of an imperial sovereign deity added to their irresistible allure.

In 1800 a sweet-tempered and reticent Englishman had conceived the modest ambition of surveying all of India. To map India a team of surveyors, beginning at an observatory in the western port of Madras, crawled toward the southernmost tip of India, before returning for a northward sweep, roughly following the arc of the seventy-eight-degree meridian. There were latitudinal forays to connect Madras and Calcutta on the east coast with Mangalore and Bombay on the west. Plagued by jungle fevers, floods, and wild animals, they steadfastly triangulated mile upon mile, year after year, using algorithms that took into account the curvature of the earth and the effect of heat on the links of the hundred-foot chain that established the seven-and-a-half-mile baselines. The longest measurement of the earth's surface ever attempted, the result was called the Great Indian Arc of the Meridian.

The use of triangles to estimate the distance between one point and another dates to antiquity. In order to survey a fixed area, lines of sight must first be established between three visible reference points. These three points demarcate the three points of a triangle, with the sight lines representing the three sides. The distance between two of the three points must be known. This is called the baseline. By measuring the angles made by the baseline with the angles of the sight line to a distant third point (a peak or a hill topped with a signal post), the distance and position of the latter can be established by trigonometry. Once its distance was determined, that side could be used as a baseline to fix the distance of another visible fixed point. Stations were thus added one by one, creating a web of triangles across the subcontinent. At critical junctures astronomical observations would be made to cross-check for accuracy.

For the Great Indian Arc, a theodolite weighing half a ton was used to measure the horizontal and vertical angles from each end of the seven-and-a-half-mile baseline to the fixed point. It required a dozen men to carry it. Where there was no fixed point on which to fix the telescopic sights of the theodolite, the survey team built one. Another man would see to the project's completion, fifty years after it was begun. His name was George Everest. The highest fixed point in the world would be named after him.

A no less monumental achievement concluded half a century later. Upon winning the right to collect revenues, the East India Company had begun mapping every inch of inhabited, cultivated, and forested land in Bengal, registering the name of each landowner or tenant in logbooks. When, in response to the Indian Rebellion of 1857, the Crown bought out the company (adding its stiff price to the long column of India's debt) the project continued. These cloth maps and logbooks were known as land records. Land records were tied in neat bundles, wrapped in red cloth, and stacked on floor-to-ceiling shelves running the length of the record room of the district collectorate. By the early twentieth century, there was a map for every village in India.

Every ICS officer spent one cold season learning the subtleties of land settlement recording. After his Midnapore posting Carritt had a stint. As soon as all the villages and fields in one district were surveyed, and the names, rents, and tenures recorded, a five-member team would move on to the next. As Bengal was made up of some twenty districts and each one took from two to four years to survey, Carritt had calculated it would take nearly fifty years to complete one round. Then the entire operation would begin again. Aerial photography to assist in drawing maps was, however, just coming into use. A light biplane flying back and forth along three-mile strips would generate a roll of images. These flights occurred in the morning or evening so that the shadows from the low mud walls surrounding each paddy could be seen and measured.

It was through land records and Survey of India maps that the Crown replaced ancient understandings governing the land with its own legalisms. The rights of hereditary ownership, from the lowliest cultivator to the most powerful landowners, could be taken away with the stroke of a patwari pen. The revised land record would then be wrapped again in red cloth and placed in the appropriate spot on the collectorate's shelves. And there it would sit collecting dust until the land once again changed hands. Yet even the smallest village has dimensions that elude measure. The offices of the collector were often overrun with litigants, gossips, and court officers agitating for recognition of the ever-shifting tides of human affairs of which any ICS officer could only ever be dimly aware.

Tax collection in Bengal was often left in the hands of local land-owners, the powerful zamindars and nawabs. On top of the revenues mandated by their British overseers, they and their minions often helped themselves to commissions, thereby sending their landless tenants spiraling into debt. The Marquis of Salisbury once said, "As India is to be bled, the lancet should be directed to those parts where the blood is congested [rather than] those which are already feeble for the want of it."

Once the wealthiest province in all India, Bengal was bled and bled.

Michael Spender wanted to lose himself in some Sisyphean project like the Great Indian Arc. The maps of the southern African veldt were woefully inaccurate, he told Arthur Hinks. What about that? Hinks knew from the Everest Committee how difficult it was now to finance Sisyphean projects. Instead, he wrote to a Zurich professor asking that he teach Spender stereographic surveying. Hinks had a mountain in mind to map.

The Wild stereoautograph was made of black cast iron, with a foot wheel and two handwheels. Between the hand wheels was an eyepiece with a high-powered double scope before which were placed two photographic plates. The whole apparatus was attached to a drafting table where a pencil clamped to a carriage plotted elevation lines on drafting paper, steered by the handwheels. Just beyond this contraption, Michael watched Herr Professor give a lecture about some nuance of spherical geometry while chalking an elaborate equation on a blackboard with his left fist clenched under the tail of his black frock coat.

"Good you have come here to work," Herr Professor said, spinning around.

Switzerland's leading expert on photogrammetry then held forth for a solid hour on the principles laid out in his opus *Die Photogrammetrie und ihre Anwendung bei der schweizerischen Grundbuchvermessung und bei der allgemeinen Landesvermessung*. The man's Swiss German dialect was nearly incomprehensible, so Michael decided to read the manuscript in German, rather than use Hinks's rough translation, so as to learn the vocabulary. He was chagrined to discover that Continental mathematicians favored meandering analytical demonstrations rather than the sort of terse proofs he was accustomed to. Within a month Michael was boasting of having mastered the false position method and having produced an elegant proof of the rotation equation. Hinks doubtless knew what he was talking about.

It is tempting to think that drawing a topographical map is like painting a portrait. A portraitist also translates the three-dimensional features of a face to the plane of a canvas. Yet however learned in the tricks of perspective, a painter in the end will trust her eye and, depending on her skill, the face she paints will be recognizable as her sitter. A map, however, requires more than a visual comparison to check its accuracy. Its inner structure, the infrastructure of triangles brought back from the field, is concealed. Only after this framework is built can visual details be fitted onto it.

Just as painters had to rethink their art after the arrival of photography, so did mapmakers. The algorithms used to account for distortion and calculate scale from photographs made for laborious computations. A black box was needed to automate them. The first was invented in 1901; the Wild (pronounced Vilt) was the latest iteration. Photogrammetry, the craft of making measurements from photographs, thus became the art of avoiding mind-bending computation so as to master the art of detailing the contours of distant surfaces, such as mountains, from photographs. Using aerial and terrestrial photography, the Swiss had spent the past five years remapping all of Switzerland.

As the Alps constituted about half of the country, the Swiss had a head start on the new technique of stereophotogrammetry, one ideally suited for mountainous terrain. In this technique, instead of a single photograph, a pair of photographs was used. Each photograph of a fixed point on a summit was taken from a slightly different base on the ground. By adjusting the left and right handwheels of the Wild the two images merged and suddenly the mountain would jump into three dimensions in the viewfinder.

This physiological phenomenon affected the geometry inasmuch as it was suddenly possible to identify and plot more accurately every feature of the visible terrain. But it also required an illustration method that could convey an illusion of depth, without overwhelming the map with useless or distracting detail. A subtle sense of light and shade,

Michael saw, enabled Swiss mapmakers to differentiate between rock and scree, between snowfield and glacier; it was a perfect marriage of art and the scientific method. The Swiss mastery of *Felszeichnung*, mountain portraiture, accounted for the popularity of prewar Swiss maps. Like the features of a human face, a skillful rendering of weathered rock, even the way its strata were arranged, gave each mountain face its individuality, its profile. After mastering *Felszeichnung*, Michael left for the Alps to photograph the mountains themselves.

Of course the mere idea of getting out of a sleeping bag an hour before dawn made him feel he was taking a ridiculous pursuit far too seriously. A cup of tea eased him past this. Together with his small team, Michael would begin to climb. If he let himself attain full consciousness the pace was unbearable, so he maintained a trancelike reverie, letting his mind wander as his boots beat out a rhythm over the frozen moraine. If he was hungry, the relentless, drumming thought of food became tedious. Even worse was having someone along who insisted on talking. Michael tended to choose the lowest mountains for his stations, ones that would give him sufficient observations but wouldn't be too difficult to climb.

At dawn, having reached over eleven thousand feet, he would call a halt. The damp patch at the small of his back beneath his rucksack would go instantly cold as the peak of the massif in front of him attained a rosy glow. He would then suit up and slather his face with cream to protect it from the sun. One of his assistants would unrope and cross to the next ridge with the target mark and two-meter rule. To distract himself from the cold, Michael would estimate the distance and the time it would take his assisstant to get there. Using a hammer and chisel to prepare a foothold, he would then remove the tripod from its case and plant it on the ground.

By the time the phototheodolite was set up, the yellow light that lay across the snowy peaks would tell him the sun was high enough to begin. A dark eyepiece was fixed and pointed at the sun to establish the longitude. While one of his assistants held an umbrella over his head, Michael would inform his booker that he was first going to take the sun's lower limb, by which he meant the lower edge of the disk. But since in the telescope everything was upside down, it was actually the upper one. When the sun reached the cross wires in the theodolite, he shouted "UP" and the booker noted down the time on his watch to the nearest half second. Then he read him the vertical angle. Twelve such observations completed the morning sights. After checking the angles twice, Michael took a photograph.

Without a set routine, the hurry to get to work might cause some small slip in the setting of the swing or the observation of the spirit levels. While this might not render the work invalid, accuracy and efficiency were Michael's bywords.

At noon the latitude was taken. After that he would sit down and tear into a tin of sardines while his assistants finished building a cairn over the spot where the tripod had been. The empty tin would be buried in the cairn and a final stone placed on top. That day's station, combined with the day before's and the next day's, would provide the three corners of a triangle. A fourth station taken the day after the next would, with the two previous, extend the network further. Eventually a latticework of triangles would overlie the area to be mapped. The Great Arc had progressed in exactly this manner.

In the early afternoon Michael would set up a detail station, choosing a spot in front of a prominent peak. Later, he would cross the glacier and ascend to the other side of the valley to take a photograph of the same fixed point from another base, leaving the phototheodolite behind under a tarp for the next day. Long before the sun set Michael would be back at the hut for a cup of Maggi soup and an early night.

Romanisches Café, Berlin,
    Winter 1931–1932

By the time his photographic plates were inserted into the Wild in Zurich, Michael Spender was in Berlin to study the Zeiss stereoplanigraph, the German version of the Wild, and to master the techniques of aerial photogrammetry. The Germans were so ferociously pro-Zeiss as to be nearly Zeiss propagandists, he wrote Hinks. They assumed the superiority of the Zeiss without ever mentioning the Wild.

For some time now, Berlin had been a city of lost souls. That winter Hitler and the Communists were preparing for civil war. Martial law had all but been declared, with paddy wagons on every corner and truckloads of police ready to haul anyone off at the slightest pretext. Though spies were everywhere, they did little to dispel the atmosphere of lawlessness. Delinquent boys and peroxide tarts whose fathers had been killed in the war haunted the beer halls. One could scarcely walk the streets for the beggars. Black markets offered every luxury and red-light establishments served every escapist or illicit desire. In this city of increasing menace, Michael met the woman who would become his wife, a runaway named Erica Haarmann. In desperate straits herself, she leapt at the chance to escape.

That winter Michael also met up with his brother at the Romanisches Café.

"There isn't a girl sitting in this place," Michael had observed in the flat and statistical tone of voice Stephen had nearly forgotten, "who hasn't got scars on her wrists where she has cut her veins in an attempt to commit suicide."

It was Stephen's habit to think of Michael as insensitive and unobservant, particularly in regard to himself, so any evidence to the contrary was grist for the mill of his reflections. Where Michael maintained a rational view of the world, Stephen nurtured an intuitive one. Where Michael immersed himself in the innermost workings of the latest technological marvel, Stephen preferred a dispassionate exhumation of his innermost feelings, particularly those inspired by his family.

Michael had been slightly more welcoming of him at Oxford than he'd been at Gresham's, but he had resolutely refused to introduce him to Wystan Auden, his former lab partner. Stephen, who cultivated literary friendships with the same care he'd once lavished on his striped caterpillars, had been crushed. Eventually, Stephen found his own way to Wystan's rooms, where he soon finagled an introduction to Wystan's school friend, Christopher Isherwood, who was also then in Berlin. Christopher never tired of hearing about Stephen's family and, like a thief emptying an unsuspecting mark of his valuables, would eagerly ply him with questions. Stephen never failed to oblige him, particularly when it came to Michael. And now that he had got over his awe of his elder brother and was making his way in the world,

Stephen could begin to regard Michael much as Michael might regard a piece of machinery that didn't quite work as it was intended to. Michael became something to be taken apart so that his flaw might be identified and, if not fixed, at least established with certainty. Stephen diagnosed his brother's flaw as "spiritual astigmatism."

So, with map and compass, rock hammer and theodolite, Michael Spender and John Auden undertook explorations of the world, one they regarded with a naked eye from a distance and close up in a viewfinder or microscope. Similarly, Wystan Auden, Christopher Isherwood, and Stephen Spender made up the three points of the literary triangle through which events in Germany and elsewhere would be sited and mapped, in poetry and prose, in the coming decade. They, too, considered the times and the world in front of them, albeit from different angles and with different implements.

CHAPTER 6

The School of Art

38 Upper Park Road, Belsize Park, London,
    October 1935

Until she left for Cheltenham Ladies' College, Nancy Sharp had spent her entire life on the Cornish coast, the daughter of the town doctor and a disapproving mother. She had no opinion on the clash between labor and capital and associated the British Empire with mottled and gnarled old men sucking down pipe slobber while droning on about their days in the colonial service. Like most girls her age, too, Nancy far preferred sea bathing, riding, and tennis to climbing mountains, arctic expeditions, and similar Boy Scout pursuits. When, in the fall of 1928, Nancy arrived at the Slade School of Fine Art in London, she came fired up with a single idea. She would transform the epic discontent of her youth into Art. To her mind this would only work if she did nothing but paint and allow everything else to go to the dogs. It was as simple as that.

An early self-portrait shows a striking young woman with chestnut hair leaning forward in a chair in front of an open door, beyond which was a window. There is a slight frown on her face, as if she can scarcely believe what she sees. When she painted she leaned forward in exactly this way. After a series of quick dabs, she would pull away to squint at what she had done. Returning her brush to the palette, she would make little circles in the pigment, her eyes darting in and out of the scene before her, fully absorbed and uncharacteristically at peace. Her work conveyed this stillness: a sleeping cat, a view from a window, a quietly contained landscape. Her sullen adolescence was not where she belonged; the painting was.

After her first year at the Slade, Nancy became privately engaged to a Kenyan coffee planter named Errol. Yet by the end of that summer, all that mattered was escaping the prison of her family home for London. That fall she shared a large studio near Hampstead with a waif-like painter raised by Augustus John's bohemian ménage in Dorset. This girl knew nothing of the social conventions that had so stifled Nancy. For her the Deity was a world-famous portrait painter in a perpetual search for sitters.

At the Slade, as at Cheltenham Ladies' College and indeed, Nancy supposed, in the world generally, the pecking order was everything. If she was going to find her way to the top, the preponderance of females— three for every male—meant she had to work fast. Where the other girls tended to huddle in groups, arranging themselves on the lawn or front hall of the Slade, Nancy aimed for more of a splash. When one of her paintings in a show of Slade students' work received a favorable mention in the *Times* and the *Manchester Guardian*, she was thrilled to be singled out. This was it, she thought.

But the Slade Boys took it sourly, scoffing at the idea that newspaper critics knew the first thing about serious art. It shouldn't have surprised her. Her brother had always been the apple of her mother's eye. So Nancy's studio—someone compared it to the stage set of a German expressionist film—became her stage. Her parties and the wild revels that accompanied them marked the boundaries of their Slade set and the shifting alliances within it. At midnight Nancy would send the Boys scattering all over Hampstead where, waking late the next morning under their coats, they would struggle to recall what had possessed them.

Engaged or not, Nancy needed a boyfriend to make her mark, and on her list of those to try for was the insufferably self-possessed Bill Coldstream. From a distance Bill had struck her as simply more alert than the rest. Thin as a pencil, with his jacket of green tweed, and immaculately polished shoes, he had a shrewd look about him. Once the director's prize student, Coldstream no longer appeared at weekly Sketch Club where she might have caught his eye. And when he did emerge from his Fitzroy Square studio he was invariably surrounded. His superior knowledge of modern art guaranteed him an entourage.

Over tea at Express Dairy, cheap meals at Bertorelli's, or beer at his studio, Bill Coldstream held forth. Pictorial art was at a dead end. Cézanne and Degas were the ones. In politics, too, his opinion was definitive. Britain's colonies held the key to its standing as the pre-eminent world power. Soviet Russia, not having any, would never pose a serious challenge to Britain's hegemony, though America needed to be watched. While his witty send-up of the Boys' fumbling grasp of aesthetics was taken as a token of affection, one thing was clear: Bill Coldstream took no one's work as seriously as his own. The only thing that unsettled him was the prospect of another war; that haunted him.

The Slade Boys all agreed they would settle for two rooms, good food, limitless art supplies, theater tickets, and one Continental holiday a year. Such modest requirements were not a measure of their ambitions, which were considerable, but of their entitlement. Like Bill, they may have feared that one day their time would come and it would be 1914 all over again. But in the meantime, the annual Remembrance Day vigil for the war dead with its two minutes of silence was wearing thin. "Herd masturbation" one of them called it. Nancy never gave it much thought. She would never have to fear a call up.

When, in December 1929, Bill finally appeared at one of Nancy's gin parties, such was his presumption that he didn't bother to introduce himself. After that she went out with him nearly every night, matching his sly remarks on the Boys tit for tat. Abstract discussions of aesthetics were as boring to Nancy as arguments over politics. But Bill's cocksure air of knowing what he was about, his unquestioned place at the top of the heap, was something she wanted more than anything for herself. Failing that, she would have him instead.

Mixed parties soon brought an end to serious discussions. Evenings now began with a frantic rush to secure the most prominent spot at the Yorkshire Grey, and invariably ended with someone making a drunken spectacle. The Boys blamed the arrival of women in their lives for this new state of affairs, Nancy foremost. Long-suppressed grievances began to be aired. Bill was now "God Coldstream" and Nancy was declared a detestable creature. Then the slump of 1930 hit and the market for paintings vanished overnight.

Money, and the lack of it, now dominated their thoughts. And beyond the indifference of the public and the Royal Academy's blinkers, the Boys suddenly had to worry about those patently sham, cleverly slick modernists like Henry Moore and Ben Nicolson. They looked to Bill not to simply explain what they were about but to show them. But Bill's paintings were closely guarded, arranged so he could tell if they had been disturbed. He couldn't draw if there was anyone watching, but if left alone he tended to dither and dawdle. He would look for a book of matches, change his trousers, shave, and hunt around for a turpentine cloth to have in close reach, though he had yet to get out his brushes. Hours were spent staring at his easel.

"Just what does Bill think he's up to?" the Boys wondered. Whatever happened to that confident chap who so charmed them all at the Slade? another asked. The milk bottle of piss kept handy to save him the trouble of a trip to the loo and the piercing eye of a pet kestrel, caged amid rotting meat scraps in a gloomy corner, contributed to the dungeon-like feel of his studio.

So there it was. Four years after leaving the Slade and three years after marrying Bill, Nancy's idea of living only for Art was in tatters. It had ended with bill collectors at the door and wails emanating from the perambulator. Flowers withered before she could paint them. Uniformed nannies invaded their lives, sniffing at the clothes on the floor and casting appalled looks at overflowing ashtrays, jam-smeared towels, and a floor running with piddle. One February, in the dead of winter, the stove exploded. Baby Juliet ended up in an oxygen tent, Bill with the flu, and Nancy with jaundice. The absolute low point had been when Bill couldn't find a canvas and one of her most treasured portraits caught his eye. Without a second thought he painted over it. The Boys were still talking about how wild Nancy had been over *that*.

Nancy looked for truth in the raw material of her life. Like a historian digging for the roots of a long-simmering feud that had ended in all-out civil war, she retraced the steps that had brought her to such straits. The beginnings were clear. Her mother had greeted the news of her engagement with a flat statement: her father would never let her marry a painter. So Nancy had left a good-bye note under a hair-brush, pinched some money, and raced back to London. Her father sent her brother to head her off. He had arrived at the Marylebone Town Hall only to discover it was the wrong registry office. She and Bill were married at St. Pancras. The next day they proceeded to her family home in Bude only to be met at the door.

"I can do nothing with your father," her mother said. Her father appeared.

"You cad!" he had shouted at Bill. "You might as well have brought her home dead on a stretcher." Nancy burst into tears.

"I'm very sorry, sir." Bill had replied. Her tears stopped.

Sorry? SORRY?!

Was it Bill's lame reply to her father? Or the ghastly black hat she had borrowed ten pounds to buy for the ceremony? (A rare instance when her taste in hats failed her.) Perhaps it was the letter that followed her back to London signed, brutally, H. C. Sharp. A long, hot, dreary summer, living on three pounds a week in a grim and sooty King's Cross flat, followed. And when her father died of a heart attack that fall, her mother hadn't hesitated to accuse her of killing him. Perhaps the curse on their marriage lay there. At least with the slump Bill's dalliances with models were behind them; they could scarcely keep themselves in pencils and milk. When Nancy wasn't mourning the loss of her youthful promise, she made herself miserable searching for the exact moment her life went wrong. She ran the reel of that race to the registry office again and again, wondering how things might have turned out differently.

Seeing Bill emerge from his studio in the back garden, Nancy would go into a rage, raining blows on his head while he stood there looking like a corpse. And when Errol, her former fiancé, reappeared one summer day, for a brief moment she imagined she might return to that point in her youth when life held other possibilities.

But it was hopeless. As soon as she had become dependent on Bill, she became a bore and a deadweight. With her frantic need for affection, she had squeezed the life out of him. Just as it hadn't occurred to Bill that he might not be the genius he took himself for, it was inconceivable to Nancy that she was not the mistress of her fate, the star of her own story. That there might be a larger canvas, one on which she was no more than a crafty painter's trick to direct the eye elsewhere, was unthinkable.

Where they had once considered Communists childishly peevish, during the slump the Boys began to rethink their political stance. The notion that abstract art was the last gasp of bourgeois decadence was the hardest to swallow. They weren't ready to abandon Picasso. Couldn't surrealism mark the final expression of bourgeois decadence? Yet how did dialectical materialism translate into painting, they wondered, once again eyeing Bill for answers.

But in February 1935 Bill had taken a job editing documentaries at the Film Unit of the General Post Office. Now he was rushing out of the house at half past nine each morning, having expensive lunches in town, and coming home in a taxi at 1:00 a.m. Bill told the Boys it was naive to believe the masses would embrace a high art celebrating the triumph of the proletariat. Cinema would satisfy the popular appetite. Cinema was more accessible. Purely representative art was not reactionary but superfluous. Socialism would put an end to society portraits as well. It was only logical. The Boys were newly impressed.

Now it was the job Nancy envied. While Bill was out and about having a damn good time, she complained to anyone who would listen, the farthest she got from the flat was Regent's Park. One Whitsun, one of the Boys ended up staying the night after seeing a Fritz Lang film. The guest bed, he noted, smelled strongly of the family bull terrier. After Bill left for work he lingered on, fending off the enormous dog's huffy snout while the char washed nappies in the bathtub. While Nancy talked, bouncing Juliet up and down on her knee, he smoked and fidgeted.

"I am trying to persuade Bill to have more children," Nancy said, "but he doesn't want to." As a child, she explained, she would go out of her way to see a baby bathed.

"Yet you needn't have one just yet, need you?" Despite Bill's job money was tight and Nancy was something of a spendthrift. She was always extremely fashionable.

"Yes, I suppose so," she said. "Still it would be bad for Juliet to be an only." Cadging a shilling from him for the gas meter and inviting him to accompany her to the shops, Nancy gathered up her drawing pads, pencils, and books and loaded them all into the pram until there was scarcely room for the baby.

"We'll just leave Juliet in the pram and the char can look out of the window every now and then and see that she's all right," she said.

The Coldstreams' ground-floor maisonette suited Bill's new colleague at the Film Unit perfectly. A "veteran enemy of compulsory hygiene," Wystan Auden never thought to task Nancy over her housekeeping. As with the Carritt family of Boars Hill, he liked the messy bosom of domesticity and had long hungered for a cozy nest of his own. When Nancy went to the shops, he would play with Juliet or lift the infant Miranda into his bed to root at his breast. He and Nancy were soon thick as thieves.

Wystan had arrived at Upper Park Road with a sturdy wooden crate of books from his father's library. These tomes treated the homo-sexual feelings between boys as a way station on the road to manhood. In Berlin Wystan had convinced himself that through intimate con-gress with the heterosexual brawn of a "truly strong man," he might imbibe the required "he-man" qualities. Much like taking Bovril, he thought. Here a sailor from Hamburg proved to be an instructive but expensive mistake. Wystan hadn't mentioned that misadventure to John, but his brother's stay in Berlin had opened yet another sluice for his thoughts on the mysterious workings of the male libido. In his own way, Wystan was a formidable explorer himself. As was his wont, his explorations took a psychoanalytic turn.

How could two brothers raised by the same woman have such dif-ferent responses to the opposite sex? he asked himself. His buggery and John's compulsive whoring implied a direct criticism and rejec-tion of Mother's values. Having received more motherly love than John had, it was perhaps easier for him to beg off women altogether, whereas John, who'd received a more punitive and castigating form of Constance Rosalie's love, must always want more and more.

Wystan also kept turning over John's dramatic account of a fron-tier skirmish, reading into it an analysis of his own struggle over his attraction to men. After a grievously wounded Indian Army officer had valiantly secured a critical border post, the officer discovered that the hill tribe he had just decimated was made up of the same tribals as his regiment. Was the violent suppression of homosexual desires as heroic and foolish as the Indian Army's violent repression of rebel insurgencies? And if so, Wystan asked himself, had he been heroic and foolish to deny himself the love of men? Wystan had yet to find a satisfying answer to this "problem" and, after settling into the ground-floor maisonette, began to hope that perhaps Nancy might unlock the heroic he-man inside him.

When Wystan wrote her a neat little note in blank verse, Nancy was pleased to discover Bill was jealous. If Bill was unable to be faithful, Wystan had told her, it was only reasonable that she, too, should have affairs. She was interested. One afternoon Wystan began turning off the lights and closing the curtains. Their experiment, alas, was brought to an early end by the sound of Bill's key in the lock.

Yet when Wystan told Nancy she reminded him of a D. H. Lawrence heroine, she'd been flustered and embarrassed. Though she hadn't yet read *Lady Chatterley's Lover* she knew perfectly well what it was about. To cover her confusion she affected outrage because it was an obvious insult for Wystan to imagine her desperation was such that she'd sleep with a *gamekeeper*.

Wystan was puzzled. He said he didn't think she'd mind. *He* wouldn't have.

PART II

The Impersonal Eye

. . . perfect monsters—remember Dracula—
Are bred on crags in castles; those unsmiling parties,
Clumping off at dawn in the gear of their mystery
For points up, are a bit alarming;
They have balance, nerve
And habit of the Spiritual, but what God
Does their Order serve?

W. H. AUDEN, "MOUNTAINS"

Let me pretend that I'm the impersonal eye of the camera
Sent out by God to shoot on location

W. H. AUDEN, "LETTER TO WILLIAM COLDSTREAM, ESQ."

CHAPTER 7

Perfect Monsters

Border of the Kingdom of Nepal and Indian Province of Bihar,
Sunday, January 15, 1934, 2:13 p.m.

A curious anomaly sets the Himalaya apart from mountains elsewhere. Scientists have known since the nineteenth century that the temperature of the rocks that make up the earth's crust increases with their proximity to the earth's mantle. The rocks at the greatest depths are subjected to higher temperatures and greater pressures than rocks nearer the surface. In the Alps, the Appalachians, and the Welsh hills early geologists noted that the rocks of the highest elevations were those least exposed to the heat and compression of the deep crust. In the Himalaya the reverse was true. The rocks at the highest elevations came from the greatest depths. Every time John Auden traveled to the High Himalaya he confirmed it.

How did he know this? A brittle or flaky rock near the earth's surface becomes denser and more malleable in the high heat of the deep crust. The deeper the rocks are buried, the older they are and the higher the grade of metamorphism. Marine limestone becomes marble. Mudstone first becomes shale then slate and schist. At the greatest depths rocks melt and form magma. Magma squeezed from partly melted rocks pools and solidifies into large granite blocks or boulders. Ascending to what is now called the Main Himalayan Range, John was also, in part, climbing down through the earth's crust. What forces propelled the older hot rocks to the surface, burying the younger, cooler ones? It was a mystery.

The Himalaya are the indirect result of the breakup of an itinerant supercontinent known as Gondwanaland. Thirty million years after Gondwanaland separated from Madagascar, a piece of this continent, the Indian Plate, collided ever so slowly with the more cumbersome Eurasian Plate. Pivoting on that first point of contact, in what is now Ladakh, the Indian Plate turned counterclockwise and, like a pair of mismatched gears, the crusts of the two continents engaged. This lifted some of the floor of the Tethys Sea to the top of the southern Tibetan plateau. The rest of the seafloor was sunk deep beneath the earth's crust and thrust into the mantle. As the Indian Plate slipped under the Eurasian Plate, its upper crust was slowly scraped off, doubling the thickness of the crust and raising both the Himalaya and the Tibetan Plateau. The rock at the top of Everest is marine limestone, but sediments from Tibet can also be found there.

Thirty million years after the plates first collided, the pressure arising from crustal thickening and rising mountains created a thrust plane or fault, oriented east west. Over time, this thrust fault enabled the deeper, more malleable rocks first to stretch in response to the tectonic shifts of the plate and then to work their way up, smeared by the stupendous weight of the mountains. For the next fifteen million years, massive blocks of stone thrust themselves into the sky, restless as a city sending skyscrapers up during a long boom. These layers of crust all tilted north, pushing southward the cooler rocks beneath them, while erosion stripped the rocks that had once lain at the bottom of the Tethys Sea off their backs. Eventually, these highly crystalline rocks arranged themselves like the uneven rows of shark's teeth into the highest chain of mountains in the world. Among them was the peak known as Chomolungma to those who lived in view of it, and Mount Everest to the Survey of India men who named it. Then the fault went quiet.

During the untold millions of years that followed, the two plates continued to butt each other like rutting bharals. Eventually, a new fault zone arose, this one to the south of the Lesser Himalaya, or Mahabharat Lekh. Shallower layers of sedimentary rocks that had been pushed aside by the earlier thrust were now heaved up. To ascend these slopes, then, is not only to travel down through the upper layers of the earth's crust but also to travel back in time, again and again, as enormous blocks of sedimentary crust pile up, one on top of another like rock sandwiches, representing discrete and vast wedges of time. This fault, too, eventually went quiet and the thrusting shifted south again, into the alluvial plain.

Few scientists of John Auden's time accepted Alfred Wegener's theory of continental drift, which first appeared in English in 1922. John was no exception. Indeed, there was a great suspicion of grand overarching theories, particularly German ones. Wegener had provided insufficient evidence, it was said, and no explanation of the mechanism by which continents moved. He wasn't even a geologist. And so without the notion of continental drift, without the means to measure the thickening of the earth's crust and to detect the persistent northward creep of India, John Auden could not explain the tectonic forces that conspired to raise mountains and create the kinds of chaotic arrangements of rocks he'd noted in the Krol Belt. What he could do was train his eye on the composition and arrangement of rocks as he traveled through jungles, across rivers, and up and down mountainsides. From his observations he wrote papers and drew intricate maps. This was the principal undertaking of exploration: to collect and to classify and to fill in blanks on maps. But as to explaining what was happening deep within the earth's crust, few dared speculate.

Then, on Sunday, January 15, 1934, an earthquake struck the border of the Kingdom of Nepal and the Indian province of Bihar. It began with a sudden, sweeping wind. The temperature dropped sharply in its wake, as if the season had changed in a moment. From the west came a rumbling. A few seconds later, the main shock hit. Lasting between two and half and five minutes, the shaking of the earth increased in intensity until the rumbling rose to a roar. Later estimates put the area of shock transmission at over three million square miles, the greatest ever recorded in the region.

In those minutes the Gangetic Plain undulated in surface waves, as if the earth had turned into water. In places of shallow alluvial soil, hundreds upon hundreds of geysers bubbled up. Fountains of hot water and fine sand spurted six feet in the air. When they subsided they left behind curious conical formations, like tiny volcanoes. Wells overflowed with sand; winter harvests were destroyed. In rockier regions, crevices thousands of feet long, thirty feet wide, and fifty feet deep opened in the earth's crust and from them poured more water, blindly furious to make sense of the new geography. People and animals became trapped in the cracks only to have the earth shift again, the clefts reopen, and eject them in a burst of water like indigestible scraps.

In Calcutta the rumbling was drowned out by the noise of vehicles colliding and the shouts and panic of people in the streets. The bell tower and steeple of St. Paul's Cathedral crashed with a clang. Bishop Foss Wescott had only enough time to rush out of his bungalow before it collapsed behind him in a tumbled mass of masonry and timber. In Kathmandu the prime minister's palace shuddered and fell thunderously into rubble before disappearing in a rising cloud of dust that shut out the sun and rendered the air unbreathable. By the time the earth stopped moving, a four-thousand-square-mile region had been devastated. Ten thousand people died in the span of five minutes; countless more were injured and made homeless.

What did those in the quiet rhododendron forests of the Himalayan foothills understand of this? Had Mara, Lord of Death, defeated once again by the Buddha, started those avalanches in a fit of rage? Was Mahasu, avatar of Shiva, chasing his rival Chasrala through the mountains and valleys? Sadhus and saints were called upon to explain what forces had brought down such a calamity. Gandhi ascribed it to the stain of untouchability; Nehru, touring the devastation, was staggered but kept his thoughts to himself. Incense and butter lamps were lit, prayers and supplications poured forth. The sounds of mourning went on through the night.

For over a century Europeans had been barred from the Kingdom of Nepal. In the course of the 1814–16 Anglo-Gurkha War, the East India Company had seized Nepal's Garhwal and Kumaon territories in the west and the Kingdom of Sikkim in the east. Since then the high ranges of the Nepal Himalaya had been more inaccessible to Europeans than Tibet. The three Everest expeditions of the 1920s were obliged to approach the mountain from the north, requiring a monthlong trek across Tibet from Sikkim. After the disappearance of Mallory and Irvine, even this access was cut.

During the 1934 earthquake, the king of Nepal, Maharaja Juddha Shumsher Jung Bahadur, lost two daughters and their maidservants in the collapse of his palace. His request that the Geological Survey of India investigate the quake was a measure of Nepal's distress. John Auden was invited to lead a team of geologists, traversing the devastated border region from west to east on royal elephants. Comparing the seismograph recordings from Kew and Bombay, where the quake had registered 8.4 on the Richter scale, Auden had estimated the epicenter to be in eastern Nepal. On reaching it he read the landscape as a detective might reconstruct a violent crime by studying the overturned furniture. Thrust faults were not always hidden deep beneath the earth; they could also be written in the surface, as they were in the Krol Belt. He decided the epicenter was farther south, beneath the Gangetic Plain, an area not known for seismicity.

Everywhere Auden went he felt the hot winds and breathed the choking dust that emerged from newly opened vents in the crust. His mouth filled with sores. His observations, however, were confined to what the quake unearthed rather than the harrowed faces surrounding him, as if human life was of no consequence when set against the colossal power of the earth itself.

Indeed, why climb Everest if not to assert the power of an Englishman over the power of nature to raise a mountain beyond his reach? Why climb the Himalaya if not for the view it afforded across time? Perhaps a man, like the rocks beneath his boots, might also be strengthened and purified of his weaker elements by such an undertaking. John Auden seemed to believe that the higher one climbed, the purer grade of man one became. Mallory, a veteran of trench warfare, was often portrayed as a near-ethereal being, a beautiful boy with his head in the clouds who, as Churchill had eulogized his friend and fellow martyr Rupert Brooke, "advanced towards the brink in perfect serenity." The fact that Mallory's body was never recovered only added to the air of legend surrounding him.

During the years Everest was off limits, attention had turned toward more accessible summits. With a limited number of mountains over eight thousand meters to go around, the race to plant national flags on the loftiest peaks began. Ten of the fourteen mountains over this height were in the Himalaya; the remaining four were in its sister range to the west, the Karakoram. Sensitive to the charge of imperial preference, the Government of India was obliged to consider permit petitions from rival nations, foremost among them France and Germany. During the 1930s permission was granted for German attempts on Kanchenjunga near Darjeeling in the eastern end of the Himalaya and Nanga Parbat in the far west. The French secured Masherbrum 1 in the Karakoram, across the Indus from Nanga Parbat. The United States also wanted in. While the three Everest expeditions of the 1920s were pitched as scientific undertakings and included botanists and geologists, those of the 1930s largely limited themselves to mountaineers and soldiers.

It was in the 1930s, too, that a new paragon was forged in Europe, one in which manhood, nationhood, and summit seeking became inextricably linked. The men who aspired to climb the highest peaks were no longer *Luftmenschen*, men in thrall to the sublime like George Mallory, but *Übermenschen*, leviathans who wanted to stand on top and look down. Summits were no longer sought after as memorials to the fallen, or in pursuit of scientific knowledge, but as means to assert or reclaim a nation's power and virility. Germany led the way in this attitude, but England and France duly followed suit, albeit in the less bombastic register befitting those who'd prevailed in the Great War. The Mount Everest Committee was equally captive to the sort of magical thinking its members imagined only their native subjects indulged in: the conquest of Everest would grant England powers more lasting and splendid than any imperial durbar. This fantasy had a flip side. Failure might unman the empire, strip the king-emperor naked for all to see.

For the sages of the Everest Committee who kept an eye on these matters, John Auden's royal invitation to visit Nepal was auspicious, raising the tantalizing possibility that access to Everest from the south might one day be granted. When writing up his account for the *Himalayan Journal*, John made sure to mention that east of Udaipur Garhi, through a scrim of mist and dust, the south face of Everest was just visible, seventy-three miles away. Had there been time to climb the Mahabharat Lekh, a fuller view of the southern approach might have been gained, but without permission to venture farther inland, he had to withdraw. Yet proximity to his mountain made him feel, briefly, less a stranger to himself.

Royal Geographical Society, 1 Kensington Gore, London,
      September 3, 1932

Two years before the earthquake, the *Madras Weekly* had carried an account of a plane flying in the vicinity of Everest on behalf of an American organization called "Knights of the Flying Carpets." Arthur Hinks, the secretary of the Royal Geographical Society, was incensed. The Yanks had already been the first to fly over the poles and the idea of them anywhere near Everest was unacceptable. In the future, Hinks wrote the India Office, German mountaineering applications should take precedence over American. In the meantime he asked that the Government of India find out if the Maharaja of Nepal had granted the Americans permission to fly over his kingdom. And while they were at it, they should ask Tibet about a new expedition to Everest. Nepal issued a weak protest regarding the "unauthorized flight," but it was five months before Hinks had an answer to his second inquiry.

Nothing had changed.

Hinks was unrelenting: if delicate reference were made to the still missing bodies of Mallory and Irvine, might that induce a change in attitude? Long silence. An application for permission for a British flight over Everest was, however, passed along to the Maharaja of Nepal. At the end of May 1932 word came back that the application was being given sympathetic consideration, and in July permission was granted. At nearly the same moment, the wind shifted, the clouds opened, and the long-hoped-for vision of the mountaintop appeared. The Dalai Lama had written a letter.

"Almost every nation on the face of the earth is desirous of ascending the high mountains in the world," the letter began. "The British are also very anxious to ascend Mount Everest," His Holiness continued before adding, undiplomatically, "They have tried twice, but so far they have failed." The British had obliged the Dalai Lama with a supply of modern weaponry and he proffered access to Everest via Tibet in return. The nine-year wait was over. Hinks was out the gate in a heartbeat.

"The first, most anxious step is the choice of a leader," Sir Francis Younghusband, the president of the Everest Committee had said, announcing the new expedition in September. "For good or ill much, perhaps all will depend upon him." Both flight and climb would take place in April or May 1933. The question now was: Who would get there first? Man or machine?

Lalbalu, Bihar, Army Dept. Landing Ground,
160 Miles South of Mount Everest, April 3, 1933

The flight over Everest's summit was to be "austerely scientific" and "based in every detail on the most serious thought." A year's testing would be required to solve the technical challenges posed by the impact of high winds, high altitudes, and frigid temperatures on the flight's aerodynamics and the frailties of the pilot's body. Each of the two prototypes would be equipped with a supercharged, nine-cylinder Bristol Pegasus S engine, capable of ascending to thirty-four thousand feet. Finally, cameras screwed to the undersides of the biplanes would generate a series of survey strips to net the semi-mythical Everest on a Survey of India grid, thirty miles square.

Lady "Poppy" Houston, a raging patriot, suffragette, and nudist, had little interest in either the survey or the science. "The chief aim of the Marquis and myself in this Adventure," she proclaimed in the peremptory voice of a woman used to getting her way, was "to show India that we are not the Degenerate Race that its leaders represent Britain to be" but "a virile and active" one.

Once a sixteen-year-old chorus dancer named Fanny, by the age of seventy-six Lady Houston had married four times and expressed her admiration for Mussolini by naming her lapdog Benito. Her feelings about the present British government were less tender. Prime Minister Ramsay MacDonald had recently suggested that India might eventually become a dominion in the British Commonwealth. Poppy was having none of it. A stalwart member of the Indian Empire Society, expressly founded to oppose Indian self-rule, she had sailed her yacht,

Liberty, along the south coast of Great Britain with a bunting proclaiming "TO HELL WITH RAMSAY MACDONALD."

Lady Houston and her ilk were known as Die Hards.

After India and Benito, aviation was closest to her heart. When MacDonald pulled funding from the Air Ministry, raising the specter that a British aeroplane might not secure the Schneider Trophy for the third year in a row, Lady Houston stepped up with a hefty offer of one hundred thousand pounds to underwrite the development of the Supermarine S.6 engine. The prototype duly won the air race at Cowes. If the Supermarine S.6 was all about speed, the Pegasus S would be about altitude. The Everest Flight Committee—Conservative MPs, earls, wing commanders, newspaper barons, and John Buchan, a writer of spy thrillers and a fixture of the Conservative establishment—was not prepared to cede Everest to anyone.

When Lady Houston had arrived with her checkbook, they were obliged to hear her out. The new India Bill before Parliament, she announced, was a shameful surrender. If India was, in Churchill's phrase, "that most truly bright and precious jewel in the crown," a successful flight over Everest's summit would fix that troubled gemstone firmly in place. Churchill was a fellow member of the India Empire Society and Poppy had shared his disgust at the sight of that "half-naked fakir" Gandhi taking tea with Viceroy Irwin two years before. Irwin, she declared, was a traitor to his class. At least his successor, the Marquess of Willingdon, had shown he had some bones in his gloves.

In the opening montage of *Wings over Everest*, Lady Houston, propped against enormous bed pillows wearing a fox stole and jeweled turban, stiffly reenacted her decision to fund the flight. The Schneider Trophy by her bedside had a close-up. Timelapse photography showed the building of the Pegasus S engine accompanied by scenes of people on telephones, at drafting tables, and rushing down steps, all in edifying contrast to a clip of natives playing pipes. In the gardens of the Maharaja of Darbhanga the pilots were shown in deep discussion, followed by a calendar with the days flying by. Twice-daily weather reports entailed further deliberations. The pages stopped at Monday, April 3, 1933. A ground crew reviewed a forty-six-item checklist. After final adjustments to their heated goggles, the two open cockpit biplanes took off to cheers. An overhead shot of natives gathering hay showed their astonishment.

As deodar thinned out into pine, ilex, birch, then juniper and rhododendron, the ramparts of cliffs and rock faces appeared. Wave upon wave of mountains rose and fell below them, stretching hundreds of miles in both directions. Climbing to 19,000 feet, the pilots had their first sight of white peaks, with Kanchenjunga rising up under their starboard wing. A moment later two tiny summits appeared just to the right of the plane's axis. A plume of crystallizing ice distinguished Everest's summit from Makalu's. The altimeter showed the plane at 33,000 feet, already 4,000 feet higher than Everest's highest point. As they began their approach the wind velocity peaked at one hundred mph and a close-up of the thermometer showed the temperature to be minus fifty degrees Fahrenheit. On a notepad the Marquis of Clydesdale wrote, "That's the NE ridge the climbers go up," as the arête on which Mallory and Irvine were last seen came into view.

The summit loomed up and passed beneath them. After the plane circled it for fifteen minutes, there was one last wide-angle shot of the Himalayan panorama to the west before the plane coasted down the airfield to applause, handshakes, and backslapping. A spokesman for the flight advised the *Times* that it would take time to study just what had been seen in those few sublime minutes "looking down on the world's last penetralia."

Who could have foreseen that the dust haze would make it impossible to see anything in the survey strips? Lady Houston's cable refused permission for another go. It was enough that an Englishman had been the first to look down upon that tiny spot of frontier, dividing this world from the heavens of the next.

Attention now turned to the mountaineers.

Base Camp, East Rongbuk Glacier,
  Mount Everest, April 25, 1933

John Auden had only just begun to study Himalayan tectonics in earnest when Margaret Marshall arrived in Calcutta to be consoled over the death of her husband. Not knowing quite what to say, he married her. No sooner was their honeymoon over than he became desperately eager to return to the mountains, disappearing for weeks at a time and leaving her alone and friendless in a tiny Calcutta flat. She took revenge by spending wildly and sleeping with his manservant. Their divorce would be finalized by the end of 1933.

In the meantime, John had finished his geological map of the Krol Belt, delineating with utmost meticulousness the stratigraphic folds of the Lesser Himalaya near Simla. He'd also done an analysis of the granites in the area, and contrary to the common understanding that all granites of the Himalaya had intruded during the Tertiary period (66 million years ago to 1.5 million years ago), he'd found evidence of far older granite intrusions, occurring as much as 250 million years ago. Intrusion was the process whereby an igneous rock like granite is forced through other rock structures in the crust without breaking the surface. The granite pebble on which his analysis was based was found to have uncanny similarities to granite he'd collected elsewhere in the high elevations, suggesting a wave of simultaneous intrusions. Should there ever be another Everest expedition, he hoped this work would secure him the spot of expedition geologist.

But when Bill Wager, whom John had known at Cambridge, arrived in Calcutta in March 1933, John realized he had missed his shot at being chosen. It was difficult not to blame Margaret for that, too. Over lunch he'd asked Wager if, as the expedition geologist, he would be surveying the East Rongbuk Glacier. The talk was all about taking the summit, Wager replied, with an unmistakable swagger. That had been galling. Not only did Wager know nothing of Himalayan geology but it was his first trip to India. Apart from Hinks's insistence that all aspirants be Englishmen, John had to wonder how the rest were selected.

Since most of the 1933 climbers were too young to have served in the war, the Mallory ideal had been rethought. Who would be the expedition's leading man? Such a man had to embody all that was noble, stirring, and sporting about the English race. Bill Wager fit Hinks's new template to a T: a first-rate English public school, membership in the Cambridge Mountaineering Club, and a thruster's hunger for the top. He was also fresh from an arctic expedition on the East Greenland coast. Still, it was impossible to predict how these chosen paragons would perform in extreme altitude. Tempers might prove as debilitating as altitude sickness. Passionate hatreds between climbers, fanned by rivalry and isolation, didn't make it into the official minutes, but there was always talk. Frank Smythe bore the brunt of it. Only Eric Shipton, a puckish twenty-five-year-old, seemed able to stand him.

From the moment they first assembled, every climber was the object of scrutiny by the leader of the expedition, Hugh Ruttledge. Out of twelve mountaineers, three two-man storming parties would be named. Until the final roster was announced each contestant eyed the others warily and did his best to appear hale and hearty. Ruttledge named the chosen when they arrived at Base Camp. To console the six who hadn't made the cut, he pointed out that if someone developed altitude sickness or, god forbid, had an accident, they might be called upon. Eric Shipton thought this tactless. It was typical of the war generation's thinking to have an excess of young men on hand to throw at the battlements, while staying well to the rear themselves. Shipton and Smythe were named the lead party.

But for his triumphant summiting of Kamet, the second-highest peak in British India and the highest ever climbed, Smythe might never have been considered. From an obscure public school he went neither into the military, university, nor colonial service. Worse, in the eyes of Arthur Hinks, he gave public lectures and interviews to the newspapers. But Smythe's leadership on Kamet, a mountain on the edge of the Tibetan Plateau in the Garhwal, had been a triumph. Two separate parties had reached the summit, including Smythe, Shipton, two porters, and a transport officer.

The selection of climbers was transparent when compared with how the committee settled on Hugh Ruttledge. "We must have a leader who has it in him right down to the nails of his toes," Younghusband had declared. Sir Francis might have tapped his protégé Smythe, but to Hinks's undoubted relief, it wasn't up to him. His impetuous invasion of Tibet had been a thorn in the side of the Dalai Lama and the less he had to do with Everest, the better. After two members of the 1924 expedition proved unavailable, Ruttledge was chosen.

A fall off a horse had left this balding, bespectacled, and nearly fifty-year-old district officer with a pronounced hitch in his gait. But he was a pukka sahib and a keen huntsman. There were striking parallels between climbing and hunting, he argued. Just as mountaineering wasn't simply about getting to the top, shikar was more than the desire to kill something. Ruttledge loved to sit around the fire telling hunting yarns and debating the best route to Everest's summit. This debate began in Sikkim and the climbers were now perfectly sick of it, but Ruttledge wouldn't let it go. His fussy habit of handing out raspberries couched in magnificent language also did not go over well.

In the years since Mallory and Irvine's disappearance on the final approach to the summit, the findings of the Everest expeditions of the 1920s had been thoroughly debated. On the 1921 reconnaissance, a surveyor had discovered that the East Rongbuk Glacier was the only possible approach to the mountain. This glacier ended at a nearly vertical 1,200-foot wall of rock and ice. From there one ascended to the snowy ridge of the North Col at 23,000 feet, the point from which any attempt on the summit from the north really begins. That was the uncontroversial part. From the Col there were two possible routes over the last 6,000 vertical feet. The first was the Northeast ridge. This ridge sported two formidable obstacles known then as Step 1 and Step 2. Step 2 was a steep rock promontory rising over 130 feet (from below it looked more like 200), the last dozen being nearly straight up.

Would they, as Mallory had, climb just below the knife-edge arête to make a direct assault on the steps while the winds off the Tibetan Plateau tried to blow them to kingdom come? Or would they choose the second option, traversing the treacherous outward-sloping and icy-smooth slabs of the Great Couloir on the North Face that at the slightest misstep would deliver them to the East Rongbuk Glacier 10,000 feet below? The climbers dutifully took turns gazing through a telescope designed to study the stars.

Ruttledge had devised a strategy that divided the route to the summit into three stages. The trek across Tibet to Base Camp was complete. The supplying of Camps I–IV up the East Rongbuk Glacier was in progress. The final stage, establishing the last two camps above the North Col and the siege of the summit, was a month away. It was for this last bit that the chosen six were husbanding their energies, curled up in their sleeping bags and fanatically checking their basal pulses. Steady acclimatization was their leader's mantra. Eric Shipton joked that they would soon be getting bedsores. Only Bill Wager was languishing at Base Camp, suffering from hill trots. Wager had only just made the third team and a case of the trots wasn't going to stop him from proving that he was of the same stamp as the rest.

Mercifully, he believed the worst was behind him and he saw no reason why he wouldn't be ready when the call came. "The mountain is not a slag heap as I had heard," Wager wrote John Auden on Expedition stationery, rubbing yet more salt in his wounds.

Camp VI, 27,400 feet, North Face of Mount Everest,
1,602 feet from the Summit, May 31, 1933

A fully recovered Bill Wager bedded down at Camp VI, his tent fixed on a tiny ledge on Everest's North Face, 1,602 feet below the summit. Two weeks before, the telegraph line strung from Base Camp brought word that the monsoon had been seen off the coast of Ceylon. No one believed this; it was far too early. The wind blew hard, the tents filled with the sound of coughs. It was a fitful night. The next morning Wager and his partner chose Mallory's route, setting off at 5:40 a.m. toward the first of the two steps on the Northeast ridge. En route Wager's partner found Mallory's ice ax. They had reached hallowed ground.

They ascended Step 1 only to find Step 2 insurmountable. Descending 200 to 300 feet below the ridge, they tried crossing the Great Couloir, picking their way over slabs covered in loose, light snow. In winter, high winds removed the snow as it fell, sweeping clean the bands of rock on the North Face. At a certain point, Wager later theorized, the balance of power shifted and the accumulation of snow exceeded the power of the wind to remove it, marking the shift from winter to monsoon conditions. They managed to cross the couloir and climb a steep buttress only to find another, smaller couloir on the far side. Nine hundred feet short of the summit, their time ran out.

On the way back they retrieved Mallory's ice ax and Wager climbed to the top of the ridge to take in the icefall on the Nepal side. Back at Camp VI Smythe and Shipton heard them out, deciding to head directly to the Great Couloir. Wager and his partner began their descent. Down on the East Rongbuk Glacier, Ruttledge knew nothing of the climbers' fate. That night there were no hunting yarns over the campfire. When no message came down the following morning, he set up the telescope and trained it on the monsoon clouds covering the North Face like a shroud. No one said a word to him.

During the night Smythe kept rolling over Shipton. Having to constantly roll him back, uphill, did not make for restful sleep. Snowfall the next day meant another night spent in this way. Finally, they were able to proceed to the couloir, following a narrowing series of ledges. Shipton realized he was as weak as a kitten and left the mountain to Smythe.

Smythe might have been a humorless and self-aggrandizing man at sea level but under the effects of hypoxia a yogi-like calm descended on him. It was in such a state that he reached the far side of the Great Couloir by 10:00 a.m. Here he planned to ascend the smaller couloir straight up the face of the final pyramid. But the snow was as soft and loose as goose down and swallowed him up to his thighs. Two weeks earlier, they had climbed 1,000 feet in an hour. Now he progressed less than a foot a minute and every step forward put him a step away from a safe return. He gave up.

The Dalai Lama ascribed the expedition's failure to the rage of the mountain's guardian deities. But Eric Shipton felt the entire vision of the expedition was suspect. The trip across the Tibetan Plateau had involved thousands of pack animals. There was a contingent of signal corps officers, armed guards, and seventy-two Sherpas and Bhotias to ferry supplies to and from the high camps. These supplies included tins of herring, smoked salmon, lobster, crab, salmon, asparagus, caviar, and foie gras. Dozens of cases had been left behind, a colossal waste of money and the porters who brought them there. Did every climber require a tent and personal servant? Including those never called? Ruttledge's obsession with acclimatization meant that the deterioration that set in at high altitudes had time to get a foothold.

Meanwhile the air commodore who flew over Everest was comparing his triumph to Alexander's conquest of India. He quoted Napoleon's "he who holds India, holds the world" to underscore the tortured conceit that Everest, a mountain that wasn't even in India, was a proxy for England's global domination. He didn't hesitate to declare the failure of the mountaineers' expedition "a splendid achievement," as if the magnetic field surrounding Everest could bend a logic that prevailed elsewhere. When, defying Lady Houston, a second flight was made, the pilots congratulated themselves on their daring. The survey strips had magnificent definition, unbroken continuity, and were precisely overlapped.

Michael Spender, who had perfected the use of aerial photography while mapping the coastal mountains of East Greenland that summer, was dismissive. Around Everest, the enormous range in mountain heights meant that the distortions of vertical photography were extreme. The plane should have carried an additional fixed camera to capture the differences in their relative heights. Then the resulting survey strips might have been plotted against existing ground surveys to create a map of the Everest region. As it was, the pilots put a pretty face on things to hit the obligatory note of triumph.

Bill Wager blamed Ruttledge for the failure of the 1933 Everest expedition. After trashing the man in a letter to John, Wager had gone on to note that John shared one of Hugh Ruttledge's mannerisms. It wasn't an India thing, or anything deplorable, he said, just some tic he had ever since he'd known him.

He stopped there, leaving John beside himself with worry over what it was. That was Wager's idea of fun.

– CHAPTER 8 –

Goddess Mother of the World

The Grand Hotel, Chowringhee Street, Calcutta,
 May 20, 1935

The Grand Hotel had an extravagant white-pillared colonnade that stretched down an entire block. This afforded the veranda above a spectacular view of the Maidan and the Victoria Memorial. But that afternoon it was the dining room of the Grand, where high officials went to see and be seen, that had the most interesting sight. Had the viceroy himself made an appearance he would not have turned as many heads as the spectacle of Eric Shipton and his ragtag entourage arriving for lunch.

Two years after the failure of the 1933 expedition, the Tibetans had once more granted England access to Everest. As it was too late in the year to put an expedition together, the Mount Everest Committee decided that a small team would first undertake a reconnaissance and thereby lay the groundwork for an all-out attempt on the summit in May 1936. Photographs of the seven members of the 1935 reconnaissance, taken on their arrival in Bombay, had been splashed all over the *Statesman*, and in these Eric Shipton, expedition leader, stood front and center. While in Calcutta Shipton planned to invite at least one member of the Himalayan Club posted in India to join them on the reconnaissance. If that man fared well, he would be asked to join the 1936 summit attempt. It was this that brought Shipton to the Grand that sweltering afternoon. John Auden's name was in the mix.

Three of the five climbers Shipton brought from London were former members of the Cambridge Mountaineering Club. The fourth was a New Zealander named Dan Bryant to whom Shipton had taken a shine. The fifth climber and the man with whom Shipton had achieved the greatest feat in the history of mountaineering was nowhere to be seen. After a hot night at the Tollygunj Club, Bill Tilman had gone directly to Darjeeling to begin requisitioning supplies and overseeing the selection of porters. He found Bengalis insufferable.

Though Eric Shipton and Bill Tilman would eventually be known as the "terrible twins" of Himalayan mountaineering, they were really more of a mismatched pair. Where Tilman was square in jaw and stature, Shipton was slim and elfin with an open face and a splayed stance like a penguin. Tilman was the son of an English sugar merchant and a veteran of the trenches. Shipton grew up on a tea plantation in Ceylon and was too young to have fought. Tilman was not known for easy affability. Shipton regarded his fellow man as an entertainment not to be missed. Tilman disdained female companionship; Shipton was a momma's boy. Indeed, Shipton's mother (Tilman called her "The Holy") was just then picking up last-minute provisions at New Market.

On Shipton's return from Everest in 1933, Tilman had invited him on a climb in the Lake District. Shipton had a better idea. Come to India for seven months, he countered. Convinced by Bill Wager that exploration was a higher calling than bagging peaks, Shipton suggested they attempt to penetrate the unexplored sanctuary surrounding Nanda Devi, the highest peak in British India.

Central to the sacred geography of Hindus, Nanda Devi was known as the earthly home of the seven Rishis. Hugh Ruttledge believed the sages had chosen it because their meditations were least likely to be disturbed, though many had tried. Ruttledge himself had attempted it three times but had been unable to penetrate the ring of thirty peaks, each over 21,000 feet, that surrounded the mountain. On the ring's western edge was a fantastic twenty-mile gorge where the Rishi Ganga had sliced a deep and narrow cut through the stone. No one had yet succeeded in forcing a way up. Shipton proposed going up the gorge, reconnoitering the inner sanctum and all possible routes to Nanda Devi's twin summits (the highest, 25,643 feet). They would then exit over the outer ring wall to the east.

Shipton and Tilman embarked from the temple town of Joshimath accompanied by three Darjeeling Sherpas. With the Rishi Ganga tumbling furiously 1,500 feet below them, they inched along, hugging cliffs, pelted by falling rocks, before finally reaching the sanctum, conducting their survey and making their exit. Shipton was thereby confirmed in his belief that smaller parties were more suited to exploration and climbing than the overstaffed military siege model Ruttledge had followed on Everest. Shipton and Tilman's 1934 season was universally hailed for the triumph it was.

For the 1935 reconnaissance, the Everest Committee told Shipton to explore the possibility of an Everest summit attempt in monsoon weather, but expressly forbid him from trying one. His main mission was to oversee a survey of as many of the glaciers surrounding Everest as he could, a far more technical undertaking than the one he'd done in the sanctum. Hinks wanted a map showing both the precise elevations of Step 1 and Step 2 on the northeast ridge, and the contours of the bands of rock that defined the Great Couloir. He believed such a map would help settle the question of which route was more likely to see an Everester to the summit. The climbers would also take calibrated photographs of the horizons from highest peaks and ridges in the immediate neighborhood of Everest and photograph what they could of the approach to Everest from Nepal. John Auden's report on the 1934 earthquake had just appeared. A change of heart in Kathmandu was always possible.

Just before setting sail for India, Shipton spent a weekend with Bill Wager. He wanted to solicit his thoughts on candidates for the reconnaissance and the 1936 summit attempt. Wager advised Shipton that every expedition needed a man "so universally disliked that the others, with a common object for their spleen, would be drawn together in close companionship." For example, in Greenland there had been this impossibly pompous man named Spender. Shipton was thus tickled to learn that Hinks's last-minute choice for chief surveyor of the 1935 reconnaissance, now sitting across from him at the Grand, was none other than Michael Spender. Wager had set him up nicely.

Michael had felt like a thief stealing off as he did. His wife, Erica, hadn't taken the news of a six-month expedition at all well, though Aunt May had kindly offered to look in on her while he was away. A crowd of family and friends appeared at the station, so even their final moments were in the public eye. In Paris he scoured the rue de Rivoli for a gift, only to get lost in the Latin Quarter. After a lonely dinner he caught the overnight train to Marseilles. Once aboard he became so absorbed in the tasks of preparing plane table sheets and holding theodolite classes for the climbers in the well decks that Erica was soon forgotten.

Over lunch at the Grand an officer of the Imperial Forest Service backed John Auden's candidacy for the open spot on the expedition roster unreservedly, as did two senior colleagues of Auden's at the Geological Survey. Shipton had once been quite keen on John Auden but he cited Bill Wager's opinion that Auden would be no good for "the top." The Calcutta contingent disagreed vociferously.

Michael Spender kept quiet. He wasn't really interested in who was chosen. He didn't know John Auden, only Wystan, and he couldn't imagine Wystan climbing anything more challenging than a flight of stairs.

"No controversy for me," he wrote in his diary.

Shipton decided to stick with the men he had.

House of the Dzongpon of Sar,
Tibet, June 19, 1935

"The less said about to-day the better," Michael wrote in his journal before launching into a long account of their travails. The march began innocuously enough. First they passed through a dense forest that looked and smelled just like Kew Gardens' Jungle House. The yaks, both the wisest and most stupid animals he had ever encountered, took the most roundabout routes and invariably got jammed between trees or tangled in vines, having forgotten they had his equipment on their backs. Above the tree line it began to rain and with that the temperature dropped and the wind, first coming from the north then switching to the west and southwest, began to roar. It was fantastic.

Staggering toward the crest of Kongra La pass they all looked like second-rate actors, miming the climbing of Everest as if on a stage, bodies curved against the wind, faces screwed into scowls. Michael was wearing his anorak over an Iceland sweater and never felt so cold and so bloody. Shipton and Bryant, the New Zealander, were hunched over the necks of their ponies, too sick to walk. Even Tilman declared it one of the most unpleasant marches he'd ever experienced. This Everest business was clearly all about making oneself deliberately ill, Michael decided. Only the Tibetan mule drivers seemed blithely unaware of the cold.

Then it was a sixteen-mile downward trek to the stony ground of the Tibetan Plateau. Michael's headache eased. His sweater came off but his knees screamed with pain. Tilman kept stumbling and retching. The last few miles were excruciating and Michael finally broke down and did the last hundred yards on horseback, another torture, but a relief from walking. When they reached the level plain dust devils spun around them as if to welcome them to hell.

"Dear, dear E, if only one could meet you at the end of a day's march," he wrote that evening in his journal, sucking on the ginger toffees his wife had packed to soothe his throat. He dreamt of trying to telephone her. Though he remembered the Hampstead number, try as he might he couldn't recall the exchange. This didn't bode well for his calculations.

For days they marched west in the searing sun, the escarpment of the Himalayan range in the distance to their left, yellow sandstone hills and empty riverbeds all around them. Michael regretted the loss of his topee and when he put a red handkerchief over his head his horse shied. When he tried an umbrella the nag took off on a tear and didn't slow until nearly a mile on. Finally, the north-south Nyonno Ri range rose before them, its peak a focal point due west of a village called Sar. This was the tangle of peaks Shipton had discovered on a ten-day sojourn with Bill Wager after the 1933 attempt. Though they were still a great distance from Everest, Shipton had decided to survey this area, too, though he hadn't received permission from the Tibetan authorities for the detour.

While everyone else began to climb and survey the valleys and ridges east of Nyonno Ri, Michael proceeded alone. Anxious about his first climb to 18,500 feet, he clung to Shipton's assurance that an extra 4,000 feet wouldn't defeat him. He did make it, but the clouds came in and he had to return two days later. Over the next ten days he secured

a good number of stations. Karma Paul, acting as both expedition interpreter and sirdar for the Sherpas taken on in Darjeeling, quickly
picked up the rhythms of his routine. Many of the Sherpas were
from Solo Khumbu, a Nepali village in the shadow of Everest, about
120 miles west of Darjeeling. They knew the mountain not as the last
penetralis or the sine qua non of fixed points but as "The Mountain So
High No Bird Can Fly Over It" or "Goddess Mother of the World."

When the weather was sufficiently clear, Michael left his tent at
two in the morning to get his tripod in place by sunrise. The RGS's
Wild phototheodolite he was using was the heaviest, the most sophisticated and fickle. It tended to seize up in the cold, so it sometimes
was a challenge to get readings, but he was usually back at camp by
10:30. After putting away his angles, they would make a start for a new
camp in midafternoon. The porters, better at managing their half-
starved ponies, stopped every so often for him to catch up, but for the
most part Michael was left to himself at the fag end of their seedy-
looking procession. The only difficulty was staving off sleep while
waiting for it to become dark enough to change the photographic
plates. Otherwise he felt fit.

At one point he found himself in a village that didn't appear on
any map. But it was the village after that one where things took a bad
turn. Just outside it two men, clad in bloody, tattered rags, stepped
from behind a rock, wailing. Corpse butchers, Karma Paul explained.
Since the ground was frozen and there was no wood for cremation, the
dead were cut up and fed to vultures. As no one had died recently, they
were hungry. Karma Paul gave them a coin.

After making camp the entire village came out to watch Michael
take a shit. When he tried to return to his tent, the village idiot, fet-
tered hand and foot, blocked his way, shaking his chains and shouting
angrily. This appeared to rouse the staring crowd from their torpor.
A hailstorm of stones came down around him before he managed to
get into his tent.

At midnight, Michael was woken by loud, unearthly music, like
trumpets and oboes and conch shells, alternating bars of G, F-sharp,
G, F-sharp, con espressione. Were the corpse butchers now coming
for him? By 2:00 a.m. the rumpus had quieted and he started off to his

station. At 2:30 an odd, twisting pain started in his belly. After hastily completing his readings he returned to his tent deathly ill.

His next memory was of looking up to see the dzongpen of the village, with the long gold pendant of his office hanging from his left ear, issuing orders. He was half carried through a kitchen filled with staring women, up a dark stairway and ushered into a cool room with a comfortable bed and a view of the night sky through an opening in the roof. He was distantly aware the dzongpen was trying to get him to take some water. Tapers of incense were lit to drive off whatever demon possessed him.

When the dzongpen left to say his prayers in the shrine room, Michael heard the ring of a bell and the stroke of a drum. He first hallucinated he was a Chinese puzzle, then that Erica had delivered a baby. At one point he opened his eyes and found the women of the house, each bearing a candle, standing around his bed looking down at him like a ring of angels. Only then did he realize he was in the same room where he'd drunk chhang in a lovely chased silver cup nine days before. The dzongpen of Sar's house was the first Tibetan house he had been in and, despite the mooing calf tied up on the ground floor, the perpetual toing and froing and salaams of the servants had left the impression of a royal court. He awoke feeling better.

In the meantime, word had come back from the Tibetan authorities that they were to stop their work in the Nyonno Ri and carry on directly to Everest to begin the reconnaissance. Shipton sent a letter of protest and five days of inactivity passed while they awaited word from on high. The ministers stood firm; their permits never allowed for a survey of the Nyonno Ri range. At their good-bye meal, Shipton produced one high compliment after another but the dzongpen was more interested in the hair on the New Zealander's legs. Bryant, in turn, treated him to a Maori rendition of "For He's a Jolly Good Fellow." After the tap dancing, high-pitched singing, the raising of toasts, Shipton braved asking why the Tibetans were so reluctant to let him explore their country.

"Western ways leave behind nothing but unhappiness," the headman replied tersely. Shipton attributed his stubbornness to "silly medievalism." Michael asked the dzongpen to explain. Karma Paul translated.

What will I do with the two hundred rupees you have paid me for the use of my ponies? Where there is no surplus there is nothing to buy. You have only to open your eyes to see that in this country, soil, crops, and people exist in a delicate balance. Money can't replenish the fodder consumed by transiting yaks. Money will simply provide grounds for the headman in the next village to be jealous, thus establishing the conditions for perpetual strife. This is the material and spiritual effect of an expedition passing through our lands. This is how unhappiness and suffering are introduced into our lives.

Everest Base Camp, East Rongbuk Glacier,
  July 16, 1935

Michael had been watching clouds move across the valley when, far higher in the sky than he had been expecting, Everest suddenly appeared, still and colossal between towering banks of slowly exploding clouds. He was glad the mountain couldn't be seen from Base Camp as the mere thought of it kept him awake with dread. At dawn he would have to ford an icy stream just below the snout of the Rongbuk Glacier. It was running balls-high.

For the next two weeks Michael worked quickly, climbing up and down slopes, collecting angles, making and breaking camp. When he returned to the Kharta valley to resupply and wait out a heavy snowstorm, he was invited to dine with a group of nomadic herders in a large yak-hair tent. The long slit in the roof that let out the smoke was closed against the falling snow. When Michael's eyes adjusted to the gloom he took in the scene. A sick goat with bloodshot eyes lay on the floor trembling violently. Patches of its fur had fallen out and it had been given a threadbare jacket to keep it warm. An absurdly tiny lamb stumbled about but when he tried to take it in his lap, it bleated in distress.

The shepherd's wife sat cross-legged on the floor tending the fire with fuel so poor the embers threatened to go out before she could deliver a new gasp of the bellows. The automatic motion of her two hands was accompanied by a rapid monologue, delivered in a monotone and directed at her husband. He replied slowly and pleadingly.

He was holding a listless toddler in his arms and rocking a wicker cradle bearing a tightly swaddled infant, as still as a doll. Michael decided the man was being rebuked by his wife for having invited a stranger to share their meal.

Everyone at home had spoken of his trip to Tibet as a great adventure. But if that was so, why was he overcome by shame? Just that morning he had been eating peppermint creams sent down from Camp I, leftover bounty from the 1933 expedition. On top of that he had unjustly suspected Karma Paul in the theft of cigarettes and sugar. And then there were his complaints about his food. Of the twenty-four eggs he was given to eat that day, only three were properly soft-boiled. Furthermore he had grumbled that not enough water had been used for his stewed fruit. His overriding worry was not survival but the lack of a letter from Erica.

Putting away his journal he looked out of his tent and saw it had finally stopped snowing; the clouds had lifted to reveal a full moon. The fixed points awaited.

Upper East Rongbuk Glacier,
in View of Makalu and Everest, July 27, 1935

On half rations for nearly a week, Michael had lost a stone in weight. His constant squitters and increasing weakness were obvious signs of dysentery. The symptoms thus far had been mild, but he had the sense of his gut digesting itself even as he staggered along stony moraines. How he would manage the trek back he had no idea (the prospect of Kongra La was unthinkable), but if it meant he would be returned to his beloved wife intact, he would suffer through whatever pain he had coming to him. Doubtless Erica thought he deserved it.

The clear culprit was a tiny piece of 1933 chocolate. It had crossed his mind as he accepted it from the Sherpa's none-too-clean hands that if Tewan had dysentery, he would get it, but he hadn't wanted to hurt his feelings. How ridiculous to take such a risk so as not to hurt a servant's feelings! And now the tsampa flour had run out. There was no paraffin to make tea and still Shipton imagined that they would be able to complete the Nyonno Ri survey on the way back. Michael had sent two other porters, Ang Tsering and Ang Tensing, off to the Kharta valley with money for food but they still hadn't returned and now there was a sea of cumulous over the valley. The chaps had no tents and would have to sleep in the open, in a blizzard. He was racked with worry and stomach cramps.

When he had last seen Shipton, all he wanted to know was how many stations he had completed. Michael was able to assure him that he had obtained enough points to draw a large-scale plan of Everest's North Face and to calculate the altitude of any point on it. While this might help with the eventual summit attempt, what of their fate in the meantime? Shipton might be fine with a small party, but with one this large he was unable to prevent the Sherpas from plundering critical stores. When one of Michael's porters caught another with a stolen tin of milk and two tins of Ovaltine there was a tremendous row. He'd had to screw up his courage and, with a look of supreme contempt on his face, intercede. It had ended without blows, but next time? The situation wasn't helped by his feeling Shipton hadn't divided the food fairly. Michael tried to look at his situation dispassionately, taking into account the effects of hunger, physical strain, and illness.

When Ang Tsering and Ang Tensing finally returned with some food, they were able to make a start on the two-day journey back to Base Camp. Despite the misery in his gut Michael maintained a sailor's sensitivity to wind. At the top of the pass there seemed to be three layers, a lower and upper layer of winds from the east, sandwiching a layer of winds from the west. The next morning Sen Tensing—he was finally beginning to learn the Sherpas' names—once again carried him over the river of glacier melt to spare him the icy water. Humiliating.

By the time they reached the fleshpots of Base Camp he had an appetite. Liver, mutton, rice, potatoes, and heavenly vegetables greeted him. This blunted the news that their stores had been ransacked. A Wild tripod, the Zeiss telephoto camera, and the RGS plane table tripod had been nicked, along with books, tsampa, a tent, a pair of his shorts, and a flask of cod liver oil. There was a letter from Granny, but again nothing from Erica. It had now been over a month since he'd discovered the loving letter she'd packed in his trunk. What was she thinking? He was left pondering her handwriting on the wrappers of the newspapers she'd forwarded.

By the end of August he was sitting out another snowstorm 20,000 feet up Everest. The endless procession of monsoon flurries rendered survey work impossible. When it finally cleared he could scarcely blame the Sherpas for refusing to continue. Warmer temperatures combined with heavy snowfall made the snow pack unstable and avalanches more likely. Shipton had come to the same conclusion about the advisability of attempting to summit Everest during the monsoon.

So, yes, the weather was *kharab*—beastly. Then the Primus died, kharab. And when they floundered around in snow and fell into thigh-high pools of freezing water en route to Camp III, the route too was pronounced kharab. So Michael sent Ang Tsering, Nyima Tsering, and Kusang with a rope to Camp III to fetch 1933 Danish butter and jam and pemmican and whatever else might be there, while he retreated to Camp II. While making a cup of Ovaltine, Michael was once more reminded that the shortage of fuel had obliged him to send three men over a dangerous route in search of food that didn't need to be heated. Sulking in his tent he nursed a grievance that dated back to an incident on Mount Kellas when someone took his supply of sugar and Shipton made off with one of his Sherpas.

Winter sports in the Alps would never be the same after this.

The three porters returned in the pitch dark, fully knackered. He'd been in a fever of anxiety over what had happened to them but the butter they brought quickly transported him far from this blasted godforsaken place to a world of grass, lowing cattle, and mild English summers. When another day of snow kept him in his tent fiddling with his instruments, Ang Tsering and whatshisname, the one with the upturned nose, showed up with news. The New Zealander and the expedition doctor were kharab, one with a bad stomach, the other a bad tooth. Both were on their way down and would soon be joining them. Ang Tsering then paused, and the other fellow, Rinzing, piped up. The route from Camp III to Camp II is, well, god, he was sick of hearing it and saying it. *Kharab!*

Given the ticklishness of the food and fuel situation, the arrival of his colleagues was a great bother. Michael wasn't about to share his carefully husbanded supplies, namely, his Ovaltine. Nor had he missed white man conversation. The sole pleasure of their company would be the opportunity to jointly curse Shipton. Sen Tensing was suffering from snow blindness: the glasses provided by the expedition were worthless. And Tilman had not only taken his Primus (stolen might be more apt) but had thrown the burner away. There were now two broken and one working Primus for the entire expedition. And Shipton had let the porters burn the remaining supply of firewood in one night, a quantity that would have lasted him six days. His men were more or less living on jam. They would soon be reduced to eating snow. Without the excess crates of the 1933 expedition what would they have done? He and Bryant took bets on who would mutiny first, the sahibs or the Sherpas.

The following day he only just made his station, snatching a few angles by working fast on rotten snow, before the clouds covered Khartaphu, his fixed point. Flurries followed. When Shipton showed up, Michael's effort to bring his attention to the expedition's organizational flaws blew over his head like the icy cloud stream over Everest.

Kharta, Lang Chu Valley,
September 5, 1935

"O Gawd! O Gawd!" Michael wrote in his journal. He'd got out of the tent at 4:30 but within minutes it began to snow. The day before had progressed from a night spent on frozen granite, to clouds at 7:00 a.m., to falling through snow up to his waist with icy water rushing into his boots because his shoelaces were broken. On top of that he couldn't see through his dark glasses, the theodolite was frozen solid, there had been a glacial stream to ford barefoot, and a forty-pound rucksack to carry to 21,000 feet. Returning to camp meant being confronted with the blocks of ice that were his boots, soaked socks, a sunburnt face, his tent a grotto of slush, no sugar, no tea, nothing to read, and no candle to read it by.

Yet the survey of the Everest region was nearly complete. With the turning of this page or the next of his diary, they would be heading home. With that in mind, when Michael awoke the next morning to yet another blizzard, he and his team of Sherpas left their tents to spend the morning playing in the snow. Snowballs were thrown. He gave them a course in sitting glissade. And about the time one arrived, red cheeked, at the Alpine lodge, to sit down to a hot breakfast of bacon and eggs before a steaming cup of tea and a roaring fire, they returned instead to camp to face their frozen and filthy tents.

And then it was over. He stood at the top of a pass and beheld yaks grazing on green grass by a crystal-blue lake, 1,500 feet below. He thought of his descent as a return to life from death and summoned a dim memory of his arrival at Cat Bells from boarding school in the summer of 1917. Suddenly there were yak herder tents and a real fire and the first human beings he had seen outside their expedition since he'd left the shepherd's tent. He pitched his tent on a carpet of grass.

And he awakened the next morning not to flurries or hailstorms or rocks under his back but a balmy air reminiscent of West Greenland in September. There was plenty of milk to drink and cheese to eat. The profusion of flowers reminded him of an exhibition at Chelsea. He identified rhododendron, Himalayan rose, and that bright little blue starflower he'd seen in the Alps. It trumped Kew for its beauty. Every blossom reminded him of Erica, who had taught him to love flowers.

But then the anticlimax: the Kharta mailbag produced a single letter . . . from Granny. Why didn't Erica write? Even the porters heard from their wives. A chhang party hosted by the dzongpen of Kharbung failed to lift his spirits. He found it impossible to get drunk on chhang and if he heard "Cats on the Housetops" sung one more time he would knife someone, Bryant most likely. Having lost a bet the New Zealander had swum in the river and they were all meant to celebrate this outstanding feat with one obscene song after another. He knew he would soon miss the Tudor scene of sitting round the fire in a smoky room filled with hungry people waiting to eat, but he was thankful to hear Nyonno Ri was out of the question. The plan was now all out for home.

Somewhere over France,
  October 11, 1935

Having seen Michael's photograph in the Bombay papers, a group of bumptious Bengalis traveling with him on the SS *Strathmore* couldn't resist offering their opinions on Everest in an exaggerated, hearty manner. Where the Arabs and Persians kept aloof, sitting upright on benches reading the Talmud (or something), these affected, half-educated Indians had no such self-possession. Michael could swear their specs were nothing but panes of glass. They had clearly drifted away from their own people and would never find a way back. Michael wondered how far he had drifted. The English residents of Darjeeling had appalled him with their obliviousness, whether to the ominous developments in Abyssinia or a gorgeous butterfly with black velvet wings. Among them he'd felt like a foreigner.

The sight of five sloops and ten destroyers at Aden confirmed his feeling that something was up. But it was the Norfolk cruiser flying an admiral's flag that compelled him to risk a flight from Marseilles. That was how he came to be sitting in an aeroplane stunned by the certainty he was about to die. The port engine had already cut out once and the pilot's landing technique at a refueling stop nearly ended in disaster. They were now flying blind in a fog along the French coast. After the months of strain the silent, high-wire tension in the cabin was too much to bear.

He stopped writing for a moment to look out the window.

Thank God. The clouds had lifted. The way home was clear.

Rudagaira Valley, Tehri Garhwal,
October 23, 1935

Before leaving Calcutta for the Garhwal John Auden had lunched with Michael Spender. Michael told him that during the reconnaissance Shipton had climbed twenty-six peaks over 20,000 feet, including twenty-four first ascents, all of it in monsoon conditions.

This had put John in the mood to prove something. He had first followed the pilgrimage trail all the way up to Gaumukh, the snout of the Gangotri Glacier, the largest glacier in the Indian Himalaya. As the wellspring of Mother Ganga, Gaumukh was considered the most sacred of all pilgrimage destinations. Here the snowmelt created a small milky stream. As this holy water trickled downward, thread-ing its way through high peaks of the Greater Himalaya, more water, from glaciated side valleys, quickened the river's pulse. Pilgrims walked against its flow. As they climbed, they accumulated merit and received blessings from the babas living in caves along the path. John carried Map 53 J from the Survey of India to check its accuracy. The pilgrims carried no maps at all.

At the temple town of Gangotri he had engaged several local porters to assist his two Darjeeling Sherpas, Dawa Tendrup and Ang Tsering. The Sherpas signaled his seriousness. The roster for the 1936 Everest expedition was still open.

Dawa Tendrup had looked after Frank Smythe when he climbed Kamet in 1931 and had been a porter on the catastrophic 1934 German expedition to Nanga Parbat. Four Germans and six Sherpas had met their deaths in the aftermath of a phenomenal blizzard; Herr Hitler himself had awarded Dawa Tendrup a medal for courage. Ang Tsering had not only survived that (though he lost several toes) but had been on earlier German attempts to climb Kanchenjunga in 1929 and 1931, and with Shipton on Everest in 1933. He was just back from the Everest reconnaissance that John had not been asked to join.

The steep alpine entrance to the Rudagaira valley was a short walk from the temple town. After a two-day trek up the valley, hanging glaciers and falling rocks thwarted his attempts on Jogin I on the east side, and two of the three Gangotri peaks. That left Gangotri III, a slightly smaller peak at 21,578 feet at the southwest end of the valley. This peak appeared to be continuous with the snow saddle he had seen from an earlier, higher camp. The closer he got to the saddle, however, the more daunting its appearance. At 19,000 feet, Dawa Tendrup called a halt, pointing out crevasses hidden by a thin crust of wind-swept snow. After descending to 15,000 feet, John turned around to look back at the summit and was shocked to discover that the snow saddle didn't even lead to the peak. Its ridge, however, led down to a pass at the southernmost end of the valley that appeared to look over yet another glacial valley. It was probably not more than 18,000 feet in height, but it seemed to be one of the few places along this part of the main Himalayan range where a route toward the temple town of Kedarnath might be forged. He vowed to return.

38 Upper Park Road, Belsize Park, London,
    New Year's Eve 1935

The Boys waited patiently in ill-fitting suits for the filming to start. They were to be playing guests at a New Year's Eve party, footage meant for some GPO film celebrating the miracle of the telephone, wireless, and postal service, in connecting Englishmen all over the empire with home over the holidays. The sitting room at Upper Park Road was as bright as day, and just like a real New Year's Eve party there were a great many bottles about. There were also two double arc lamps and four single ones, a platform for the camera and its spotlight. Sprigs of holly graced a mantel strung with paper chains. Wystan Auden was demonstrating the dance he wanted them to perform. Of course he had to dominate; he was the director. They heard he was once a schoolmaster.

Though it had been less than six months, Wystan was already tiring of the Film Unit. The GPO left him little time to write and the atmosphere was too public school, too upper middle, for his taste. And the present film was not at all the sort of film he was interested in making. He did enjoy working with Benjamin Britten. Benjamin had proved as effortless a composer as he was a lyricist. Wystan was just then mulling over writing a play about mountain climbers with Christopher Isherwood. Benjamin would provide the score. Himalayan expeditions were once again all the rage.

The dramatic premise of *The Ascent of F6* would revolve around a race between climbing parties of rival colonial powers for a summit strategically placed on the contested border of a prize colony. The quest for F6 was an expansive metaphor. Not only did it capture the jockeying for power in proxy wars then under way in Spain and Africa, but it also neatly dramatized Britain's struggle, in its ongoing quest for Everest's summit, to project its imperial power over a restive India.

That past fall Wystan had seen quite a bit of Michael Spender, not long returned from Everest. Michael had introduced him to Shipton and had sung John's praises, Wystan reported to his brother. Yet when the list of those chosen for the upcoming attempt on Everest was published, once again John hadn't made the cut. Only Bill Tilman's exclusion had excited comment. After his and Shipton's reconnaissance of

Nanda Devi, they were thought inseparable. But Tilman had failed to acclimatize during the 1935 reconnaissance. Shipton had made the difficult call.

For his play, Wystan decided to base the lead climber and dramatic hero of *The Ascent of F6* on Michael Spender. Echoing the colonial rivalry would be a fraternal one between the mountaineer hero and his politician brother. The politician's scheme to exploit the expedition for imperialist propaganda is at first thwarted by the mountaineer's refusal to sully his beloved mountain with great power politics. Only when their mother arrives to compel him to take the commission does the mountaineer hero relent. Wystan could never resist an Oedipal theme.

There would also be a lot about marriage in the play, Wystan told John. Wystan had once likened heterosexuality to watching a game of cricket, but in its domesticated form it hadn't proved nearly as boring as he had once supposed. Six months of living with Bill and Nancy had made him a marriage expert. The climbers' progress up the mountain would be relayed over the wireless into the living room of a similarly bickering couple. They never went anywhere exciting, the wife complained.

Knowing John was still bitter about Margaret, Wystan reported that Michael Spender was also in dire marital straits. And while he was on the subject of Michaels, Wystan asked that John convey his best wishes to Michael Carritt. Mrs. Carritt had been happy to hear that her eldest son had finally found someone to talk to in Calcutta. But how had he abused the Carritts' hospitality while at Oxford? He was a model house-guest; Mrs. Carritt adored him, as did Nancy.

Carritt had regaled John with tales of Wystan at Boars Hill. Wystan had complained about the "tepid piss" of his mother's tea, made midnight raids on the pantry, and pulled up the stair carpets to add to the blankets on his bed. Wystan had also kept his brother Gabriel awake till all hours going on about poets no one had ever heard of.

The Morning Post, *London,*
    October 17, 1936

"We are beginning to make ourselves look very ridiculous," the headline in the *Morning Post* had read, quoting Captain George Finch, a member of the legendary 1922 Everest expedition. "We ought not to treat the climbing of Mount Everest as a domestic issue. It is an issue of National and Imperial importance."

Such an assertion was scarcely ever uttered aloud, much less published in the morning papers. While the 1936 Everest expedition was under way a hopefulness mixed with dread had stilled any criticism. Even after it became clear the climbers had once again failed, any disagreement over how the Mount Everest Committee had choreographed the enterprise was limited to grumbling and backbiting. Now, with the *Morning Post* headline, the frustration of those with a stake in Everest had exploded into the open. Captain Finch was leading the charge and Bill Wager was egging him on. Like Wager, in 1922 Finch had been defeated by the Great Couloir on Everest's North Face. Since then he had run afoul of committee members over their resistance to his pioneering use of oxygen. In twice placing its bets on Hugh Ruttledge, Finch continued, the Everest Committee had wasted precious time. The conquest of Everest should not be left in the hands of those whose climbing days, if they ever had any, were long behind them. Nor should the committee be choosing an expedition's members and leader.

A clipping of the article and its offending headline quickly found its way to the External Affairs Department of the Government of India, the Foreign Office, the desk of the secretary of the RGS, and the members of the Everest Committee. Few needed to be reminded of the stalemate in the trenches. Soldiers trapped by enemy fire had been unable to advance, sometimes for months. The decision to limit the Everest roster to Englishmen, Rutledge insisted, had nothing to do with chauvinism. Everest's summit would admit only those who approached the mountain as votaries, unsullied by the lust for fame, fortune, and national glory that had become so shamefully evident in continental climbing parties. Ruttledge didn't name the offending nation but Nazi flags would soon be photographed flying over camps on Nanga Parbat. To Finch, an Australian, this was tantamount to embracing mediocrity. Men had been left out of leadership positions, he held, because certain individuals considered them to be unduly driven by personal ambition.

"In a venture of this kind," Finch continued, "personal ambition is a valuable quality." Everest leadership should be in the hands of a proven climber, no older than thirty-five, with solid Himalayan experience. He alone should choose his team. It was absurd to appoint a leader without the power to compel climbers to risk their lives. "The instruction, 'you must not take any risks' is tantamount to saying that you must not get there." Only a climber could ask others to face the same peril he did; only a climber could judge the risks fully. He should not be down on the East Rongbuk squinting through a telescope whose sights are obscured by a blizzard.

While the wireless on Everest in 1933 made it possible for Ruttledge to receive weather reports from Calcutta, it also meant London expected progress reports every twenty-four hours. Just as India's viceroys were now at the mercy of cables from the Secretary of State for India, obliging them to make up in pomp what had been lost in power, so Hugh Ruttledge had to answer to an overbearing Hinks and the second-guessing of the Everest Committee. In this way the distance between Kensington Gore and Base Camp was uncomfortably close, impossibly distant, and, like the relationship between Westminster and Delhi, prey to the armchair misconstructions of men hoping to relive their prime.

The question was no longer about how best to climb Mount Everest but how much longer Britain's global hegemony would last. Though an Australian, Finch fully identified with all that was at stake. He'd heard the Germans and the Americans now had their eye on Everest. "Unless we put up a better show," he concluded, "it will be difficult to argue that we are justified in keeping Mount Everest for ourselves."

Eric Shipton, for one, was ready to hand the mountain over. Had it not been for Everest, he wouldn't have wasted an entire climbing season stuck on the East Rongbuk Glacier freezing to death. He would have been with Bill Tilman when he, and a handful of American undergraduates, summited Nanda Devi, the highest peak in British India.

– CHAPTER 9 –

I Spy

Viceroy's Residency, New Delhi,
April 18, 1936

According to the book Winston Churchill pressed on first-time visitors to India, the viceroy of India was a veiled prophet, the axis around which the British Empire turned. Screened from all knowledge of the people he ruled, the viceroy perceived, dimly, a "dark indistinguishable mass" far below his unfocused gaze. Indeed, if India was the plant, the viceroy was its flower.

At six feet four the 2nd Marquess of Linlithgow was a very tall flower.

Due to a bout of childhood polio that left him stiff-necked, if Linlithgow wanted to address a man at his side he had to pivot his entire body. In his official portrait the blue velvet mantle of the Star of India rests on a cape with ermine trimmings. Beneath the cape is an embroidered Kashmiri vest and below that knee breeches and white stockings, ending in pointy patent leather slippers. The delicate effect is somewhat ruined by his swollen ankles, but the formal pose is softened by the figure of his four-year-old granddaughter, Sarah Jane, looking up at him, bobbed head atilt, and arms crossed in a huff.

Linlithgow had chaired the panel of worthies responsible for drawing up the 1935 Government of India Act that had so exercised Lady Houston. This act was initially intended to tamp down the political passions stirred up by Gandhi's Salt March of 1930 but the Die Hards, led by Winston Churchill, had tied up negotiations for years. The *Daily Mail* had published Churchill's fanatical rants suggesting that sectarian wars would break out should even the most nominal autonomy be granted. When that argument didn't succeed, he asked why Britain should feebly surrender power just when other countries were carving out their own empires and turning their backs on democracy altogether?

Though the 1935 act was pitched as a great step forward, to get the bill past the Die Hards, a back door of safeguards was installed to reclaim all that was brought in the front door of regional autonomy. As before, the fine print enabled the viceroy to dismiss ministers, dissolve legislatures, and suspend the constitution. Defense, foreign policy, finance, and police were again excluded from Indian oversight. The British business community in Calcutta exploded with relief. The government would not be turned over to baboos.

Linlithgow arrived in India hoping that both Nehru and Gandhi would embrace the spirit in which the 1935 act was written. Though Gandhi had resigned from Congress in 1934 to focus on the plight of low-caste Hindus, the Government of India no longer fooled itself that he was in any way a spent force. Linlithgow appreciated the feeling that in the past there had been instances of bad faith, but this time things would be different. It all came down to trust. Secretly, Linlithgow had misgivings about his predecessor, the Marquess of Willingdon, though less for his iron-hand rule than for his misplaced priorities. Lady Willingdon had every room in all three viceregal residences painted lilac. The Calcutta residence had been done up with enough mirrors and chandeliers to suggest Versailles. Everywhere Linlithgow looked he saw a lack of initiative and a sorry neglect of duties.

For his maiden speech in April 1936, the viceroy chose the easily grasped metaphor of family, promising to understand and cherish the differences between Muslims, Hindus, Sikhs, and tribals, just as he did with his own children. He would never favor one over the other. His first task, however, was to oversee regional elections.

The dyarchy of the 1919 Government of India Act would be abolished and replaced by representative assemblies of elected Indian members in each of the eleven provinces of India. The viceroy's second task was to persuade all six hundred and sixty nizams, nawabs, rajahs, and maharajas of India's princely states, protectorates, petty states, agencies, and unions of states to sign the Instruments of Accession,

surrendering their sovereignty to answer to an All India federation
of provinces and princely states. The territory under royal rule constituted one-third of the Indian subcontinent. It was made up of private fiefdoms of varying sizes, their princely rulers all staunch allies of
the Raj. Linlithgow was eager to get to know these royals, not having
had the opportunity in his earlier seat on the Royal Commission on
Indian Agriculture, given that many of them preferred hunting, gam-
bling, and carousing in European capitals over the quiet cultivation
of the soil.

Next came the question of a meeting with Congress leaders. His
predecessor had believed that because Gandhi's methods of argument
were so slippery and oriental the wisest course was to avoid him altogether. Linlithgow was more concerned that a meeting might enhance
Congress's prestige or create unrealistic expectations. He needed to
bear in mind, too, the peace of mind of the princes and Muhammad
Ali Jinnah. Though still based in London Jinnah remained the leader of
the nearly moribund Muslim League. Any sudden overture to Congress
might be regarded as a betrayal of his loyal standing. Such were the
concerns that kept the viceroy at his desk all hours composing lengthy
missives to the Secretary of State for India and to the king.

The king found his letters exceedingly tiresome.

Archbishop Acland's Residence,
     Malabar Hill, Bombay, March 1936

Reverend Scott's clandestine meetings with Indian Communists took
place in public so that they might more easily be passed off as chance
encounters. In Bombay their rendezvous point was Juhu Beach. To
arrange a meeting he would leave a stray mark on a specified pillar.
His contact would see it on his way to work and know a note would
be waiting at the usual drop. Retrieving it, he would leave another
note confirming the meet. In this way, Scott maintained contact with
Communist Party leaders such as S. S. Mirajkar or Chief Secretary
P. C. Joshi. Despite the best efforts of Special Branch to keep tabs on
them, their whereabouts were presently unknown.

That day Scott had used his usual evasion technique en route to the drop point. Tram hopping involved getting off at alternate stations then, at the last moment, jumping back on to see if anyone followed suit. He'd picked this up reading about how the Communists evaded the Nazis. That was before Hitler. There probably weren't any Communists left in Germany now, he thought.

But then, just as he approached the rolled-up missive tucked into a hollow railing, a large black crow swooped down, picked out the piece of paper, and flew off with it. He was stunned, incredulous. It occurred to him that his Indian comrades would not find this amusing. Worse, they might not believe him. He scarcely believed it himself. Once again, he decided he wasn't really cut out for this work.

Reverend Michael Scott came from a long line of vicars.

He had first been recruited to the Communist cause while working as a lowly assistant priest in Hackney. In 1933 Oswald Mosley's Blackshirts were squaring off against the Communists, and Hunger Marchers were arriving in droves from the North and Northeast. The streets of London's East End had become a battleground and he'd had to choose sides. On his departure for India he had offered his services to the Communists as long as what they asked of him didn't clash with his Christian conscience. As he understood it, the mission of the Communist Party of Great Britian was to encourage Indian peasants and factory workers to join the global uprising against their capitalist and imperialist overseers.

Posted as a domestic chaplain and assistant to the archbishop of Bombay, the reverend had been shocked by the wealth of the European community and its Indian supporters. For official functions this crowd would glide up the long drive to Government House in gleaming motorcars driven by liveried chauffeurs to emerge one by one in all their feathered finery. There were the savvy merchants and bejeweled princes and the small but powerful Parsee community. He was never comfortable in such a crowd. Except for tobacco—he smoked like a chimney—the reverend had an abstinent disposition. And everywhere he went he overheard the same withering remarks about the nationalists.

Congress: a crop of worthless agitators who in no way represent the starving and ignorant masses. Gandhi: a bowler-hatted solicitor who had taken to native attire to deceive the unwitting peasant into thinking he was one of them.

From the high windows of the archbishop's palatial residence in the fashionable heights of Bombay's Malabar Hill, Reverend Scott watched the mass political rallies taking place on Chowpatt Beach. Brightly colored banners fluttered among cheering crowds. Though the Communist mission was more ambitious than the strictly nationalist goals of the All India Congress Party, he was sympathetic to their cause. When a Congress deputation gave him proof that police had beaten their cadres with long canes and inflicted shocking forms of torture he had pleaded with His Eminence to compel the governor to prosecute the men involved. The archbishop had no immediate response.

On a trip outside the city, however, the archbishop gently suggested that it was time for Scott to face reality. Wasn't it better for a few agitators to suffer than to have whole tracts of the country laid waste when the realization hit that the hopes these troublemakers were raising among innocent villagers were destined to be disappointed?

The question did worry him. But he found it impossible to accept that there was nothing to be done. So Reverend Scott fell back on the Gospels. Yes, he argued with himself, the Communists were the first to grasp the perils of fascism, the first to fight it on the ground. Similarly, Marx offered a convincing critique of imperialism. Yet Scott found the idea of perpetual class warfare inimical to his Christian beliefs and a materialist view of ethics wanting. And it was no help at all, alas, when it came to explaining the vagaries of individual conduct, or even chance events. Like that crow.

And so he censured himself over the pride he took in his own cunning. He prayed he would be forgiven for the lies and duplicities of his double life, telling himself that God would understand that helping the Communist Party of India was the very least he could do. Periodically, the strain would overwhelm him and he would ask his contacts to find someone else. In the spring of 1936, not long before he was transferred to Calcutta, they had. That person was ICS Special Officer Michael John Carritt.

It was during his last rainy season as a subdivisional district officer in Tangail that Carritt had finally begun to grasp the true nature of the British Empire. Tangail was located in the plains of the Bengal

Delta. Barely a town, it had no club and no machinery in place for any kind of socializing. Because a previous district officer had been shot on an inspection round, neither his DO nor the police chief visited during Carritt's yearlong tenure. Yet he had asked for this post. Had he wanted to prove he was as much a man as the assassinated district officers of Midnapore? Did he hope to disarm the Raj's most implacable foes with a demonstration of his due diligence?

On his arrival in Tangail a nearly unbearable tension hung in the air, as if the entire district might explode. Even the local police were on edge. But when the rains came, the flat, shimmering world of heat and dust vanished overnight. Paddy and jute fields filled with water. Swollen rivers coursed through the countryside. Once planting was done, country boats were provisioned and suddenly village life was on the move. There were visits to relatives, singing parties, and exchanges of presents and gossip. In Calcutta, there was no escaping the pestilence that came with the rains; one simmered in a stupor that passed for stoicism. In Tangail it was blissful.

Carritt followed the villagers' lead, making his inspection rounds in a rickety and leaky government barge. The crew lived on the front deck and roof; at the back, his servant, armed guard, and cook. He shared the main cabin with an assistant police inspector, fresh out of public school, who did little but drink away his boredom and sexual frustration. It was during this rainy season, listening at night to the cries of jackals, the badinage of boatmen, and the sounds of village festivities carrying across the water, that Carritt fell in love.

He fell in love first with the Bengali people. Then he fell in love with the gentle light on the waterways at dusk, the rippling curtains of rain splashing the riverbank. And as he watched the silken currents of the Brahmaputra make their way through loosening skeins toward the Bay of Bengal, he realized he no longer regretted not having served in the North-West Frontier Province. And with this realization he began to reflect upon all he had seen as an ICS officer in Midnapore, in Calcutta, and in Tangail. Too busy learning the ropes or hunting snipe, Carritt had never pulled back to regard the Raj with an impersonal eye. Now he did.

He began to see how power happens.

When a third district officer in Midnapore was shot on the football field at halftime, matches were suspended. The DO had been using them to cultivate informers. After six Indian Army battalions were transferred from the frontier to establish order, military intelligence began to bypass the local magistrates. Special tribunals tried political cases without juries, in front of politically reliable judges. Bespectacled youths were condemned to death on the testimony of paid informers. If Carritt dismissed a case for lack of evidence, the police simply appealed to a higher court, leading to far harsher sentences than he would have imposed had he believed the charges in the first place.

Every once in a while Carritt would strip off his clothes and dive naked into the center of the river's current. The crew was aghast. The rivers were infested with crocodiles. The assistant police inspector was horrified. Carritt was letting the white man down. He ignored them both, returning to his chair feeling refreshed.

While posted as a special officer in the Political and Home Department in Calcutta, one of Carritt's duties was to administer the camps where political prisoners were held. Where Midnapore criminals had languished in shackles between festering ankles, or fetters that chained them to the walls of their cells, the five hundred détenus lodged at the jails of Deoli, Hijli, and Berhampur received his speedy attention. Every petition for medicine, family allowance, and reading material was swiftly addressed. Complaints about police abuse were thoroughly investigated and invariably dismissed. In this way the consciences of the Indian members of the regional assemblies were assuaged and the appearance of English impartiality, fairness, and decency sustained. Carritt knew better. A police officer had once described to him with great relish how a condemned political prisoner had responded to the tortures inflicted upon him.

In Writers' Building, the ugly red-stone block of offices housing the government secretariat in Calcutta, Carritt was no longer master of a district. He was simply a writer, one more popinjay among the secretaries, additional secretaries, deputy secretaries, and under-secretaries desperate to grab the next rung on the professional and social ladder. Whatever the amount of gold braid on his ceremonial uniform—and as a third-class special officer Carritt didn't have much—

they were all writers. How many spies, watchers, and informers were on the books of the Political and Home Department? No one was saying. The rule among writers was simple. They signed what the police told them to sign, where the police told them to sign it.

After Tangail he had been promised a plum post in Calcutta. This prospect had contributed to his introspection and restlessness. During those long and lazy days on the river, Carritt, who rarely read more than month-old copies of the *New Statesman*, began reading the standard editions of Marx and Lenin. Gabriel, the youngest of the golden Carritt boys, once the love object of Wystan Auden and now a full-time worker in the Communist Party of Great Britain, had sent them to him.

Carritt's superiors had initially looked upon nationalism as a more serious threat than communism, but with each new circular from the Bureau of the Public Prosecutor, the list of banned titles by purportedly Communist authors grew: *Revolt on the Clyde*, by William Gallacher, *Reporter in Spain*, by Claud Cockburn, *Ten Days That Shook the World*, by John Reed, and *Coolie*, by Mulk Raj Anand. Even suspicious titles, such as Maxim Gorky's *The Mother* or a biography of Genghis Khan, could be seized for study. In time the police became more learned in Marxist philosophy than the political prisoners at Deoli or Berhampur.

But though such works were prohibited under the Sea Customs Act, ADO Carritt's book parcels were never tampered with. He continued his education while on home furlough. In the Welsh hills and in wayside pubs he now debated the scourge of capitalism and the evils of imperialism with his brothers, all keen hill walkers. The coming conflict would not arise between Germany and England or France, he learned, but between the working classes and bourgeois capitalist imperialism. Before Carritt returned to India, Gabriel introduced him to Ben Bradley of the League Against Imperialism.

Bradley had been arrested and tried in the Meerut Conspiracy Case. Twenty-four men, mostly Indians, had been charged with acting on the orders of the Comintern "to deprive the King Emperor of the sovereignty of British India." During the four-and-a-half-year trial, the Communist line on class warfare was systematically explained from the stand. When convicted, the sentences of the Meerut conspirators ranged from transportation to twelve years' imprisonment. But as it was feared they would wreak even more havoc as prisoners, their sentences were overturned. After their release, many went underground; Ben Bradley had returned to England.

The day after Carritt arrived in Bombay he went to a photographer's shop deep in the crowded lanes of Bombay Bazaar. Purposefully dressed in shabby clothes, he felt faintly ridiculous. The two toothless old men behind the counter became alarmed when he asked to speak to S. S. Mirajkar. Mirajkar had been one of Bradley's codefendants in the Meerut Conspiracy Case. Carritt was meant to ask for his photo to be taken and inquire into Mirajkar's health. They were then to make inquiries and provide him an answer when he picked up his prints. That way they could check the face in the photo against the one they'd been sent. When Carritt failed to follow protocol, they fell at his feet in supplication.

Mirajkar had just left! They didn't know anyone named Mirajkar! Mirajkar had just that morning been arrested!

When Carritt tried to produce Bradley's letter, they pushed him out of the shop and locked the door behind him. When passersby became curious, he returned to his hotel to weigh his options. He could put the entire thing out of his mind and quietly take up his Calcutta post. But Bradley told him that if he failed to establish contact, as a last resort he was to go to the archbishop's residence and ask to see Reverend Michael Scott.

The manicured lawn and flower border of the residence made him feel just as conspicuous on Malabar Hill as he had in the bazaar. At first the sharp-eyed chaprasi refused to relay his message, taking him for a suspicious character. Then he was made to wait on the veranda until Reverend Scott arose from his siesta. No sooner had Carritt sat down to explain himself than the chaprasi reappeared to convey His Lordship's hope that the reverend's guest would honor them with his presence at dinner.

Over a formal table, with servants rolling out one course after another, Carritt and His Lordship discussed the arrival of the new viceroy. The twitchy young curate seemed entirely lacking in social graces, Carritt thought. The food, however, was delicious and after dessert and a final grace, they excused themselves. Carritt was relieved to hand over the copies of speeches from the Seventh World Congress held the previous year. The Comintern had previously denounced Gandhi and Nehru as petit bourgeois, regarding the Indian nationalists much as the English did, as social-climbing baboos who did not truly represent the masses. But henceforth the Communist Party of India was directed to join forces with Congress in a Popular Front against fascism and imperialism. With the rise of Hitler and Mussolini, the new thinking went, now was not the time for ideological nitpicking and divisive class warfare. All democratic, socialist, reformist, and constitutionally in- clined political parties should now be gathered under the Popular Front umbrella.

Carritt had hoped to leave that night for Calcutta, but Scott in- sisted they meet the following day at Juhu Beach so that he might be more fully "put into the picture."

Hatibagan, 139 Cornwallis Street, Calcutta,
April 17, 1936

The rise and fall of empires was a much-visited subject at Sudhin Datta's Friday night adda. With the proliferation of dictators, fascists, and tyrants around the world, new issues of *Parichay* were in great demand. The contributions of a newcomer named Susobhan Sarkar on current affairs were now hotly anticipated. Basanta Kumar Mallik, avid consumer of samosas and tireless purveyor of his theory of con- flict, had found in the young Susobhan a most able sparring partner. The adda's secret diarist never failed to follow their exchanges closely. Susobhan was just as steeped in learning as Mallik-da, he found, but he had rare personal qualities. Unlike Mallik-da he was forbearing of the more eccentric members. And he was humble. Until Sudhin in- duced Susobhan to write for *Parichay*, he hadn't considered himself a writer. Now he was called upon to elucidate everything from the history of pre- and postrevolutionary Russia to the disparate origins of the Bengal Renaissance. His critical appraisal of Arnold Toynbee's three-volume *A Study of History* was eagerly discussed.

On this particular evening in 1936, the conversation began on a rather esoteric note: what influence did religious belief have on the framing of imperial ideologies? Susobhan floated the idea that Hindus, believing in the existence of many gods, were more broad-minded than the Calvinist monotheist. Yet their polytheistic tendencies had a drawback, too, leading many to worship Mussolini, Hitler, Lenin, Stalin, Kamal Pasha, Reza Khan, Sun Yat-sen, and Gandhi simultaneously.

There followed a lot of pointless talk before global politics resurfaced. This was happening more and more. The 1933 collapse of the Social Democrats in Weimar Germany, and the fall of four successive governments in France in two years, had not struck adda members as unduly alarming. Mussolini's dream of resuscitating the Roman Empire with the dispatch of a general to Eritrea had been greeted with hoots of ridicule. Eritrea! But Susobhan had lately begun to use his *Parichay* essays to express his indignation at British inaction over Mussolini's Abyssinian adventures and Hitler's forays in Spain. A general consensus soon arose that France and Germany would go to war only if England desired it. By turning a blind eye, England was acquiescing to Hitler's and Mussolini's muscular expansionism.

The subject of communism's prospects in India was also coming up a lot, largely due to another recent arrival from Oxford. Hirendranath Mukherjee always arrived with a retinue of young admirers at his heels, young men who could be counted on to parrot his opinions. The more senior adda members found Hiren-da something of an upstart but were keen to hear what he knew about the April 1936 Lucknow session of the Indian National Congress. Nationalist politics were also getting a more extended hearing.

At Lucknow, Hiren-da said, Nehru had reiterated his objection to the 1935 Government of India Act. He argued that Congress should contest the coming provincial elections to take advantage of the opportunity to outline their program and educate the masses. Then, so as not to surrender their revolutionary agenda, they would refuse to take office. Hiren asserted confidently that Nehru's decision to contest would come back to haunt him, that the entire exercise was an elaborate British trap. Viceroy Linlithgow would use the elections either to dissipate Congress's power or divide them. The adda diarist noted that Hiren-da tended to lightly lick his lips before delivering his little bons mots.

"Wasn't it most unwise for Nehru to become so closely aligned with Congress?" one of Hiren-da's acolytes asked. "It was bound to stymie the spread of Communism, wasn't it?"

Before Hiren could reply, Susobhan spoke up. "Congress provides a better platform for progressive, nationalist politics than Communism does."

Though Susobhan was on the Special Branch of Police's radar as a suspected radical, he was also a government servant with a family to support and could not afford to air his political sympathies openly. Chief Secretary P. C. Joshi had recently moved the headquarters of the Communist Party of India to Calcutta from Bombay, hoping to bring the various terrorist, left-nationalist, and left-student groups under the CPI umbrella. While Susobhan's ablest students had signed on as Joshi's foot soldiers, he was limiting his activities to slipping Joshi envelopes of money.

A divide between the recent Oxford arrivals and the older adda members was taking shape. Susobhan and Hiren-da shared the conviction that no political system yet devised by man was as benevolent as Soviet Russia's. Sudhin Datta and Shahid Suhrawardy had signed on with the Decadent Bourgeois Party. Sudhin said he fully expected to be found swinging from the nearest lamppost the day the Great Reckoning with communism arrived. When the Comintern turned on the French writer André Gide after the publication of his book on Russia, Sudhin understood all he needed to about Stalin. The secret adda diarist was as yet uncommitted.

That evening all the young Communists came to life when Susobhan turned an obscure discussion of Kant and Hegel to Marx, the dictatorship of the proletariat, and the brotherhood of workers. Sudhin listened for a moment before interrupting impatiently.

"What could you *possibly know* about the life of a landless tenant farmer? It is nearly impossible to imagine such poor souls are part of our own society, much less imagine becoming one of them through the medium of communist ideology. What can bookish, middle-class bhadralok like ourselves ever have in common with them?"

A flurry of protest was swiftly countered by Sudhin's claim that having gone hungry during his last months in Europe did not mean he knew anything about the hunger that followed a bad harvest in Midnapore district.

This was the sort of argument the adda lived for, bubbling like a pot of soup thickening on a stovetop. Tension mounted until Hiren accused Sudhin of being too class conscious.

The fat hit the fire.

"Such talk is the height of stupidity! There is no such thing as class struggle among middle-class Bengalis," Sudhin replied excitedly.

One of the young poets was taken aback. He could feel in his bones that his bosses were exploiting him. Most definitely! Everyone began talking at once.

It was then that an Englishman, yet another recent arrival from Oxford, spoke up. From the adda's earliest days the presence of sahibs brought a touch of novelty and a frisson of tension to their evenings. Apurba Chanda, who had accompanied Sudhin and Tagore to America in 1929, often complained that Sudhin attracted foreigners like a magnet. He was never as ebullient when they were present. Otherwise Apurba liked to boast of how he, a lowly babu, had outfoxed his English superiors at Writers' Building.

Humphry House struck the adda's secret diarist as an English version of a Brahmin pundit from ancient India, a man who married a sagelike wisdom with beautiful manners. Indeed, House had been ordained into the Episcopal ministry and was briefly a deacon at an Oxford college until a crisis of faith obliged him to resign. Twice rejected for a fellowship at All Souls, he was offered only a Calcutta University teaching job, though taking it meant leaving his wife behind for a year. On the voyage out, he had been hopeful, planning to finish a book on Gerard Manley Hopkins in the peace and quiet of Calcutta.

His department head had been there to meet him when he arrived to accompany him to temporary lodgings at the United Services Club. Humphry was to stay there until he could find himself a bungalow. When he said he'd already arranged to stay on Dharamtallah Street with a friend from Oxford named Susobhan Sarkar, the department head's discomfiture was blisteringly evident.

From that moment Humphry House was a marked man. The Special Branch of Police assigned a watcher to sit on the wall outside his bungalow, ready to pad after him whenever he went out. Humphry's watchers tended to carry cheap umbrellas and wear heavy shoes. They would sidle up to him at the Esplanade tram stop, wiggle their eyebrows suggestively, and ask him questions.

"You are going home, isn't it?"

"Yes, I am going home."

"My nephew has a friend who was your student."

"Oh, yes."

"How do you find our boys?"

"I like them very well."

"Do you find they talk freely to you? I think they do; they talk about many things."

"Yes, they talk about many things."

Having weathered the hothouse of Oxford gossips like Isaiah Berlin, Stephen Spender, and Wystan Auden, Humphry found the machinations of the Criminal Investigation Department of the Special Branch of Police laughable. He might as well have stayed in Oxford. And when Susobhan Sarkar brought him to the Parichay adda, it seemed as if he had.

Clearing his throat and speaking gently, Humphry turned to the youth who felt in his bones his bosses were exploiting him.

"Do you also feel in your bones you are exploiting the servants in your home?"

A desperate look crossed the young man's face.

"There are times," he acknowledged solemnly, "when I realize this may be true."

"Class struggle cannot take place in a country where the caste system is so strong," Mallik-da suggested, tentative on this new ground and nervously reaching for a samosa.

"The driver of my car and I may belong to the same caste but I cannot imagine sitting and eating at the same table with him," Sudhin observed sagely, suggesting caste and class might work at cross-purposes.

Hesitantly but with a hint of daring, a young Communist volunteered that he had once shared a meal with his brother's driver. After a

long moment of stunned silence, the adda broke up and they all made
their way home.

Writers' Building, Dalhousie Square, Calcutta,
    late October 1936

One of Michael John Carritt's first responsibilities as a special officer
in Calcutta was to encode and decode messages arriving from London
and Delhi for His Excellency the Governor. To this end he was given
a small black box made out of steel and secured with a padlock. The
box, which contained cipher codes and secret files, went with him
everywhere. One of his orderlies liked to carry it on his head. The
other liked to carry it in gloved hands, like a butler carrying a tea tray.
Carritt relished being called away from a posh dinner table by the
delivery of a top-secret telegram. This would oblige him to retire to
a study to decipher its contents, sipping slowly from a large whiskey
thoughtfully provided by his host.

Carritt was often disappointed to discover that more than half
of the files marked "Highly Secret" had more to do with the sender's
sense of self-importance than anything remotely sensitive. Another
twenty-five percent were designated "Secret" to keep them from being
circulated to Indian members of the General Assembly. That left only
about a quarter of files marked secret on the grounds of law and order.
Naturally, these proved the most valuable. He alerted his contacts
when the police had intercepted letters at "suspect" addresses. Weekly
police reports and encrypted correspondence from London were cheer-
fully passed along.

Apart from Reverend Scott, John Auden and Humphry House
were the only ones who knew of Carritt's secret life. When John was
in Calcutta, the four of them would meet at John's flat. Though John's
voice was uncannily similar to Wystan's, Carritt found him to be cut
from a different cloth. When they first met, John hadn't yet begun to
question British rule; his conversation was more about his Himalayan
work than politics. It took a few pegs of whiskey before he was freed
of his nearly Old World reserve. Only then did his sardonic humor and
dry sense of the absurd come to light. As time passed, he became even

more forthcoming, as if he hadn't had anyone to share his thoughts with before.

Humphry, in contrast, was more of an anarchist; his outrageous (and often drunken) behavior at the most formal official durbars left Carritt gasping with terror and exaltation. Reverend Scott, alas, was rarely the life of the party; he was unable to fully appreciate the ridiculousness of their position. He saw nothing funny in having been asked to conduct Sunday services over an altar draped with a Union Jack. Regrettably, too, alcohol disagreed with his sensitive stomach.

They had an easier time of it on Sundays, when the reverend was otherwise occupied. Carritt would ride off to the Tolly, sending his boy ahead with a change of clothes and his groom to bring back his horse and kit. Just as he took great pleasure in the rituals of his office, brushing down his dress uniform and admiring the knifelike crease in his trousers, Carritt luxuriated in this immaculately kept club, far from the crowds, noise, and dirt of the city. Amid pleasantly vacuous talk over tables of mah-jongg, with the smell of jasmine mixing with that of scented talcum powder, Carritt felt perfectly at ease. When the three of them sat with cold mugs of beer, the laughter of unmarried maidens playing lawn tennis coming down the causeway, it summoned the England of their childhoods, before the war. On such mornings Carritt was nearly convinced the Raj would endure forever.

But then he would down his beer and excuse himself, off to meet an organizer in some distant bustee, ferrying a message from a labor leader on the lam in need of money or a safe house. Or he would meet the young reverend, still in his Sunday robes, and hand over the briefs he'd worked up, drawn from articles in the *New Statesman* or *Labour Monthly*, on the worldwide struggle against fascism. There were also impenetrable Marxist tracts from London to pass along to Indian comrades. Lord only knew what they made of them.

If Carritt couldn't take his underground work as seriously as Reverend Scott, it was no less important to him. Equally dear was the conspiracy of sentiment he shared with John Auden and Humphry House. They made up their own united front against the casual arrogance on display beneath the Tolly Club's high green canopy of mango and neem.

The Viceroy's Residency, New Delhi,
     April 12, 1937

By the end of Linlithgow's first year as viceroy, a face-to-face meeting with Gandhi had become unavoidable. Regional elections had been held, and Congress had secured absolute majorities in eight out of the eleven provincial ministries. In the remaining three it had received the largest block of votes. The Muslim League had not even achieved majorities in the two Muslim-majority states, the Punjab and Bengal. In the wake of the landslide, Nehru had changed his mind. Congress candidates would take office after all, provided the viceroy could assure him the British governors would not interfere with their mandate by veto or the invocation of special powers. When assurances were not forthcoming, Gandhi began to call for a judicial tribunal to rule on the matter. Though he had resigned from Congress office in 1934 and described his role as a humble adviser and moral influence, Gandhi made it clear to Viceroy Linlithgow he was not going away.

First, however, there were those devilish questions of protocol to be settled. Would Gandhi sign the guest book? Would his visit be mentioned in the Court Circular? Could the viceroy insist upon decent dress? And what would his ADCs wear? The scarlet-and-gold uniform was generally reserved for royal birthdays but might strike just the right note of unassailable dignity. Otherwise, yes, the dark frock coats with gold buttons.

Clearly Gandhi could not be received in the throne room. The throne room of Buckingham Palace was modest by comparison with the viceroy's, the largest in the world. His private study was more modest; only the size of two Oval Offices.

Gandhi of course would have to make the first move. A formal application for an interview would be required. And the veiled prophet wouldn't reply right off. It would not do to make it easy.

CHAPTER 10

The Moscow Agent

38 Upper Park Road, Belsize Park, London,
January 7, 1937

In the wake of Bill Tilman's triumphant ascent of Nanda Devi, Wystan Auden bestirred himself to undertake an expedition himself. In the fall of 1936 he and his poet friend from Oxford, Louis MacNeice, set out to explore Iceland. Under contract to write a travel book, they shared a pup tent missing one of its tent poles. A pack of schoolboys and their schoolmaster filled out the expedition roster. "When roughing it in this way it is always a good thing to think of the discomforts of the people climbing Everest," the schoolmaster would chide his young charges when they complained of the cold and rain. Wystan quipped he was far happier in the cold and rain than dining at the Ritz. While writing *The Ascent of F6*, Wystan had begun to think he needed to leave England altogether.

Stephen Spender had been quick to publish his critical assessment of Wystan and Christopher's play. Stephen had recently become a Communist and this provided him a clarifying view both of his brother Michael and the mountaineer hero at the center of the geopolitical drama. The most interesting thing about the hero, he explained, more important than his nascent fascism, was that he was a self-righteous prig. The play's climax had the mountaineer hero reaching the summit before his colonial rivals only to fall to his death after a hallucinatory encounter with the summit's resident demon. Yet Stephen felt the consequences of being a fascist and a prig were insufficiently dramatized.

John, to whom the play was dedicated, found the hero silly. Wystan pointed out it wasn't meant to be a realistic portrayal but more in the way of a pantomime. But he agreed revisions were needed. He hadn't wanted his hero to come across as a prig; he wanted him to be, much like Michael Spender, an autodidact, appealingly eccentric and isolated. The Mother character, too, needed development. Wystan wanted her Oedipal hold over the hero to be explicitly political. Just as the Nuremberg throngs had spawned Hitler, he explained, so her demand that her son climb F6 had created a monster, feeding an itch to conquer that could never be quenched. Set against the all-consuming roar of the crowds was the abbot's offer: a complete retreat from the public sphere into a monastery.

In London Wystan feared he was becoming something of a monster himself. His last play had been a critical and commercial success and he was now a sought-after voice on the burning issues of the day, leaving him consumed with fears of becoming a fraud, or eager-to-please court poet. But Wystan wasn't retreating to a monastery. Following two of the four Carritt brothers, he was heading for the civil war in Spain. The fight against fascism was now the struggle. Wystan would either join the International Brigades or drive an ambulance. He hoped the latter as he didn't think he would be a very good soldier, discounting the fact that he was a terrible driver. There remained, however, one loose end to tie up before he left.

If London was a parlor filled with madly flirting sherry drinkers oblivious to anything but their own wit and ironclad sense of self-importance, Louis MacNeice, Wystan's tentmate from Iceland, would be found standing to one side, smoking in the semidarkness to watch from a safe remove. Originally from the coast of Northern Ireland, Louis had long felt like a rustic interloper among the London highbrows. So just before the holidays, Wystan brought him to Upper Park Road for dinner. Ever the matchmaker, Wystan whispered to Nancy:

"Isn't he handsome?"

Nancy regarded Louis's long, equine face with a painter's eye.

"No, he looks like a horse who might shy but not kick."

When Wystan left for Madrid in early January 1937, Louis and Nancy saw him off at Victoria.

Later, Louis would say that until he'd met Nancy, he'd been color blind. He praised her still lifes and took her out for expensive meals. He paid her to accompany him to the Hebrides to illustrate a travel book on the islands. In the Hebrides Louis hardly registered the appalling weather and scarcely took in the landscape; he had eyes only for Nancy. On their return to London she rang Bill from the station call box and announced she was leaving him. She was taking the girls and moving in with Louis. When Bill tried to respond, his childhood stutter resurfaced and she knew at once she couldn't go through with it.

Louis returned to the Hebrides alone, shattered. Humphry House's book on Hopkins became his lone bedtime companion. He was meant to review it but no sooner did he open it than he would fall into a troubled sleep.

GSI Camp, Somewhere in the Tehri Garhwal,
March 1937

"He simply mustn't risk himself," Humphry House had insisted in a letter to John, as if John, sitting in a tent in the Siwaliks, could stop Wystan from going to Spain. It was the first John had heard of his brother's plans. Humphry had the news from Carritt, who had it from his brother Gabriel. Carritt had said that going off to fight was bourgeois romanticism; Wystan's job as a poet was to think and write. Humphry agreed. Sudhin Datta had yet to comment.

It was only on meeting Humphry House and, through him, Susobhan Sarkar, Shahid Suhrawardy, and most of all Sudhin Datta that John had finally realized how isolated he had become in India. Apart from a handful of Indian GSI colleagues, he rarely even spoke to Indians. But the quality of Sudhin's intellect and the grace of his manners were a revelation to him. And it was through his conversations with Sudhin that he began to see India and its aspirations in a new light. This naturally forced him to reflect on what part he would be called upon to play once British rule came to an end.

Calcutta might appear unchanged, John wrote Sudhin from the Garhwal, but elsewhere in India it was a different story. In every village he passed through, porters now refused to carry his kit and equipment boxes no matter how much he offered. It now dawned on him that he represented those who had repeatedly imprisoned their political leaders. He blamed himself for this impasse. He'd been too wrapped up in himself to reach out to Indians. Whereas Carritt's "hobby" enabled him to make up for the years he spent carrying water for the Raj, John had no such defense. Beyond its rocks and tectonics, he knew nothing about India. Ten years simply wasted.

Of course he was happy the empire was coming to an end. True friendship was possible only now that the balance of power had shifted. The tide of history was all on Sudhin's side. Yet with independence inevitable if not imminent he was left uncertain about his future. The prospect of returning to England galled him. England's objection to Nazi Germany had nothing to do with that country's treatment of Jews, John explained to Sudhin, though it now suited their book to make a fuss. England's real fear was that Germany's hegemony would usurp its own. How could he go back to that?

But how could he remain in India?

And of course the news that Wystan was heading for Spain unsettled him; the last headline he'd seen before he left suggested Madrid was about to fall to the Fascists. John had once shared with his brother his abstract concern at being complicit in British rule. It was indeed wicked to keep the ship going, Wystan had lectured. Yet Wystan also thought he made too much of himself and his difficulties, telling him that if he threw his life in India away, he was a coward. What Wystan didn't understand was how little he had to offer India, and the little he did have was of dubious value. What was the point of his geological surveys? Would he ever collect his speculations about the structure of the Himalaya? To whom would it matter if he did? And however much bile there was now, it would be nothing next to what would arise once British rule was finished and Indians were left to contemplate all those statues of men on horseback. And the railways and canals; the English wouldn't fail to remind them of those. There would be hell to pay, and those who stayed behind would pay it. Sudhin was far more understanding of his fears and uncertainties than Wystan.

Sudhin had long been schooled to think Bengalis were too emotional. They affected flippancy or flowery language as a means of dis-

guising their most passionate feelings. He knew that if he wanted to
be taken seriously by an Englishman, he had to subdue his natural
exuberance and affect a frigid manner and halting speech. With John
Auden he'd been too lazy to bother. From the moment they first met,
John had spoken to him like a man released from solitary, bursting
with things he needed to get off his chest. And now the poor man was
alone in some godforsaken wilderness writing him about his overwhelming sense of doom.

Sudhin knew Englishmen were often overcome by sentiment when
it came to India. Only a handful went as far as John did in extending
their affection to Indians. Yet he risked overstepping if he presumed to
offer him advice and had begun several letters before abandoning
them. Weary of his bleak bombast, he also worried about how it would
sound to a person living in solitary seclusion, seemingly near the end
of his tether. In the end he prayed John would not be shocked when
he told him just how much he missed him and how much he hated he
was so far away. Seeking to reassure him as to the value of his work,
however, Sudhin confused geology with geography. "You have only to
look at China to realize where a celestial contempt for Geography will
land you."

Sudhin had begun to see the Bengali in John Auden. "We live in a
curiously perverse age which is not only morbidly self-conscious but
at the same time is absurdly afraid of feelings. This results in a sort
of inverted sentimentality that, by cramping our outward expression
excessively makes our inner turmoil the more turbulent." Sudhin was
on intimate terms with such turmoil, though he was far more reluctant than John to speak of it. Even those closest to him heard nothing
of his loveless marriage and loneliness. To John he admitted only that
he had stopped writing. That he hadn't written a poem or felt a fresh
emotion in four years. Humphry's book on Hopkins was the first thing
he'd read in a long time that excited him, but when he tried to put his
thoughts on paper, his writing seemed intolerable. So he could readily
identify with John's thwarted creative ambitions.

Sadly, the sufferings of others were rarely as compelling to John as
his own. More to the point, in the same post as Sudhin's thoughtful
and affectionate letter was a telegram from Michael Spender inviting

him to join him on a survey expedition with Bill Tilman and Eric
Shipton. It wasn't the long-awaited invitation to Everest but rather an
opportunity to explore the remote glacial wilds of the Karakoram.

During the return march across Tibet after the failed 1936 Everest
expedition, Shipton had begun thinking about the Karakoram. A sister range of the Himalaya, it was located west of the Main Himalayan
Range, separated from it by the north-south Indus River. It was distinguished by its remoteness, its spiraling towers of granite, and a great
number of colossal glaciers. The Karakoram also held four of the fourteen peaks in the world over 8,000 meters, including K2, the second-
highest mountain in the world.

Before settling on this region, Shipton had consulted the maps.
While the southern Karakoram watershed had been surveyed, as the
map got closer to the range's major peaks and glaciers, the ridges and
valleys became increasingly chaotic before suddenly ending in a blank
space near K2 identified by one word: "Unexplored." By the time Shipton
arrived in Calcutta he had a plan. The plan was not to climb K2 with an
invading army of signal officers, armed guards, porters, and pack animals. The plan was to map K2 and the blank space surrounding it.

On receiving Michael's telegram, John promptly wrote letters to
Humphry and Sudhin begging them to tell him what he should do. To
accept meant completely scrapping the plans he'd made for his upcoming furlough. He admitted he was already toying with the idea of
going, but only on the condition that the time he spent there be counted
as time on duty. He didn't mention that contributing to a survey expedition by helping to map an uncharted territory would extend
and strengthen Britain's grip on the subcontinent. "I feel so useless
and unable to help in ways which come easily to you, Richard, and
Wystan," he wrote Humphry, as if asking to be forgiven. Richard was
their code name for Carritt. Humphry never bothered with it.

Like Sudhin, Humphry didn't entirely grasp what John did out in
the field but he told John he had the technical know-how an independent India would find useful. He also had the stamina to overcome
the physical hardships his work entailed. The one thing he lacked was
self-confidence and an expedition to the Karakoram wouldn't provide
him a sense of what he had to contribute. Europe or America would.

Sudhin also chimed in. It would be a terrible pity if John sacrificed his leave for this. Hadn't he been slaving away at just that sort of work all this time? Shouldn't he be thinking of resting rather than introducing more exhaustion and hardship into his life? Russia, England, or America would be more pleasant and welcoming destinations for his expertise than the glorious Karakoram. And if he went, what would he do when he came back? Would there be time for him to make a start on his book? Finally, it was a grave mistake to let his fantasies of personal failure loom so large. And how could he possibly insist he was unloved and a fraud with friends like Humphry and Susobhan? Were they more gullible than the common run of man? Was he?

"I know it is unpardonably cheeky to say all this, but you will please remember in extenuation that I am a slightly older man and have made such a dreadful mess of so many things that my opinion as to what is failure and what not should, at least, be worth a moment's consideration?"

Sudhin Datta's grasp of what failure and greatness entailed paled beside John Auden's. And he couldn't well tell him what this invitation meant without giving away just how grandiose his ambitions were. Either Shipton or Tilman would be chosen to lead the 1938 Everest expedition. One of them would decide the roster. More than writing any book, more than joining any cause, he wanted his shot at that mountain.

While John was off in the Garhwal, Carritt and House had gone out one Saturday night, returning at 4:00 a.m. to the chummery Humphry now shared with John. Fully soused or, as Humphry put it, "bottled up to the eyelids," they announced their arrival by crashing the car into the fence and shouting drunkenly in the company of two women of uncertain reputation. The missionaries who lived in the flat above had been rudely awakened.

On another evening, this time with Reverend Scott, both "politicals" had been sober as death when they left around midnight. Though Madrid was still hanging on, the war in Spain had reached a breaking point, and Carritt was worried about his brothers. Later that same night, while preparing for bed Humphry and his visiting wife found themselves with "midnight buttock stirrings." After a quietly serious

excavation of "all the usual pleasure purlieus and crannies," there ensued, Humphry explained in great detail to John, a prolonged, ener-
getic, and deeply rewarding fuck. The crashing and rattling of the bed
had again woken up their god-fearing neighbors. A letter of eviction
arrived the next morning. Humphry's antisocial behavior made his
continued residence impossible. There was a feeling in the residency,
the letter said, that he thought himself superior. This was undoubtedly
true, he admitted.

It was too bad, really, he wrote John, because the Amherst Street
place was such an excellent setup. Sudhin, Hiren-da, and Minnie
Bonnerjee, a new addition to adda and wicked fun, had been coming to his parties to smoke, drink, and argue about politics. When
Humphry told Hiren-da that the real objection to Mrs. Simpson was
not that she was a divorcée but that she circulated in the social milieu of Oswald Mosley's British Union of Fascists, thereby raising the
specter of a "Churchill Mosley right wing Press Fascist King's Party,"
Hiren-da got very excited. The adda was now abuzz with anticipation
of a Churchill–Hitler pact. An alliance between the arch-imperialist
anti-Communist Royalist and the arch-Fascist anti-Communist made
perfect sense, they agreed.

John was disappointed to lose their chummery but in an unusually
chipper mood, he composed a homily:

> *We'll hear how Humphry fell*
> *To the lowest pits of hell*
> *Was ever a Devil's proselyte*
> *More sudden in his appetite?*
>
> *God above knows all you do*
> *From Amherst Street to Timbuctoo*
> *From Heaven's walls He can see*
> *Into the darkest lavatory*
>
> *Let this be an awful warning*
> *To boys and girls on Sunday morning*
> *The blessed blood, though wine perhaps,*
> *Does only good to holy chaps*

Soon after Humphry found a new flat De Sahib, the Englishman from the adda who was a suspected Special Branch informant, dropped by Hiren-da's house to chat. Insisting that he and Humphry had been at school together, he proceeded to inquire about Professor House's doings. This gave Humphry an idea. He would immortalize De Sahib, along with the watchers who had been following him all year, in a book titled *I Spy with My Little Eye* and dedicate it to John and Sudhin. Humphry's time in Calcutta was nearly up.

Humphry's new landlord was a judge of the High Court, half Muslim, one-quarter Italian, one-quarter Austrian, and, like John, a Marlburian. Unfortunately, those pan-chewing men with wiggling eyebrows were once again squatting outside his door. Leaving behind his ancient jalopy, Humphry was walking all over the city now, stopping to talk with all and sundry in fluent Bengali. His watchers could scarcely keep pace.

"Jesus what a town!" he wrote John.

Undersecretary's Office, Writers' Building,
     Dalhousie Square, Calcutta, March 1937

With the grim news out of Spain, Carritt's mind had not been entirely on his work, either for His Excellency the Governor or the Communist underground. His brothers' brigade had been through hell; he was waiting to hear if they had survived. Some days Carritt could convince himself that for every life lost in Spain, one hundred new recruits to the cause were won. But on bad days he thought he should become a rare bird egg collector and pretend he didn't know any better. It was on such a day that he was approached by the deputy commissioner of police (Intelligence Branch) of Calcutta.

"Carritt, old boy. I'm worried. Am I in trouble for not producing results? Are they likely to push me out of the IB into some God forsaken up-country dung-hill with my wife and young babies? For God's sake, old man, tell me what they are saying."

Carritt turned to the DCP and replied offhandedly.

"I've heard nothing. No complaints about your reports, all quiet as usual. I doubt the Chief even reads them. Don't worry."

Carritt had been reading Wystan's articles; it was good, effective stuff. He appreciated what Wystan had to say about the role men like them were to play in the coming struggle. That it was no good pretending they were workers, or Indians for that matter. Really, everything Wystan wrote made sense. The present crisis wasn't simply about the expansionist aims of Germany and Italy. No, what was happening was precisely what Marx had foretold: the international working class in arms. It wasn't going to be 1914 again.

For one thing Indians had suffered the full crop of terror, imprisonment, shootings, massacres, and vicious exploitation. Two decades of unceasing struggle, all crushed by the brutal imperialist hand. Late as it was, the Indians were beginning to grasp things. Carritt had once feared that the nationalist movement would simply make way for a "babu raj." Instead, the movement was passing from the hands of the petit bourgeois to the workers and peasants. Glassblowers, tea workers, hand carters, dockhands, Chinese cobblers and sailors, hawkers, sweet shop assistants, printers, and workers in the rope, saloon, tobacco, and hosiery industries were all organizing. Even ordnance factory workers had a union and the Calcutta police were agitating for a salary increase. However many files they opened, Special Branch couldn't keep pace.

The deputy commissioner of police was still talking.

"For weeks we haven't laid our hands on a single bastard. How do they slip away? There's something about it all. It's a game of Blind Man's Buff, and I am the poor blind buffer in the middle. They spin me around and I just get hold of a suspect and he disappears into thin air whilst I go on spinning round and round."

Carritt finally turned to the poor sod, suddenly appreciating the irony that the DCP was venting his frustration to the very man who had tied his blindfold. The DCP was earnest, hardworking, and more intelligent than most of his colleagues at Writers' Building. To get rid of him, Carritt suggested it might be the handiwork of a foreign agent. The man left his office transfixed by the thought that deeper and darker forces than he could possibly imagine were at work.

Carritt had entirely forgotten their exchange by the time word of a Moscow agent on the loose began percolating through Intelligence Branch reports. He asked Reverend Scott what he knew. Had the

Comintern sent someone to keep an eye on them? Chief Secretary P. C. Joshi asked around but his contacts, too, were mystified. They decided to sit back and see what else IB came up with. Weeks passed.

Then suddenly the Moscow agent appeared, in the flesh, right on the streets of Ballygunj! According to the new reports, he was a tall, thin, sallow creature with an enormous head, sporting a shabby topee and dressed in a dhoti so inexpertly tied it threatened to un-ravel. The watcher who reported the sighting said he had been seen in the company of Muzzafar Ahmed. Though everyone knew the union leader was at that moment serving a jail sentence, the IB lapped it up. Informants were popping up everywhere, swearing they had seen him, here, there, all over the city.

Finally, a report crossed Carritt's desk in which it was suggested that the Moscow agent might be a lecturer at Calcutta University named Humphry House.

The first newspaper John Auden saw on getting back from the Garhwal had virtually the same headline as the one he'd seen before he left; Madrid was on the verge of falling. With only three weeks in town be-fore leaving to join Shipton, Tilman, and Spender in Srinagar, he didn't bother to shave his beard before showing up at the Tolly for Sunday lunch. Carritt, too, was preparing for the twice-yearly Darjeeling retreat that preceded and followed the monsoons. And as Humphry's Hopkins book was being well received in London, he was in a fine fettle. He took the news that Special Branch was on to him in stride.

"What does a Moscow agent wear?" he asked Carritt. He wanted to look the part. When he proposed a toast to his international celebrity, Carritt had to remind him his name had appeared in only one confi-dential police report.

"Nonsense, old boy; absolute nonsense. The police force is a public service and recognition by it is therefore essentially public. Moreover, they have me down as an appointed agent of an international body, the Comintern, thereby granting me international status."

After Carritt left for Darjeeling and John for the Karakoram, Humphry unexpectedly secured a berth on an earlier boat. He spent his last night in Calcutta drinking with Sudhin Datta and Shahid Suhrawardy. When he left them to finish his packing, he wasn't at all surprised to find a subinspector waiting for him on the veranda. The man welcomed him in, apologizing for his intrusion as he did so. No sooner had Humphry lit the lamp than the man's eyes went straight to his bookshelves.

There were two types of police officers, Humphry had once explained to Carritt. The first were bullyboys who liked a good lathi, either to tap you on the shoulder or poke you in the balls. Then there was the cringing sort who told you how much they hated their jobs but, what to do? His guest was of the latter sort, so unctuous that, forgetting himself, Humphry offered him a peg. The man declined, citing his Hindu beliefs, but begged him not to deprive himself of his vital sustenance. The subinspector began by saying how saddened he was by the news that Humphry was leaving. On behalf of everyone at Special Branch he wanted to convey their most sincere love and affection. Humphry, in turn, promised he would never forget them. After several rounds of this, the officer turned to Humphry's bookshelf.

"You are a literary man, Professor? Yes, I can see you have many books."

"Yes, I suppose you could say I am a literary sort of man. . . . Do you read many books, Inspector?"

"Not books, not books . . . I read many . . . reports."

"Ah yes, of course. *Reports.* These reports must be very interesting, a very interesting field of Literature. I would myself like to read your reports—some time."

Humphry pulled out some books that the subinspector's eye seemed particularly drawn to and passed them over. In anticipation of this visit, he had dolled up *A Christmas Carol* with a cover of *The Coming Struggle for Power. Northanger Abbey* cross-dressed as Orwell's banned book on the mill workers of Lancashire, *The Road to Wigan Pier.* Other Victorian worthies masqueraded as main selections from the Left Book Club. The man glanced at them distractedly, not quite sure what was going on. Then Humphry took down *Selections from the Writings of Karl Marx*, holding it reverently with both hands, like an offering.

"This may be of special interest to you. It is an exceedingly valuable book. Please have a look at the inscription." Humphry opened the page and moved alongside the subinspector. He had written it himself.

"To my good friend, Humphry House from D . . . R . . . Deputy Commissioner of Police (IB) Calcutta."

A copy of *I Spy with My Little Eye* eventually found its way to Isaiah Berlin at Oxford. Isaiah Berlin had always taken an unhealthy interest in all Humphry's doings. But the idea that Humphry's letters and packages were being opened and he was being followed by the secret police struck Berlin as fantastic and wildly paranoid.

"I tremble to think," Berlin wrote Stephen Spender, "what, with his natural rankness of mind . . . must have happened to [Humphry] in the congenial society of a lot of inferior Mulk Anands." Mulk Raj Anand was the one Indian writer of note in London; the idea there might be others, in India no less, was inconceivable.

A Boardinghouse in Darjeeling, Bengal,
   late July 1937

Carritt had first visited Darjeeling on compassionate leave after the assassination of yet another Midnapore DO. Sometime during the night of his arrival his manservant had awakened him, pointing excitedly to the window. Coming out from under his mosquito net Carritt saw the light of a ghostly form floating in the sky. It looked like a massive white breast topped with a rosy nipple: Kanchenjunga.

Six years later, the hill station was little changed. His landlady had greeted his arrival with a chatty explosion of relief that he wasn't an Anglo-Indian but a proper Englishman. She went on to explain that as long as men like him kept the Indians divided, they could all remain in India and make money. Of course, Indians didn't really smell, she whispered, sotto voce, especially respectable ones. "But it pays to pretend they do."

Carritt retired to his tiny room with a bottle of whiskey. He had been dreading this Darjeeling interlude, his letter to John Auden began, but he now realized this was just what he needed. He wanted the letter to catch John on his return from the Karakoram, before he left for England. Perhaps he was slightly drunk. No. He was quite *clearly* drunk, but he wouldn't let that stop him from getting to the point. After a long aside about a drunken encounter with a red pillar box of His Majesty's Postal Service, and another about having caught "the last train out of the desert of barren desires" and some indecipherable scribbles, Carritt stopped himself.

"Where was I going?"

He began again. He was coming out of the woods now. The pillar boxes were still there but he had learned to treat them with respect.

He forgot where he was going with that.

This didn't mean all loneliness and pain were gone, not at all. But he could no longer find it in himself to say that life was meaningless or to ask himself why he bothered. That was the refuge of all those Englishmen who had been having such a good time only to bump painfully against that pillar box. As he imagined John had.

"I want to help you catch this train John."

If John could just take a look at the faces of his traveling companions, take in the tawdry decorations of the imperial carriage, he would *see*. They had both been pawns in the empire game; the Secretary of State for India had appealed to their vanity by offering them a shot at adventure and moral greatness. Humphry's book had diagnosed them both. "The Lakes are a training ground for ambition," he had written; "they breed ideals." Carritt had joined the ICS, John the GSI with those ideals and ambitions only to find themselves radicalized by the fear of becoming pukka sahibs instead. Maybe his own work for the Communist underground arose from a similar assumption of lofty superiority, as Humphry said, or even a lust for power. What did it matter? His party work remained the one thing he was sure of.

John might not have Humphry's self-confidence, Carritt wrote, but he did have a need to say things worth being said. He was by far the nicest of them. But he was trapped by his enchantment with the mountains, and could not see what was coming.

Was he sounding like a beastly ICS wallah, taking an interest in his Jat?

The truth was, if Humphry hadn't been there when he received the news of his brother's death after the battle of Brunete in Spain, he wouldn't have tided over the last month with any grace at all. The one thing Carritt was grateful for was that he'd given away no hint of his grief to the bloody fascists at Government House. He was proud of that. But as soon as he was alone he couldn't think of his brother without tears starting. He was crying now.

"Do you ever cry?" Carritt wasn't ashamed to admit that he did, all too easily, really, and at all kinds of silly things. Certain poems, jazz tunes, when people try to be sympathetic, things like that. Wildest of all, he wept at the sight of a woman's breasts. What could *that* mean? Did he ever think about dying and what it was like? Did he think it was better to know or not know when death was coming?

Anyway, the point was, he had "friends" in London. If John decided to join the cause, they would help him. Regardless, he hoped John would have a grand time. Calcutta wouldn't be the same without him and Humphry.

"Tell the chaps at home what a hero I am—all lies, but tell them, 'cos I wanna be loved! Do I write balls? Well forgive me; I mean well but am so very *very* bourgeois."

Carritt's elation dissipated quickly. Work was slow, weighty decisions were always being put off. Every official communication, even from adjacent offices, had to be routed through the Indian clerical staff left behind in sweltering Calcutta. And once the sun went down, it was as if a curtain had dropped. Darjeeling's small lanes took on a sinister aspect and he began to wonder how much longer he could play his cat-and-mouse game with the DCP.

The governor of Bengal had also begun to worry him. Formerly a hard-faced administrator of the Black and Tans in Ireland, Sir John Anderson had been brought in to govern Bengal with a similar ruthlessness. Carritt had sat in on a conference of senior district officers discussing what further measures might be taken against the nationalists. In the eight out of eleven provinces where Congress had prevailed, elected officials were already opening the jails and freeing their colleagues. In Bengal, where they had received only the largest block of votes, Governor Anderson was advocating the adoption of Nazi tactics and a return to wholesale arrests of union organizers and activists.

Both Carritt and Reverend Scott had also been hearing rumors about changes in Communist Party leadership. It had been a relatively easy matter for Carritt to ask for a few days' leave for a quick trip to Bombay. Back on Juhu Beach, he was meant to be looking out for his underground contact, but his eyes kept drifting toward the breaking waves. There was something truly hopeless in the sight of a fisherman casting his net, again and again, coming up empty every time.

Finally, two sweaty figures rose up before him in the noonday sun. One was tall and thin, the other short and squat. Both looked left and right, as if they were checking traffic, before crossing toward him to settle in the dunes. The tall chap was Ajay Ghosh, a member of the CPI politburo. He had once organized armed raids, but while in jail he had been converted to propaganda work. Ghosh addressed Carritt by his code name, Bashir.

Come meet *Our Friend* here, he said, indicating his tubby companion.

A former terrorist being brought into the CPI fold, Carritt supposed, nodding.

Such meetings followed a predictable course. He took notes to pass along to Ben Bradley, at the League Against Imperialism. He conveyed Bradley's promises that cash for party work would be forthcoming. Generally, however, the funds disappeared en route or were never sent. Carritt had complained to London that it was impossible to carry out resolutions without funds, that P. C. Joshi was sitting on his arse. Furthermore, the disappearance of courier links because of arrests or someone being forced underground meant that no one knew where party leadership was at any given time. At one point Joshi had to hide out from Special Branch at *his* flat. And if they couldn't keep tabs on each other, keeping channels open with Congress was impossible. They were more of a Divided Front than a Popular one.

But neither of his companions was interested in rehashing party problems. Events in Europe were moving quickly, Our Friend began. He had proof that the Bengali firebrand Subhas Chandra Bose was in contact with Hitler and Mussolini, proof that the latter was funding him. The previous year, having failed to get Congress to take a more militant stand, Bose had launched his own mass protest against British rule and was kicked out of the party. His arrest brought Calcutta to a standstill. Released from prison in March, he was now using the example of Lenin's exile in the kaiser's Germany to justify his efforts to raise an army. This line was pitched squarely at radical Communist cadres and those on the left in Congress impatient with Gandhi's quasi-religious nonviolent tactics. Should it come to war, some believed, neither nonviolence nor those newly elected Congress officials of the provincial ministries could protect them. For this reason alone, Bose posed a danger. There were elements in the Indian Army and the upper echelons of Indian society that might well opt to work with Hitler. The avenue to national liberation must not be through an alliance with the Fascists.

It was dark by the time Ghosh's companion stopped speaking.

Carritt was ready with questions. Where did that leave the British Empire? How should the Communist Party of Great Britain respond? What did the Comintern have to say? What was the greater evil, imperialism or fascism? Weren't they simply two faces of the same enemy? And what part was he to play? Neither man had any answers.

It was hard not to feel it was their show now.

But if his fight was no longer in India, where was it?

CHAPTER 11

In the Ice Mountains

Woyil Bridge, outside Srinagar,
 Kashmir, May 5, 1937

The sound of hobnailed boots on the Rawalpindi platform woke Michael Spender from a deep sleep in the station waiting room. After four days and four nights on the train from Darjeeling, Angtharkay, Sen Tensing, and Ang Tensing from the 1935 Everest reconnaissance had finally arrived, a day overdue, accompanied by four new smiling faces. Wearing pyjama trousers with tweed jackets, windproofs with flannels, the seven Sherpas made a theatrical entrance. The sleepy crowd on the platform couldn't stop staring. John Auden, who had seen them off from Howrah station in Calcutta, would follow in a few days.

Eight hours later, at the border of the princely state of Kashmir, they ran into problems. Somewhere along the way the Nazis had acquired the belief that the Himalaya were the true homeland of the Aryans. Three years before, ten German climbers had died in a reckless try for the summit of Nanga Parbat and now a German mountaineer named Karl Wien intended to reclaim German honor. Nanga Parbat was Germany's mountain of destiny and Wien had insisted that while his expedition was under way, no other expeditions be in the field. As with Germany's other territorial claims, British officials down the line were making every effort to keep Hitler happy. Eric Shipton's permit application was refused. After an entire day was wasted haggling, the impasse was eventually breached by Shipton's bold assertion that they were not really on an expedition. In a narrow sense, this was true. They were there not as mountain climbers but as surveyors; the summit of K2 was their fixed point, not their destination.

Later, over dinner at the Srinagar Club, the subject of *The Ascent of F6* arose. Shipton had seen the play, and the idea of a race to seize a summit on the contested border of a prize colony reminded him of all he hated about the massive, siege-style Everest expeditions. Bill Tilman, who wouldn't have been found dead in a West End theater, much less a Group Theatre production, expressed his opinion that music hall humor was demeaning to women. An awkward silence fell over the table. Shipton changed the subject. On a walk later that night, he aired his irritation to Michael; Tilman, who had spent the entire sea journey in his cabin and had vowed to walk all the way to the Baltoro Glacier in short pants, was becoming a feminist crank. Thereafter Michael assigned Tilman the code name of F6 in his journal.

A letter from Granny awaited him in Srinagar: she was pleased to report that Erica and the new baby were getting by perfectly well on no allowance whatsoever—just as she would have had to had she remained in Germany. Fearful that England might contest Italy's colonial claims, Granny wanted to know whether Michael had seen any sign that Indian sepoys were leaving for Abyssinia. The German people wouldn't now be starving and enslaved, she wrote, if they hadn't been robbed of their colonies. One of her German relations had said that and she wondered what Michael thought. Finally, she wanted to know if he had heard anything of the German expedition to Nanga Parbat.

While the English party was accommodated on the lawns of the residence of Sir Peter and Lady Clutterbuck, the Germans were staying on houseboats that lined the shores of the Jhelum River. Michael, who went to visit Karl Wien to practice his German, was briefly taken with the idea of living on a leaky houseboat for two shillings and six pence a day. Three shillings, if a woman was thrown in. "The lotus flower floats and blooms on those lakes as an enduring symbol of reposeful life," Francis Younghusband had written in one houseboat's guest book after his epic journey from Peking to Kashmir, exactly fifty years before. Younghusband was the last man to have visited the area they intended to survey.

The nineteen-day, 275-mile journey north began the next day. On John Auden's arrival, they left wheeled civilization behind at the Soyil Bridge, enjoying a lavish picnic with the Clutterbucks before crossing. At the point of departure, Michael suffered a moment of panic. Shipton was jumpy, too, certain he'd forgotten something. He confessed to Michael that he really hated climbing mountains and deeply disliked being above the tree line. He was already praying for the moment they would return.

As the bird flies, the distance between Askole, the southernmost outpost before the uplift of the Great Karakoram, and the Upper Yarkand River, near the unmarked border of Chinese Turkestan, was about seventy miles. But here even birds ran into trouble. In the course of the expedition they would come across countless bird skeletons. Not being greatly learned in ornithology, Shipton supposed they were some sort of duck. One had legs as long as his arm. Some still had their plumage. Had the ancestors of these birds established this migratory path before the high ranges existed, trapping them into flying over a frigid and inhospitable terrain? There had to be an easier way, Shipton thought. For the surveyors there wasn't.

The area of their proposed survey was divided into two unequal parts, bisected by the Shaksgam River. The Shaksgam ran east to west and drained the Karakoram's northern watershed. Sandwiched between the Shaksgam River and the Upper Yarkand River on the border of Chinese Turkestan was the Aghil Range. In 1926 Kenneth Mason, the director of the Survey of India and president of the Himalayan Club, had mapped the region just east of the area Shipton had his eye on. Michael's map would eventually join up with Mason's, encompass the route of Younghusband's final marches from Turkestan to Kashmir, and extend as far west as they could get before running out of food and fuel.

By crossing the Shaksgam River, climbing and passing over the Aghil Range and descending to the Upper Yarkand, they would be extending the northernmost borders of India, not with an invading army, but with a subtense bar. Auden and Spender would lead separate parties of Baltis and Sherpas in radial journeys outward, methodically triangulating. Tilman and Shipton would be given the highest stations to do their part and get in some climbing. Periodically, Spender would collect all their work on plane table sheets from which he would later work up a final map.

The exact location of the pass over the Aghil Range that Younghusband crossed was of abiding interest to the Foreign and Political Department, the ministry responsible for India's border security. Younghusband had explored the northern passes leading into India, those through which an invasion might conceivably take place. After fixing the position of Sir Francis's Aghil Pass, surveying the far side of the Aghil range, the parties would join up and return south. Shipton scoffed at the idea that an incursion into this delicate border region might be dangerous. The chief bogey was to finish with the Aghil Range and recross the Shaksgam before the summer floods swelled it to the point where it became impassable, stranding them in no-man's-land.

At the heart of Shipton's proposed survey were some of the largest glaciers outside the Arctic Circle. Not far from where they hoped to establish their supply dump was a confluence of immense glacial streams—the K2, the Sarpo Laggo, the Skyang, and the Crevasse Glaciers. This would be their first Base Camp. Younghusband had named this spot Sughet Jangal, maintaining that he had found evidence here of an ancient caravan route between Turkestan and India.

To get to the Shaksgam River, they had first to reach the Sarpo Laggo Glacier. Younghusband had crossed the East Muztagh Pass from the glacier, but an Italian explorer had seen another, more easily accessed one at the head of one of the side valleys leading off the Trango Glacier on the southern edge of the Karakoram. When they reached there Shipton and Auden went off to see which of the two to try. Sighting the twin summits of the toothy Muztagh Tower, itself over 7,000 meters high, Shipton made a guess where each was. The tangle of huge rock precipices and surreal-looking granite spires might have put him off, but the fun of crossing a new pass trumped the sure thing of the East Muztagh.

To support themselves for three and a half months, the expedition required the services of nearly a hundred local porters, in large part

Muslim Baltis from Askole. These men would ferry one and a half tons of food and supplies over the yet-to-be-found pass to the supply dump at Sughet Jangal, and then return home. After that there would be no runners bringing letters from Granny and no dated issues of the *Spectator* bearing news of Hitler's mischief.

The Baltis were dubious. Even if they succeeded in crossing the pass and dumping their loads, they feared they would find themselves trapped on the glacier, unable to return. Nonetheless, Shipton prevailed upon them and after a great deal of wrangling all were assembled and loaded. It was at this moment that Tilman and Sen Tensing suffered malarial relapses. Rather than see their food supply disappear, John volunteered to stay back with them while Michael and Shipton accompanied the rope gang and their loads over the promised pass. When the fevers lifted they would follow.

In Shipton and Tilman's zeal to strip the party down to the essentials, however, quinine supplies had been jettisoned, as well as sticking plasters and most of John's geological equipment. Shipton had initially considered his rock hammer and ungainly Mannlicher-Schonauer hunting rifle unnecessary but was voted down. Michael only just managed to hang on to his coffee but had to bind up his blisters with a handkerchief.

Uli Biafo Pass, 12,600 feet,
    Greater Karakoram, May 29, 1937

The Darjeeling Sherpas took pride in their reputation as mountain men. However hard the work, it was nothing like tea plantation labor or pulling rickshaws up and down the slopes of Darjeeling. The mountains recalled for them the summer days of their youth when they herded the family yaks to high pastures. They had all been young boys when they first heard about the effort to climb Chomolungma. It wasn't long before they knew the details of every Everest expedition. Secondhand accounts of Mallory and Irvine, Dr. Kellas, and General Bruce had all been passed down. The *chilingna* were an endless source of fascination, with their strange clothes and large, heavy boots.

They regarded the Baltis, at that moment intent on mending their paboo slippers with bradawls, twine, and goatskin, more warily. Baltis were neither Hindus like the Gurkhas nor Buddhists like themselves. No one knew what they believed or why they couldn't eat meat they hadn't butchered. So that first evening the Sherpas kept to themselves, occupied with the usual camp tasks. Ang Tensing had found and killed seven fleas in Michael's sleeping bag. Lhakpa Tensing, one of the new faces from Darjeeling, was sneaking a rock into Nukku's pack. Sherpas never grew tired of this prank and as Nukku, another newby, was a bit slow he was often a target. A dinner of curried goat was being prepared; Angtharkay had a heavy hand with the chili powder and had to be watched.

Regarding this domestic scene Michael couldn't help but wonder how things were at home. Unlike the journal he kept on the 1935 reconnaissance, it had taken only a single page to get from Victoria Station, where Erica, Granny, and his sister Christine had seen him off, to the Kashmir border. There was no mention of his infant son. There was no worry over Erica's fate in his absence. It was as if he expected the baby would keep her company, absolving him of any further concern. But now a touch of homesickness came over him.

It was the end of May. The trees would soon be coming into leaf. Erica would be getting out their summer clothes. Had anyone gone to visit her in the little thatched cottage Granny had bought them in Essex? Had the strawberries come in? Had she managed to put away some jars of spring rhubarb? He wondered now if he should have renounced marriage, as the others here had, before taking up this life. Adding to his introspection was the fact that while crossing another river he had fallen into a hole and nearly drowned. Yet his first panicked thought was not of Erica or his son but of his ice ax, which he only just managed to save.

After dinner the Baltis formed a ring around the fire and began singing. The Sherpas watched silently. As the night wore on the Baltis grew more and more ecstatic, clapping their hands, slightly off beat, one man after another breaking away to dance in the middle, drawing from a seemingly inexhaustible repertoire. Michael's sense of contentment was only slightly darkened by apprehension of what awaited them all in the morning.

They set off at 8:00 a.m. in bright sunshine. By noon a light snow began falling and a cold wind picked up. The moment they stopped at the snout of the Trango the flurries became a snowstorm and within minutes transformed their camp into a scene off a Christmas card. By six a cup of water froze solid in half an hour. Of course the Baltis were unhappy. A few of them were barefoot. There was no dancing around a fire that night and no tents to crawl into. Some staged strikes in the hopes of getting a blanket. Was this an omen of what awaited them? Even inside his tent Michael felt like a block of ice. At daybreak he lifted his tent flap and saw no sign of anyone. The Baltis had absconded, taking all their supplies.

But what he'd taken for snow-covered boulders turned out to be Baltis under blankets. Still, two loads of firewood were gone. Within an hour the Baltis had thawed sufficiently to get up, grab their sixty-pound loads, and begin their way up the moraine. After an hour Shipton called a halt. The sun was fierce on the newly fallen snow, the men didn't have dark glasses, and their paboos gave them no traction. Furthermore, the side valley he had chosen made a turn and Shipton couldn't be certain they were heading toward the pass. He and Michael started for a ridge to get a quick look. They ended up slogging their way in thigh-deep snow for what turned out to be hours. Michael fell out in exhaustion, but Shipton continued on to confirm what they feared. They had taken the wrong valley and wasted an entire day. The Baltis would have to spend another night in the open.

When they returned with this news, a melee broke out and eventually ten were given their rations and pay and let go. Boots and dark glasses were distributed, then rations, then blankets. Some complained they had no glasses, others that they had no boots. Some had boils, some were snow blind, some lay on the ground holding their heads and groaning in pain. Everyone, Michael noted drily, had a great deal to say. At last all were fixed up and fed. As quiet descended over the camp Michael wondered how the Baltis would survive another night. It rivaled Everest during the monsoons for misery. "Such fun to go exploring!" He and Shipton went over what they would do if a revolt broke out in the morning.

They broke camp before daybreak to try another side valley. By 9:15

Shipton had found a hard shelf from where he was sure he could see the pass. When they reached it, it proved an illusion. The pass was another two miles farther on and some six hundred feet higher in soft snow. They decided to stand between the false and the true pass and beckon the Baltis to cross the snowfield with their loads in order to receive their pay. The Baltis balked, eying a hairy-looking icefall. A standoff ensued until Angtharkay traipsed back and, through some miracle of Sherpa persuasion or dire threat, got them to advance.

After paying off the mutineers, they were still left stuck in the middle of a pass at 18,650 feet with all their supplies. High winds prevented them from camping there and it was a severe drop to the Sarpo Laggo Glacier. Worse still, there was bloody awful-looking snow on it. Clearly, Michael thought, it was too early to be there. Nonetheless by June 4 Shipton was directing the movement of loads down to Sughet Jangal by the seventeen Baltis who had stuck it out and a few men they had taken on in Skardu. Michael was at his first station; K2 was in his sights, standing out "like a cathedral spire above the roofs of a provincial town." K2 was the fixed point from which the entire summer survey would grow. To complete the moment John Auden showed up with the news that Tilman and Sen Tensing were on their way. The bandobast was over. The expedition proper had begun.

Shaksgam Valley to the Aghil Pass,
    Greater Karakoram, June 20, 1937

All along the path of the Sarpo Laggo Glacier they found remains of encampments, both the rectangular shapes of Younghusband's tents and the circular rings of nomadic yak herders'. Sheep bones, the jawbone of a horse, and the ruins of a hut were all signs of human habitation. Perhaps Younghusband had been right about an old caravan route, Michael thought. But when was it abandoned and why? After crossing the Shaksgam River they climbed through a narrow defile that opened onto a forked valley, turning west then north. Was this the right way to the Aghil Pass? A single iron nail found underfoot was proof enough for Shipton.

Suddenly, much sooner than expected, they were upon the crest of the Aghil Range. Below them the ground fell away into a valley and beyond that lay the Upper Yarkand River and the snowcapped mountains of Central Asia. Behind them lay the vast Karakoram. Of this view Younghusband wrote, "There arranged before me across the valley, was a glistening line of splendid peaks, all radiant in the sunshine. . . . Where I had reached no white man had ever reached before." For Shipton nothing could spoil the moment.

Michael, however, was stunned, scanning the horizon behind them in alarm. He had counted on being able to see at least one of the fixed points he had already established. But in the sea of peaks behind him, he couldn't recognize any of them, not even K2. He had made a tremendous blunder. Back at the Sughet Jangal depot lay the Wild Precision Invar subtense bar in its box alongside its tripod. With the subtense bar he might have measured the distance between K2 and the Aghil indirectly, via an astronomical azimuth and latitude. How many times had Ang Tensing asked him if he needed it? It would be a two-day journey to retrieve it and return.

And now, when Michael broke the news, Ang Tensing, the most helpful and cheerful bloke of the lot, rebelled: I'm not going, he said. "*Na jaayega.*" Ang Tensing had nearly been swept away crossing the Shaksgam. He had been severely shaken, having only just managed to hang on to the twenty-two-pound plane table. Where the Baltis were blasé about river crossings, the Sherpas simply hated them. So naturally Ang Tensing was angry. But one of the principal aims of their entire enterprise was to determine the position of the Aghil Pass.

Well, there it was and Michael was sick about it. They sat down for tea in silence. Finally, he asked Auden to explain in Hindustani. So John Auden made a little speech on why it had been entirely reasonable for Michael to imagine he would see some peak from this height and distance. After a minute of strained silence, Ang Tensing relented.

"*Ham jaenge.*" I'll go.

More than anything Michael hadn't wanted to carry any more weight and the subtense bar, made from nickel iron alloy, weighed fourteen pounds. When he realized that they were going to have to carry fifty pounds apiece for the Aghil survey, his heart sank. As it was, he arrived at camp behind the slowest coolie, having turned into a kind of insensible rock plant. But he wasn't a rock plant; he was a tender sapling. It was the old problem: they weren't workers; they weren't natives. Unlike Tilman, they weren't even soldiers. They were upper middle. Auden agreed.

Both he and Auden had also left behind their tape measures but rather than confess to this as well, they made do with a tent pole, a rope, and Spender's slide rule to establish a base.

Ang Tensing left without turning around to wave good-bye.

Aghil Pass to the Yarkand River,
  Chinese Turkestan, June 26, 1937

Heading down from the pass, Michael came across a makeshift shelter. There were lashings of yak shit, remains of abandoned dwellings, and a good source of water. Bedding down within the walls of a roofless hut, sheltered from the wind, gave him a sense of security. It was a relief to be out of the cramped confines that work among the high glaciers involved. He enjoyed being on his own with four Sherpas and a Balti, as he had been on the 1935 Everest reconnaissance. It spared him having to accommodate other people's idiosyncrasies. He didn't expect to see Shipton or Tilman for at least a week.

At times, though, the hoary phrase "His first thought was for the welfare of his men" haunted him. What if they ran out of food? What if his porters refused to share his tent when the rain turned to snow in the night? The Sherpas missed the lavish rations they'd had on Everest and they were already running dangerously low on salt. Michael had come upon a herd of wild sheep that afternoon but Tilman had Auden's rifle. And of all the vegetables, he would find one—chives—that couldn't be eaten in quantity. Finally, he knew damn all about where he was but was expected to be decisive about where to camp. Every day he found himself tied into knots over this. After Ang Tensing returned with the subtense bar, he'd tried to get him to weigh in.

"If we go up it will mean an easier climb tomorrow but a vile camp tonight. What shall we do?" Only to have Ang Tensing reply:

"Are we staying here or going on?"

He said quickly, "Going on."

There was another worry. Ang Tensing reported the Shaksgam was already rising. There would be an awful row if Shipton didn't show but a far greater crisis would ensue if they were forced to cross the river on their own. For these reasons it was a relief to have someone to talk to when his route happened to cross John Auden's a few days later.

When Auden first joined them in Srinagar, Shipton had teased him about his beard, impressed by his ability to flout Calcutta's pukka grooming code. Privately, Michael sniggered at his silly hat. Halfway through the march to Askole, he'd asked Auden if he'd ever met Christopher Isherwood.

"The last time I saw him was the night before my divorce proceedings went through," Auden had replied. There was then a long silence, giving Michael time to reflect that his reply had the very shape of a sentence by Somerset Maugham. Only a Maugham character would continue his story, not leave his listener hanging. He'd been annoyed. Still, right now he was hoping Auden would reassure him about the river crossing and the ration supply.

After a brief visit, the two men parted at the foot of a desolate gully-like valley, one that appeared to climb 400 meters every kilometer. At the head of this valley would be Michael's next station, giving him an entire afternoon to ruminate on his conversation with John Auden.

The essential quality of life on an expedition, Michael decided, was that it was stimulating, but in predictable ways. There was either something to eat or nothing at all. The temperature was either hot as the blazes or deathly cold. One's mood was either that of dreading a descent to some nasty river, an ascent to a fearsome height, or rejoicing in a cozy and tidy camp. Finally, the day either threatened you with bad weather or promised clear skies. There was never a moment of indifference.

In a similar vein, Auden either said too little or too much. When Michael told him what Ang Tensing had said about the rising Shaksgam, he expected to be reassured. Instead, it was if a dam had burst. Auden launched into his own anxious litany about the river. And on the subject of running short of rations, Auden told him he had left a Balti in charge of his tent for two days while he and Lhakpa reconnoitered the no-man's-land bordering the Upper Yarkand River and the Balti had eaten more than his share of rations. To this he added another concern. Lhakpa had seen two Yarkandi boys tending a flock of goats on the far side of the river. They were all now at risk of capture by Chinese border patrols.

Shipton and Tilman were not expected back from their high stations until July 3, Michael reflected. He should have told Auden that wits and a rope would get them across the Shaksgam and if someone drowned, well, it couldn't be helped, but why not wait before starting to grumble? And there was no use in pointing out the flaws in Shipton's running of an expedition. It was his show. Michael decided that Auden suffered from the neurotic's habit of fretting about things that couldn't be helped, conveniently forgetting that he had been fretting about the same things.

After settling these matters, not even the ever-multiplying lice in his shirt could keep him from sleeping.

Junction of Sarpo Laggo and Crevasse Glaciers,
   Greater Karakoram, July 19, 1937

George Mallory wasn't the only graduate of trench warfare to find solace in the high mountains. To walk roped to another man, along a high ridge, a precipice on one side, a snowy slope falling away on the other, felt both familiar and necessary to Bill Tilman. At high altitudes the deep sleep of exhaustion kept nightmares at bay. The endless rigors settled the soul. Peace might be found sitting on a mountaintop with a pipe looking out over an undulating cloud cover, or at a fireside slurping tea in the company of younger, more lighthearted, men.

Because of his successful ascent of Nanda Devi in 1936, that past March Tilman had been elected by a jury of his peers (Shipton among them) to lead the next attempt on Everest. On his return from the Karakoram he would be choosing his team. Tilman may have appeared misanthropic and crusty, but on Nandi Devi he'd had a strong rapport with the young Americans who accompanied him. Until the 1935 reconnaissance of Everest, he'd had that with Shipton. But he never found his feet that year. Plagued by altitude sickness and nameless fevers, he fell behind while Shipton shot ahead of him, disappearing into the mists. In the Aghil Range they had recovered their easy rhythm. Yet the day after recrossing the Shaksgam (which went smoothly after all the fretting) and starting up the Crevasse Glacier, their settled arrangement began to shift.

Of the glaciers that met at Sughet Jangal, the Crevasse was the largest. It ran like a sclerotic east–west artery across the Karakoram with major branches leading off north and south. The third part of the survey would bring them down the Crevasse to those glaciers lying between the Sarpo Laggo valley and the Shimshal Pass in the far west. This area alone was about 1,000 square miles. From Shimshal they would make their way back to Srinagar. On July 17 all the porters were mustered to help Shipton and Tilman shift their food and supplies from the Sughet Jangal depot to another some distance up the Crevasse.

Michael had a hellish time managing without his Sherpas. When his tent flooded with glacier melt he'd had to move to a more uncomfortable spot on higher ground. Then there was the damned business of getting a fire going. He'd had to use a bit of his precious plane table sheets to get it started. And doing his own cooking and washing up prevented him from adding the angles and fixed points they had all amassed to his sheets.

Tilman had no patience for Michael's carping about the sparse rations and the disgusting food, often breaking out in hysterical fits of laughter by way of a reply. These fits mystified Michael. As for survey work, Tilman regarded it much as "not too patient uncle might regard his nephews playing trains on the table on which he was shortly expecting his lunch." He preferred climbing without the nuisance of heavy survey equipment. So when Michael started in on not being able to put the finishing touches on his plane table sheets because his Sherpas were otherwise occupied, Tilman finally lost it.

"If everyone was carrying bloody heavy loads up," Tilman had raged, "we'd be doing double relays instead of treble." Tilman obviously expected Michael to help with the ferrying of supplies and was furious when he acted as though he was meant for more important tasks (Auden was suffering from fever). But once again Michael was baffled by what F6 was going on about. When Tilman protested at how the scientific nonsense was holding them up, did that mean he wanted to go home? When Shipton got to this incident in his expedition narrative, he mentioned only that extreme isolation could impose a considerable strain on a party. He later claimed it was the scientists who needed to be kept apart, but that was disingenuous.

Shipton was a man of great focus. His thoughts on the people who lived in the foothills revolved around how suitable they proved as porters, what food they had to offer, and how likely they were to importune him for baksheesh. While he admired and respected the Sherpas, he was doubtful they would ever achieve the technical competence of the best Alpine guides. The following year Tenzing Norgay would note that when a porter became dazed at Camp 4 on Everest's North Col, though Shipton was in charge of the camp, he had left him there. Tenzing did not think that was right. Sherpas had been known to keep the dying company, even if it meant certain death. Eventually Tilman, descending from a higher camp and with the assistance of other Sherpas, helped the man reach safety.

Finally, though Shipton respected scientific expertise more than Tilman did, it was an abstract respect. He didn't pretend to understand what Auden was doing with his rock hammer. Maps, however, he knew. The thrill of summit seeking with Tilman paled beside the opportunity to fill in a blank space marked "unexplored." While he might write vivid descriptions of landscapes and the feelings they evoked in him, only plane tables, subtense bars, and theodolites could deliver a map that would accurately convey the high concentration of dangerous peaks and glaciers of the Karakoram. And for that he needed Michael Spender.

More to the point, topographical maps of sensitive border regions, where the line between one country and another was imprecise, were of particular interest to those with a say in funding expeditions. The Sino-Burmese Frontier Commission had recently demarcated Burma's border with China. In his grant application, Shipton argued that the Shaksgam region had equal geopolitical importance; identifying the exact location of Aghil Pass was a critical security task. In a calculating aside, he mentioned that Soviet agents were said to have shown up in the capital of Chinese Turkestan. Rumors of Soviet agents always got attention from the ministry for border security, the Foreign and Political Department.

For his Royal Geographical Society audience, Shipton made a more sentimental appeal. With so much of the Himalaya untrammeled, he argued, exploration should take precedence over summit seeking. Shipton may have accepted the notion that the mountaineer's desire to climb ever higher peaks was being exploited to further imperial or jingoistic ends, but the enduring attraction of being the first man, the first nation to take a summit remained irresistible, even for him. He struggled to hit the right note but ended back on the expected one. Only if undertaken in "the right spirit" could tackling Everest "demonstrate our modern superiority!"

Bill Tilman wanted no part of Shipton's "modern superiority." The advantages of the Western way of life were far from obvious to him. On the 1935 Everest reconnaissance, he had viewed the dzongpen of Sar's wariness of Western ways as a testament to the native wisdom of the Tibetans. And what was the value of a precise border where before there had been a vague one? Did such specificity deter the invader or provide reason for a scrap? Why couldn't the exact location of passes, the intimate knowledge of mountains, and the seasonal ebb and flow of rivers be left to the memories of goatherds?

As a young subaltern fresh out of the Royal Military College at Sandhurst, Winston Churchill asked himself similar questions. On the one hand he saw no profit in the holding of garrisons on the Afghan border. It was a blunder to have made a stand there. Let the devil hill tribes take out their devilry on one another, he wrote. On the other hand, the strategic importance of high passes was undeniable. A Russian force descending from Chitral would have an easy way to Jalalabad. If they didn't make a stand there, a Russian agent would make it his business to get the hill tribes to make a stand against the British.

"Can you ever, having advanced against Asiatics, safely retire?" asked G. W. Steevens, Churchill's favorite Victorian journalist. What was there to show for these border wars? Only more wars, equally inconclusive, one after another. No sooner had they crowned one height than another rose up in front of them. And as Chitral was just one tiny point on a long, infinitely tangled frontier, "it was precisely thus that the frontier lures you on." The English might show the hill tribes how they could occupy their valleys by driving them into the winter snows to freeze to death. Or they might exterminate the lot outright. Then again that might draw Russia into the void. And if the Indian Army engaged the Russian on the frontier, there would be mutiny among the disaffected at their rear, in India.

It went round and round, this Great Game, all in all a good-natured amusement for gentlemen of leisure who found the settled life tedious. Predictably, for all the blood and treasure expended on the North-West Frontier, when the threat to Britain's hold on India finally arrived, it would not come in the form of Communist hordes spilling over 20,000-foot passes, led by some latter-day Alexander the Great. It would come from the air.

Focused on connecting one fixed point to the next, Michael had no idea what purpose his maps would serve. But they were now six weeks out of Askole and if they didn't reach some settlement in another six weeks, they would starve. The Wild phototheodolite was broken. Their boots were in an appalling state. F6's had lasted the longest. Where the Sherpas had "Om Mane Padme Hum," Michael had settled upon chants of "onandonandon" and "upandupandup." Fridtjof Nansen must have chanted the Danish equivalent while crossing Greenland by dogsled, he supposed.

"The further we go, the stronger the Nansen flavor, the only way to safety, ahead," Michael wrote in his journal. "There is no retreat."

Camp near Head of the Crevasse Glacier,
Greater Karakoram, August 11, 1937

A shortage of fuel decided it. A party of fifteen couldn't manage on a pint of paraffin a day. Given all that remained to be surveyed, Shipton decided that they should now split up; one pair to continue due west and the other lay to rest two longstanding geographical controversies concerning two regional legends.

A nineteenth-century explorer named Martin Conway had seen a large pool of smooth white ice out of which mountains rose like islands. He named it "Snow Lake." A few years later, Dr. and Mrs. Workman, two intrepid Americans, saw Snow Lake from a distance. Perhaps owing to the beauty of Conway's description the idea arose that Snow Lake was something like an ice cap. The Workmans went further, insisting that a nearby glacier, contrary to every other known glacier, had no outlet, no snout. Other explorers followed, including John Auden in 1933, but none was able to get close enough to investigate.

When Conway questioned the idea of a glacier without an outlet, Dr. Workman angrily told him he should go see for himself before casting aspersions. Grateful for something new to argue about, Tilman championed the Workmans' position, pleased to call into question scientific expertise and come to the defense of a lady. Auden backed him. Shipton and Spender backed Conway. Michael ridiculed the accuracy of the Workmans' observations, their atrocious prose, and their amateurish maps. In this way the terrible twins of Shipton and Tilman, of Auden and Spender had an awkward exchange of partners.

Since Tilman was restless to begin preparing for Everest and Auden needed to return to Calcutta in advance of his furlough, Shipton tasked them both with settling the controversy over Snow Lake and the Cornice Glacier before finding their separate ways back home. Shipton knew that John wanted to be chosen for the 1938 Everest expedition. And Tilman shared Auden's pawky sense of humor. It might have worked.

But no one thought to ask the Baltis. They refused to proceed in any but a southerly direction. This, combined with a broken Primus, left Tilman to solve these geographical riddles alone. Shipton allotted him two Sherpas and twenty-two days of food. Auden, with the four Baltis, was given sufficient food to last twelve. The two men parted at a pass they had discovered together. Had the Baltis not balked, had they had an extra Primus and a week or two alone together, would Tilman have asked Auden to join him on Everest? Perhaps.

Instead, John's last view of Tilman was upside down through the sights of the theodolite telescope from a survey station at 17,300 feet. Then he turned away from the panorama, away from Tilman and the dream of Everest, to head south. Descending to the Nobande Sobande Glacier he lost a day trying to find a way through a terrifying maze of towering ice pinnacles. His Baltis invoked Allah throughout the night.

Early the next morning he sent two of them to prospect a route. They returned jubilant and covered with mud. They raced down, bombarded by boulders released by melting ice. As they reached the snout of the Panmah, a mudflow carrying a 120-ton boulder swept past them. For the Baltis this was "one more proof that God exists and was favorably disposed." They flew like jailbirds.

Then came the march down valleys, uphill and downhill, through pine forests and over trout-filled streams. Tobacco and eggs were restored to them in Askole. Apricots were plentiful in Skoro La. At Skardu John received three months worth of mail, including Carritt's drunken Darjeeling letter pleading with him to join the Communist cause. Madrid was still holding on but the Japanese Army was now in Peking and Shanghai was on the verge of falling. Closer to home, a massive avalanche had buried seven Germans and nine porters on Nanga Parbat, nearly the entire expedition, in the middle of the night. Karl Wien was among those who had found a lasting repose. John read, too, that Gandhi had finally been granted an audience with Linlithgow. Despite Congress's assumption of power in the regional ministries, the ban on the Communist Party remained; only the viceroy could remedy that. So it was business as usual for Special Branch on Lord Sinha Road.

John Auden walked in long, fast strides. Milestones passed one after another. A countdown that began with weeks turned to days, then hours, and finally minutes. The last mile passed in a blur of anticipation of Lady Clutterbuck's food hamper. After the deprivations of glacier work, the exhaustion of carrying a heavy pack over hundreds of miles of inhospitable terrain, England was now his only fixed point.

Junction of Wesm-i-Dur and Snout of the Braldu Glacier,
*   Greater Karakoram, September 2, 1937*

Side by side in their sleeping bags, Shipton talked to Michael of his early climbs in the High Dauphiné, where he first fell in love with mountains. Michael spoke of the impact of Europe on his Englishness. They dreamed of boarding school and the boys and masters they once knew. Some nights, kept awake by Shipton's perpetual cough,

Michael worried about money, wondering whether he could still afford to keep a car.

Shipton and Tilman both shunned the "caviar and aspic" quest
for glory. Though Tilman preferred steerage to first class, the recent
death of his parents meant he would never have to work again owing
to dividends from West Indian sugar. Shipton carried a hundred-
pound note in his pocket; Michael never had more than forty shillings in his. He had turned over his Leverhulme Fellowship money to
Erica and posted articles to the *Spectator* from Skardu and Askole for
money. John Auden, having no Granny Schuster to call on in a pinch,
was even more hard up. The GSI wouldn't even buy him an ice ax. At
the end of the expedition he owed Shipton 250 rupees.

When Shipton pressed him to climb a serious peak, Michael quailed.
Wary of approaching clouds, he protested he might lose the lower
station if he risked going higher, though a higher station meant more
ground covered. He also asked himself if he really felt any closer to
the Unspeakable at 20,000 feet. Shipton and Tilman clearly did. But
he saw only a chaotic arrangement of peaks, ridge upon ridge of ice
and snow and rock, sometimes rising to a misshapen and loutish summit. Truth be told, Michael preferred sailing.

Which pass would lead them to the Braldu Glacier, the one Shipton
had stumbled on or the one Michael had? Shipton agreed to try
Michael's in hope that it might spark his interest in exploration. And
indeed, the limestone walls of his valley were filled with marine fossils. Michael saw enough whelks, periwinkles, mussels, and sea ur-
chins to be reminded of his beachcombing days on the Great Barrier
Reef expedition. But a few days in it dawned on them that their route
didn't meet up with the Braldu Glacier until very near its end and the
valley they'd just walked had a name: Wesm-i-Dur. "Whatever that
means," Michael wrote, content to be back among named places. The
detour meant an eight-day journey back up the Braldu to complete
the survey.

So much for any idea of himself as an explorer.

K2 was once again the world's most stupid mountain, good for only
one thing: a fixed point. But what meaning, he wondered, did the sacrifice and suffering they underwent for the sake of a map really serve?

In *A Passage to India*, which Michael had been rereading each night, E. M. Forster wrote that babas went to the mountains to submit to rigors that would free them from the curse of property. In Christianity asceticism was undertaken as self-punishment for one's sins. But Michael was inclined to subscribe to the Tibetan belief that their suffering had no meaning at all. The high mountains were really all about one thing: death. After three months in their grip, the farther he got from them, the happier and more alive he felt.

Adding the last stations to the plane table sheets, Michael joined Shipton in a celebratory meal of two extra large grouse. The next morning they set off down the glacier with the sight of the grass and trees of the Shimshal Valley beckoning them in the distance. Soon they came upon the Braldu River, divided into numerous fast-flowing channels. The farther down they walked, the more its channels proliferated. Eventually, the valley on the other side became too enticing. They decided to try and cross.

On the way over, however, they had a furious argument.

What real difference had the various rulers of India made to the lives of the Baltis? Michael had asked. The Moghuls might have imposed a new religion, the English higher taxes, but what did those amount to in the elementary facts of their existence? Beyond a sound house and sufficient food to eat, Baltis required little. Did they even know who ruled them? Kashmiris filled the role of district officers. The only evidence of English rule he could find was the king's face on the postage stamp and the baksheesh they had distributed on Coronation Day. "Our big Sahib is being given a golden topee," Auden had explained in Hindustani. But the Baltis simply thought Shipton was getting a new hat. If the Baltis didn't care about all that nonsense, why should anyone? They were fooling themselves with this pompous Raj business.

It was at a Copenhagen coffeehouse crowded with Danish explorers in deep conversation that Michael had begun to question the notion of empire. These men shared one idée fixe: that Greenland should "take its place in the modern world." How might the Eskimo be protected from exploitation and reach the point of doing without the protection of the Danish government? Greenland was a source of rare minerals, but all mining profits were turned over to the literate West Greenland men of mixed Danish and Eskimo blood who administered the country. Michael had been struck by the idea of administering a country entirely for the benefit of the people who lived there. He doubted the same would ever be said of the British Empire.

The British Empire, Shipton countered, was predicated on the be-lief in the tremendous power of personal example. It was the responsi-bility of explorers and mountaineers, of superior men like themselves, to establish friendships in foreign lands and be done with talk of poli-tics and war. "Even a philosophy of Empire could be worked out on the basis of personal relationships," Shipton insisted.

To set oneself up as a paragon of Western civilization or the em-bodiment of a heroic ideal, Michael countered, was a romantic delu-sion. Once a person decided what was worth doing—whether that was growing potatoes or mapping the Crevasse Glacier—he should just do it. If Shipton thought climbing Everest worthwhile, he was welcome to it, but it didn't mean anything more than that. It was a mountain, not a metaphor.

Shipton felt Michael was apt to argue for the delight of it, espous-ing views he didn't necessarily hold very firmly. But before he could respond Michael fell with a splash into the Braldu. He lay there for a moment like a beetle upended on his back, arms and legs waving help-lessly while the waters washed over him as if in a tremendous hurry to join the Upper Shaksgam fourteen miles downstream. Michael finally emerged on the other side of the river, fully soaked and freezing cold once again.

Three hundred more miles to Srinagar.

38 Upper Park Road, Belsize Park,
    London, July 1937

Constance Rosalie Auden had been in the audience at the tiny but packed Mercury Theatre in Notting Hill for the debut of Wystan and Christopher's play, *The Ascent of F6*. Wystan was still in Spain and she had been beside herself with a mother's worry. Christopher Isherwood's mother was there too, sitting behind E. M. Forster and his friends.

When the lights went up Kathleen Bradshaw-Isherwood had seen that the play's dramatic climax had upset Mrs. Auden. The demon haunting the summit of F6, it developed, was the hero's mother. It was the Mother who had sent her son to his premature death.

"Poor Mrs. Auden," she thought.

William Butler Yeats thought the play simply brilliant. His one complaint touched on the Mother demon's final appearance on the summit. The play wasn't about the making of a fascist megalomaniac, or an Oedipal struggle. The play was about India. Auden and Isherwood had missed a great opportunity to skewer the British Empire, he wrote the director. The white garments should fall away to show the demon in profile as the face of the Mother Country, a snow-white Britannia on an imperial rocking chair.

"That I think would be good theatre."

Wystan hadn't needed to stay long in Spain to see that the Republican cause was not the struggle he took it for. In July 1937 he was back at 38 Upper Park Road when Nancy rang from Cornwall, looking to berate Bill for not answering her letters.

Wystan promised to pass along her "connubial requests." He had also mentioned an erotic dream in which she figured.

"Up the Old Flag," he had said.

"That was cheering," Nancy wrote Louis MacNeice, still heartbroken in the Hebrides.

CHAPTER 12

Taking a Hat off a Mouse

Hotel St. Peter, Zurich, Switzerland,
March 27, 1938

Driving to Zurich from London with Erica, Michael Spender systematically itemized the portents of war. Factories and mines in the Saar district were running three shifts a day. When he asked at a shop for cream he was told no one used cream any longer. Animals were being butchered to save grain, pastures put to plow. The newspapers were so filled with rabid Jew baiting and saber rattling, it was hard to find an intelligible voice. A headline "Have We Still Any Private Life?" castigated those who "missed sitting in cafés and listening to nigger bands." A good German scorned such Jewish entertainments. Finally, the road to Saarbrucken led down one Adolf Hitler Strasse after another, each town filled with youths in cheap, ill-fitting uniforms. In the wan faces of these young Germans, in their quickness to violence, Michael saw unsettling signs.

Michael knew what Stephen thought was needed. Six days after Hitler's Anschluss of Austria, the Group Theatre premiered his brother's play *Trial of a Judge* to an audience of high-strung leftists. The play concerned a judge presiding over a trial of Communist conspirators. After first siding with the Fascists the judge recants and becomes a Communist, thereby joining the conspirators on the firing line. In the wake of the Anschluss everyone in the audience was presented with the same stark choice. Stephen had made his.

But how did becoming a Communist alter anything? Michael wondered. He ascribed the rise of the Nazis to the failure of England and France to grasp Germany's desperation and imagined Hitler might welcome a friendly alliance with Britain. At the Alsace border, every seam of Erica's clothing was minutely fingered for the crackle of hidden papers. It was a sensitive border region, Michael supposed. The mobilization of mines and factories was essential to Germany's survival, not, as he once thought, the reason for its distress. It was the closeness of French guns that posed the real threat. He admired the punctuality of German trains. Efficiency always impressed Michael.

Still, he was relieved to reach Zurich. The annual spring festival was under way and the city streets were festooned with bunting and alive with parades. Shops were fully stocked. On Sunday night men dressed as clowns carried the Boog, representing Old Man Winter, through a jeering crowd. At sunset he was impaled above his funeral pyre and set alight. But even here, at every banquet table in every guildhall, the talk was of the Anschluss. Fearing they'd be next, the Swiss were anxious to distance themselves. When Churchill pointed out that with Austria gone, the Czechs were isolated, his reception was similar to Old Man Winter's. No one wanted to hear it. Though the 1938 expedition was well under way, when Michael and Erica met up with John Auden, in Zurich to confer with an eminent Swiss geologist of the Alps, the subject of Tilman and Shipton's progress up Everest was quickly dispensed with. Instead, the question that had dogged them since childhood was now on the table. What would they do if there was a war?

As a member of the Calcutta Flying Club, John hoped to join the Royal Air Force as a pilot. Though Michael was leery of flying, he also wanted to join the RAF. The Ordnance Survey had recently completed a three-year triangulation of the British Isles but had contracted the mapmaking to civilian air survey concerns. Michael had argued in the *Spectator* that private firms were incapable, that the Air Ministry should take charge. Armed with a stereoplotter and a fleet of specially equipped planes, he and the RAF could do for Britain what he had once done for Switzerland.

Erica was far more interested in hearing about John Auden's search for a wife than listening to Michael go on about the competing qualities of the German and Swiss stereoplotters. She had had enough of being a mapmaker's wife. After the Karakoram, Michael had stayed on in India for another six months to work on the Shaksgam map. Now, while he worked on his map of the Everest region at the Wild factory, she planned to take the baby and visit her friends in Germany. She no longer understood Michael. They had lost whatever connection they once had.

That past Christmas in Brussels, John had once more proposed to a woman Wystan had found for him. He had been relieved when she refused him. In January he traveled to London to attend Shipton's RGS lecture on the Karakoram expedition and for a meeting at the Geological Survey and Museum. Wystan's old bed on Upper Park Road was offered and gratefully accepted, though he'd relinquished it when Wystan passed through London en route to China; he and Christopher were to write a book about its war with Japan.

John's recent paper for the *Records of the Geological Survey of India*, "The Structure of the Himalaya in Garhwal," was a lithological and stratigraphic analysis of a two-hundred-kilometer-wide segment, from the Gangetic Plain in the south up into the Main Himalayan Range. The culmination of eight years of fieldwork, it was hedged with enough conditional clauses to render it well-nigh impenetrable. The paper aroused little interest. The director of the Geological Survey and Museum told him he was welcome to bring it along but he was more interested in hearing his views on Askell's excellent work on Dorset.

Nancy Coldstream, too, would have been hard pressed to find the Garhwal on a map, but she had been keen to meet Wystan's brother. Before leaving London John had taken her out for dinner. During a long candlelit meal he described his work while she lost herself in the dark blue of his eyes. There was something helpless and innocent in there, she decided, as if a veil hid the man within. He reminded her of Errol, her former fiancé.

Nancy had finally read an unexpurgated copy of *Lady Chatterley's Lover* to see what the fuss was about. It had taken her two days and left her in raptures. Perhaps the gamekeeper was a prig. But she had been deeply roused by his encounters with Lady Chatterley. She was now resolved to become the D. H. Lawrence heroine Wystan once saw in her. Interrupting John's description of his summer plans for the Alps, Nancy leaned over the table and arched one shapely black brow.

"Any other man would have kissed me by now," she said.

He was instantly out of his chair and lunging across the table.

The idea had been to kiss her but instead he knocked her flat. Picking herself up, she was gratified by how suddenly John Auden's uninviting reserve had been overtaken by enthusiasm. An easy conquest. Her affair with Louis had begun with a similar pounce, but that had been uninvited. She had stormed out of his flat in a rage at his presumption.

That was before Lady Chatterley.

In Zurich John Auden felt like a man arisen, freed of his crypt and blinking in the sunshine. He was bewitched: women like Nancy weren't to be found in Calcutta. She said whatever was on her mind and assumed he knew everyone she did. No one had ever called him "Oh Johnnie my sweet my love" or "my bull calf" before. He had to wonder: would *she* marry him? He scarcely registered the presence of Louis MacNeice in her life, though Louis was a frequent visitor and came up often enough in her conversation. As did Bill and the state of her marriage. And someone named Errol.

The memories of 38 Upper Park Road followed him everywhere: the taste of sherry, the taxi home, the key under the mat. Wherever he went he saw her bedroom door closing, blinds being drawn against the dark, the electric stove ticking over and glowing. He recalled the texture of her hair under his hands, her smile willing him on and hungrily taking him in. He now felt capable of anything, as if magnetized to a new pole. She was all he had longed for during those cold dak bungalow nights. A fixed point.

It was perhaps this vision that blinded him to the little warnings embedded in the missives that followed him to Zurich. While Nancy overflowed with affectionate thoughts—"I do feel your going so poignantly" and "Darling if I can be of any use to you, you know I am at your disposal"—there were also provisos: "as long as it doesn't hurt Louis or interfere with Bill." She went so far as to admit she had a tendency to get carried away with feverish declarations. But John registered only her excitement at the prospect of seeing him again.

After being bombarded with letters from Zurich, Nancy invited John to visit her in Cornwall. In Bude he carried Miranda up and down the cliffs and showed Juliet the fossilized wave patterns on the cliff face. Nancy had been gratified. Louis regarded her daughters with a baffled stare whenever they appeared, she told him. So it was with a light heart that John returned to Zurich to join the foremost authority on nappe structures of the Western Alps on a brief expedition. A letter from Nancy awaited him on his return.

His heart sank on reading it. Nancy wrote that it was simply the case that Bill had more of the really important qualities, "with a few known exceptions," than he did. And however shaky their marriage, she wasn't ready to leave it. She regretted her waspishness during his Bude visit but admitted she would most likely behave exactly the same way had she the weekend to do over again. "The thing to be aimed at was independence," she had advised him. He shouldn't think marriage was the answer; marriage made no difference one way or the other. Only by thinking and acting independently was happiness possible.

While she had once loved him, it appeared, she no longer did.

He supposed it wasn't entirely unexpected. Yet, reading her letter carefully, John noted that while Nancy drew a sharp distinction between her feelings before and her feelings now, she did still claim to love him quite a lot. He couldn't help but wonder if their connection had, after all, suffered any revision. Perhaps this was what true love entailed, an inviting smile followed by a plate of soup in one's face. His brief experience of freedom, of absolute mastery in the art of making a woman like Nancy happy, now gave way to something more compelling: the prospect of torment.

He planned another trip to London, writing Nancy that on May 28 he would fly from Zurich to Croydon, arriving at Victoria terminus at 1:35 p.m. If it suited her, might he stay Saturday, Sunday, and Monday, returning to Zurich on Tuesday, May 31?

By the time Nancy received his letter her memory of the Bude weekend had faded. Against her better judgment she became quite excited at the prospect of seeing him again.

"So my puss I expect I shall be very surly next weekend but just now I am very warm."

Café Royal, 68 Regent Street,
London, July 1, 1938

Though his May visit was no more a success than the weekend in Bude, John was back at the end of June for another try. He'd been invited to the annual Himalayan Club Dinner at the Café Royal on July 1 and asked Nancy to accompany him (eight shillings, six pence per head, excluding drinks). She didn't say no. The Café Royal was the epicenter of fashionable London. Augustus John, Noël Coward, and Winston Churchill were among those frequently seen at this vast, mirrored, and gilded establishment. Brigadier General, the Hon. C. G. Bruce, C.B. M.V.O., leader of the legendary 1922 and 1924 Everest expeditions, was presiding.

All John Auden wanted was in the room that evening. The Himalayan Club Dinner would be attended by men of distinction and renown. In such company Nancy couldn't help but see him as a man among men. Members of the Everest Committee and the higher-ups of the RGS would not fail to note Nancy, dressed to the nines. Maybe that would open their eyes to him, John Auden, explorer and scientist, author of an excellent paper on the structure of the Garhwal Himalaya. Somehow it would all come together that evening at the Café Royal; his mountain, this woman, and the man he believed he might yet become.

Somewhere in the crowded room was Eric Shipton, just returned from Everest. The Tilman-led 1938 expedition, like the three previous, had been a bust and once again an early monsoon was said to be the culprit. There was not yet talk of another but Shipton was looking to speak with John about returning to the Karakoram. Shipton wanted to survey the Turkestan border west of the Aghil Pass, a sixteen-month undertaking. Michael Spender had already signed on. Spender was also milling about.

While the polar explorers and Everesters were still standing, whiskies and pipes in hand, John saw Bill Wager or Eric Shipton or Bill Tilman or some other worthy with whom he could claim acquaintance across the room. Whoever it was, John was intent on introducing him to Nancy. But before they could reach him, Nancy's eyes lit on another. Did John know *him*? So veering away from his original quarry, John introduced Nancy to Michael Spender instead.

The first thing she noticed was that his eyes were the color of cornflowers.

On his return to Zurich several days later John had a letter from Erica Spender. There wasn't the slightest reason for her to write him, she admitted. Still, she couldn't bear knowing how unhappy and lonely he was. This was something they had in common. She mentioned, too, that Michael had gone off sailing on the Scottish coast, but he would always be welcome to stay with her in London, or to write whenever he liked.

But John already knew that Michael was in Scotland. At Nancy's suggestion, they had dropped him off at Stansted. John's own departure had been disastrous. Nancy had declared the final curtain had dropped on their affair. Henceforth it would be entirely spiritual between them. Her letters, which had once arrived regularly, stopped. On the telephone she sounded distracted. Louis was with her, helping with the children, she couldn't talk. His need to see her grew desperate. Knowing now that her moods were changeable, and hoping she might reconsider, John booked another flight.

Louis MacNeice might have warned him.

John found her consumed with anxiety over an ailing Juliet. When she embarked upon a new round of confidences, he pressed her to give him more of that love she had once given so freely. Before he knew it he had lost his temper and behaved in what Nancy called a violently selfish manner. Didn't he see how upset she was over Juliet? But no, John thought only of himself and gave no thought to her happiness.

He drafted a letter of apology on his return to Zurich. Of course he had no right to be possessive. And perhaps he *ought* to have felt happy that she had found a valuable new correspondent in Cornflower but it was difficult to sustain that degree of objectivity. How could he rejoice in her happiness unless he was the one causing it? And then to hear that while she might be feeling only spiritual toward him and yet not necessarily so with Cornflower—he couldn't bring himself to write Michael's name—filled him with bitterness.

In the meantime, he asked if he might once more take up her guest bed on a trip to London. She wouldn't have to change the sheets. Wystan's sweaty ones would do. Wystan had since returned from China. John would be following him to Brussels from London. India was so very near now, and he needed to see her one last time before he left.

So yes, Louis might have warned him.

38 Upper Park Road, Belsize Park,
*   London, Summer 1938*

Throughout the spring and summer of 1938 Louis MacNeice had met Nancy's demand for letters, dishing out generous portions of London gossip he knew would please her while she was away in Cornwall. Had Nancy heard Augustus John had resigned from the Royal Academy? It was all over the *Evening Standard*. At the flat Rosina the nanny had washed the nursery walls; he was arranging the bookshelves. "And tomorrow, dearest, I shall do your drawers," Louis added, naughtily. In the coming week there would be tea with Stephen to hear more of his muddled views on painting. "Speaking quite frigidly and leaving all sex out of it," he told her that Stephen's conversation suffered by comparison with hers and he awaited their next reunion with intense anticipation. In the meantime, he sent her a poem, asking that she keep it to herself.

She didn't. She sent a copy to John Auden.

Seeing his rival approaching the doors of Lyons Corner House while he was having breakfast with Nancy, Louis had abandoned a half-finished plate of eggs and bacon and fled. Fantasies of violence and torture invaded his dreams. When he wasn't having nightmares he was sleepless, spending half the night writing Nancy letters only to burn them in the morning. The mere appearance of her handwriting on envelopes awakened all his hopes and sent common sense flying. He knew how frantically a heart might beat waiting for a call. Hour upon hour he had listened with focused excitement for her taxi to pull up below his window, the impatient frenzy that awaited the step of her feet at the door. Dashed expectations of an assignation drove him to the point of madness.

There were times when he hated her, times when he was desperate to expunge every trace of her from his life. He told himself she was feckless, superficial, given to gossip and overstatement; she could be morose, intractable, and unbelievably nasty. He hated rows and Nancy's temper was frightening. She never became violent, but she seemed to be daring him to. If he took what she said seriously, she would say she was pulling his leg. But if he failed to take her seriously, she might throw a cup of tea in his face. It was a neat little trap and Louis was not the first to fall into it. Even Wystan had found himself ducking a teacup and making the penitential return, flowers in hand.

But then there was her eagerness, her curiosity and ready sexual responsiveness, her deep distrust of those abstract notions that had tied them all up in knots these past ten years. Louis was haunted by a vision of her sleeping, like the beauty in the grove of thorns, inaccessible and lost. Yet on those nights when she finally arrived in his arms, a voice in his head accompanied the rhythmic knock of the bedstead against the wall:

Is this love? When will it end? When will it begin?

Such questions echoed in Westminster clubs, at 10 Downing Street, and all over London that summer.

Is this peace? When will it end? When will it begin? When Louis could take it no longer, he left London for Dublin.

So Louis might have warned John Auden, who calmly finished the plate of eggs and bacon Louis had abandoned, as he repeatedly warned himself. Louis would have told him to think of his pride and "in the name of reason, to cut his losses." He would have schooled him, as he schooled himself, in how doubt, looking for a loophole, would compel him, like Chamberlain's feverish pursuit of Hitler, "to gamble on another rendezvous."

But John Auden was compelled to gamble that August and it wasn't the last time he would. A week before his departure for India, John flew from Brussels and took Nancy, in town briefly from Cornwall, to lunch. He wanted to end his stay on a peaceful and composed note, even as the world itself appeared headed elsewhere. Then she borrowed a pound note off him and was gone.

When Eric Shipton rang 38 Upper Park Road in late September, hoping to speak with John about returning to the Karakoram in 1939 for his survey, he was only briefly flummoxed when he reached Michael Spender instead.

Victoria Station, London,
Wednesday, September 28, 1938, 2:00 p.m.

"I am so glad I'm here," Stephen Spender had said, standing by the stove on the opening day of the 1938 fall term at the Euston Road School of Drawing and Painting. "It is such a relief to have finally decided to give up writing, even if I start painting so late." Stephen wasn't much of a painter, but the Boys had needed his fees.

"Oh, are you giving up writing?" the painter standing next to him had replied. "How strange, I have decided to write and to give up painting."

A plumb line and a twelve-inch ruler were the principal teaching tools of the school, which had been founded by Bill Coldstream and a few of the Boys from the Slade. The ruler, held at arm's length, verified distance; the plumb line was dropped in front of the model to establish how her body parts aligned, as if she were a conquered territory needing a new map. Like Michael Spender's matrix of triangles, it was an empirical approach to the feat of representation, which enabled them all to firmly turn their backs on abstract art and political ideology. Stephen regarded the plumb line with alarm; his first brushstroke on the canvas was invariably his signature.

Three weeks into fall term, Stephen invited Bill Coldstream to the family Sunday tea with Granny. Perhaps Stephen thought Granny might benefit from Bill's views on the Czech crisis. Bill had only just met Michael. When Erica found out Michael was having an affair with Nancy, Michael had moved to Upper Park Road to hide out. He arrived with his luggage just as John Auden departed for Brussels. There, at Wystan's implacable insistence, John tore up the enraged telegram he had prepared to send Nancy. He phoned her in Cornwall instead, accusing her of deliberately timing his departure with Cornflower's arrival. It was a bitter ending to all his hopes. He was cursed.

That was where things stood with everyone when tea was poured.

The argument that ensued, however, was not about Michael's affair with Bill's wife but about Chamberlain, due to return that day from Germany. The PM had forwarded Hitler's demand for the Sudetenland to the Czech cabinet. They had until two o'clock Wednesday afternoon to surrender it. The Czech cabinet promptly resigned, throwing the ball back in Chamberlain's court. Protesters were just then marching on Whitehall, crowding Trafalgar Square and shouting, "Stand by the Czechs! Concessions Mean War! Chamberlain Must Go!"

If further concessions to Hitler meant war, what did standing by the Czechs mean? The air was filled with an unfocused fear that made it difficult for anyone to think clearly. Bill appeared to be the exception. Had Chamberlain suddenly become as rabidly pro-Nazi as Lady Astor? Of course not, he assured everyone. Chamberlain wasn't stupid or ill informed, just desperate for peace. As they all were, really. Bill was pulling every string possible to avoid being called up.

Stephen didn't want war either but neither did he agree with Granny that peace was worth any price. And what price was he, personally, willing to pay? He wasn't entirely sure. Christine lit into her brother, defending both Granny and Chamberlain. Though Michael sat there stone-faced, saying nothing, Stephen blamed him for setting Granny against him. Tea ended with Christine in tears.

Nancy, stewing in Cornwall, resisted being lumped together with those who had left the city as the crisis over the Sudetenland intensified. She was desperate to get back to London. She supposed Wystan had an earful from John about her wickedness and that her stock must have sunk quite low. Wystan was the one who told her neighbor of her affair with Michael. The busybody then promptly went and told Erica. Despite Wystan's betrayal, she still expected him at Upper Park Road that coming Wednesday. Nancy instructed Michael to give Wystan a kiss for her and to make sure there was cream and butter in the flat for his breakfast.

In Cornwall everyone was listening to the wireless five times a day. Nancy's mother was fretting incessantly that the girls' pregnant

nanny would give birth at any moment. An ultimatum was broadcast at every meal: Rosina must return to London by the end of the
week, not a day later. Nancy was desperate. If Rosina left, she would
be trapped for the duration with evacuated, bridge-playing relations. Then, on the morning of Hitler's 2:00 p.m. deadline, Wednesday,
September 28, an ominous telegram arrived at the breakfast table
in Bude: SUGGEST MOMENT UNSUITABLE TO SEND ROSINA TO
LONDON STOP MICHAEL.

For the past month Christopher Isherwood had been feeling like a
man in debt up to his ears, begging his creditors for more time, in the
full knowledge that it was hopeless. He'd asked the war correspondent
Peter Fleming if the crisis over Czechoslovakia meant certain war. It
was like taking a hat off a mouse, Fleming said; it may run in any
direction. As the two o'clock deadline approached, Christopher arrived
at Victoria to meet Wystan's train and found it teeming with weeping women. He bought some gum and a newspaper just as Big Ben
tolled twice. There were now new editions every twenty minutes; the
newsboys peeled them off like they were shucking corn. After stowing
Wystan's luggage in a taxi, they saw that new placards had been posted:
DRAMATIC PEACE MOVE. Christopher bought another paper.

At the end of a long speech in the House of Commons, Chamberlain
announced he was returning once more to Germany. Trunk calls overwhelmed the telephone exchanges. Letters from Cornwall crossed in
the post with ones from Belsize Park. Wystan was dropped off at Upper
Park Road, sunburned and wearing a very loud suit. Michael Spender
let him in without a kiss. In Brussels, John finished packing, preparing
to leave for India the next day. In Cornwall, Nancy wrote him a good-
bye letter.

She hoped he would find another upon whom to fix his "as always,"
reminding him of what Wystan had said about women being natural
destroyers. Several of the war jobs going were paying ones; war would
provide her the freedom and independence she had long sought. Of
course her mother said her only *job* was to look after her children,
but if she had to answer one more question about how Juliet liked her
rice pudding, she would kill herself. She regretted they couldn't have
spoken before he left, but the lines were hopelessly tied up.

Nancy had managed to get a call through to Dublin. Louis MacNeice's letters had studiously avoided the crisis. When she pressed him he purred as calmly as a cat that there wouldn't be a war. War would come when least expected and since everyone was expecting it, they would all be proved wrong. In the silences that hung between them on the telephone, the sound of his slow, even breathing calmed her.

Even before Chamberlain returned from Munich, Wystan had made plans to leave London. He was sick of listening to the wireless, sick of a press that "turned forests into lies." For all the English paeans to liberty and justice, Hitler had called England's bluff, exposing the venality Wystan had witnessed during his tour of the British Empire's eastern strongholds. En route to Hong Kong, he'd asked a rubber planter based in Malaya whether England would ever leave India. Not while there is either a virgin or a rupee left, the man had replied smugly.

Wystan had told John he would welcome war when it came. He planned to enlist, not as a patriot—he hoped the empire would be shattered in the coming conflict—but because war would bring an end to his years of lonely isolation. After leaving London he completed a sonnet sequence that would close *Journey to a War*, his and Christopher's book about what they had witnessed of Japan's war on China. To Wystan's mind the war had already begun and there would be no refuge. London would be as vulnerable as Nanking.

A Calcutta Hospital,
  Saturday Evening, October 1, 1938

Bishop Foss Wescott was a kind man, Reverend Scott thought as he lay in his hospital bed listening to him talk. The bishop had never paid much mind to what his young curate was doing in his off hours. As long as he showed up on time for Sunday services and prepared a decent homily the bishop was happy. And when a watcher from Special Branch had reported to him that he had seen Reverend Scott's red sports car on Karaya Road the bishop had gently suggested that, if he must visit these establishments, it would be more discreet to take a taxi. Scott sometimes met underground contacts on Karaya Road. He would have laughed at the memory, if he didn't hurt so much.

His sports car: well that was done for. He had taken a Moth out for a brief flight, hoping to clear his head of the Munich farce. Hitler and Mussolini in ear-to-ear grins were all over the papers, photographs of Chamberlain standing in an open car, acknowledging the *Heil*s of the Munich crowds, and again at Heston airfield, bowler hats hailing him as if he were Caesar. The long line of expensive cars said it all. Before the day was out Hitler's troops had reached Sudetenland.

Scott had ascended above the clouds of the receding monsoon as the sun set. He was still feeling aloft when he started back to the city. His last thought before his car collided with a bus was that it was Saturday night and he had yet to write his Sunday sermon. He broke the steering wheel with his chest.

Wasn't it better for a few agitators to suffer than see all of India laid waste? The archbishop of Bombay's question still haunted him. But what of those Bengali villages, where British soldiers, maddened by their support for the nationalists, beat children, raped women, and burned their homes to the ground? British rule had now substituted vengeance for justice. And if England with its empire had not the will to stop the evil of Nazism, then what, truly, did it have to offer India? Bishop Wescott was still talking at his bedside, counseling Scott not to lose heart, telling him there remained a great deal of work to be done. He considered confessing everything to the old man.

Instead, he went to Kasauli to convalesce. There he and Carritt wrote a pamphlet describing the short and brutal lives of landless peasants in Bengal. It was their last hurrah.

Hatibagan, 139 Cornwallis Street, Calcutta,
    December 24, 1938

At the Parichay adda Sudhin Datta dismissed female writers in one word: "petty." George Eliot was insufferable. He was indifferent to Emily Brontë. Jane Austen was the least offensive, but her prose had the air of cut flowers. A member of Calcutta's Progressive Writers' Association listened with his head tilted to one side. The secret diarist noted that with his oiled black hair brushed straight back over his head, the man looked very much like a curious, long-necked bird.

When Sudhin finished pillorying nineteenth-century lady novelists, the birdlike man asked him about Virginia Woolf.

"You can get her measure only if you compare her to a male writer of her education and range, say Aldous Huxley."

Sudhin was not without his blind spots.

In keeping with the partisan tone that had invaded the adda of late, one of the young Communists challenged Nehru's private secretary, a guest that evening, to name even one progressive English writer.

Surely, the man offered, *A Passage to India* expressed an anti-imperialist mind-set?

Didn't *The Ascent of F6* qualify? Sudhin asked. Auden and Isherwood's play had been recently staged at Calcutta University.

Yet for the Communists, a recent Left Book Club anthology told the real story. *Poems of Freedom* did not include a single poem addressed to the question of *India's* freedom, its Bengali reviewer had noted. In the introduction, W. H. Auden had backed away from the stance that English poets had any role to play in politics, even in instances of injustice carried out in the name of British rule. For all the left's hand-wringing over Spain, Germany's treatment of Jews, or the cutthroat greed of capital, as far as the brutality of British rule in India went, there was now a clear conspiracy among English writers to maintain a deadly silence. They dithered over whether to become Communists or socialists as if it were a choice between dinner jackets. They financed excursions to Spain with Indian dividends.

Mulk Raj Anand, visiting Calcutta from London that December, agreed. Anand was a small, handsome, and fast-talking novelist partial to scarlet shirts. On the outer rings of Bloomsbury, he was a friend of Louis MacNeice and had met George Orwell in Spain. Anand had done his best to argue the cause of India's freedom before the British public. Only MI6 showed any real interest. And Special Branch returned the favor when Anand had arrived in Calcutta. On a previous visit to the adda, Anand had clashed with Shahid Suhrawardy over his sympathy for the downtrodden, as evident in his banned book, *Coolie*.

Anand had also crossed paths with Stephen Spender in Spain. He found him insufferable and patronizing. Stephen had stated plainly that he didn't believe India was ready for independence. Though Stephen seemed to grasp imperialism's fascist nature, he was more concerned with what that meant for artistic freedom in England, his own particularly, than with India's political aspirations.

Stephen's views didn't surprise Orwell, Anand told his Calcutta friends. Orwell was just beginning to see that the left's call to dismantle England's economic order was complete humbug. England was not some rustic village of their school holidays, but a world power dependent upon the unlimited cheap labor the empire afforded them. Invariably overlooked in the left's concern for the working class, he pointed out, was the fact that Indians made up the greater portion of the British proletariat. They labored in the tens of thousands on East African railways, Malayan rubber plantations, Burmese teak forests, and Ranigunj coal mines. Yet while Orwell had none of Stephen's middle-class haughtiness, Anand said, on hearing Stephen's views on India, he had simply chided him for being silly.

Sudhin might then have gone to his bookshelves to pull out *I Spy with My Little Eye*:

> *Mill was a clerk in India House;*
> *Carlyle approved of Governor Eyre;*
> *A hundred poets roared and cawed*
> *Behind the imperial rocking-chair.*

– CHAPTER 13 –

The Truth about Love

38 Upper Park Road, Belsize Park, London,
January 17, 1939

With the immediate threat of war receding, Wystan was leaving the guest bed at Upper Park Road once more. The previous January it had been for China; the January before that, Spain; this time it was for New York. When Bill had asked Wystan what he would do in New York, he got a reasonable reply. He promised Nancy he would be back if war broke out but until then he planned to make the most of what freedom remained to him. Indeed, the time had come for everyone to grab a brass ring. Some loyalties, those arising from patriotism or political partisanship, were already spoken for, but hearts were still up for grabs. It was as if no one could bear to be found in the same bed when the war music started up again and the world began to spin ever faster.

As everyone knew it would.

At the farewell party at Benjamin Britten's new flat, Stephen Spender was standoffish, as if he didn't want to be compromised by a room full of pansies. Wystan had encouraged Britten to be more playful in his compositions, assuring him it was perfectly all right to be vulgar or silly. Stephen couldn't stomach that; he was a highbrow. He told Benjamin that his music was too homosexual. Periodically Stephen would sidle up to Nancy and hold her hand, as if he needed to be reassured while in hostile territory.

Stephen was too soft, red faced, and puffy, Nancy thought. Michael was more of a real man. Nancy's plan for a cozy winter had taken form the moment the Munich Agreement was signed. Michael would write a book while she painted. Yet on the eve of her return to London Michael had told her he wasn't in a fit state to run off with her and had applied for a job in the west of England. A poisonous letter followed. Michael was a pig. Why not Manchester or Perth? Did he imagine he could be home for dinner by seven? He didn't rise to the bait. Wystan had heard them go at it over the telephone.

"Why are you behaving like that? You know, don't you, that you are only cutting your own throat?" Nancy was no match for Michael, Wystan wrote a disconsolate John in Calcutta. Michael could take the indifferent line far better than she could.

Hedli Anderson, a late arrival at the party, upstaged all the little dramas by heading straight for the piano to belt out Cole Porter's "You're the Top." Classically trained, exiled from the cabarets of Berlin, Hedli had been cast in several plays at the Group Theatre, including *The Ascent of F6*. To Nancy's chagrin, Hedli would marry Louis before the war ended. But that night she was intent on giving Wystan a memorable send-off. After the Porter tune, she launched into a new song by Wystan called "O Tell Me the Truth about Love."

It was to be their last night together at Upper Park Road; their landlord hadn't renewed the lease. While Wystan drew a bath, Bill made him a cup of Ovaltine and Nancy went to bed. They talked for a bit before Bill tottered off. Snug in their separate beds, they were soon fast asleep, dreaming separate dreams.

> *Will it come like a change in the weather?*
> *Will its greeting be courteous or rough?*
> *Will it alter my life altogether?*
> *O tell me the truth about love.*

Lansdowne, above Mussoorie, Garhwal District,
  February 1939

With both Michael John Carritt and Humphry House back in England, John Auden was again drinking alone among strangers. He'd been trying to convince Sudhin to come with him to the Garhwal in January, but for a man who complained unceasingly of Calcutta, it was hard to get him out of it. The one time Sudhin had gone up into the mountains he said he had nearly frozen to death. When Reverend Scott returned from his convalescence in Kasauli, John took him to dinner at Firpo's to mark his recovery.

The beau monde could always be found at Firpo's. With its faux Louis XIV chairs and white tablecloths, the dining experience was akin to that of first class on a P & O steamship. The table d'hôte was excellent. There was a nightclub featuring European cabaret acts and, for the spendthrift, American cocktails with free cocktail sausages at the bar. Signor Barazini, the Italian proprietor and maître d', had been raised in one of the whorehouses on Karaya Road. A thick layer of white powder covered his wife's face, as if to turn her into an Italian as well.

No sooner had John and the reverend seated themselves than the Bonnerjee brothers, dressed in shabby suits and carrying rolled-up umbrellas, sat down at the next table. For a while they pretended not to see each other, but the reverend eventually waved them over. As they pulled up chairs, Scott introduced them to John Auden.

"Yes, of course I've heard of you," Protap Bonnerjee said. "I know your name, your brother's name well. I've just been reading criticism of his work in the *New Yorker*. Of course they have got him all wrong, haven't they? They haven't any idea really what he's about, isn't it? Don't you agree?"

"Well, I don't really know," John said.

"Won't you have some more bacon and eggs?" Protap asked. Before John had a chance to reply, he rattled on.

"Top you up? I say, won't you have something to eat? Won't you have a club sandwich? Very American meal this, isn't it?"

"What, bacon and eggs?"

"Oh no. *Ham* and eggs. A great difference. This place reminds me of the Café Royal. The waiters there are all taught to play their part— don't you think so, Mr. Auden?"

Protap gave him a searching look as if a great deal depended upon their seeing eye to eye. John was at a loss.

"Might I ask you a very personal question, Mr. Auden? What school was your brother at?"

"Gresham's."

"Oh, how odd. One of the new schools. Of course there was only one man there. Sanderson. And what school were you at?"

"I was at Marlborough."

"Oh I know Marlborough well. One of the safe schools, isn't it? In India the safe schools are thought to be Marlborough and Wellington. I suppose Beverley Nichols was before your time."

He is just like his father, Ratna, Auden thought.

If John Auden wearied of being known simply as Wystan Auden's brother, Protap's father, Ratna Bonnerjee, though a distinguished barrister himself, was only ever the son of Womesh Chandra Bonnerjee. W. C. Bonnerjee was the first Indian president of the Indian National Congress, a fantastically wealthy luminary of the Calcutta barristocracy, and a social pillar of the Set.

W. C. had been a great believer in an English education. When his eldest was ready for Oxford, he had purchased a three-story, ten-bedroom mansion just outside London, adding a new wing to accommodate a billiard room and smoking den. Named Kidderpore after the family ancestral estate on the Hooghly River, the spread included tennis courts, an orchard, gardens, and a stable. After settling his wife and eight children under its roof, W. C. returned to Calcutta to amass his wealth and reside in an equally grand residence on Park Street. Its grounds also included a tennis court and stable, as well as an aviary, two fern houses, and a veranda wide enough for a coach and four. For the legions of W. C.'s grandchildren, Kidderpore and the Park Street mansion where Protap spent his childhood represented a golden age as legendary as the man behind it.

Ratna had read Greats at Balliol before following in W. C.'s footsteps to practice law. Once, in a righteous fusillade of damnation aimed at an accused criminal sitting in the dock, Ratna suddenly realized he was meant to be acting in the man's defense. He pivoted, deftly turning his own narrative on its head. Ratna's four formidable sisters went to Cambridge; two became doctors, one studied at the

Sorbonne. If an Englishwoman condescended to talk to her, she either replied in French or pretended she was a halfwit.

Ratna married Kitty Roy, the daughter of one of W. C.'s oldest friends. They had six children and lived on the top floor of the Park Street mansion. Ratna spoiled his four daughters with too many cakes, leaving Kitty to stay up all night holding their heads as they relieved themselves of them. He raised them on Shakespeare and Shelley, Browning and Tennyson, and on Greek, Roman, and Hindu mythology. They threw extravagant dinner parties in the English style, with everyone retiring to the music room for piano recitals and singing after. They were regular visitors to the Tagore and Datta households; indeed it was an uncle of Sudhin's who had first introduced W. C. to Rabindranath.

The rumor was that Protap and Bharat, Ratna's only sons, had their English education cut short after Kitty's sudden death. A heart attack, it was said, brought on from worry over Ratna's drinking and debts. The mansion on Park Street was sold: each of the six Bonnerjee children received a small settlement. Protap had a "grace and favor" job but was more likely found at the racecourse and the establishments of Karaya Road. Only one of his four sisters was married. Bharat was said to be cuckoo. When Bharat looked as if he were about to say something, Protap told him to shut up, scarcely pausing long enough to take a breath.

"I say—you must have another drink. You Reverend Scott, you Mr. Auden. What will you have?" He flagged a distant waiter.

"Boy! Brandy lao!"

"No really. I think I've had enough," Reverend Scott said.

"Oh no you must drink with us." He shouted again. "Boy! Brandy lao!"

But they couldn't. Protap invited them back to the family flat for brandy. More excuses were produced; Protap didn't give in easily.

"Well, can I phone you?" he finally said.

"By all means," Reverend Scott said, graciously. They said their good-byes.

Protap Bonnerjee was yet another instance of all that England had to answer for, John and Reverend Scott agreed as they stepped out. At nearly the same time, they brought up Sudhin. Only Sudhin managed to sustain a dignity and inner integrity, preserving the best qualities of both Europe and India. They didn't think to ask themselves whether his poise, artfully balanced between one civilization and another, could survive a war.

Reflecting on Protap's melancholy fate, John Auden gained a little purchase on his own. The Christmas holidays were fast approaching and as memories of Nancy receded, he began to think more fondly about the woman in Brussels who had turned down his marriage proposal the previous Christmas. Perhaps he had shortchanged her. Unlike Nancy she was never impatient and there was never any fear of disaster in bed. More simply: she had been kind. Perhaps if Sudhin wouldn't accompany him to the Garhwal, he would invite her instead.

When Betty Boggins arrived in Calcutta Sudhin regretted not having taken John up on his invitation to the mountains. What was John thinking? But he kept quiet. On New Year's Day John took Betty to Barrackpore. With dhows with lateen sails and dhoti-clad helmsmen, Barrackpore was one of Calcutta's most picturesque sights. Betty was so taken with the spectacle she said if his marriage proposal was still good, she would now accept. As soon as John produced a ring, she mentioned that her father would need to see his divorce papers. It was perhaps then that John dimly recalled that his last visit to Barrackpore had been with Margaret. He was flying blind once again.

Two weeks later they were motoring across the cool plains, skirting the edge of Nepal before tacking north. A water supply problem in the Aravalli Range twelve hundred kilometers to the south diverted him, but he was soon back north writing up his report. In Roorkee there was a map of London on the wall of his room. Nancy's new address on Provost Road was near the shortcut they often took to Regent's Park, he noted. Suddenly, an urgent memory of Nancy's red dressing gown eclipsed all thought of water supply problems and Betty in the next room.

When he fell ill on their arrival at Lansdowne Betty brought him steaming cups of tea, lined up the pencils on his desk, and arranged his books in a tidy stack on the bedside table. John received her ministrations meekly, wondering if this was the fever that would finish him off. Sweating through the sheets, fading in and out of sleep, he was dimly aware of a profusion of darlings and dearests wafting about him on a breeze of eau de cologne. Betty, efficiently plumping his pillows, had decided their wedding would be in late July, followed by a honeymoon in Ceylon. She would assemble her trousseau in Brussels while he finished up whatever it was he did.

When he began feeling better he became ruthlessly eager for Betty to be off. Outside his window the familiar white peaks of the High Himalaya beckoned him. He studied the blueprints of the new maps of the Nelang-Gangotri region. He hoped to bring his structural study of the Garhwal up to the Tibet border. The day after Betty left a letter from the GSI arrived, asking him if he would be interested in a long-term posting in Afghanistan. A secret reserve of coal near the Oxus River needed mapping. A flight to Kabul, a three-week march through the Hindu Kush, an indefinite number of months spent mapping coalfields near the Russian border suddenly sounded infinitely more exciting than marriage. John cabled yes, he would be only too glad, only to hear back that nothing might come of it. The GSI would be in touch.

He was off to his mountains.

Hoping to spark some conviviality at an evening halt, he threw a campfire party for the porters who'd come with him from Lansdowne, supplying several gallons of local spirits and three Hurkiya women to sing and dance. He dressed one of his porters in Wystan's Chinese dressing gown and invited him to open the festivities. By custom men were there to sing and clap sticks together, not dance, so the Hurkiya stalked off, insulted. Inevitably the men followed them and failed to turn up the next day.

That evening he'd had to sleep on straw in a flea-infested village hut. That, the 103-degree heat, and the Potu fly bites that peppered his face, arms, and legs meant he arrived in the sacred confluence town of Devprayag, where the Ganges met the Bhagirathi River, in a foul mood. A letter from Eric Shipton awaited him, expressing hope John might still join him in the Karakoram for their sixteen-month survey expedition. He was sorry to have missed speaking with him about it while he was in London. There was also a wire from Betty, sent from the Bombay docks, professing her love and perpetual devotion.

Christ, he thought.

If the GSI missed him at Harsil he would stop at Gangotri on the twentieth of June. After declining Shipton's invitation and cabling Betty to suggest they postpone their wedding, he was off again.

Sachthol Bad Balgach, Switzerland,
April 29, 1939

Michael Spender could never escape the thought that, at least when compared to a well-maintained machine, a man's mind was a second-rate device. Hard work, accurate measurements, and the right instruments had gotten him far in life. Yet he had begun to suspect that such things offered little in the way of answers to the questions that really mattered. Personal happiness, for a start. He had met Karl Jung the previous year sailing back from India. Over the course of their passage, Dr. Jung outlined his theory of the collective unconscious. Michael was sufficiently taken with it to submit himself to a course of Jungian analysis on his return to London.

It was not a success. He'd had to ask Stephen to answer the analyst's questions about his childhood as he recalled very little of it. After that he'd resigned himself to being shut out of ordinary, instinctual understandings that other people seemed to grasp quite readily. He called this capacity "the elusive element," and imagined that it helped explain certain human behaviors, such as Nancy's rages or Tilman's hysterical laughter, or Erica's neediness, he found unfathomable. His analyst had advised him not to get involved with anyone unless that person had a placid nature. That ruled out Nancy. So he'd left London for a placid village in Switzerland where the Wild factory was located.

From 7:00 a.m. to 7:00 p.m. Michael and Shipton fitted the photograph pairs from the 1935 reconnaissance of Everest into a Wild A5 stereoautograph. The Wild A5 was an advance upon the stereoplotter he'd worked with in Zurich in 1931 as it accommodated the crow's-eye view of aerial photography. The A5 minimized the distortions of magnified aerial photographs automatically, thereby enabling him to make use of the 1933 Everest flight survey strips that had been gathering dust at the RGS. Combined with the photographs taken on the 1935 reconnaissance, he could finally draw Everest's *Felszeichnung.* Sitting beneath the A5's high arch of olive-green steel, his eyes watched for the moment when the split pairs aligned themselves in the viewfinder and Everest was brought into the room. Raising the pairs brought different elevations and bands of rock into sharp focus, as if he were climbing the North Face himself.

If only he could see himself as clearly. If only he had a black box to automate the calculations involved in mapping a way forward in his life. He saw his prospects for happiness slipping away like sand in an hourglass. At 4:00 a.m. on May 13, 1939, Michael was expected at the Marseilles dock to join Shipton for his sixteen-month survey expedition in the Karakoram. The reckless possibility of begging off was stayed by the thought of Hinks's fury, Shipton's disappointment, and unemployment.

Michael decided to send letters off to Hinks and Shipton, reference the current war scares, and express concern at being away from Europe at this critical time. These would be followed a week later by a "definite decree of non-cooperation." But before he had time to post the second batch he had a blistering note from Hinks telling him his only "duty" was to the Karakoram. Shipton was sick at the thought of losing him. But then the rest of Czechoslovakia fell to Hitler and an English civil air survey concern offered him a job plotting an aerial survey of the Iraq oil fields. Oil was the new coal.

Shipton left for the Karakoram without him.

Unnamed Pass between Rudagaira Valley and Gatling Glacier,
   18,200 feet, June 29, 1939

On his arrival in Harsil to continue his structural study, John Auden realized it was a year to the day he'd flown from Zurich to see Nancy. How eagerly he had anticipated their reunions! And what disasters had lain in wait. Beset with longing and loneliness, and under the influence of some very strong chhang, John tried to fathom the truth about love.

For the women on Karaya Road sex was not a sacrifice, a gift, or a dream of a leafy bower. It was a straightforward matter, its price known in advance and its success guaranteed. What an ecstasy it was to be freed of the fetters of respectability for an hour! He left the beds of these women lighthearted, unaccompanied by a sense of loss. But with Betty the price of love had kept rising. The chhang awakened memories he had tried to stifle, assaulting him like a fusillade. There were her yes darlings, no darlings, and my-goodness-gracious-mes. There were her atrocious dresses and letters filled with mysterious nothings. That time she put Beethoven on the gramophone, timing it for his return like a scene from a Hollywood film. The oppressively silent hours she had spent studying her fingernails, the Krishnamurthy on her bedside table aside a volume of Rupert Brooke marked with red silk tabs, all the while his loan of Frank Smythe's account of his triumph on Kamet remained unopened.

It got worse. The time she had sat with her legs carelessly apart, exposing her pussy.

Exposing her pussy!

The night before Betty left Lansdowne he'd had a dream in which he was in a motorcar racing up a dark mountain road. Signs written in Hindustani loomed out of the darkness, only to disappear behind him before he could make out what they said. What on earth had possessed him to agree to marry her? It was a failure of courage. He would have to live with that. "It had better never be," he wrote in his journal a few days after leaving Harsil.

There was still no reply from Betty. And Afghanistan had fallen through.

The Jadh Ganga Valley in the upper Garhwal was a meeting ground of Shiva and the Buddha. Here lichen-crusted gompas and Shiva lingams coexisted peacefully. Boundary pillars, on the other hand, those heathen idols worshipped by Survey of India pundits, were constantly being uprooted and moved. To John's eye the valley, with its arid wastes and rock spirals, was unquestionably Tibetan. But when had the character of a landscape ever determined the location of a border? Mapmakers drew the lines, boundary pillars marked them, and soldiers defended them.

The new maps didn't cover his intended route, so John had to guess which pass wouldn't find him crossing into Tibet, though by Tibetan lights he already had. After a day of struggle up a slope of sticky snow he reached a pass just as a blizzard arrived. Only when it cleared did he realize that he was in the wrong valley. He saw another pass to the south; the map gave it a height of 19,300 feet. Shouldering his heavy pack, he marched off.

As lightning flashed and thunder cracked around him, he and his porters humped for hours over one ugly scree heap after another, walking along the flanks of a gorge in dismal clouds, debris crumbling beneath their boots like a rotten slagheap. His efforts seemed preposterous. Whether he succeeded in extending his tectonic study to the edge of Tibet or forged a new route from one part of the Himalaya to another, what did it matter? Scott and Carritt at least tried to do something on India's behalf. He felt exhausted and defenseless.

They finally made camp in the pouring rain. Looking ahead John thought there might be a pass from the Mana Glacier to the Arwa Valley, but the last 1,000 feet were too steep and didn't appear oriented in the right direction. There may have been a more roundabout route at the end of the glacier, but given the ugliness of the moraines and the rubbishy weather, he was disinclined to try a pass over 20,000 feet. With the excuse of having to check his mail at Gangotri, he was able to hide how relieved he was not to be facing three nights without fuel, camping on a glacier.

As they reached a large alpine meadow, an eagle dropped a wolf cub in front of them. Christened Jimsie, the cub joined the expedition, soaking John's sleeping bag with pee but providing some warmth and lifting his spirits. At Nelang, halfway down the Jadh Ganga, Jimsie had her first taste of fresh meat and the porters got plastered on four gallons of chhang. John had hoped to get them to dance, but they passed out too soon. At Gangotri there was still no word from Betty.

After resupplying, they crossed over the Bhagirathi River and turned south up the Kedarganga Valley, weaving their way through pine and rhododendron in pouring rain. They ascended a ridge on the west side of the valley and descended into the Rudagaira Valley, using a compass to navigate through the clouds. He'd been in this valley in 1935, when he had tried and failed to climb the Jogin and Gangotri peaks with Dawa Tendrup and Ang Tsering. This time he had only local porters, but one of them, Juin Singh, had been with him that year.

The rain continued steadily for twenty-five hours and then off and on again for three more days. Auden finished a Spanish Civil War novel for the third time and brought his field notebook up to date. A porter returned from Gangotri to report the babas were saying it was written in the shastras that the rain would continue for nine more days. He also brought a letter from the director of the GSI. Auden was being transferred to work on mineral springs. This spelled the end of his Himalayan work. So John Auden was now resolved. It was now or never. He would attempt a new pass over the main range even if it killed him. Juin Singh was as eager as he was.

· They moved camp to the southern end of the valley, in the shadow of hanging glaciers from the previous ice age, dirty with debris from bygone rock falls. The skies gradually cleared. Before them rose a pristine and nearly vertical wall of snow with a sharp crystalline crest. The sunset that night was the most beautiful he had ever seen. The moon rose in a blue-green night sky. Here, in the heart of the High Himalaya, there were no superior or inferior races. Here, in the deep time in which these mountains came into existence there was no such thing as British rule or God's inscrutable wisdom. There was only the simultaneous feeling of pain and peace, of sound and suspended quiet. His heart was full.

If luck is with him, an explorer will return home to tell his story and collect his laurels. Few will grasp the dangers he has faced or the knowledge he has brought back. Maps can't convey what it is like to submit to a cold that grips a body at sunset or the hours spent under an unforgiving sun and a heavy pack. Even more difficult is the realization that the man who has returned is little changed from the one who left and that soon the longing to go back will return. Maps will be taken out and an even more treacherous route plotted. In this way the explorer exists suspended between the longing for home and the longing for extinction.

John Auden knew he had done nothing that summer that was not done as a matter of necessity by the people of the Jadh Ganga Valley. Their lives were a silent reproach to the lofty notions of men like him. Unlike babas and mountaineers, they accumulated no merit in the course of extracting a meager living from an unforgiving land. Without benefit of ice ax, tricouni nails, and Players cigarettes brought up from the plains, they simply made their way from one high valley to another to graze their sheep.

They broke camp at dawn and started up the pass. Every so often John would stop and lean on his ice ax to wait for his breathing to slow. They reached the pass by 8:20 a.m. but the precipitous drop to the glacier below gave him pause. There was a fierce wind and a long moment when the pounding in his chest nearly undid him. "Fear is the enemy of love and the destroyer of life," he told himself, summoning the god Krishna's admonition to the fearful warrior Arjuna in the Bhagavad Gita. Then he got out his line and roped up. Juin Singh went first, committing him to follow. And he did.

After a slippery descent to a virgin snowfield, after hours of struggle through fresh and sticky snow, they were faced with an icefall that appeared to extend the length of the valley. John was reminded of his troubled crossing of the Karakoram, alone with his Baltis, and the impatient march back to the road that would take him to Srinagar, Calcutta, and thence to London and Nancy. What awaited them all now?

But on this bright morning, with a wolf cub strapped to the top of his rucksack, Juin Singh was fearless on the heavily crevassed ice, hopping from rock to rock, never losing his footing, never wavering. The hour, the day, the triumph, was all his.

The last six marches were so hot they took to walking at night in the light of the nearly full moon. On arrival in Mussoorie, John was relieved of his beard and lice-infested clothes. For three months he had heard only the wind and rain slapping his tent, the thunder of avalanches, and the pistol shot of rock falls. Now an army band tortured a Gilbert and Sullivan number at the bandstand. Ladies under parasols on the arms of men in oversized topees strolled along the green. That Mussoorie was not even a first-rank hill station made this parade seem all the more desperate. Amid the Savoy's shabby grandeur, his men were suddenly timid and self-conscious. Juin Singh alone strutted about, whistling to get the attention of the waiters. John cringed, only to flush at his cringing. They moved to a more modest establishment down the mall, accompanied by Jimsie.

Juin Singh had once asked John what the English words "quite, quite" meant. It was no easier trying to explain the prospect of war. If Juin Singh had never seen an airplane, what could he tell him of bombs dropped from the sky? Or gas masks and concentration camps? But Juin Singh did understand that at their journey's end he would once again become the sahib's porter and John the sahib. And so it was. After a day's rest, John paid them all off and saw them on their way. He turned to finishing a letter to Wystan.

In London the previous summer John had learned from Christopher Isherwood that Wystan had had a tearful breakdown on their way back from China, confessing to Isherwood his fear that he was unlovable. Yet John had been so upset over Nancy he never thought to inquire further. Bitter heartache was his province; Wystan was impregnable. Wystan had all the luck. Now, from the Mussoorie mail, he learned Wystan had fallen in love with an American named Chester Kallman. They were celebrating their honeymoon in New Orleans.

In his reply John described the nightmare he would face on his return to Calcutta. He had a cable from Betty; she had set sail for India. She expected him at the dock, marriage license in hand. Of course he was in the wrong. He had played the stricken card one time too many. He vowed never to play it again. If she sued him for breach of promise, so be it. Whatever price he had to pay, his freedom was worth it. He cabled her boat.

There isn't much visible ahead, he wrote gloomily, having entirely forgotten to wish his brother every happiness.

Hatibagan, 139 Cornwallis Street, Calcutta,
   May 12, 1939

Near about the time John Auden was recording his reflections on love in Harsil, the three unmarried Bonnerjee sisters arrived at Sudhin Datta's adda in a phalanx of colorful saris to settle like tittering birds around the leading literary light of the Congress Party, a fifty-eight-year-old poet named Sarojini Naidu. That evening her wide, expressive face was framed by hair done up with flowers. A Congress legend and a great raconteur, Sarojini was the daughter of a revolutionary who had been executed by Stalin two years before. Her own resistance to British rule began with the 1905 partition of Bengal. She had accompanied that "little Mickey-Mouse of a Man" on the Dandi Salt March and been imprisoned during the civil disobedience campaign that followed. The first thing she said that evening was that Muhammad Ali Jinnah's relations with Congress had gotten so unfriendly of late she needed a coat to ward off the chill. Gandhi was warmer. Unlike Nehru, with his hangdog eyes, he was just as quick to laugh as she was. Sarojini made India's nationalist leaders seem like part of a one large and bickering joint family household. The adda lapped it up.

While Sarojini told a mischievous story about Tagore, Sudhin introduced the Bonnerjee sisters to a young friend of Hiren-da's, a flaming Red. Sudhin knew perfectly well that neither Minnie nor Sheila Bonnerjee was in the least political, though Anila was something of a smoldering Pink. Slim and sharp as a knitting needle, Anila had recently returned from Russia, accompanied by a love-struck and penniless Pushkin scholar from England. The previous Friday she had gotten into a fierce argument with a man who worshipped Adolf Hitler as an incarnation of Vishnu.

After the death of their mother, Kitty, Minnie, the eldest and most brilliant of the sisters, had tried to step up but had never quite managed to master the art of running a household. A scholar of Smollett with a teaching position at a women's college, she had long been the sole female of the adda regulars, much to the dismay of the secret diarist. He couldn't abide intellectual women, particularly unattractive ones. But what Minnie lacked in looks or domestic skills, she made up for with her enormous fund of gossip concerning the private lives of the Set, making her terrifically popular at dinner parties. She was often found in the company of Hiren-da and Lindsay Emmerson, a *Statesman* editor. Humphry House had adored her. Beneath Minnie's badly draped saris was a stout heart.

Sheila, both the prettiest and the family artist, shared Minnie's fatalistic view of life and her sense of the absurd. After attending Calcutta's Oriental School of Art, she had received a scholarship to attend Munich's Deutsche Akademie until the Nazis obliged her to shift to London. Recently returned to Calcutta, she was working with Jamini Roy, a classically trained painter turned folk artist whose current exhibition they had all just attended. Had he not needed the money, Jamini whispered to the adda diarist (who thought Sheila's English accent overdone), he would have given Sheila Bonnerjee a wide berth. She was far too westernized. Sudhin had been coming to his studio to watch Sheila paint; Jamini doubtless suspected something was afoot between them.

However often Sudhin reminded himself that, at nearly forty, he was an old man to this pensive, wry, and beautiful twenty-seven-year-old painter, he fell hard for her. Unlike the lover he'd left behind in Germany in 1929, Sheila Bonnerjee came from his own betwixt-and-between world. She made him laugh. She teased him. She was a talented painter. In her company he felt like a free man. But what could he offer her? He was not a free man. He had never been free. It was not just the British who ruled him, or even the oppressive propriety of his joint family household. It was his aged and gentle father's good opinion that bound him. So even if he had the money to keep a mistress, Sudhin didn't want to become the sort of profligate he'd often disparaged. Sheila deserved better. As the dog days of May gave way to June monsoons, with a European war threatening and promising to upend everything, Sudhin struggled. The longer he carried on with Sheila, the more impossible it would become. While outwardly he smiled as easily as before, inwardly he raged to see this chance, too, slip away.

Ever so slowly, he resigned himself to losing her.

One evening a month after the rains had arrived, Sudhin told Sheila she must meet his friend John Auden when he returned from the mountains. He tried to describe him.

"John Auden sounds like a cold fish," she said with a laugh. Soon "John Auden" became an ongoing joke between them. Only once did she take it too far. After putting up green curtains in her room at the family flat on Bright Street, she teased Sudhin that she wanted it to have the light of an aquarium so as to make the cold fish feel at home in her bedroom. He gave her a pained look. She was more careful after that.

Sheila had been fifteen years old when her father's drinking and debts caught up with him. She had been there, too, when Protap and

Bharat returned from boarding school, their education permanently
curtailed. She had watched a procession of carts pull up at her childhood home, the Park Street mansion where her legendary grandfather had once presided over an elaborately set table. The bailiffs had
packed up the gilded imitation Louis XIV furnishings, rolled up the
carpets, and stripped paintings from the walls before hauling everything off to a Russell Street auction house. Beloved cousins, aunts,
uncles, servants, and pets were all dispersed.

After that Sheila vowed to travel light and pretended to be more
frivolous than she was. While she and Sudhin flirted madly and drank
too much, she wondered what would become of her. Yet while he
might tease her for her highborn airs, she saw in him a sense of loss
that ran even more deeply than her own.

De Sahib, the Special Branch officer who sometimes attended Parichay
adda, must have been otherwise occupied the evening Lindsay
Emmerson declared that he was entirely in favor of an armed uprising
in India. If political necessity required that Europeans be killed, so be
it. Sudhin, smiling, pointed out that arms weren't so easily come by.
Was it really so difficult, Lindsay persisted, couldn't they be smuggled
in? From Siam? The Irish had managed some rather sensational assas-
sinations, he pointed out.

Minnie had cackled sweetly; though Lindsay was an Etonian and
Oxford man, they shared the anarchic spirit of the Calcutta born. Still,
en route to Cornwallis Street for a drink and stand-up that August,
Minnie pleaded with her sisters to behave like the grown women
they were, and not act like silly schoolgirls without a thought in their
heads. Sudhin might well put up with that but such behavior would
not go down well with John Auden.

So this John Auden was a pompous prig, too, Sheila whispered
to Anila.

Sheila was struck first by his unearthly pallor, his blazing cheeks.
Some silly woman asked if he used rouge. His white-blond hair reminded her of those Munich Hitlerites who would pull her roughly aside
on the street to ask if she was a Jewess. She began a nervous digression
on the exotic allure of blonds. She wouldn't have blamed him if he de-

cided she was a shallow flirt. His reticence flustered her. She may have been overconscious, too, of Sudhin watching from across the room.

At Cathay, in Chinatown, Sheila left it to Minnie to make conversation while she ate an enormous number of dishes. When John Auden next invited them out, she was on her own as Minnie was off with Lindsay. She ate just as much at Chung Wa but the dinner passed in strained silence. Then came the Saturday lunch at Firpo's with Sudhin.

The previous night's adda had left Sudhin despondent. The diarist had been the first to arrive, and as soon as he walked through the door Sudhin asked him if there would be a war. The Nazi–Soviet Pact had been signed on Wednesday, and it seemed to Sudhin as if England was going to let Hitler get away with whatever he liked in Poland by blaming it all on France.

Despite England's failure to abide by its stated ideals, whether in regard to India or to its European alliances, Sudhin had made up his mind to join the Indian Army. Whether this was a decision born of a broken heart, a high-minded commitment to the rule of law and democracy, or a hatred of fascism he couldn't be certain; perhaps it was all these things.

Then the adda's Naziphile, an ICS officer and Muslim League member, sashayed in with a smirk on his face.

"Sudhin, didn't I tell you ages ago? You people don't understand politics at all. You have no idea what's going on. You'll never be able to understand why I admire Stalin. Britain's foreign policy is absolutely useless. They should all be given the boot. And why is Nehru going on about protecting democracy when this is India's chance to get out from under the British? You have to admit that Hitler is a genius. Have you seen how easily—"

Sudhin raised his hand in surrender. "I can't disagree with anything you say. Still, I am prepared to enlist in any military capacity the British need me for."

"What has Germany ever done to you?" the Naziphile shrieked, dropping his smug demeanor.

The diarist was taken aback at this outrageous departure from civility.

"There is no point bickering," Sudhin had replied mildly, gracefully offering him a cigarette before lapsing into silence.

At Firpo's the next day Sudhin was the first to get tight. He suddenly began talking wildly about how he and John might share Sheila by having her on alternate nights. John promptly offered to marry Sheila only to clap his head. A fortune-teller in Dehra Dun had foretold a marriage to someone named Doris. He was stymied.

"Perhaps you might change your name?"

"Would you marry me if I did?"

"Well, I don't know. You seem a little snooty."

"How can you *say* that?" Sheila said, rattled.

"Indeed," Sudhin interrupted. "Much as I admire you, John, I never thought you were a good judge of a woman's character." He was thinking of Betty Boggins.

It was settled then. They would both live with her. By then they had had so much to drink they were making very little sense. After John promised to take them both on a night flight over Calcutta that evening, they went their separate ways. John returned to his office and stood there ecstatically admiring his maps.

Neither Sheila nor Sudhin was entirely recovered when John went round to pick them up. Perhaps it was a mistake to have tried to extend the giddy afternoon into the evening. Sheila was ill on the drive, recovering briefly while they were in the air. John dropped Sudhin home first. When he got to Bright Street Sheila rushed out of the car. He supposed she was afraid he would try to kiss her.

Too restless to return to Alipore, John drove to Lizzie's. Expensive cars lined Karaya Road, hidden by the trees. As he entered, Lola, the bewigged and fat Yugoslav housekeeper, asked him if there would be a war.

"Why yes, of course," he said. He was feeling unusually lighthearted.

Upon inquiring he found that Eileen, Baby, and both Peggys were taken. It was clearly a very busy Saturday night.

"Take Babs," Madam Lizzie said. "As a memsahib I tell you honest. She's a nice girl, a fine girl."

He took Babs. The sound of a German broadcast followed them into her room.

"Will they bomb us?" Babs asked.

"You're safe as houses," he told her and then took off his pants.

PART III

The Fall of the Gods

The eyes of the crow and the eye of the camera open
Onto Homer's world, not ours. First and last
They magnify earth, the abiding
Mother of gods and men

W. H. AUDEN, "MEMORIAL FOR THE CITY" (1949)

You see the fall of the Gods of yesterday
And the fall of the Gods of the morrow
Yet never a sigh or regret you say
For the infinite ocean of sorrow

W. H. AUDEN, "EVEREST" (DECEMBER 1922)

CHAPTER 14

Somewhere a Strange
and Shrewd Tomorrow

Sunday Lunch, Penwether's House,
  Bude, Cornwall, August 27, 1939

For nearly six months, Nancy Coldstream had plotted to rekindle Michael Spender's interest. Yet when she lamented having to go to her mother's because it *again* looked like war, he refused to listen. She hadn't spoken to him since. When her train to London reached Okehampton, she rang him from the platform to ask that he meet her at Waterloo. He told her he couldn't. He was going out for dinner in Hampstead.

You sound upset, Michael remarked.

Nancy had run away, abandoning her children after Sunday lunch. Bill had run out after her, jumping on the train, pleading with her to be reasonable: London was too dangerous, he argued.

Nancy began to tell Michael of her argument with her mother but he interrupted her.

"Why do you insist on foisting your troubles on other people?" She hung up.

The next day she called him again. Michael said it would be unseemly to go to a nice restaurant so they went to a dreary one. He wasn't pleased to hear Bill was with her in London and did not see her home. Back at Provost Road, Bill was warm and affectionate, insisting their marriage was not over. Nancy succumbed. The next morning he convinced her to return to Cornwall.

Wystan had got Bill to scrap all his ideas about cinema and return to painting. Though Sonia Brownell had been modeling at his
art school for nearly a year, Bill had only just met the woman the Boys
called the Euston Road Venus. In her diary the previous Friday, Sonia
had written, "Bill. Bad teeth, good hands, a ring I think." Not that a
ring bothered her. She also noted his slight stoop. "Not really an apolo-
getic one," she added, shrewdly. Sonia had agreed to sit for Bill when
he returned from the weekend in Cornwall, hence the earnest desire
to see Nancy safely out of London. It was only when war was declared
the following Sunday that Nancy realized she'd been tricked.

Two calls to Michael found him implacable. He cursed her. He was
writing her off. She was terrified she was pregnant. This was the state
she was in when a parcel from John Auden arrived. The sight of it ban-
ished her bitterness. Was he really coming back? Had he married that
Brussels girl? Louis was in Ireland having a breakdown, she told him.
His letters were those of a man rotting in his grave. It might be years
before she saw him again. And Michael Spender was a bloody hypocrite. She didn't mention the war. The war was the least of her concerns.

When Nancy made her way back to London three months later,
the prospect of a fire-breathing wife catching him with Sonia briefly
eclipsed Bill's fear of being called up. Among the Boys the state of the
Coldstream marriage was by then a well-worn subject. Nancy suspected everyone knew more about Bill's doings than they let on, and
they did. Sonia suspected everyone of trying to marry her off to Bill.
And they were. Had Louis MacNeice not left London, the Boys said,
had Bill not become so famous, he might not have found himself so
trapped. Heads nodded up and down Charlotte Street. Nancy tried
to brazen it out by talking about her ambulance training. Everyone
listened politely. She was humiliated.

Louis wrote her a stream of consoling letters from Ireland. By then
he knew his love for her was doomed, yet to abandon it entirely meant
facing an unspeakable abyss. Some days he thought he might as well
go out and sit under a bomb. When a job in Dublin fell through, Louis
accepted a lectureship at Cornell University. Nancy assumed that, like
Wystan, he wouldn't be back. He managed to see her just before he left.
She'd been beastly.

"Do go on painting, puss. Don't let the boys frighten you away from London," Louis wrote from the docks.

A fortnight after his departure, finally convinced that she'd lost Bill to Sonia, Nancy bought a bottle of poison and downed the lot in front of the Boys. They got her to hospital to have her stomach pumped while Bill hid under a bed somewhere at the back of a Baker Street hotel. It would take a bomb dropping on Nancy to free Bill, one of the Boys remarked.

"Stomach pump and many horrors," Nancy said of her stay in University College Hospital. In the morning the doctor she'd been seeing began sternly:

"Either you promise to . . ."

"I promise," she replied before he could finish.

Within a month of leaving hospital Nancy was assigned to ambulance station no. 49, on St. Pancras Way at the back of Camden Town. In twice-weekly letters to Louis, she itemized her complaints. The men, retired taxi drivers or ex-army officers, were not in the least tempting. It was too icy to practice driving (never her strong suit), so the work involved sitting in a circle around an electric fire from 3:30 to 11:30 p.m. knitting woolens for soldiers. This, too, proved a challenge: she soon disgraced herself by not following the pattern.

The ladies were all refined and deadly and spoke only of getting home to their hubbies and home fires. For Nancy, a little of her Percy Street room went a long way. The winter was the coldest in ninety years. Ice on the tracks prevented coal deliveries. Everyone and everything was frozen, including the war. She said nothing to Louis about her attempt to end it all, and nothing at all about Sonia.

George Washington Hotel, 23 Lexington Avenue,
New York City, September 3, 1939

Having heard from home that John was going out for the RAF, Wystan sent off a cable, accusing his brother of doing so to spite himself, as if he had nothing to live for. He begged him to wait for his letter before signing up.

Wystan had once written that a writer's duty was to "make action urgent and its nature clear." In 1938, as with Spain in 1937, he'd been ready to sacrifice everything. He believed death would solve his "problem." But he had changed since he'd left England, and his ideas about where duty lay changed with him. He no longer had a death wish, no longer aspired to become a he-man. He had burst into tears when war was declared, and took that as a sign he was not meant to be a soldier.

But what argument could he use with his brother?

The day Hitler invaded Poland, Wystan renounced all his previous fiats. His new credo was, "We must love one another or die." The primacy of love underlay the four-point argument he set out in his letter to John.

Point 1. If John had found a love that made him happy and then made the choice to sacrifice it, that would indeed be heroic. What difference did it make that Sheila was Bengali, or that Chester was a Mister not a Miss? John had another life ahead of him—"don't imagine you won't find it." The search for that life trumped whatever compelled him now.

Point 2. The war was a showdown between the Nazi-Soviet war machine and Big Business Imperialism. Wystan failed to see what use John had for either. Letting his hatred of the Nazis drive him into the arms of England made as much sense as letting his hatred of the British Raj drive him into the arms of Hitler. "This war is not our war," he insisted, as if he might decide that for them both.

Point 3. As a member of the intellectual elite, John's duty was to understand what was happening. With that he might incubate in his own life a brighter future. "It went without saying that this would take as much courage and hard work as flying an aeroplane." He begged John to stay in India or find a way to come to America.

In California Wystan and Christopher had studied yoga with a California swami. This was Point no. 4. Leaving aside the mumbo jumbo, Wystan said, there was a great deal of profit in Raja Yoga. If a pacifist position is taken, every effort must be made to be genuinely nonviolent in one's private as well as one's public life. Louis MacNeice, struggling with whether to stay in America or return to England and join up, had parted company with Wystan here. He didn't see how pacifism could be justified, given that they weren't pacifists at the time of Spain and Munich.

Left unsaid in all four points was Wystan's fear of losing John.

John had just been to the cinema to see Edward G. Robinson in *Confessions of a Nazi Spy* when the declaration of war came over the wireless. He asked himself if Wystan was right. Was he joining up to spite himself? He decided: no, he wasn't. And when Wystan's letter arrived, he answered it point for point. Yoga held no interest. Making war to create a new order from the ruins was hopeless. Even the idea of a war to end Nazism meant nothing to him. With Sudhin now his closest friend and Sheila his lover, he certainly didn't believe in racial superiority, an English *Blut und Boden*. England's cause for him meant the cause of Sugar Loaf near Abergavenny, the burrows on the Downs, the Cotswolds, the Roman Wall, and the Pennine Fells. For these relics of childhood, he would give his life. Nothing else. He hoped his ability to read maps and fly planes would prove useful.

Sudhin knew that he and Sheila were together, at least for now. There had been an awkward drunken moment when Sudhin, sensing John's ambivalence, tried to renew his claims on her. Later, he'd written a letter of profuse apology, begging John's forgiveness and expressing his hope that John's relationship with Sheila and their friendship with him could continue on as before.

Since then John and Sheila had spent nearly every evening dancing at Firpo's till the wee hours. After sleepless nights in her arms, John would drop her back at Bright Street at dawn, driving the car in his bedroom slippers. He would continue on to the Dum Dum aerodrome to practice takeoffs and landings. By ten he was asleep on his desk.

But after a month of this he felt he needed to get a handle on himself. The late nights would have to stop. His nerves were shot. He hadn't qualified in the first round of the RAF pilot's test, having failed to nail a three-point landing. His hands shook and there was a hollow in the pit of his stomach. He hadn't told Wystan the real reason he was enlisting, knowing he would disapprove. He wanted to see himself in an airman's uniform; he wanted to fly a Blenheim bomber.

Were he and Sheila of the same race or living somewhere other than Calcutta they might have had a chance to be happy. But the bald truth was, they weren't. And he'd rather die than brave the hostility of those English who would view his relationship with an Indian with the same revulsion as the Nazis. Sheila would soon be off to Bombay for an exhibition of her paintings and that would be the end of it. The RAF would keep him from falling back into the mire.

Sheila had the right attitude: nothing really mattered.

Stay in America, John had written Wystan. Nothing he could write would save England. Only the wholesale murder of the bunglers on Downing Street and the twits in A Class bungalows orchestrating the evils and bloodshed in India would accomplish that. If Wystan decided to become an American, he wouldn't judge him.

Others would. Questions would be raised in Parliament as to why W. H. Auden was not returning to England in his country's time of need. But long before His Majesty's Government decided to take up the fight against fascism, Wystan had fought it and lost. He was surrendering his weapons and retiring from the field. As he had broken the contract he imagined he would be the first to honor, he expected no forgiveness.

Viceroy's Palace, New Delhi,
  September 3, 1939

Viceroy Linlithgow had been unable to assemble the All India federation of provinces and princely states as called for in the 1935 Government of India Act. No matter how eloquently he had appealed to the nizams, nawabs, rajahs, and maharajas of India to surrender their sovereignty and sign the Instruments of Accession, the princes had hemmed and hawed. They knew full well Churchill had said they weren't to be forced. This was one measure of the extent to which the viceroy's office practiced the diligent performance of good intentions and what might generously be termed a delusion of candor. The charade had ended that summer when a large coalition of royals flatly refused. Then Hitler invaded Poland and Linlithgow promptly declared war on India's behalf.

"Confronted with the demand that she should accept the dictation of a foreign power, India has decided to stand firm," he said, thereby reminding everyone there was only one foreign power dictating any-thing where India was concerned. He was fully prepared to cite chap-ter and verse from the 1935 act giving him the right to do so, should anyone object.

The viceroy and the Secretary of State for India both assumed that Gandhi's belief in nonviolence would mean he could not be drawn in to support the Crown, though of course they didn't know for certain as Linlithgow had never raised the subject with him. To Linlithgow's surprise Gandhi, speaking only for himself, offered his unconditional support for England. The prospect of London being bombed had upset him. "I was greatly struck with the depth of real feeling . . . Gandhi showed at this part of our conversation," Linlithgow reported, "his emotion at times being so marked as to make it impossible for him to continue."

Jinnah, who had by then shuttered his London law practice and sold his house in Hampstead, had a cooler head. Having simmered for two years watching Congress rule in the eight provinces, with two non–Muslim League governments in power in the Muslim-majority states of the Punjab and Bengal, he welcomed the abandonment of the All India federation and was thrilled to be invited to the viceregal palace to weigh in on what role India was to play in the conflict. The war provided Jinnah a lifeline out of political irrelevance and a new hearing for his dream of a separate nation for India's Muslims. He was calling it Pakistan.

Nehru had been making speeches condemning Hitler since 1936. He'd visited Spain in 1938 and had been in London to witness Neville Chamberlain's capitulation at Munich. He was on record express-ing his full support for the Western democracies, should it come to war: "I should like India to play its full part," he had said, assuming Congress leaders would be consulted. When they weren't, he asked Linlithgow what England's war aims were, suggesting, without actu-ally saying so, that a written commitment to a free India would be the price of his support. Congress then sat back to see how far the viceroy would go.

What sort of ultimatum is couched as a polite request for impe-rialism to commit suicide? M. N. Roy had thundered. An occasional visitor to Sudhin Datta's Parichay adda, Roy had cut his teeth as a boy of fourteen on terrorist intrigues of the Bengal underground. He had founded both the Mexican and Indian Communist parties. When he ran afoul of Stalin he returned to India and was promptly arrested. During six years of imprisonment, Roy rethought his political philosophy and upon his release made common cause with Nehru and Congress. He also became a close friend of Sudhin's.

Roy had pressed Nehru to remain neutral. The smart move, he held, was to maintain Congress's power in the provincial ministries so as to protect Indian civil liberties when war was declared. Yet when Nehru finally learned that all His Majesty's Government was prepared to offer was a seat on an advisory war committee and perhaps one or two on the Viceroy's Executive Council, he ordered Congress members to resign en masse. Roy was appalled. And when Nehru demanded complete and immediate independence, he threw up his hands. Predictably, Linlithgow turned away to embrace Jinnah as the perfect obstacle to any further engagement with Congress.

Meanwhile, in London, in the wake of the Narvik naval disaster of April 1940, a Conservative politician and former *Times* correspondent named Leo Amery stood up in the House of Commons and, after a mesmerizing itemization of the government's many failures, turned to Chamberlain and paraphrased Oliver Cromwell's denunciation of the Long Parliament. "You have sat too long here for any good you have been doing. Depart, I say, and let us have done with you. In the name of God, go!" A fine moment. When Winston Churchill formed a new government, he made Amery, his contemporary at Harrow, the new Secretary of State for India.

Germany's blitzkrieg over the Continent soon led Amery to rethink His Majesty's Government's India policy. He floated offering India dominion status after the war. At first Churchill roundly denounced the spectacle of His Majesty's Government running after Gandhi. Then he saw that the mere suggestion of dominion status was acting as a cat among pigeons. "Winston rejoiced in the quarrel which had broken out afresh between Hindus and Moslems, said he hoped it would remain bitter and bloody," his private secretary wrote assiduously in his diary. In the end the War Cabinet decided that the time had not come to give anything away. Following Churchill's lead, they agreed: "We must remain firm as a rock."

49C Hazra Road, Ballygunj, Calcutta,
   June 21, 1940

Sudhin had never spoken to his father about the rift in his marriage. A child would have provided some solace, but he and Chhabi remained childless. His father might have wondered if Sudhin's brother, a young widower, had become overfamiliar with Chhabi. In a joint family household such things happened. Or maybe his father had intuited his recent heartbreak. Whatever the reason, Sudhin knew his distress did not go unnoted. Perhaps this was behind his father's decision to rent a south Calcutta flat for the couple. There he and Chhabi might have a degree of freedom from joint family life.

The adda regulars left Hatibagan for Hazra Road reluctantly. Hiren-da promised he would continue to supply sweets from his secret sources in north Calcutta. South Calcutta confectioneries were universally disparaged. Sudhin furnished the Hazra Road parlor, not with settees and tea tables, but in the traditional Bengali way, with mattresses on the floor covered in white sheets and bolsters upholstered in colorful silk fabrics. Hand-block saris hung from the doorways. Only the books remained the same.

A month after the move, that veteran of revolutions on three continents made an appearance. Since the outbreak of war M. N. Roy had made more enemies than allies. Perhaps this accounted for his sullen temper that day; the great revolutionary uttered not one word. After he left, Hiren-da said he had been hoping someone would ask him, in all innocence, the *real* reason he had left Russia. Hiren-da couldn't believe Stalin would really have executed the man Lenin had hailed as "the symbol of revolution in the East."

"Manabendra can speak to the point when he wants to," Sudhin said, disappointed that Roy hadn't proved a more forceful ally in his arguments with Hiren-da. "He just wasn't in the mood."

"Yeeees, he can be rude," Minnie Bonnerjee drawled.

The secret diarist noted that with Minnie around no one else could get a word in. Conjectures about the European war had whipped back and forth between her and Roy's foreign wife, leaving the younger, less worldly poets too intimidated to say anything. The diarist had recently begun warming to Minnie, though he still heartily disapproved of women smoking.

As Germany began its European offensive in the spring of 1940, members of the adda began choosing teams. On Fridays the fireworks could be heard from down the street. Separate arguments started up in different corners; England and France here, Russia there, India near the sweets table; everyone at cross-purposes. They no longer got carried away citing the advantages of kurta pyjamas over Western attire or the intricacies of the inswings and off cutters of the Town Club's fearsome star bowler. Instead there were white-hot debates over the respective strengths of the various European navies and air forces. Sudhin, whom they all depended upon to lighten the most entrenched views with sly quips, was unusually silent or, the secret diarist noted, unaccountably irritable.

Apropos of England's dithering, someone told a joke about a dying old man being tended by his loving family. After months of waiting for him to die, they were at their wits' end. Then a mad man passing by the scene shouted, "He's done for, just burn him!" Everyone laughed but Sudhin.

Sudhin had long taken England to task for its failure to rearm and contend with Hitler's growing menace. When the bombing of Warsaw began, he had felt certain that England would come to the immediate aid of the Poles. When that didn't happen, he agreed with Lindsay Emmerson of the *Statesman* that once Belgium was attacked, swift military action would be taken. But it was not until mid-April 1940 that his confusion over England's war objectives was dispelled. It was simple: England wasn't going to lift a finger to defend Europe. This realization, coming on the heels of heartbreak, distressed him deeply. Even an atrocious pun from some fool at adda, something about "Narvik" and "nerve weak," failed to ignite his exasperation. But it was the invasion of France and the fall of Paris that proved his final undoing. Sudhin had introduced the work of Paul Valéry and André Malraux to *Parichay*: Stéphane Mallarmé was his poetic ideal. France stood for something unshakable.

When the talk turned to France's sudden downfall clouds of pipe smoke billowed ominously around the adda's most ardent Francophile, as if he were about to combust.

"France's collapse does not mean that it wasn't as strong, militarily, as Germany, just that it was more peace loving," he said. Sudhin laughed bitterly before replying.

"Did it not occur to the French that some defensive preparations might be required?"

The man had no answer. No one did. Congress, too, had faltered in the wake of the fall of France. A new initiative to cooperate with the war effort was being discussed in meetings of its working committee. Friday-night adda continued, seemingly rudderless.

Someone ventured that if Hitler were now to invade England, Russia would swoop down on Constantinople. A few heads swiveled to see Sudhin's response, but he had gone to look for a book on his shelves. "Germany would have to establish air supremacy before invading," Sudhin finally said, returning to his seat. "Though its air force is large, its planes are too slow to evade the much faster Spitfires. They will never reach London."

The question of what India stood to gain if Britain were to be defeated was taken up. It was narrowly decided that at present India would not be well served by Britain's defeat, but the future was another matter. Many were eager to entertain the prospect of the English being taken down a peg or two.

"The British are calling Dunkirk a huge victory," Sinbad Sinclair had told Sudhin. Sinclair was yet another of Sudhin's sahibs. A silver-haired Oxonian with hairy knuckles who worked for Burmah Shell, he was a gifted talker. His wife, Elinor, was something of a memsahib, Sudhin said, but had excellent legs.

"Never before in history have so many people been transported from one place to another in such a short period and at such a limited loss of life," Humphry's friend from Oxford, Susobhan Sarkar, chimed in. "I have no hesitation in congratulating the British authorities on such an absolute success." This was intended as an olive branch. They had all begun to worry about Sudhin. He'd been needling Hiren for weeks.

"Are you happy or pleased to see the Nazis on the march all over Europe?" Sudhin asked Hiren-da, unable to temper his scorn.

"Pleased, certainly, who wouldn't be? The Brits being cornered is a matter of hope."

"Surely we don't think that after the war the Germans would be preferable as rulers than the English?" one of his acolytes asked.

"Accepting foreign domination is not something we ever think about," Hiren-da said calmly. "What we do understand is that the waning of British hegemony will lead to large-scale changes the world over. We also know that of all the imperialist powers none has been more crafty, cruel, pitiless, arrogant, and brutal than the British."

"Romans did not want in arrogance and the Germans are incomparable when it comes to cruelty," Sudhin countered.

"The Germans will incapacitate Britain and thereby weaken themselves. Class warfare will then begin and the workers will eventually triumph." Hiren doubtless knew that the Communist Party was secretly fomenting strikes in local munitions factories supplying the Middle Eastern front with war matériel. "The west has yet to grasp the war's revolutionary significance," he added; "they are approaching it simply as soldiers—tanks here, aeroplanes there."

"*Alternately*," Sudhin replied with equal smoothness, "what will happen is that the Nazis will become so confident of their military prowess that they will turn on the Soviets and that will be the end of Communism."

Sudhin's coeditor at *Parichay* had long shared Sudhin's view that the British Empire would last as long after the death of the Mahatma as the Roman Empire did after the death of Christ. But that evening he was silent, seemingly distracted by the ghugni and sandesh on the sweets table. When he could eat no more he suddenly came to life.

"I support Hiren-babu," he said, in a dramatic shift of allegiance. "However fast Germany may spread its reign, the raw material from the British and French colonies cannot be put to use overnight. If Germany and England carry on at this pace, both their economies will collapse and the workers of the world will rise up."

Sudhin ignored him, once again directing his ire at Hiren-da. Adda was nearing full boil. "When it comes to arms, Germany will always find a way. Even if the Wehrmacht is unable to secure the whole of France, the might of Britain and Free France won't be sufficient to topple it. Is that what you want? Are you now a fascist sympathizer?"

At this Hiren-da exploded.

"It was the leaders of Britain's Labour and Liberal Parties who joined hands with the capitalist moneylenders and conspired to corner Russia! This is what led them to make a hero out of Hitler!"

Even the adda diarist was inspired to speak up in Hiren-da's defense.

"From the very first, Soviet Russia has been steadfast in its efforts to join together the forces of anti-Fascism!"

When Sudhin tried to blame the rise of Hitler on the German Communist Party, Hiren was ready with facts about the paltry number of seats the party held in the Weimar government. "It was the French and English who conspired to build up the German war machine. They imagined the Nazi forces would turn on Moscow to dismantle the Soviet state. But Hitler's nerve failed. And Stalin outsmarted them all. He turned the fascists on the imperialists instead."

The diarist had never heard Hiren-babu speak at such length and with such passion.

Hiren now collected himself and turned to look at Sudhin's bookshelves.

"There are so many books in this room," he began sorrowfully, "but there is not even one monograph on the Soviet system of restructuring society."

Sudhin protested. It was unfair to say he is biased about books—to argue that amounted to an abuse of reason. It was not a compelling rejoinder. The gravitational pull Sudhin had long exerted over adda was weakening. Major planets in his solar system were drifting into another sun's orbit. The voice of Calcutta was finding a new register.

Susobhan, who'd said little all evening, turned to the watchful diarist.

"What was the reaction of your British colleagues to the fall of Paris?"

"They haven't expressed any deep sorrow," the diarist reported, "but they are jittery. They see fifth columnists under every rock, even in the most ordinary train crash. Even my Japanese customers are perplexed. 'What are the British up to?' they ask. 'Can England really afford to do nothing?' They seem more excited than anxious, as if Germany's overrunning Europe was a bonanza for them. Indeed, my British colleagues are as eager as ever to export the manganese and iron Japan requires for steel production."

He suddenly caught himself, abashed at having spoken at such length. Sudhin broke the silence.

"There are no friends or enemies when it comes to making a profit." On this all could agree.

"There is scarcely a loyalist of any note who is not bitter at heart," the editor of the *Statesman* had written Leo Amery, the new Secretary of State for India. His friend Sudhin Datta was foremost among the embittered. The editor had begged Amery to come out and salvage things with Nehru and Congress. For weeks now Amery had been after Linlithgow to call the Indian leaders together. Without the support and governance of Congress leaders, he feared India might drift into civil war and England would be held accountable. He spent the first two weeks of July lobbying the War Cabinet and frantically drafting a proposal for India to be granted full dominion status immediately after the war.

Linlithgow came round. Perhaps not having fixed a date for dominion status had left a mistaken impression, he wrote in a long cable from Delhi. Suddenly, it was not impossible that "HMG might . . . say that . . . they would spare no effort to bring about Dominion Status within a year after the conclusion of the war." A deadline was a capital idea. Should Congress stick to their demand for independence, Amery argued in his covering minute to Churchill, they could easily be portrayed as unreasonable.

Bypassing Amery, Churchill replied directly to Linlithgow. Did he truly think it wise to make promises when England was on the verge of being invaded? Churchill regarded an invasion as highly unlikely but he was happy to stoke fears of one to keep everyone on their mettle. Accordingly, the viceroy folded like a cheap umbrella, but not before blaming Amery for misleading him about the extent of his support in the War Cabinet. His cable was so long it had to be sent in installments.

"A piece of hypocrisy from beginning to end," Churchill hissed to his secretary.

– CHAPTER 15 –

The Magnified Earth

Aircraft Operating Company Factory, Wembley,
Northwest London, February 10, 1940

Michael Spender's expertise with the Wild A5 gave him an air of high-handed independence his more deskbound colleagues at the Aircraft Operating Company (AOC) could only marvel at. They had to admit that once he got his nose into a job there was no stopping him. After working straight through the night, he would go off and there was no telling when he would be back. A restless chap.

In February 1940 Michael had been sitting on his stool in the drafting office when his boss handed him a batch of five-by-five-inch transparencies. With his black eye patch and salt-and-pepper moustache, Major Harold "Lemnos" Hemming cut a cavalier figure. A former pilot with the Royal Flying Corps, he'd lost an eye during the last war and founded an aerial survey and mapmaking firm. He'd written a rejoinder to Michael's *Spectator* article defending the role of private firms in civil mapmaking. Michael convinced him to buy a Wild A5 and hire him to work on it.

Though Hemming hadn't been told where the photographs he'd handed Michael had been taken, he had an idea. He simply told Michael to extract as much information from them as possible. Entering the "Holy of Holies," the all-glass, air-conditioned room where the Wild A5 was kept, Michael inserted the first pair of photographs into the instrument and brought them into focus.

The next day a long red Hotchkiss Saloon came speeding up the drive to the factory, turning sharply in a hail of gravel before the entrance. A chauffeur jumped out and opened the rear door. A tall man unfolded his legs and emerged with a briefcase. In a few long strides Sidney Cotton stood before his former business partner and retrieved a roll of film from his briefcase.

"I've brought some more," he said. "How are you getting on?"

"Come and see," Hemming replied.

When war was declared Sidney Cotton was tasked with recruiting staff for a secret RAF unit. Before that he had been employed by France and MI6 to take clandestine aerial photographs of critical German military installations. MI6 had provided him with a customized Lockheed 12A aeroplane painted duck-egg green. He equipped it with concealed Leicas controlled by switches under the pilot's seat. On a flight pitched as a joyride, he'd managed to photograph German airfields while a Luftwaffe general sat at the controls with Cotton's fingers surreptitiously working the cameras beneath him. On the last plane out of Berlin before war was declared, Cotton saw most of the German fleet anchored at the port of Wilhelmshaven and Emden, a smaller port on the border with the Netherlands and the one closest to England. The *Tirpitz*, a sister battleship to the *Bismarck*, was in dry dock. He photographed all of it.

Michael was so intent on the photographs he'd received the day before he didn't look up until Hemming asked him about his progress.

"The scale's absurdly small," he said curtly, "which isn't surprising as I've determined the photographs were taken from a fantastic height. But I'm getting quite a lot out of them. I can plot or measure just about anything as long as I can see its outline."

Hemming translated. "The Wild gives nine times magnification."

As Cotton's photographs were at a scale of 1:80,000 (about one mile per inch), Air Intelligence had believed the images were too small to make anything out. Yet to maintain a watch on Germany at 10,000 feet would be suicidal for pilots.

"Don't worry about scale just now," Cotton said. "The cameras that took those photographs were meant to be operated from 8,000 feet. But it won't be long before we have something better."

Cotton had managed to wangle two Spitfires from the Air Ministry and was in a fierce contest for more. Despite being an honorary wing commander, despite the fact that the pilots of his secret unit had photographed the entire Ruhr district and most of the Siegfried Line without losing a single plane, the Air Ministry was doing its utmost to obstruct him. But even Spitfires couldn't accommodate cameras with the 25 mm lenses he wanted. For the moment lenses half that size had to be used, with a corresponding shrinkage in scale. A five-by-five-inch print would capture sixteen square miles instead of eight. Cotton moved over to the drafting table to look at Michael's calculations.

"I see you can measure some of the buildings all right." He paused. "And there's no reason why you shouldn't measure ships." The Admiralty was dependent on the Air Ministry for reconnaissance but they, too, were cast in the role of abject petitioners. Michael said that if he could make out their outlines, it should be possible to measure and identify ships. This was what Cotton wanted to hear. To increase flying range he planned to enlarge the gas tanks of his two Spitfires by stripping the planes of their guns. In the meantime he swore the Wembley factory to secrecy, sent a steady stream of film to Michael, and pleaded with the Air Ministry to requisition the Wild and the AOC's technical staff.

They ignored him.

Then Naval Intelligence received a report that the *Tirpitz* was no longer in dry dock at Wilhelmshaven. By the time the Admiralty approached Cotton one modified Spitfire was ready. It roared off at a hundred miles an hour, ascending to five miles above sea level. A short while later the Spitfire returned with photographs of both Wilhelmshaven and Emden. Cotton brought the film to Michael, along with a liaison officer trained in the identification of enemy ships. Less than forty-eight hours later, at 2:10 a.m. on a Sunday morning, Michael had plans for both ports drawn up, including the number and types of ships at dock, all drawn to scale. The *Tirpitz* was still in dry dock.

His report sparked incredulity. Plans of military installations couldn't be drawn from aerial photographs. Ships couldn't be identified in this way. The Air Ministry refused to let Cotton send Michael's report to the Admiralty; they wanted to sit on it. When the Admiralty still hadn't gotten word by Monday night and, furthermore, learned that Bomber Command was preparing an attack on the sixty subs at

Emden (Michael had pegged them as river barges), Cotton defied orders and sent the report directly to Naval Intelligence. That did it. The chief of naval staff alerted the then first lord of the Admiralty, Winston Churchill, that the Air Ministry had been withholding critical intelligence. Churchill was astonished that this intelligence had come through civilian channels. Wheels began to turn. Cotton was summoned.

If the Air Ministry wasn't interested, Churchill let it be known that the Admiralty would be only too happy to acquire Cotton's services along with the civilians at Wembley and this miracle machine. The air marshall in charge denied he'd ever been told about the A5, and then he and the chief of naval staff went at each other hammer and tongs. Cotton looked on bemused. Four days after the fall of France he would be sacked for having made the Air Ministry look incompetent.

That April Michael was given photographs of Kiel harbor on Germany's border with Norway. The port was crammed with ships and the nearby fields were packed with enemy bombers. As he had no previous photographs of Kiel he was at a loss to say whether this was unusual. Only then did he realize that one set of photographs was insufficient; a series marked chronologically was needed to establish historical continuity. With such a series he could intuit not only what the enemy was doing there but what their plans were. It wasn't until Germany invaded Denmark and Norway two days later that the Admiralty grasped that Cotton's photographs had captured the moment the seven-month "Bore War" came to an end. Michael's insight became known as "comparative cover" and would define the field of photographic interpretation, or PI.

Thereafter reconnaissance aircraft fitted with cameras would fly out again and again from airfields around Great Britain to photograph a predetermined area of occupied territory. As soon as the planes returned the film was developed, printed, and labeled so that the photographic interpreter on duty might recognize when a landscape or harbor configuration had changed. Photographs taken after a bombing sortie could show the aftereffects of bomb drops. If targets remained intact, the bombers went out again.

Antoine Saint-Exupéry compared this work to that of bacteriologists studying slides under a microscope. "They seek on the vulnerable body . . . traces of the virus which devours." Michael was a skilled pathologist. He developed a photographic memory of the Channel coastline and Norwegian fjords. He could refer to a previous cover, by date, sortie number, and photo number, off the top of his head.

He was born for this.

Inter-service Meeting, Whitehall, London,
   June 10, 1940

The first meeting of the Invasion Warning Sub-committee took place at the Admiralty on May 31, 1940, in the middle of the evacuation of Dunkirk. Where might the German invasion of England be launched? A number of possibilities, from the Baltic ports to Eire, were considered. Then a stray rumor reached them. A report of a conversation between the German military attaché in Ankara and a senior Turkish officer suggested that the Germans might attempt an invasion across the Channel. This seemed preposterously obvious, but Churchill agreed that the chiefs of staff should consider it.

Ten days later senior officers from Bomber Command and the Royal Navy met for a showdown over who should get Cotton's unit, his modified Spitfires, his pilots at Heston, the Wild A5, and Chief Technician Michael Spender. Bomber Command was adamant that the identification of military targets should take precedence. The Admiralty disagreed; reconnaissance should be focused on the ports and coastline. Coastal Command stepped between them, and the Air Ministry, now fully awake to the intelligence gifts coming out of the ramshackle factory at Wembley, moved in.

One-eyed Hemming and Michael Spender received Class CC commissions. Michael was made a flight lieutenant in the General Duties Branch of the RAF Reserve, intended for civilian officers. When the king and queen visited at the beginning of June 1940 they had only just received their uniforms. Seeing a file marked WILD PLANS, the king gave Hemming a royal wink and said, "You wouldn't like to show me what's in those, would you?" The more Michael gleaned from the photographs, the more the Admiralty and RAF pressed for flights, photographs, and his cornflower-blue eyes.

By the summer of 1940 there were thirty trained photographic interpreters at Wembley, twelve of them WAAFs who had once been typists. Cotton believed women, with their experience darning socks, had more patience and focus than men. Michael induced a handful of academics to join them. Everest thruster Bill Wager, his geologist colleague in East Greenland, was made pilot officer. A Cambridge archaeologist was another. Others just turned up. A plant fossil expert set up an industry section to determine how critical specific factories were to the German war effort. The retreat from Dunkirk produced a specialist in wireless and radar installations. A female aircraft journalist started an aircraft section. Michael headed up the "specialized interpreters" section. Dons, actors, choreographers, newspaper editors, writers, and one of Churchill's daughters swelled the PI ranks. Michael eventually arranged for his brother Humphrey to be brought on. Nothing would induce him to put up Stephen.

When Stephen heard that Michael was saying he wasn't taking the war seriously, he felt obliged to remind him of the time he accused him of being a warmonger. With Wystan and Christopher gone, Stephen argued, he alone had sufficient stature to finish what they had begun. He provided Michael a list of his war work. He was writing a play and a book of poems. He was often on the BBC. He wrote a monthly essay for Penguin New Writing and something for the *Listener* or the *New Statesman* every week. Finally a high official at the Ministry of Information had told him that *Horizon*, where he was on staff, was the most valuable propaganda England had for neutral countries, that is, America.

By July the photographs showed signs of unusual activity. A latticework of footpaths scoring the dove gray of a formerly pristine patchwork of fields and pasture appeared on the north coast of France. New telephone lines, identified by the early-morning shadows cast by telephone poles, pinpointed the local military headquarters. The heavy tread of truck tires exposed the white clay beneath the topsoil five miles inland from Calais, marking the locations of ammo depots. The War Office kept up a drumbeat for more covers.

In the final days of August, forty to fifty merchant ships showed up at Kiel, with another 350 large launches of a type not previously seen appearing at Emden. Fifty-six barges were suddenly missing from Amsterdam. Michael noticed that the bows of five 130-foot barges in the Rotterdam shipyards had been modified. Conceivably this might enable them to offload tanks and troops. Modified barges began showing up at the ports of Antwerp, Rotterdam, and Amsterdam. Launches and other craft were also photographed progressing down the coast toward the ports and estuaries of the Netherlands, Belgium, and northern France.

Wembley acquired an airfield section to keep a tight focus on the French coast. Every clear day Spitfires took covers of Boulogne, Calais, and Dunkirk. One hundred modified barges suddenly left Antwerp while eighteen popped up at Ostend. Photographic intelligence saw more and more movement as barges hopscotched down the coast to arrive at embarkation points opposite the white cliffs of Dover. By Friday, September 6, two hundred barges were assembled at Ostend.

69 Oriental Road, Silvertown, London,
Saturday, September 7, 1940

When the sirens went at 4:43 p.m. Nancy climbed out onto the station roof to watch for dogfights. The late-afternoon sky was pale blue with not even a scrap of cirrus. Only in the east was there an oddly shaped pink-tinged cumulus. A call came for her to collect a man who, fearing the worst, had blown out his brains. By the time she returned there was some lingering apprehension, but it was all over by 6:00 p.m. One hour after the first incendiary fell, the bomb racks were empty and the planes headed back across the Channel. Fire engines raced through the city, clanging their bells. A call went out for emergency transport. When she next ventured out the small cloud she had seen earlier had ballooned out, billowing and exploding, its color a menacing red with blackened edges.

Intelligence maps had called for German bomber pilots to focus their bomb drops on a place called Silvertown in London's docklands. After crossing the Channel the bombers had flown over the southeast coast, following the Thames west. The British chiefs of staff, meeting that afternoon in Whitehall, had been caught by surprise when the roar of the engines reached them. They had always understood that a heavy bombardment of London would precede an invasion. Was this it?

By 7:00 p.m. there was still no all clear. At 8:10 the sirens went again. A second wave of bombers was en route, the glow of the fires their beacon. Nancy's call to attend came an hour later. Two ambulances were needed at 69 Oriental Road, somewhere south of West Ham. The driver assigned to her was about fifty and balding and had driven an ambulance in the First World War. Nancy grabbed her tin hat from its peg and a load of blankets.

The ambulance took off down Holloway Road with no headlights and Nancy in the passenger seat watching bombs fall in the distance. They were driving at about forty miles an hour, but Nancy wanted to go faster. She grew testy. Her driver calmly told her they would get there in the end and that quieted her. Every few miles men in white hats holding torches waved them on. They swerved to avoid hitting a dog only to have the ambulance behind run over it. The red glow before them gave a sharp outline to the jet-black silhouette of houses. They reached the rendezvous point in West Ham where a number of Greenline buses and ambulances were parked. After waiting a bit she saw an incident officer.

"Is this right for Oriental Road?"

"Good gracious, no," he said. "Oriental Road's in Silvertown." Nine miles on. They had some trouble starting the ambulance up but with a push from some men they set off again. They dodged and dipped between streets that became more twisted and narrow as the red glow they glimpsed between houses got closer and brighter. They stopped again to ask a man the way to Silvertown. He said it was another two miles on, but there was no point in trying: the docks were aflame from the Tower of London to Tilbury. Soon there wasn't a soul to be seen.

To envision the scale of London's dockland, as critical to the enterprise of empire as the square mile of the City, one must pull back, rise several thousand feet, and view it as if one were a goggle-eyed airman. From this vantage the network of piers, warehouses, false quays, sluices, culverts, channels, entrance locks, and basins looks more like an engineering diagram than a landscape. The warehouses of the London and St. Katharine Docks began below the Tower of

London. Here derricks offloaded sacks of Australian wool and strips of Malayan rubber. The commercial docks of Surrey on the south side of the river followed. Three times bigger, they were designed to accommodate dairy produce and grain from Canada and resinous cedar, pine, Douglas fir, and spruce. Across the landward side of the hairpin loop of the Isle of Dogs were the piers of the West India and Millwall Docks. The West India Docks handled Burmese mahogany and teak, tropical fruits, molasses, and raw sugar from the West Indies. Millwall Dock was built to store grain. Adjacent to Millwall were the deepwater East India Docks. These had once serviced the thousand-ton East Indiamen carrying tea, spices, indigo, silk, and Persian carpets, ships plying every port between the Cape of Good Hope and Cape Horn. Continuing downstream hugging the north shore were the vast Royal Victoria, Albert, and King George V Docks, equipped to unload frozen meat, grain, and tobacco.

After the Isle of Dogs they drove onto a narrow swing bridge. Warehouses lit up like blazing cathedrals were collapsing in front of them. Dark-red flames enveloped the tenements crowded between the docks and the factories. Two steamers and an ocean liner were entirely alight. Bonfires of smaller craft drifted between the burning shores of the Thames. A warehouse collapsed into the river, spewing beans like a sudden downpour. Every so often a gas main would explode and another building would go up like a fountain. A dense pall of smoke arose from snaking rivers of burning tar flowing into bomb craters. And the entire scene before them was reflected in the water of the canals, basins, and locks.

Suddenly there was a line of vehicles in front of them, a few ambulances but mostly firefighting pumps, pulling water from the canals. They couldn't see what was holding things up and so they tried to pass, but a warehouse crashed across the road in front of them, burning debris thudding across the ambulance's roof. With the firemen helping them, they turned around. All the other ambulance drivers shouted there was no way to get through.

"We know another way," Nancy's driver said. He was winging it.

"Wait for us," the ambulance drivers shouted.

"We can't wait for you," Nancy shouted back. "We can't stop here;

we're jamming the roads." Antiaircraft fire could no longer be heard above the roar of fire. Searchlights rolled across the night sky like the spokes of a tremendous wheel. They found their way back to the swing bridge that, miraculously, was still there, and after trying several roads and finding them blocked, her driver left the road to cut across the burning wharf, driving over tangles of hosepipes and cinder tracks.

How quickly the fire moved, Nancy marveled, as if it was desperate to burn down everything at once. Each warehouse seemed to harbor a different sort of fire. Stacks of Canadian timber exploded, showering sparks. Barrels of West Indian rum detonated like bombs while liquefied West Indian sugar coated the surface of the Thames with fire. The smoke of smoldering peppercorns from Ceylon seared the lungs. Assamese and Darjeeling tea burned with a sickeningly sweet smoke. Clouds of flies moved over walls in a black swarm. Singed pigeons flew in confused circles above the flames while rivers of panicked rats streamed over the burning ground.

They drove up and over chairs, prams, bedsteads, roof slates, and piles of bricks. Every time they got stuck firemen would launch them forward again. At every turn another house would explode. They came to a ghastly and towering wall of flame and, in a terrific burst of speed, drove through that, too. Pulling up to a group of firemen wearing masks, Nancy rolled down the window and called out:

"Anybody hurt here?" A man removed his mask to answer: "All dead, go on."

They finally reached Silvertown, "the warehouse of the world." The construction of the Royal Docks had left Silvertown a virtual island. Factories and sweatshops took up most of the square mile between the Victoria Dock and the Thames, but there were also lodgings for thirteen thousand dock laborers and seafarers. All were without shelters. The water table was too high for cellars.

They came across a man covered in soot who had lost his wife and his mother's house was gone. They took him in. It would be weeks before men of the docklands learned whether the families they left that morning were alive or dead. The next person they asked for directions said Oriental Road was an inferno. They passed a place that looked like a deserted village, where not one two-story cottage had a roof. Finally, they arrived at a spot where no walls remained, where there was nothing but enormous empty craters ringed with debris and a jet of canary-yellow fire burning off gas in the center. This was Oriental Road.

Heads of people digging in the rubble for survivors popped out of holes in the ground. Nancy thought it looked like a scene from Wystan's war in China. Her ambulance was the first to arrive since the bombs began falling the previous night.

"Is this Oriental Road?" Nancy shouted.

"Ambulance?" one head shouted back.

"Yes, anybody hurt?"

"Over in the shelter," another head said, pointing at the large brick arches holding up an aqueduct in the smoky distance. "You can't get your ambulance there; you'll have to leave it." Nancy pulled out a stretcher, and she and the driver made their way over the rubble. She looked into what seemed like a cave under the arches and saw about forty people.

"Anybody hurt?" she asked, but was met with blank faces. She went up to a woman and grabbed her shoulder. The woman turned and pointed out another woman with a newborn baby. They had just been dug out. Two more were catatonic. The warden was dead. They loaded sixteen people into the ambulance and closed the curtains to shut out the glow of the fires. No one said a word. Later Nancy learned they had been given the wrong address; that Oriental Road wasn't in any ambulance station.

The all clear sounded sometime after dawn. The barges of Burma teak that had been set adrift to burn themselves out on the river returned with the tide on Sunday morning, still burning. The survivors of Silvertown had to be evacuated by water. A national day of prayer was called. Reverend Scott, sharing a London flat with Michael Carritt, was working as an air raid warden that night. The civil authorities, constrained by their "bowler hatted little money values," had failed to anticipate the scale of suffering, he wrote later. As he raced about in the confusion he said a prayer for Gandhi, who had.

Three weeks later entire families were still living and foraging among vistas of rubble. They were discovered taking sanctuary with the dead in the crypts of dockside churches. Still liable for rent on homes with no water, electricity, gas, or roofs, some returned home and lived under tarps. A year later, they were still there. By then the press ferreted out that Sir John Anderson, the "Home Front Prime Minister," had made more provisions for the dead than the living. When he was forced from office Winston Churchill invited him to join the war cabinet, taking the seat of the dying Neville Chamberlain. He had the former governor of Bengal in mind to replace Linlithgow as viceroy. He called Anderson Jehovah, and counted on his support to save the empire.

By the time a bomb rendered Nancy's maisonette unsafe, the windows had been shattered three times. For a while she was homeless. The editor of *Horizon* asked her to write about the first night of the Blitz but Sonia Brownell promptly handed it back, pronouncing her effort "not literature." That December, en route to a new posting Bill came by Nancy's new flat in a sentimental mood. He absolutely hated military life. Though they could never live together, he said, they could also never divorce because of their long history. They wept. Sonia had dumped him.

In the coming months Nancy would often stand on the roof of Camden station to watch the red lights of fire trucks humping their way through a dark maze of ruined streets. Wrapped in smoke against the night sky, she cut a solitary figure, secure in the knowledge that when all the East End was ablaze and five hundred ambulances were sent for, she alone had traveled sixteen miles into its fiery heart.

Aircraft Operating Company Factory,
   Wembley, Northwest London, September 17, 1940

While his squadron leader shouted over a bad phone line, Michael Spender followed the German advance sortie by sortie. Ten days after the dockland bombings, photographs showed fully stocked supply bases, an armada of merchant vessels and convoys, and 266 barges at Calais, twenty-two miles from Dover. There were another 220 at Dunkirk and 600 lined up side by side at Antwerp. When Michael arrived at midnight to check over the PI reports, the factory buzzed with anxiety. Michael calculated that 130 barges had arrived in four days. Suddenly, he threw down his stereoscope and approached a Cambridge archaeologist he had trained in PI.

"Haven't you had enough of counting barges? The invasion will happen tomorrow or the next day. Shouldn't we go down to Kent? If we could each kill one German, even if we both were killed in the attempt, it would be a good thing for this country and for history."

It was late and the man was tired after three straight shifts counting barges. The factory had been under constant bombardment. He thought for a moment while Michael's eyes bored into him.

"Your next night on duty is the day after tomorrow," the archaeologist finally said. "I shall have a car ready: we will drive to Dover."

By the time the archaeologist returned, the photographs showed barges parallel to the quays instead of perpendicular. The numbers had declined. No one knew why. When Michael came on duty at midnight, he gave the archaeologist a hard look.

"So we don't have to go to Dover," the man prompted.

"No, and just as well. You told me you were a bad shot," Michael said with his usual delicacy. "Would you now please concentrate on the occupied French ports?"

– CHAPTER 16 –

A Representative Indian

49C Hazra Road, Ballygunj, Calcutta,
  August–October 1940

The secret diarist arrived in the middle of a debate over the devastation being inflicted on the English Channel counties. All agreed that aerial bombardment was destined to take a greater human toll on land than any lives lost at sea from torpedoes. It was well-nigh impossible to make defense arrangements, Sudhin pointed out, when one out of four English citizens lived within range of German bombers. With the Spitfire, someone else volunteered, the RAF made up in skill and technology what it lacked in numbers, but how long could Great Britain sustain such losses? Not that he believed everything he heard on the wireless, he added quickly, looking at Hiren-da.

"England will surrender in a month's time," Hiren-da said with the utmost assurance.

"Germany is on the verge of collapse," Sudhin countered. "The barbaric aerial bombardment of England is a clear sign of Hitler's desperation."

Before they could start another argument, Apurba Chanda made a late but stately entrance. Since he'd begun working as Shaheed Suhrawardy's private secretary, Apurba's attendance had been spotty. Everyone eagerly anticipated his tiffins of gossip from the back corridors of Simla and Delhi. As soon as Apurba had his tea, Sudhin pounced.

"What was Congress saying about the viceroy's 'August Proposals'"?

After the fall of France Congress had once more offered to support the Allied war effort in exchange for recognition of India's right to self-rule. Linlithgow, ignoring the opening, presented his own offer several months later. He would make a few more Executive Council seats available to "representative Indians." After the war, with the *least possible delay,* he would *recommend* that His Majesty's Government call a constitutional congress to prepare a new constitution. That is, another Government of India Act, dictated from London. He was now prepared to talk but only on his terms, thereby opening and closing the door at the same time.

Linlithgow was as dim-witted as a rock, Nehru had by now decided, with a rock's corresponding self-awareness.

Apurba paused long enough for Hiren-da to jump in.

"Congress will have to reject that proposal. It has no choice but to do so."

"Will Jinnah accept it?" Sudhin asked Apurba, ignoring Hiren-da. Six months earlier Shaheed Suhrawardy had been one of the signatories of the Lahore Resolution, Jinnah's call for the creation of Pakistan, a nation of separate Muslim-majority states to be carved out of India like choice cuts of meat. When first conceived, the idea of a Muslim homeland did not include Bengal; Jinnah's focus was on the North-West Frontier Province, Baluchistan, Sindh, and the Punjab. But now Bengal was considered part and parcel of Jinnah's Pakistan scheme. Knowing Shaheed, Sudhin supposed he was already anticipating living the life of a nawab as Bengal's first native-born governor. He feared Jinnah would agree to the viceroy's offer in exchange for British support for Pakistan, with inevitably fatal consequences for Bengal.

Apurba cleared his voice and the room went quiet.

"A well-placed bureaucrat I know in Simla told me that the arrogance and bragging of each and every white bureaucrat from the viceroy on down had risen manifold since the publication of the August Offer." Apurba summed up the official mood: "Whether we win or lose the war, at least we won't be stupid enough to hand over power to the natives."

When the wireless began broadcasting news of air attacks on London and the signing of a tripartite treaty between Japan, Italy, and Germany, Hiren-da made every effort not to gloat. By October at the latest, he said quietly, it would be all over. Britain would collapse and Stalin would demand that India be freed.

At the end of September, the assembled shouted at the sight of Shahid Suhrawardy at the door. Despite all he had undergone in the last few months, his pince-nez was still firmly secured and his coiffed pate remained as sleek as a seal's. He began by reading a lengthy letter addressed to the adda from Basanta Kumar Mallik, now back at Oxford. The war would not distract him from committing to paper his theory of conflict, Mallik-da wrote; the work *must* go on. The secret diarist was impatient for Shahid to get to the real story—his escape from Nazi-occupied Paris.

When the Wehrmacht first marched in, Shahid began, the wireless went dead, the water, electricity, and gas were shut off, and the city was enveloped in a thick black smoke from burning fuel stocks. Once the Germans were in position at the major arterial crossings the connections were promptly restored. There was absolutely no resistance. Even the traffic police stayed at their posts. It took him three days to acquire one hundred liters of petrol and make his escape. Driving at night to avoid aircraft machine-gun fire, their caravan of vehicles raced through the countryside at high speeds. They were an assortment of Russian and Indian intellectuals, British generals, French citizens and Jews, all subsisting on nothing but fine red wine until they got to Bordeaux. There Shahid boarded a British vessel already filled with Jewish refugees, each having paid handsomely for a berth.

Shahid spared a few words of praise for the British Navy, but it was the single-minded discipline of the Wehrmacht in Paris that he found remarkable. Only one restaurant in every arrondissement was open to them and hotels were entirely off limits. He saw no looting or any show of indiscipline, remarking only on the sight of German soldiers transfixed by the department store window displays.

Listening intently, the adda's resident Francophile disappeared in clouds of smoke, winding his chadder even more tightly round his neck as if to throttle himself. Sudhin had already heard most of it and was quiet. The adda diarist had heard Sudhin was suffering from an obscure malaise. His mother had even made a rare appearance,

arriving from Hatibagan to check on him. It was the first time the
diarist had ever seen her. She was said to be very traditional. Indeed,
he noted, she was careful not to come into contact with the doorway
curtain in fear of caste pollution. When Sudhin assured her he was
feeling better, he lifted it up so she could pass through cleanly.

October passed and still England hung on and there was not a peep
from Stalin on the subject of India's freedom. When someone ventured
to speculate on Stalin's motives, Hiren-da laughed.

"Okay, fine," Sudhin said sharply. "Why don't you enlighten us?"

Where Susobhan argued that Stalin was simply using his pact with
Hitler to buy time to prepare Russia for war with Germany, Hiren-da
believed England was Soviet Russia's real enemy and India her natural
ally. If Stalin hadn't as yet demanded India's freedom, Hiren-da supposed it was only because he didn't want to impugn India's self-respect.

"Stalin knows that Britain's hold on its colonies can be loosened
only by attacking London. Oppressed people everywhere are fed up
and desperate. Any opening will create opportunities for socialism to
flourish." The adda diarist looked at Sudhin for his reply.

"It is absurd to think that the people of India will tolerate Soviet
Communism," Sudhin said. Apurba piped up, red faced and indignant.

"Do you think our rulers are any less cruel and ruthless than the
Nazis?"

"There is nothing as barbaric as Nazi brutality in the whole of human
history," Sudhin said, his voice breaking into a high pitch. "What can
be more heartless than indiscriminately eliminating a large section of
people who have built up the nation over the centuries, just because
they are Jews?" Boatloads of Jews had arrived in Calcutta with Shahid
Suhrawardy, their faces worn with exhaustion. "I will take you to a
man in this city, a peaceful, learned man who never had anything to
do with politics and whose only luxury was collecting art. They seized
ten of his paintings and forced him to leave Germany destitute! What
can be more barbaric than this?"

"You have no idea of the sort of torture practiced by our civilized
rulers on the Chittagong revolutionaries," Apurba replied heatedly.
"They are the real barbarians—do you know how much pleasure they
derived from tying up people's hands and feet and inserting chilies

into their orifices? Have you heard of how, in village after village, the young and old, whether human or animal, were locked up in their homes and burnt alive?"

"Whatever you may say, I am talking about a people uprooted wholesale from their homeland."

However much he despaired over the state of Calcutta, Sudhin Datta could not imagine a worse fate than exile. Granted, the British were obtuse fools. What would it have cost them to acknowledge India's right to self-rule? Nothing. But he was now deeply concerned about Jinnah's designs on Bengal. He hoped Gandhi's call for a return to satyagraha would cut the ground from under the Muslim League. Chosen individuals had been enlisted to read out seditious statements to court imprisonment; Nehru was one of the first to be arrested. He had just begun a four-year prison sentence.

"Muslims in Madras are doing satyagraha now," Sudhin said. Any expression of solidarity from Muslims was a sign of hope.

"Gandhi will lose his nerve," Hiren-da predicted. A number of his Communist comrades were signing the satyagraha pledge with the sole intention of exposing Gandhi's nonviolent strategy as toothless. Muslims might well be doing the same.

Sudhin had it from a reliable source that Germany intended to apply more economic pressure on England before attempting an invasion. He prayed England could hold them off.

"It won't be easy to separate England from its empire and its enormous resources spread all across the globe," Hiren-da responded, impressed despite himself that England was still standing, three months into the Blitz.

Nether Worton House, Worton, Oxfordshire,
    Spring 1941

At first glance a pocket stereoscope looks like a pair of metal spectacles standing upright like a tiny table, on four stems rather than two. Two round apertures are fitted with magnifying lenses; an indentation accommodates a nose. The device is placed on a desk over a pair of images. A photographic interpreter would then hunch over to peer through the lenses, manipulating the images with his hands until that moment when the two views of the object of interest, taken from two slightly different bases, pop up in three dimensions.

Here one has to pull back and imagine a far larger stereoscope, one fitted with lenses of a magnifying power as yet unknown, so as to square London's view of the war with Calcutta's. This would require a photograph of the war be taken from each city and placed under the stereoscope so as to obtain a three-dimensional view. In the spring of 1941 Michael Spender's uncle, Sir George Ernest Schuster MP, had a similar idea.

India's former finance minister was then in the feverish throes of completing his magnum opus, *India and Democracy*. The *Times* and the *Spectator* carried his editorials on how to break the viceroy's deadlock with Congress. His pet proposal addressed just this misalignment of Indian and English views. A representative Indian, he suggested, should be invited to London to witness the courageous spirit awakened by the Blitz. By seeing the British people and the war they were fighting from nearly the same angle as George Schuster saw it, such an Indian might better convey to India that England, and all it stood for, was worth fighting for.

And what did England stand for? The image of London's elegant terraced streets reduced to rubble had wholly eclipsed the shame of the Munich Agreement. For the Ministry of Information there was no better propaganda for visiting American dignitaries apt to question the legitimacy of the British Empire than a night of bombing. Those envoys to Berlin who, two years before, had treated the Reich Chancellor's designs on Austria and Czechoslovakia as not entirely illegitimate, those statesmen who had proposed bartering a French or Portuguese colony here or there in exchange for business as usual, were never mentioned. Winston Churchill was the man of the hour. If only India would see it.

Upon his appointment as viceroy Linlithgow had received a lecture from a cranky backbencher whose political career was said to be finished. Any effort to open channels between the Congress Party and the Muslim League, this MP said, was to his mind "distressing and repugnant in the last degree." Winston Churchill hadn't been setting India policy then. Now he was and for him, the solemn promise of Commonwealth status for India was one that might be endlessly deferred. "As you have laid it down yourself," Amery reminded him, the basis of British policy was to insist "Indian divisions and not our refusal to surrender authority [was] holding back India's march towards the 'declared goal.'" Amery assured him he could hold the line.

But the line wasn't holding. *Time* magazine was openly skeptical. The *New York Daily News* was talking of "Imperialistic exploitation" and portraying Gandhi as the "greatest single man in India." Eleanor Roosevelt, friendly with a journalist who had Gandhi's ear, was pressing her husband on the subject. FDR's secretary of state, in turn, pressed the British ambassador. Where was India in the "partnership of Nations"? Repeating the ritual invocation, the ambassador cited the Hindu-Muslim deadlock.

Once blithely indifferent to the impact of the price of salt on the Bengali peasant, Sir George Schuster was now more receptive to India's plight. England took India too much for granted, he said. He lay awake at night wondering how best to mobilize the spirit of India. He had visions of Nehru and Gandhi addressing crowds of hundreds of thousands, whipping up war enthusiasm in native hearts. "What a story that might be!"

On top of India's spiritual wealth, there was also the more pressing question of its material contribution. As Sir George was then working in war production, this was paramount; no one understood India's critical importance as well as he did. Here was India's chance to become an arsenal of democracy, to join the ranks of the great industrial powers, equal to any in the Commonwealth, including, he dared say, Great Britain. Nearly two years into the war it was a scandal that India's total expenditures were only up 30 percent. Uncle George had this from Leo Amery. Blessed with the largest high-grade iron ore deposits in the world, India somehow had less than 1 percent of America's industry. The manufacture of automobiles and aircraft remained a distant dream; even wireless sets and power tools had to be imported. "Can anyone be satisfied that India's possible contribution has yet been visualised on anything approaching the full scale?" Sir George asked. What was the holdup? The Americans had wondered the same thing, eventually sending over a captain of industry to find out.

Crisscrossing the subcontinent, John Auden was writing feasibility reports on various hydroelectric schemes, while bemoaning his rejection by the RAF. The GSI director had penned a confidential memo suggesting steel mills be constructed near coal-fired power stations, such as the one at Ranigunj. But if attached to existing reservoirs, hydroelectric power stations fed by the great rivers cascading from the Himalaya might supply electricity even more cheaply. John imagined he was working on behalf of a postwar India, but the groundwork being laid for a manifold increase in India's industrial capacity was not for India's defense and well-being but the empire's.

Sir George posed a delicate question: were British industrial interests perhaps fearful of an unfettered India? He knew very well they were. The tycoon in charge of aircraft production suspected Amery of conspiring to produce "Baboo" aeroplanes. But England was now fighting for its life, Sir George argued. Congress must be made to understand that England's war aims were in complete accord with India's aspirations. There was only one man who could invite India to be an equal partner. Only one man could convince Nehru and Gandhi that England was in earnest. One speech from Winston Churchill could have as catalytic an impact on India as it had on the home front.

"He need only tell the truth," Sir George implored, "truth as to the urgency of the peril—truth that this is India's war as much as ours—truth as to the greatness of India's opportunity—truth as to the British people's desire to see India grasp this opportunity to rise to her full stature, and then take her place as one of the most powerful partners in our Commonwealth—a British Commonwealth now, but to be enlarged, it may be, to a wider family of free nations when the war is over."

49C Hazra Road, Ballygunj, Calcutta,
     March 18, 1941

Sudhin was in the middle of an argument with Protap Bonnerjee when Minnie Bonnerjee arrived with M. N. Roy and his wife. Everyone rose. Roy was unshaven and disheveled, as if he hadn't seen a barber in some time. Recent personal attacks had clearly taken a toll.

After the fall of Paris Roy, too, had had a change of heart. Neutrality was no longer an option. He'd called for Congress to join a global mass mobilization against fascism, without preconditions. For his efforts, he was derided as a British lackey and condemned as a traitor and a quisling. Nehru stripped him of his Congress membership for a year. "How do I become less of a patriot," he responded angrily, "less of a freedom fighter by supplying a spade to Mr. Winston Churchill, to dig the very grave of the British Empire he has sworn never to liquidate?" This was a war of attrition, he argued; England had a chance to prevail but its empire would never survive. No one was listening. He'd been away too long.

Sudhin asked Roy if the Germans were using the confiscated wealth of the Jews to buy raw materials to sustain their war effort. Roy's wife piped up. Loans advanced by London banks before the war enabled Germany to stockpile raw materials.

"Let us have tea rather than talk," her husband interrupted. "We have come here to have tea." As if to make up for his rudeness, Roy praised the chire bhaja.

Once again, the secret diarist wrote, the great revolutionary wasn't going to join any serious discussion with nobodies like them. But he was pleased to get a closer look at the man. He sketched a mental cartoon; with a slight exaggeration of Roy's teeth and his wild crop of hair, he might get a good likeness. Roy's foreign wife switched subjects.

"My husband is quite indifferent to a woman's looks. He can scarcely tell one from another."

"That is why we are such good friends," Minnie replied, laughing.

Sudhin was taking a book from his bookshelf when yet another Bonnerjee sister arrived.

"Carry on," Anila said. "I am in a quandary over a baby bear—I can't think of what to feed him." Anila, like Minnie, talked too much, the diarist noted.

"Ask Uncle Joe," Sudhin said, nodding at Anila's Pushkin scholar, a Stalinist, sprawled on one of the sheet-covered mattresses.

"Or Rosa Luxemburg," Uncle Joe parried, indicating Roy's wife, a German Jew.

"Why worry, when M. N. Roy is here?" someone else suggested, with shocking irreverence. The diarist was trying not to look at Roy to see if he had heard when Anila sat down next to him. He told her he had twice tried to tame bear cubs but each time they burrowed into the floor of their cages and escaped.

But before he could continue, the geologist brother of the poet arrived with his pregnant wife. The adda was now officially overrun with women, he thought, grumpily. Lindsay Emmerson was said to have recently proposed to Minnie over the telephone. After accepting, she asked, "Who *is* this?" All that remained now, the diarist reflected, was for Anila to marry her Pushkin scholar. Then three out of four Bonnerjee sisters would have married Englishmen. Sheila Auden had begun the trend; he supposed babies were next.

It had taken Sheila Bonnerjee's departure for Bombay in November 1939 for John to think of marrying her. Her exhibition had been a great success. Her letters had been full of soirees at the homes of wealthy and cultured Parsees. There was a dance hosted by a baronet and a dinner with an industrialist from the Tata family. John became haunted by the fear that she'd meet and marry a rich Parsee. Engaged just after Christmas, they were wed in February 1940.

When John wrote his mother that he had married Sheila Bonnerjee her response was so mild he was sure she hadn't understood. He wrote again. "I quite realized that Sheila is an Indian," Constance Rosalie replied, telling him that people treated the subject rather differently nowadays. Though she was pleased to learn that the Bonnerjees were high-caste Brahmins, she did hope Sheila would become a Christian. As far as having children, she felt it might be better if they didn't, but of course it was up to them. A baby was expected in May; Constance Rosalie died in her sleep not long after receiving a photograph of her granddaughter.

"Since I began coming to this adda membership has been dwindling," Minnie observed, when the talk turned desultory. It was true; the adda was withering away. The diarist was not alone in blaming the women for that.

"Perhaps I should stop coming," Minnie prodded. Silence descended.

"We value quality over quantity," the diarist finally said, gallantly.

At the same time Rabindranath Tagore was dying, as if some mystical connection bound Parichay adda, Tagore, together with the fate of Bengal. Sudhin was preparing a *Parichay* festschrift on the poet;

they were all working on essays. Even more unexpected, Sudhin had taken to praising Hiren-da, remarking that many were saying that given his rhetorical gifts he was Bengal's only hope. Hiren-da ignored him. Privately, Sudhin was convinced the world had gone stark raving mad and even so drastic a remedy as communism couldn't cure it. The times seemed to call for a more cosmic disruption, he told John, a large die-off like the mass extinctions evident in the geological record. With Nehru's imprisonment, the quick collapse of Gandhi's satyagraha, and the resurgence of the Muslim League under Shaheed in Bengal, it seemed unlikely Bengal would survive the war intact.

Shahid Suhrawardy was among the adda's Muslims. He had shared Sudhin's hope that the Muslim leaders of the Punjab and Bengal might derail Jinnah's call for the creation of Pakistan. If a majority of Muslims in these two provinces could be won over, Jinnah's plan would fall on its face, it was thought. Now that seemed wishful, in large part due to his own brother.

Sudhin blamed Shaheed Suhrawardy for actively manipulating genuine Muslim grievances to shore up his flailing political career and tighten the Muslim League's hold on Bengal. British commercial concerns, equally invested in fanning and financing Muslim unrest, were among his patrons. The British governor appointed him to powerful positions. No one needed to be reminded of how Viceroy Curzon had purchased the support of a powerful Muslim nobleman of Dacca for the 1905 partition of Bengal with a loan of one hundred thousand pounds.

Jinnah's dream of Pakistan was beginning to feel inevitable.

"It's not as if the Muslims of India are limited to Bengal or the Punjab," Sudhin protested; they were everywhere. "The entire notion is impractical." Did Jinnah imagine that both provinces would be his? What would that even look like? Bengal was more than a thousand miles from the Punjab. He feared Jinnah was prepared to incite a civil war between Hindus and Muslims to get his way. The man compromised with no one, Sudhin said, neither the viceroy nor Gandhi.

"Perhaps only communism can unite us," another of the adda's Muslims said, looking quite defeated.

"If India were to become more of an industrial power than a rural one," Sudhin said, "perhaps socialism might have a chance." Hiren-da was quiet.

When someone mentioned Subhas Bose, everyone wanted to know where he was hiding. After feigning illness to get out of jail, he had escaped from house arrest. Everyone at the adda was eager to speculate. Someone said he had disguised himself as a Sikh and was now in Japan raising an army to march on India. At the mention of Japan, the adda diarist piped up.

"Our firm is giving greater importance than ever to the export of manganese and iron to Japan." This was the last entry in what survives of his secret diary.

And so, as late as March 18, 1941, at least one English firm in Calcutta was still selling iron and manganese to Japan. Japan was believed to be China's problem. Even the governor of Bengal couldn't figure out what Japan was up to. With the best Indian divisions off fighting Germans in the North African desert, or marooned in the foothills of the Hindu Kush awaiting the Russians, the real danger to the empire had yet to be divined.

Hatibagan, 129 Cornwallis Street, Calcutta,
    December 23, 1941

Sudhin at thirty-nine was considered too old to be eligible for military duty, so he accepted a post as deputy officer-in-charge of Air Raid Precautions (ARP), relinquishing the adda to the Communists and stepping down from the editorship of *Parichay*. The end of Sudhin's adda meant that when the Blitz ended abruptly that May there was no one to note Susobhan Sarkar's thoughts on Hitler's decision not to invade England. And when, on June 22, the Wehrmacht suddenly began its march on Moscow, there was no one to ask Hiren-da whether Stalin still planned to come to India's rescue. Finally, in a development too head snapping for many to absorb, when the viceroy lifted the ban on the Communist Party, Hiren-da began calling on everyone to support the Allied fight against the Fascists. The Popular Front was dead and once again Gandhi and Congress represented the voices of the petit bourgeois, the baboos.

Nor would there be anyone to record Sudhin's response to the death of Rabindranath Tagore on August 7, 1941. As the barbarity reached new levels in the heart of Europe, Tagore had also suffered a loss of faith. Before his death he had voiced the anguish for which Sudhin could no longer find the words.

"I had hoped that the leaders of the British nation, who had grown apathetic to our suffering and forgetful of their own sacred trust in India ... would at last, in the time of their own great trial, awake to the justice and humanity of our cause," Tagore wrote in a letter to Bishop Foss Wescott. "It has been a most grievous disappointment to me to find that fondly cherished hope receding farther and farther from realization each day."

By the end of 1941, Sudhin had returned to live with the joint family at Hatibagan and threw himself into his work at Air Raid Precautions. By then England had been forcibly reminded that it had an empire to defend. Twenty light bombers were all that were on hand to meet the Japanese attack on December 10 off the coast of Malaya that left the prize battleships, the *Repulse* and the *Prince of Wales*, on the bottom of the South China Sea, along with a hundred thousand tons of merchant shipping. Two weeks later, Rangoon was bombed, sending a cascade of refugees towards Calcutta. Hong Kong surrendered on Christmas Day.

"[Should India] be attacked and find herself without any of the necessary materials and equipment for defence, the political effect would be disastrous," the newly appointed commander-in-chief of the Indian Army had warned Churchill four months before. His predecessor had requested tanks to make up at least one armored division but the prime minister had demurred, asking him, "How do you know that they wouldn't turn and fire the wrong way?" Two million raw British recruits were sent to India instead, not to defend it, but to maintain law and order.

Exactly one year after the viceroy's "August Offer" of 1940, Roosevelt and Churchill had signed the Atlantic Charter. The second clause of the third point read, "Sovereign rights and self-government may be restored to those from whom it has been forcibly removed." FDR and Churchill were thinking of those countries occupied by the Axis powers, but that was not how the Atlantic Charter was read in India. When, in the wake of Pearl Harbor, Roosevelt raised the question of India with him directly, Churchill threw one of those spectacular tantrums so familiar to Leo Amery. When it came to India, Amery confided to his diary, the PM was "really not quite normal." FDR backed down.

But the question of whether the charter applied to India could not be so easily brushed off. At the end of the year Churchill stood before the House of Commons to proclaim in language calculated to set India on fire: "I have not become the King's First Minister in order to preside over the liquidation of the British Empire." The following morning the entire War Cabinet looked down their noses while Churchill launched into an apoplectic rant at the humiliating prospect of being kicked out of India by "the beastliest people in the world next to the Germans." He wasn't referring to the Japanese.

In these months of upheaval Sudhin disappeared from view, throwing himself into the task of readying bomb shelters and conducting ARP training sessions. Even in happier times his closest friends often found Sudhin inaccessible, his true feelings masked by a warm yet enigmatic smile. When his beloved father passed away and Hatibagan filled with weeping women this smile, combined with his navy blue ARP uniform, set him apart. John Auden once asked him about his grief, only to retreat when he didn't reply. Had he trespassed upon a private reserve? Had he not tried hard enough to break through?

He didn't ask again.

Nether Worton House, Worton, Oxfordshire,
late 1941

While Wystan Auden and Christopher Isherwood might have been justified leaving Chamberlain's England, they had missed an opportunity by not returning once the Blitz began. That, at least, was Stephen Spender's view. "We are where we are, because we believe what we believe," he now declared. Yet when Michael had refused to recommend him for something lofty in Naval Intelligence, Stephen had become huffy at having to join the Civil Defence Corps, having divested himself fully of his communist robes. Why should he accede to the "vulgar demand" from the "mass life outside?" By his lights there was sufficient valor in having stayed put.

Stephen eventually relented and joined the fire brigades. His duty largely confined him to a stuffy recreation room where the wireless was always tuned to the lowbrow BBC Light Programme. He lasted five months before securing a post leading civic discussion groups. Having washed his hands of all European isms, there was now a virtue in being "simply English," albeit of a superior sort. Wystan accused him of becoming his father or, worse, a literary version of his uncle.

Uncle George was just as eager as his nephew to broadcast England's rediscovered virtue. Amid the turmoil in the East, however, Sir George Schuster's *India and Democracy* had had few takers. As India would doubtless be Japan's next destination and target, Linlithgow didn't feel that seeing to the proper distribution of George Schuster's book was the business of his government. When Sir George asked the British ambassador in Washington if anything could be done to improve American sales, he received no reply.

The Secretary of State for India did his best. Amery sent two dozen copies to the Propaganda Ministry. The Empire Division purchased 426 copies for itself and the Colonial Office. As it was quite the tome, a précis of the book's conclusions was requested. Someone suggested the summary convey that responsible public men in England were genuinely anxious to see India succeed. The sole problem was to settle on the ways and means. Linlithgow found this fatuous.

In a final effort to portray relations between England and India in a more agreeable light, for the concluding chapter of *India and Democracy* Sir George orchestrated a debate between himself and a representative Indian, albeit an imaginary one.

"I think it's too late to talk as you do," this Indian told him frankly. "We don't trust you any more. Your proposals involve asking us to be satisfied with something less than full self-government, and to trust the British to make a final surrender in the end."

"Of course we have made many mistakes," Uncle George parried, "and missed many opportunities but the fault isn't all ours. . . . The 'too late' formula [is] an easy excuse for never being ready to take responsibility."

"I think you are rather too simple-minded when you talk like that," his Indian replied.

The worm had turned.

A war is not a stone cairn on a mountain peak. It has neither a fixed point nor is there a fixed stance from which to view it. Even those men standing over maps laid out on tables cannot see it. Theirs is the gaze from the summit. They have mapped in advance the location of coal mines and steel mills, oil fields and airfields. They can call up a million men, a million tons of grain, at the snap of their fingers. Intelligence cables from across the globe feed their calculations. Histories written about them or by them will reenact the conflict in front of maps showing the ebb and flow of their power. All will confuse the map for the war itself. In this way history erases the nameless millions, those lives heedlessly set adrift on tides beyond their control, without even a shallow grave to mark their passing.

Had Sudhin Datta been George Schuster's representative Indian, he would never have seen the war the way Schuster longed for it to be seen. Whenever Sudhin immersed himself in Western books or perspectives, he was haunted by the thought that he was betraying something essential to the man he was. Yet whatever his pride as an Indian, and however highly he regarded Bengali literature or the traditions of Indian philosophy, when he explored Indian modes of thinking it was his Western mind that gave him no rest.

Sudhin lost his voice after the fall of France. His once elliptical and passionate prose now conveyed the impression of having been written by a foreigner writing in his second or third language. He abandoned his father's belief that Bengal had been revitalized by its marriage with English thought. In his darkest, most defeated moods he would come to suspect there was something unstable about a mind that was a compound of East and West.

And therein lay his marital impasse. Sudhin couldn't participate in the daily domestic life of his household because he was never wholeheartedly of it. He could never find that sweet spot where two views of the same mountain became one.

− CHAPTER 17 −
An Infinite Ocean of Sorrow

During the Great War over sixty-four thousand Indian soldiers died defending the British Empire. The cost of outfitting, arming, and employing all of them, for a cause that was unclear even to those over whose borders the war was fought, fell upon India's treasury. India forgave £100 million of Britain's war debt, leading to a fiscal crisis that lasted into the 1930s. In 1940 Great Britain reluctantly agreed to shoulder the lion's share of the cost of men and military stores India exported to foreign theaters. Conceivably, at a certain point India might go from a nation in perpetual debt to Great Britain, to one in whose debt Great Britain would find itself. After that, the longer the war, the greater the debt.

The idea of His Majesty's Government owing India anything was an abomination to Winston Churchill. When India wasn't the Jewel in the Crown, it was the cross "the shoulders of our small island" had to bear. The only way to halt the rise in sterling balances, Secretary of State for India Leo Amery told him, was to stop mobilizing Indian soldiers. At the war's peak over fifty thousand recruits were being added to the Indian army every month. Linlithgow described the two and a half million sepoys who would eventually serve in Africa, the Near East, Burma, Malaya, and Europe as the "largest volunteer force in history," as if they had all signed up in a burst of indignation at the trampled freedoms of the Poles.

To George Schuster's evident satisfaction, along with providing soldiers India had also begun churning out shipments of boots and blankets, millions of yards of jute for sandbags and textiles for uniforms, tents, and parachutes, as well as consignments of iron, steel, coal, and timber. With the sudden access to American financing, even "Baboo aeroplanes" began rolling out. Over two hundred aerodromes supplanted rice paddies all over Bengal and Bihar. While Nehru tended vegetables in his jail yard, every class of Indian, from the wealthiest Parsee to the lowliest munitions worker, was mobilized. This was not an expression of support for the Allies. Rather, it was a simpler calculation: there was money to be made. Great Britain's sterling debt began to rise.

Even so there was a hitch; accounts would be settled only after the war. Until then, India was as powerless to stem the outflow of money as of men. Since the viceroy was unable to impose sufficient measures to fund the war, the Government of India mostly just printed money. Before the war three billion rupees were in circulation; by the end it was twenty-two billion. More than any of the back-channel intrigues between the prime minister and his viceroy, this arrangement would dictate who the victors were when the guns went quiet, who the vanquished. In no place would this be more true than the province of Bengal.

Memo from Intelligence Bureau, Home Dept.,
  New Delhi to Special Branch, Calcutta, March 12, 1942

"A new station calling itself FREEDOM INDIA has recently been picked up broadcasting on 9400 KC/S in Hindustani from 16.00 to 16.15 hours BST and in English 16:15–16.30 hours BST. It has been located at a place about 75 miles south of Dresden. This Bureau would be grateful for your report on the effect of this station's broadcasts in your jurisdiction.

"Uses abusive language against the British and constantly describes them as 'dogs' or 'jackals.' It also recapitulates alleged horrors perpetrated by the British on Indians, extols the Axis powers to seventh heaven and exhorts Indians to rebel and throw off the shackles of slavery."

Reply from Special Branch,
  Lord Sinha Road, Calcutta

"The effect of this station on the listener is not bad as they . . . use filthy language. No information about any other station known as Freedom India or Azad Hind could be obtained."

Portmore Nursing Home, Simla,
     August 8, 1942

Sheila Auden was visiting friends in Delhi when another effort to break the impasse between the viceroy and Congress was launched. It was a tremendous tamasha. In the wake of the fall of Singapore and Burma, Sir Stafford Cripps arrived in Delhi in March 1942 bearing a new offer from His Majesty's Government to run by Congress leadership.

Cripps's arrival coincided with the appearance in the Bay of Bengal of the fleet of Admiral Chuichi Nagumo, carrying the squadrons that had laid waste to Pearl Harbor four months earlier. The world press, in town to report on the Cripps proceedings, took bets. Who would get to India first: Cripps with his piece of paper or Japanese Zeros? India was wide open: there was not one armored car or tank, bomber or fighter plane, in the entire country. While Delhi was teeming with princes and politicians out to get what they could, Bengal was bracing for an air attack and a Japanese landing force; its coast was better supplied with carrier pigeons than warships.

Everyone was violently excited, Sheila wrote John from Delhi.

The first thing the foreign press noted was how few Englishmen they spoke to had ever even met Jinnah, Nehru, or Gandhi. And they thought it odd that during the three weeks of talks not one Congress leader was allowed to speak directly with Jinnah. It was like a game of blindman's buff, one journalist said. Roosevelt's envoy, there to assist in the militarization of India's economy, was drawn into the negotiations only to see Cripps undermined by subterfuge and sophistry. To all appearances Churchill had played him.

"Everyone was frightfully disappointed in the Cripps proposals," Sheila wrote John when it was all over. After that she resolutely refused to read the papers. For the sake of her daughter, Anita, and the new baby she was carrying, she felt obliged to remain calm and composed, averting her eyes even from the headlines. She was glad that John was in Calcutta with Sudhin, Sushoban, Shahid, and Minnie. That is, if social life was even possible. Prices were a scandal. The cost of living was up 400 percent. Minnie was dead broke.

Poor Minnie. She'd had no word from Lindsay since the fall of Singapore and was fretting over reports of Japanese atrocities. A part of Sheila understood how years of being mortified at the hands of Europeans might breed an insane hatred. She had frankly relished the prospect of those who had so lorded their invincibility over others being humiliated in return. She wasn't proud of that, but there it was. John agreed that it would be unwise for her to return to Calcutta for the baby's birth, so Sheila traveled to Simla to await the birth of her second child. Without Elinor Sinclair for company, the hill station would have been impossibly lonely.

Sheila had met Elinor and Sinbad Sinclair at one of Sudhin's drink and stand-ups. That evening Chhabi had made a rare appearance. She had quietly set out prawn and chicken curries, along with crisp puris blown up like small balloons and decorated with a sprinkling of red pepper. While her guests drank, talked, and ate around her, Chhabi had stood as still as a Jamini Roy portrait. Elinor had been sitting by herself watching her when Sheila, then hugely pregnant with Anita, approached to ask for baby advice. They talked until 2:00 a.m. Elinor had shown up at her flat the next morning with her old pram, begging her to accept it. The Audens were soon dining at the Sinclair's home upon beef stroganov and chocolate pudding or meeting at Shahid Suhrawardy's for games of badminton and tennis.

At their flat at the bottom of Jakhu Hill in Simla, they hung hand-loom curtains. Sheila painted ballet dancers on the sitting room wall. Monkeys came in through the windows, snatching precious fruit off the table and frightening the children. They tortured themselves remi-niscing about the crab soup, sweet-and-sour pork, and fried prawns at Nanking restaurant, those breakfasts with tinned fruit and cream or ham omelets served with proper marmalade and not the glutinous mess they all had now. The food in Simla was revolting. And then the rains came.

Whenever Sheila heard "J'attendrai" on the neighbor's wireless she would long for those evenings when the Firpo's orchestra would strike up this song as soon as she and John walked through the doors. But the music program was always followed by Subhas Bose's hectoring broadcasts declaiming Axis triumphs on every front, the pending an-nihilation of Britain, and the coming liberation of India. Sheila would leave the room. But for the arrival of refugees who had survived the

nine-hundred-mile journey from Burma, the war felt a million miles
away. Indeed, a fortnight after the baby's birth, John was still awaiting
word of it. None of Sheila's Express telegrams had reached him. His
letters had become increasingly frantic.

"We shall either free India or die in the attempt. We shall not live
to see the perpetuation of our slavery," Gandhi had said as the police
closed in, days after Sheila entered the Portmore Nursing Home for
her confinement. The last of Gandhi's mass protests, the Quit India
Movement, had begun. By way of a reply, Linlithgow declaimed that
the time for "appeasement" was over; Congress would now be crushed.
While Sheila was giving birth, peaceful protests in Calcutta were met
with lathi charges and tear gas. A mob descended on Cornwallis Street,
attacking a tram with brickbats and setting it on fire, along with the
street's gas and electric meter boxes. Rioting crowds were fired upon.
Congressites were rounded up by the tens of thousands and put behind bars in secret locations. While John Auden waited for word of
the birth of his second child and Sheila listened to a deafening rain
batter the tin roof, bridges were being blown up, rail lines dismantled,
telegraph and telephone lines cut. "A peculiar feature of the disturbances," a puzzled editorial writer noted, "has been hostility to post
offices and pillar boxes."

Referencing "secret evidence," Leo Amery denounced Nehru and his
lot as wicked men and saboteurs on the Empire Service, rebroadcast
on All-India Radio. Viceroy Linlithgow piled on, accusing Congress
of directing "bomb outrages and other acts of terrorism." Calcutta's
Special Branch pounced on an informer who provided details of the
courier system between Subhas Bose's fifth columnists and Gandhi's
ashram. When questioned, the man admitted his source was a swami
with mystic powers but Special Branch went with it.

One of Subhas Bose's broadcasts suggested it wasn't the imprisoned Congress leaders directing the sabotage but the BBC Eastern
Service. Bose, who listened to George Orwell's broadcasts as closely
as Orwell listened to his, had heard him speculate about what effect
"unchecked sabotage" might have on German war operations. "A few
blows from a sledgehammer in the right place can stop a power station
working. One tug at the wrong signal lever can wreck a train. Quite a

small charge of explosive can sink a ship." Perhaps Indian saboteurs had taken up his suggestions, Bose hinted, mischievously. They had. In response to police atrocities, rebels in Midnapore district embarked on an insurgent campaign of assassination, sabotage, and extortion that would last for two years.

Unaware of the insurgency under way, Sheila sent another cable to John and wrote letter after letter. She couldn't bear Lila as a name for the baby. She would always think of that pretentious Lila Ghosh and inevitably Lila would be called Lily at school and that would be just too awful. Elinor had suggested Romila. Could John ask Sudhin what it meant? Sudhin had been promising to visit all summer, only to beg off by citing his work with Air Raid Precautions. She would have so loved a visit. Simla was overrun with women and healthy men were a rare sight. The only men there were recovering from dreadful diseases picked up in Burmese jungles.

Sheila confessed a growing allegiance to India, something she'd never really felt before. She saw something of her country's vulnerability in the lives that stretched out before her half-and-half daughters. She hoped they would love both India and England, yet be worldly enough to see the faults of both. She supposed that once the rains stopped, it would be "Enter the Japanese and goodbye Bengal." Either way, Elinor would soon return to Delhi and she would have to manage an infant and a toddler on her own. Ayahs were impossible to find. Was John disappointed to have another daughter? She was relieved. A mixed boy would have a difficult time. She hoped they would stop at two and resolved to be less vague about Dutch caps. Yet for a man who feared he was sterile, they hadn't done too badly.

Sheila rambled on and on. Save putting a notice in the *Statesman*, she wasn't sure what else she could do. She felt obscurely responsible.

When his first daughter was born, John had played Beethoven's Seventh at top volume on Minnie's gramophone. When he finally received news of the birth of his second daughter, he played it again. He supposed one day his daughters would find their suspicions they were different confirmed and would need to understand the meaning of their heritage. Where would they call home? England was out. Even India was doubtful; the words "a touch of the tar brush" shadowed anyone whose hair was not positively flaxen. John feared the virus of racial arrogance, the myth of the superior Nordic races that Hitler had unleashed, would prove contagious. In defeat, Germany might prove resistant, but he was less sure of the vengeful Anglo-Saxons. He no longer trusted anything England claimed it stood for.

In the early years of the war Sheila would move from rooming house to rooming house, living in lonely hill stations where she could be near family or friends while John traveled all over India writing engineering reports. Wrapped in blankets against the cold, her daughters sharing her bed for warmth, she wrote her husband long and loving letters with her gloves on. Sheila liked to relive the early days of their courtship, the predawn flights to see the sun rise over the Sunderbans and the dancing till the small hours. How many Dundee cakes and Firpo's chocolates she had once consumed! How many plates of oysters! She hoped her daughters would know these little luxuries. They eased one's way through life's difficulties.

Of course compared to those women whose husbands were off in the desert or jungles facing lord knows what danger, Sheila knew she was lucky. Were she to die tomorrow she was certain people would say of her: that woman never had a day's trouble in her life.

Subhas Chandra Bose, Free India Broadcast,
    August 17, 1942

"The whole world now sees that the velvet glove, which ordinarily hides the mailed fist of Britain, has now been cast away and brute force—naked and unashamed—rules over India. Behind the thick screen of gas, underneath the heavy blows of police batons, amid the continual whistle of bullets and the angry defiance of the injured and the dying—the soul of India asks—'Where are the Four Freedoms?' The words float over the seven seas to all corners of the globe—but Washington does not reply. After a pause, the soul of India asks again—'Where is the Atlantic Charter, which guaranteed to every nation its own government?' This time Downing Street and White House reply simultaneously: 'That Charter was not meant for India.'"

War Rumors File, 1942, Special Branch,
  Lord Sinha Road, Calcutta

"Letters by soldiers stationed abroad are written by the post office. In Singapore a British high official was made to pull a rickshaw mounted by two Indians. Lorry loads of wounded civilians were taken from a Rangoon hospital into a forest; those slightly injured were told to leave while those more seriously injured were burnt alive. During the Rangoon retreat Indians were denied passage on steamers and were forced to go by jungle tracks bristling with thugs and dacoits. Thousands went mad with hunger.

"Japanese infiltration through the Sunderbans is imminent. The Japs are marching towards Chittagong along routes taken by the evacuees from Burma. A recent air raid alarm was not a practice alert but a real one and the information was suppressed to prevent a panicked exodus from Calcutta. Dynamite has been placed at Howrah and Ballygunj Bridges, at Howrah and Sealdah rail stations wired to blow up when the Japanese invade. A European was overheard in a railway waiting room saying Rudolph Hess's visit to England had yielded a joint plan to crush the Soviets. Once Russia was defeated, peace would be declared. It is believed that Britain has mortgaged India to the U.S.A. and that Hess has become an American."

The Streets of Calcutta, 1943

On September 5, 1942, the U.S. State Department received a long telegram regarding the widespread political upheaval from the American Mission in New Delhi. One paragraph noted that consular officers all over India were reporting food shortages. The following month a cyclone leveled the winter paddy crop in Midnapore and Chittagong districts, killing thirty thousand people. It was nearly a month before news of the cyclone appeared in the Calcutta papers. Referencing the central role these districts had played in the Quit India uprising, the district officer suggested that relief be withheld "in view of the political misdeeds of the people." Most of the dead were farmers who had rushed out to protect their crops.

The cyclone was the one precipitating condition for famine that was not of human doing. The fall of Burma, long Bengal's reserve granary of rice, headed the list of the conditions that were. A scorched-earth policy had targeted Midnapore and other rice-growing areas on the Bay of Bengal. All forms of local transport that might fall into Japanese hands were seized. Rail lines were taken up. Oxcarts were broken into pieces. Twenty-five thousand boats, the means by which grains were moved from cultivators to markets in Calcutta, were destroyed. In this way, the British governor of Bengal argued, the Japanese would be prevented from invading Calcutta.

They could, however, bomb it. Beginning on December 20, 1942, Zeros made three nighttime raids, killing a thousand dockworkers and destroying critical infrastructure. The raids precipitated a massive panic. Rickshaw wallahs, street sweepers, and petty bureaucrats fled Calcutta. Englishmen commandeered all transport and evacuated the city in droves, causing further disruption to food supplies and leaving Sudhin and his ARP colleagues to fend for themselves. Crows, kites, and pye-dogs fought over the garbage that filled the streets. The following month the War Cabinet denied Linlithgow's request for six hundred thousand tons of additional wheat shipments to feed the influx of soldiers to Calcutta and to maintain the level of munitions production. The shipping could not be spared. Instead, during the first seven months of 1943, seventy-one thousand tons of grain, enough to feed four hundred thousand Indians for a year, were shipped to Ceylon, Persia, and South Africa. Bulk purchases of rice for government employees and those industries critical to the war effort both inflated prices and reduced supply stocks still further.

With thousands of Congressites imprisoned, Gandhi's Quit India Movement had foundered four months after it began. When the viceroy refused to meet with him, Gandhi announced a twenty-one-day fast, beginning February 8, 1943. The War Cabinet, boosted by German defeats at El Alamein and Stalingrad, decided he would be allowed to die. "This is our hour of triumph everywhere in the world," Churchill pointed out. "It is not the time to crawl before a miserable old man." If the "blackamoors" on the viceroy's council made good their threats to resign if Gandhi was not allowed to die in freedom, what did it matter? Gandhi survived.

The week Gandhi's hunger strike began, *Time* magazine ran a cover story on reports of Indian food shortages, ridiculing the doublespeak of Leo Amery's denial. Any report of food shortage was a famine marker and mandated that precise steps be taken in response. The first step was to declare a famine. By April landless laborers began arriving in Calcutta, overwhelming suburban rail stations. This was another marker. Encampments grew at each end of Howrah Bridge and under the trees on the Maidan. An autopsy on a corpse retrieved from the streets revealed a stomach stuffed with grass. The sudden appearance of a vast number of beggars on Calcutta's pavements was thought to be the work of Subhas Bose's fifth columnists. When it appeared the Japanese were not going to invade, British authorities began seeing fifth columnists everywhere.

"It is difficult to believe that they are all here of their own initiative," a Special Branch officer wrote, noting that the beggars employed strikingly similar "professional techniques." At first they touched people they importuned for food, but they soon began to put themselves deliberately in the path of pedestrians, wrapping their arms around legs. Did they have a natural-born right to make such a nuisance of themselves? He wondered how the soldiers kept their tempers. Calcutta was now the base of operations and supply hub for the war against Japan. Soldiers were everywhere, spending freely, inflating prices, and increasing food shortages. The officer recommended passing an ordinance closing off Chowringhee so that they might walk in comfort.

That same month, the Secretary of State for India was aghast to learn that Linlithgow had let a letter from Gandhi journey on to Muhammad Jinnah. It appeared that Jinnah had publicly remarked on Gandhi's correspondence with the viceroy while under house arrest. Jinnah asked, why did Gandhi not write him as well? The Government of India wouldn't dare stop a letter from reaching him. A clever snare indeed, Amery thought, and Linlithgow had fallen right into it. The viceroy had intercepted the letter but only to make a copy of it. Helpfully, he forwarded this to London before sending the original on its way.

After panicking that it was too late to stop its delivery, Linlithgow managed to swoop in and retrieve it. Still, Amery was flabbergasted to learn he was still considering a face-to-face meeting between the two.

The sentiments expressed in the letter were perfectly innocuous, but the whole point was to keep the two sides from talking. An interminable telegram arrived from Delhi, setting out the viceregal reasoning for having let the letter go, and so on, and so on. Amery wasn't nearly convinced; Churchill cabled his agreement from Washington. Amery had never bucked Linlithgow so strongly before. He was curious to see how he would respond. He hoped he would be gracious.

Would the letter's existence and its subsequent suppression be made public? Linlithgow now asked. This would simply open the door to further chicanery, Amery cabled back. The sound policy was to announce that Gandhi, detained for promoting an illegal mass movement that had gravely interfered with India's war effort, and who had thus far shown no intention of abandoning his methods, was unavailable to communicate with Jinnah or, indeed, with anyone. Roosevelt's newest envoy to India, a patrician and pedigreed Bostonian, was struck by the absurdity of the government's claim that the major parties were unable to come an agreement while holding all parties incommunicado. Even he was refused permission to speak with Gandhi.

The hullabaloo over Gandhi's letter absorbed the War Cabinet for three weeks. Six weeks later Linlithgow was still revisiting the episode. Many telegrams were exchanged. Detailed minutes were kept. All the while the famine in Bengal continued unabated. While the viceroy argued over whether Gandhi's letter should be made public or whether, as a matter of courtesy, Jinnah should be informed of its contents, Shaheed Suhrawardy, now the Muslim League minister of civil supplies in Bengal, insisted that sufficient rice was on hand. While the various British governors reported on the public response to Gandhi's letter, Shaheed was in secret talks about procuring surplus stocks. While Linlithgow ruminated over Churchill's demand that the letter be kept secret and accepted praise for his skillful handling of Gandhi, the price of rice had risen 600 percent. Hoarding was rampant. And still famine hadn't been declared.

By July the pavements of Calcutta were lined with the dying, and a member of the Bengal Assembly asked Shaheed about declaring a famine. He refused. When a relief worker begged him he raged that rumors of famine were an opposition conspiracy to undermine his

Muslim League government. Everywhere Shaheed went the roly-poly Apurba Chanda and an honor guard of goondas from the bustees of Howrah accompanied him. When anyone crossed Shaheed, Apurba noted, he could be quite vindictive.

That same month, the U.S. Board of Economic Warfare issued a report predicting that unless substantial quantities of foodstuffs were immediately imported, hundreds of thousands of Indians would starve. The average Indian had been subsisting on a daily diet equaling about a thousand calories, it reported. A minimum subsistence was thought to be two thousand, and the average American or Englishman tucked away nearly twice that. Linlithgow, still toiling away fourteen hours a day at his desk, had finally put in another request for additional grain shipments, seven months after his last one had been denied. "Famine conditions have begun to appear in parts of southern India and in Bengal," he wrote in July. If his new request for three hundred thousand tons of grain went unheeded, he warned, he was not answerable for the consequences. As if the consequences were not now upon him.

In August the wheels came off. Reports of rural peasants selling their children coincided with a cholera epidemic. On Cornwallis Street someone found a child's corpse partially eaten by dogs. Vultures lined up on tree branches and rooftops to wait out those dying below them. Jackals were less patient. The burning ghats at the river's edge were overwhelmed; corpses piled up like stacks of charred wood. According to the doms who worked the pyres, they burned easily. In the villages few had the strength to dig graves or cut wood, so the dead were cast adrift on the river, washing up downriver rubbery and whitened. The footpaths of South Calcutta were rendered impassable by shit. The smell of death was everywhere.

On August 22, 1943, the first in a series of shocking photographs appeared in the *Sunday Statesman* accompanied by editorials slamming the government for inaction. The *Statesman* was edited by Englishmen and generally toed the line drawn by Calcutta's merchant community, so this was a departure. The photographs, of skeletal mothers and their children mobbing a free kitchen, of a man laid out on a pavement on the precipice of death, caused a stir at the U.S. State Department. The following Sunday even more terrible images appeared. No statement was forthcoming from either the viceregal palace or Governor's House. Finally, two weeks after the second batch of photographs appeared, the Viceroy's spokesperson suggested that Bengal's distress was being "overdramatized." And still famine had not been declared.

In early October Linlithgow finally departed, filled with expansive regrets that he had been unable to convince India's politicians to put aside their rivalries. Ten days later Shaheed announced Bengal was in the grip of "an unprecedented famine." The city's death toll was reaching eighteen hundred per week. The *Statesman* ran a new series of photographs, timed to coincide with the new viceroy's arrival in the city. The famine had finally displaced the war in Europe on the paper's front pages.

The finger-pointing soon began. Following Amery's lead the London papers ascribed the famine to the political incompetence of the provincial ministry, rising tensions between the Muslim and Hindu communities, and the greed of speculators eager to capitalize on the misery of their own people. It was also said that Calcutta's wealthier citizens treated the proliferation of beggars as a civic nuisance. Linlithgow had been hesitant to interfere, it was held, not wanting to undermine the principle of regional autonomy. But he hadn't hesitated to arrest twenty elected members of the Bengal Provincial Assembly. And the British governor of Bengal hadn't hesitated to force the leader of the majority ministry out of office after he promised an investigation into the gang rape of dozens of women in three villages of Midnapore district by hundreds of police officers and soldiers. Such moves had cynically empowered Muslim League gangsters like Shaheed Suhrawardy. Shaheed used his access to relief supplies to consolidate his power.

When the House of Commons finally met to discuss the famine in November, only fifty-three MPs attended. A member of the Bengal Assembly noted, "This knocks the bottom out of the old superstition that these 600 and odd men can govern India from 7,000 miles away. Is it not time that this Punch and Judy show was ended?"

When the famine was reaching its end, one of the 43,600 American soldiers arriving in the city, the writer Howard Fast, asked the new host of the Parichay adda, a trade unionist, for his thoughts. At first the man was silent. Then he told him a story.

One night the whining drone of women and cries of children for rice water came in through his window. He did not get up from the table where he and three fellow unionists were eating their one meal of the day. He asked Fast what he would have done.

"I would have given the poor devils my dinner."

"We did not give them our dinner," the trade unionist said. "And in the morning five dead bodies were on my doorstep, two women and three children."

Fast didn't know what to say.

"Those five would have died anyway, a day later, two days later," the trade unionist went on. "And they will die like that until India is free. There is always a price put on freedom, and part of the price we pay is to stay alive."

According to many accounts of the famine, an estimated one hundred thousand destitute flocked to Calcutta in search of food. Sudhin would later write that when Air Raid Precautions bomb shelters were taken over by the starving, they were turned into relief kitchens. It was characteristic of him not to mention that he was instrumental in this, as by then he was director of ARP. Then there is this. In the wake of the uproar over the *Statesman*'s photographs, the dying began to be forcibly removed from the streets. On the insistence of the governor of Bengal, an ordinance—the Bengal Destitute Persons (Repatriation and Relief)—was passed in late October. Under this Orwellian "improvement scheme," forty-three thousand "sick destitutes" were packed into vans and driven back to the countryside to die outside public view. To evade patrols, the starving often died hiding in stairwells. After the war Sudhin would tell Louis MacNeice that the famished often found their way into the stairwells of the apartment building on Russell Street where he had a new flat.

Sudhin left no account of the Bengal famine. Many years later he would sit at a desk in Chicago trying to write the story of his life, the story of the city he both hated and loved. He left his Chicago fellowship midway, never having progressed in his writing beyond his childhood. And just as his delicacy barred him from speaking of the reasons for his despair, pride stopped him from writing about what Calcutta went through during those years. Nobility and shame conspired to silence him. Sudhin would tell Louis that at the famine's peak two thousand dead were removed from the streets every day, but not what it was like to be greeted each morning with loudspeakers on trucks crisscrossing the city, calling for people to clear the dead from their doorsteps.

It is inconceivable that Sudhin regarded the dying as a civic nuisance. Imagine him instead in his navy blue ARP uniform, stopping in the stairwell with a plate of rice for its tenants. In that brief moment of proximity and intimacy, there would be an exchange of some sort, a nod or greeting. Or they would simply smell the food and he would smell them. And then Sudhin would continue on his way, backing his car smartly out of the drive, a smile covering his face like a mask.

Shipments of grain and rice began to arrive in 1944 but the death toll continued to rise. Station platforms in the countryside remained crowded with the starving. A bumper rice crop came in but in many villages no one was left to harvest it; skeletons littered the paddy fields of Chittagong, Midnapore, and Mymensingh districts. The new viceroy kept up a drumbeat for more grain shipments, but the War Cabinet decided that eighteen Australian ships laden with wheat should bypass a starving Bengal to enhance the stockpiles awaiting the liberation of the Greeks and the Yugoslavs. For these men it went without saying that some lives were worth more than others. An estimated 3.5 million Bengalis died of starvation, typhoid, cholera, malaria, and dysentery, possibly far more. They were the truly vanquished, sacrificed by design and willed indifference.

Was it a coincidence that in the midst of the famine England's debt to India had reached £800 million? Until mid-1943, the repatriation of India's long-term debt to England had kept sterling balances in check, but after that the debt exploded. Churchill demanded to know why India couldn't be charged the equivalent for having been saved from the Japanese (as if India had been stoutly defended instead of violently policed). But India paid for its own defense, Amery explained. By then England had extracted more from India than he ever imagined possible; even Linlithgow had judged India to be at the breaking point. While J. M. Keynes was telling Churchill the Crown might repudiate England's debt or arrive at some scaled-down sum after the war, Churchill was telling Amery to inform India he would reserve the right to renege. Perhaps Churchill feared that to honor such a debt might one day oblige the Crown to acknowledge that England owed something of its survival to India. He needn't have worried.

Instead, in one of his arias, Churchill warned that India was threatening England with starvation. The British workingman would be reduced to rags, enslaved to filthy-rich Indian mill owners, he roared, were the deficit in sterling balances to be honored. In November 1943, on the eve of another meeting on grain shipments, Churchill's minister of food had suggested that after the war India might "spend her huge hoards of sterling on buying food and thus increase the population still more." "They breed like rabbits," Churchill echoed, complaining to his private secretary that Indians were "a foul race protected by their mere pullulation from the doom that is their due." If RAF Bomber Command could have spared the bombers, he said he would have happily done to India what he'd done to Hamburg.

This was power in the shadow of its end.

Meanwhile, the British public was informed that in anticipation of Europe's liberation, their chocolate rations would be cut.

– CHAPTER 18 –

A Boy Falling Out of the Sky

30 Upper Park Road, Belsize Park, London,
Boxing Day, December 26, 1943

For twenty months Michael Spender had flown restlessly between airfields. He reviewed covers, briefed pilots, and sent them back out. He kept his eyes on the entire theater; a view captured in an unending series of filmstrips, unwound, cut, and enlarged into five-by-five-inch prints. He was so focused on tiny changes to the industrial and military infrastructure of Nazi-occupied Europe that he had no time to reflect. He stayed up so many nights his face took on a deathly pallor. An old case of malaria flared up. His hair became more salt than pepper. His cornflower-blue eyes turned gray, acquiring the same hunted look as his mother's had during the Great War.

Was that a camouflaged battleship? What might a fake haystack hide? By studying the wake of a cruising vessel Michael could calculate its speed and direction so that Bomber Command might find it again. If he needed a closer view there was a risky flying maneuver called dicing. A Spitfire would dive down through cloud cover, photograph obliquely, and zoom back up before fighter planes could be scrambled. Reconnaissance planes had perfected nighttime photography, with a lead aircraft flying low and dropping flash bombs. The photographs they took provided the next installment in the game of ships, submarines, armies, and aircraft moving like chess pieces over a vast board of land and water.

There was always a flap when a ship he'd been keeping his eye on suddenly vanished. The disappearance of the *Bismarck* became a "permanent super-flap." There had been a panic about the battleship getting loose in the Atlantic, as the *Admiral Scheer, Admiral Hipper, Scharnhorst,* and *Gneisenau* had. RAF St. Eval reconnaissance aircraft flew out, scanning for a sight of the *Bismarck* in shipyards and docks in and around Brest, the German-occupied Channel ports, and even the Atlantic, while planes from Wick scoured the vast North Sea, from Statlandet in the Shetland Narrows on down the Norwegian coast. There was shouting over bad telephone connections and no rest for anyone until the *Bismarck* was sighted and sunk.

Under the press of work, spit and polish fell by the wayside; Michael didn't always bathe. His imperious voice carried over everyone's desks. He was brusque with new arrivals, treating them like pieces of luggage. He made no secret of his belief that half of the unit's personnel were useless. He kept three kittens at Benson, oblivious to a fuming group captain who would bat at them with a rolled-up newspaper. He played classical music on the rec room's piano. Long nights never made up for absences. He was often caught out.

However exasperating Michael found official ineptitude, he always held out hope that once the promised reorganization of his unit got under way, the final acronym settled upon, and the civilian nucleus of Harold "One-Eyed" Hemming's Aircraft Operating Company fully absorbed into RAF Medmenham, all inefficiencies would be discovered and all the idiots removed. When a new commanding officer arrived, he thought that time had come. But the man understood nothing! Red tape doubled the time it took to write reports. Michael railed at the way certain men acquired large RAF contracts. Though their unit remained short of skilled personnel, his former squadron leader, a man with more experience interpreting than anyone, was put on a list of officers "for disposal."

After that, Michael spent as little time as possible at Benson. St. Eval was only marginally better. It was under constant bombardment, as if the Germans knew exactly what went on there. Wick, on the northeast coast of Scotland, was more congenial. To get there from St. Eval, Michael would fly up the Welsh coast. From the cockpit he could look across the Minch to see the Hebrides looking something like the map

Nancy had done for Louis's book. Once, the pilot ceded him the controls and cavalierly fell asleep.

Fraternizing between civilian officers and RAF pilots was frowned upon. Michael ignored this; he was as bewitched by them as he had been by the Eskimo, Sherpas, and Baltis. After six pints of local ale they would lose their reserve and describe to him what it was like to fly over the North Sea. He eavesdropped on their arguments over whether Blenheims could be rolled and marveled at the rituals with which they appeased the gremlins inhabiting their aircraft. These machines were so delicate, he once explained to Stephen, they couldn't help acting up. When they hooted at his affection for the humble and slow Moth, he flushed like a girl. It was a Wick pilot who finally found the *Bismarck*, a tiny kayak shape hidden in the filigree of one of over a thousand Norwegian fjords.

One night the mess loudspeaker announced that a Spitfire and a Blenheim carrying a pilot Michael was fond of had failed to return. The mess fell into a helpless silence. Airmen, like the Eskimo, were filled with superstitions. They shared the Eskimo's reluctance to talk of the dead. And when, three hours overdue, the Spitfire miraculously reported in, a tide of elation surged through camp, leaving his friend's Blenheim entirely forgotten. Four nights later eight aircraft, out on minor missions, went missing. And so it went.

It had felt dishonorable to be living a charmed life among men who were almost certain to be killed. If he could have wangled a seat, Michael might have been relieved of the shame that assaulted him whenever a plane failed to return. When his name went up on the unit roll of honor as "Mentioned in Despatches" he was mortified to find himself listed alongside pilots who had won Distinguished Flying Crosses.

In the second winter of the war Michael lay in his sleeping bag on a hard airman's bed and thought of Nancy. She had rung him up one day, inviting him for coffee. In the course of their conversation he'd asked her to explain why the Women's Auxiliary Air Force girls at the factory should be so ready to give him their all when he really only needed two-thirds. She had laughed at him. He persisted; he really wanted to know what he was missing. This made her laugh even more. After having quite a lot to drink, they found themselves kissing madly in his parked car.

Now, he wondered: Were the pipes still frozen and if so where was Nancy taking her baths? When the Thames overflowed its banks, when water streamed down the walls at Benson and mushrooms sprouted in the barrack's dark corners, he recalled her love of baths. When spring failed to arrive by Easter, when he'd grown tired of a life that had him living with her in patches instead of all the time, the thought of her warmed him. He found it strange that the simple thought of another person could light him up like a stove. And when the wireless reported bombs falling heavily on London he put aside his pocket stereoscope to write her a letter:

"Do lie low, my love. . . . p.s. You took my pajamas."

At Station 49 in Camden Town, Nancy also had a pallet and a sleeping bag. She would answer Michael's letters in the middle of the night sitting by the phone waiting for an ambulance call. Around her drivers and attendants lay snoring on stretchers. That first winter she had found her way back to Upper Park Road, house number 30, first floor. She had hung curtains and sewn a new bedspread for the double bed in the corner of the living room. When Juliet and Miranda visited from her mother's they were impressed by her newfound patience and domesticity.

If, on the phone with Michael, Nancy spoke in an Old Testament voice he would know that the girl who spelled *casualty* with a *K* in the ambulance station's incident book was listening. She wrote him of arriving home one afternoon and remembering there was snow in the back garden. She'd fired up the stove and flung open the window to paint the view for two hours with her coat on. There were lunches with Bill (an official war artist) and dates with Stephen and Louis. But if the weather deteriorated, she would cancel on any one of them at the drop of a hat. Michael could only work when the skies were clear.

Throughout the long winter and spring of 1941 she had sketched Michael reading the newspaper, sketched him leaning over a sink washing his face. She drew his shoes. A drawing showed him at work, one hand grasping his jaw, thumb in cheek, a pencil laced in his fingers.

It was up to Michael. She could always be found, no? With a little vision our hero might arrange a meeting, yes? Would that not be a treat? And in reply, Michael Spender's arms reached out and closed around her. She drew their bodies clasped together like hands in supplication. And when they parted, she to her station and he to his airfields, their letters kept up their conversation. When the summer of 1941 finally arrived, Michael wished he could stop the war for a week so they could spend more than a night together.

And then, in late summer, the war had stopped for him. Thinking the notice he'd received must be a clerical error, he'd gone from office to office to sort things out. Finally, the assistant director (photo intelligence) informed him his services were no longer needed. Michael turned to his commanding officer, who consulted the director of intelligence. Would it affect operations if Michael Spender left the service? the DI had asked. "Definitely yes," his CO had replied. Michael should remain in his post while his application for an honorary commission, intended for the handful of civilians the RAF deemed critical for the war effort, proceeded.

It didn't proceed. When Michael inquired about the delay he was told by the assistant director, buttressed now by an air commodore, that he was unfit for intelligence work on grounds of security. Was it the German wife he had yet to divorce? Articles for the *Spectator* conveying sympathy for the prewar plight of the German people? The talk at RAF Medmenham traced Michael's troubles to his monumental tactlessness. In August 1941 he was stripped of his smart sky-blue uniform with three lines of gold braid and told to leave the aerodrome within sixteen hours. The assistant director ripped up his identity card in his face.

One-Eyed Hemming called it a "slap in the face with a wet fish." But for Michael, it was disastrous. He wrote outraged letters to his uncles, referencing his "unimpeachable correctitude" and the failings of the "miserable creature" who fired him. "Parliament exists to prevent such abuses," he railed, describing an intrigue of Elizabethan proportions. Part of him hoped the Air Ministry would soon see how important he was, part of him knew he'd be wasted anywhere else. He was heartbroken. People he had barely noticed overwhelmed him with expressions of dismay and support. With no movement on his application for a new commission, he withdrew it.

Michael turned to his Admiralty contacts and was given a post in propaganda. After a while he asked to be shifted to Operational Intelligence only to realize this, too, was a dead end. Uncle Alfred warned him that if he didn't learn to cultivate at least an appearance of modesty, he would be marked down as an impossible man and written off. When he raised the possibility of renewing his application for an RAF commission, he was told it was safer to be the only PI specialist at the Admiralty, than one of several hundred at the RAF. Once he might have been content with that. But he had received his share of eviscerating letters from Nancy. After a careful study he'd concluded that she would be appeased only if he achieved something noteworthy.

"For people like us," he wrote her, "there cannot be any accepting of an inferior position without hope or possibility of betterment." He knew he had it in him and that if he remained hopeful, eventually a superior position with good pay would materialize. If it didn't, Nancy would strangle the life out of him, of that he was certain. There was also her tendency to want to die when things got difficult. This didn't frighten him or mean that it would be a mistake to carry on with her. He knew only that if he took the safer course, she would eventually come to doubt him. So he took his chances with the RAF once again.

On the understanding that he would look out for the Admiralty's interests, Michael obtained the support of the admirals for an application to return to work in RAF photo intelligence. As acting pilot officer on probation, he was to report to Squadron Leader Bill Wager, the Greenland geologist he had trained in PI and the man who had spiked John Auden's shot at Everest. And when Bill Wager took the man he once described as universally despised and gleefully cut him down to size, Michael Spender said nothing.

Instead, while sitting in his car in front of 30 Upper Park Road in the midst of a fusillade of buzz bombs, he presented Nancy with a ring. He followed up with a stilted letter that set out his reasons for marrying her. Foremost among them was her beautiful body and the pleasures it would bring to both of them. He acknowledged that a wartime marriage might be a shady deal; he had seen too many surprises sprung to be complacent. Less tactfully, he rationalized marrying her by concluding she would be no better off if he didn't. He also undertook to look after her in illness and old age. "Though we need not search the horizon for portents," he added cautiously, knowing how she felt about turning thirty-three. Lastly, he vowed to figure out how marriage worked, as if he was prepared to take it apart and tinker with it.

After Erica agreed to a divorce, Nancy and Michael were wed in March 1943. A son was born the day after Christmas. "Juliet and Miranda adore him and so do I," Nancy wrote John Auden after a lapse of four years, "but his father is a funny chap and might like an engine nearly as much." Though there were days when she hated being a mother again, when she missed the ambulance terribly, Nancy was content. And she was immensely proud of having produced a "bootiful boy" (had it been a girl, she had threatened to drown it). Wystan agreed to be godfather.

It wasn't long before Michael was writing of young Philip's sound instincts as a climber. He expected his son would develop a superb sense of balance, since Nancy wasn't likely to have a fit every time he got into trouble. He ascribed his own difficulty following Eric Shipton to having had an overanxious nanny.

Melsbroek Aerodrome, outside Brussels,
   February 1, 1945

When Michael arrived back at RAF Medmenham, he was changed, as if he had at last mastered what it was to be human. Then, just after Philip was born, he was transferred to 34 Wing, the Strategic Reconnaissance Wing of the Second Tactical Air Force. Based out of an aerodrome in Hampshire, its three squadrons would supply reconnaissance for the planning and execution of the Normandy landings. Spitfires, Mosquitos, and Vickers Wellingtons snapped coastal installations, provided maps of landing sites and, on the eve of D-day, undertook night reconnaissance, using flares to track troop movements. Four months later, in early September 1944, 34 Wing followed General Eisenhower into France, dropping flash bombs to illuminate pockets of resistance. By October 1944 the pilots and officers of 34 Wing were in Melsbroek, an aerodrome in Belgium.

In his early weeks on the Continent, Michael expected the war to end at any moment. He could see the launch of V1 rockets toward London, a sign of Germany's desperation. But as a sea of mud and slush rose around them, the Wehrmacht fought on. Tents threatened to take flight in the high winds, much as they had on Everest. There was rarely time to remove his seaboots and greatcoat before falling into bed. He had to travel to Brussels, "amongst the shades of John Auden's erotic adventures," for hot baths and hot meals. That was his memory of the last nine months of war: no hot water to shave with, unbroken nights of work in the bitter cold, overwhelming fatigue, and the acrid taste of canteen tea. He was often flying between various aerodromes on the front, debriefing pilots, collecting photographs.

Still, he found time to take a motorbike over pitted roads to practice his schoolboy French on stationmasters, priests, children, and members of the Resistance with whom he bartered his chocolate rations for eggs. He heard stories of inconceivable suffering under German occupation. And when Nancy related some fresh outrage of her mother, Stephen, Bill, or the Slade Boys, he wondered how people dared to behave so shamelessly while soldiers and civilians alike were still dying.

"I have to use all my imagination and memory to realize that this little group does actually behave like that. It is behavior so far from normal, so far from the ordinary human give and take that exists everywhere else, that one wonders how they ever produce anything satisfactory. . . . It stinks of all that is worst in England, the dregs left behind for us to fight and get killed for." Against such behavior, he offered the soulfulness of his men, whose letters home he censored. Riddled with misspellings, grammatical errors, XX's and OO's, they conveyed a love and devotion that these London people would never know. No one in England dared contemplate the horrors these men had lived through, he wrote.

Clear skies over Christmas had Michael working through the night. Air-raid sirens woke him thinking he was back in London during the Blitz. On New Year's Day Melsbroek was attacked and two out of three squadrons were lost, including all its Mosquitos, five Spitfires, and eleven Wellingtons. Michael had since gained the gold braid marking him as a squadron leader. The *London Gazette* included his name, for the second time, on the New Year's list of those mentioned in despatches.

But home leave in February was difficult. All three children came down with chicken pox and there was little coal to be had. Nancy was near despair, convinced that he would be killed before the war ended. He took responsibility for having married her in wartime, for having saddled her with an infant, for not knowing for certain how everything would turn out. He didn't dare mention that PI officers were being posted to India in preparation for the war against Japan. Instead, he warned her that as soon as a person loses faith in their future, nothing would ever happen to help them. She had to keep hope.

The Dalai Lama was once told that a successful ascent of Everest would bring about scientific breakthroughs that would benefit all humanity. Even unsuccessful ascents had brought about knowledge of the impact of high altitudes on human physiology and cognition. This, in turn, led to the development of oxygen tanks that enabled pilots to fly to impossible heights. The use of stereophotogrammetry to map the North Face of Everest was repurposed for intelligence. And how would the Battle of Britain have been won without Lady Houston, whose Supermarine engine had launched the development of the Spitfire?

Yet the benefits to humanity must be weighed against cost. Rabindranath Tagore once cursed the desecration of the heavens with planes bearing man's fratricidal wrath. What had Michael Spender seen of this wrath from 30,000 feet? For six years he had followed the progress of the damage done. He saw more clearly than most the scale and thoroughness of the destruction. When Michael realized that RAF Bomber Command had begun targeting German civilians, he was appalled. Operation Gomorrah, the nighttime firebombing of Hamburg, outraged him.

On the night of July 27, 1943, in a raid lasting forty-five minutes, over a million firebombs and hundreds of two-ton "block-busters" had rained down in the dark, setting off a tremendous firestorm. A 6,500-foot tornado of fire lit up the old city, generating hurricane-force winds that shrieked and howled like trapped animals. Tidal waves of flames barreled down residential streets at ninety miles an hour. Within minutes tens of thousands of people were incinerated, swept up like dry leaves into the rolling flames or suffocated in air-raid shelters and cellars as the fire sucked all oxygen into the maelstrom. When the air temperature reached a certain point, clothing burst into flames and bodies boiled away on streets of sizzling tar.

"The bombing of Hamburg cannot be justified as necessary to victory," Michael explained to Stephen. "It's the destruction, not just of Germany, but of an essential part of Europe." One and a quarter million survivors stumbled away from the city, dumb with shock. In the course of four nighttime raids and two daytime ones, forty-five thousand civilians were killed, a number surpassing those killed during the entirety of the Blitz, and twice that in London alone.

On April 26, 1945, Michael took a small plane over the Ruhr district to see for himself. What he'd seen in dove grays and blacks was now before him in monochromatic rust. Factories and railways lay in ruins. Not a single bridge over the Rhine was intact. The streets of Cologne were empty. Lines of washing that fluttered like Tibetan prayer flags over the rubble were the only sign of life. "Although I have been watching for years the gradual build up of this damage, it still appalls by its horror when you see it," he wrote Nancy. What sort of broken humanity would emerge, he wondered, when Cologne, Hamburg, Düsseldorf, Essen, Dortmund, and the rest were liberated?

When the liberation of towns and cities had first begun, Michael had had an anxious feeling that some kind of sabotage was under way. There had been arguments in the mess over the disarming of the Belgian resistance by force. Churchill's speech in Parliament defending, in the name of democracy, the aerial bombing of the Greek Resistance, he'd deemed mendacious. "I'm sure he knew he was being a dishonest old pig, because nowhere in the speech was there a fine turn of phrase or even a resort to the reserves of English morality." When, long after the German war machine had ground to a halt, the Ruhr was burned to the ground, he'd suspected wicked men behind the front and in England working to get things back the way they were before the war. Propaganda programs on the wireless showed their handiwork, sickening him nearly as much as the firebombing of

Hamburg. The intellectuals had drifted away from the business of getting better ideas into people's heads, he'd written Nancy.

"It's been too long for them, and it is only we who get the bombs and the casualties now." Upon viewing the Ruhr's devastation three months later, he couldn't conceive of the effort it would take to rebuild Europe. All he could think of was going home. Reading between the lines of the newspapers, he felt it was quite possible that Downing Street was cooking up a statement at that very moment. A small leap of joy surged through him. By the end of his letter to Nancy, he allowed himself to fully exult.

"This is the end!"

125th American Evacuation Hospital
   outside München-Gladbach, Germany, May 5, 1945

Michael liked to say that he had walked higher in the Himalaya than he had ever flown, as if he had convinced himself that if he didn't ascend over 21,000 feet, he would be safe. But when he left for Germany the last time he told his brother Humphrey he knew he was going to die. The numbers were against him. There had been scares before—an emergency crash landing in Devon and, that past January, Humphrey had phoned Nancy to tell her Michael's plane was reported missing. It was hours before he was able to phone the flat to assure her he was fine.

But on the return cross-Channel flight, Nancy's weeping and distress had replayed in his ears over the thrum of the Mosquito. In his mind's eye Michael had seen her, alone with her grief in the living room at 30 Upper Park Road, his son by her side. Two months later that was where Nancy was when the phone rang and she learned that Michael's plane had crashed in a forest in Germany. Early the next morning she caught a flight across the Channel from RAF Northolt. She was with him when he died a day later. He never regained consciousness.

Late in the war, Michael enclosed a cutting of a poem by Wystan in a letter to Nancy. The poem was based on a painting ascribed to Brueghel that Wystan had seen in Brussels in 1938. Coincidentally, on the day of

Michael's death, Wystan himself arrived in Germany. On an overseas mission of the U.S. Strategic Bombing Survey, he was there to assess the impact of area bombing on civilian morale. Given the rank and uniform of a U.S. Army major, Wystan spent two months asking Germans how they felt about being bombed. Though he was often near tears, he was never surprised by what they had to say. Yet had he not seen it himself, he wrote a friend, he wouldn't have believed it possible that a city like Darmstadt could be 92 percent destroyed in thirty minutes.

During the Great War the poet Wilfred Owen called out Horace's perennial "it is sweet and right to die for your country" as "the old Lie." He had seen too many boys die in panic and terror for that ever to be true again. Owen wanted his readers not to expect consolation from his poems but the bitter truth. Wystan had once aspired to follow in Owen's path, to discover what his generation's "bitter truth" would be. In the last week of World War II he found it. Compared to what Germany had undergone, W. H. Auden told Stephen Spender, London hadn't been bombed at all.

That went over well.

For Michael, Wystan's "Palais des beaux arts" captured another bitter truth: what it felt like to watch planes falling out of the sky in full knowledge that in England there were people getting on with their lives, unaware or scarcely registering the loss.

> In Brueghel's Icarus, for instance: how everything turns away
> Quite leisurely from the disaster; the ploughman may
> Have heard the splash, the forsaken cry,
> But for him it was not an important failure; the sun shone
> As it had to on the white legs disappearing into the green
> Water; and the expensive delicate ship that must have seen
> Something amazing, a boy falling out of the sky,
> Had somewhere to get to and sailed calmly on.

Squadron Leader Michael Alfred Spender was buried in Eindhoven General Cemetery on VE Day while crowds of people the world over celebrated the end of the war in Europe. The sun shone somewhere that day, as it had to, and England sailed calmly on.

– CHAPTER 19 –

Incompatible Gods,
Irreconcilable Differences

Geological Survey of India, 27 Chowringhee, Calcutta,
Direct Action Day, August 16, 1946

"I read the papers rather anxiously and hope you are not all dead—caught between two fires," Wystan wrote John when the riots first began in Calcutta. "Kipling and Elgar must be positively tossing in their graves at what's happening to the B.E."

By the time Congress's leadership had been released from prison at the close of the war, India was changed. When new provincial elections were held, Congress still carried the majority of the provinces, but Muhammad Jinnah's Muslim League had finally gained the mandate that had eluded it in 1937. Nehru still thought the entire notion of Pakistan impractical and absurd. After the viceroy invited Nehru to form a provisional government and he and Jinnah were unable to agree on what form it would take, Jinnah decided to force Nehru into accepting Pakistan by showing what would happen if he refused.

Shaheed Suhrawardy, now Bengal's chief minister, followed Jinnah's directive to announce a "Direct Action Day" rally on the Calcutta Maidan on Friday, August 16, 1946, in response to the formation by Nehru of a provisional government. Similar rallies were to be held all over India, but Shaheed also mandated a citywide holiday. Moreover, he threatened to declare Bengal independent if Congress took office in Delhi. "Bloodshed and disorder are not necessarily evil in themselves," he told a reporter for the *Statesman*, "if resorted to in a noble cause."

When Hindu shopkeepers opened their shutters on the sixteenth, Muslim goondas, inexplicably well supplied with trucks and scarce petrol rations, set their shops on fire. "It is not a ridiculous assumption that they had been provided for in advance," Sudhin wrote in disgust in an unsigned editorial for the *Sunday Statesman*. With their men away at the mass rally on the Maidan, Muslim bustees filled with women and children were set on fire by vengeful Hindu mobs. At the Park Circus roundabout, Shahid Suhrawardy witnessed a lone Hindu being surrounded by a crowd of young men. While the Hindu was being questioned, another youth stood by. When he raised his finger, the mob closed in, knifing the man in the stomach and melting away. Though a British tank was posted in plain sight, the armed sentry standing guard did nothing but watch as the encounter unfolded. By midnight, cadres of Hindus spread out across the city. There were three Hindus for every Muslim in Calcutta. For forty-eight hours the police were nowhere to be seen.

Over four days and three nights, as many as fifteen thousand people were stabbed, stoned, speared, attacked with acid and brickbats, hacked to death with axes, or set on fire. The vast majority of them were Muslims. Shops and tenements were turned into smoldering shells, and vultures once again made lazy circles over the city. Roving mobs ransacked trains, stopped cars, killed their occupants, and then set all alight. Looting was indiscriminate and bodies were everywhere. John Auden went out in a jeep to check on his office staff, bringing food and provisions. If they were Muslim he moved them to Park Circus; if they were Hindu he drove them to South Calcutta. He took Sudhin to check on his mother on Cornwallis Street, passing by the decomposing bodies of a dozen Muslim hawkers en route. A neighbor, an alumnus of an English university, had incited their deaths, Sudhin learned. "Those in possession of their senses kept their doors bolted," he would write, "and if thus they missed the fine glow imparted to the monsoon sky by houses blazing away at night, nowhere was there any escape from the stench of rotting carcasses." The *Statesman* first described the days of bloodshed as the "Fury" before settling upon the "Great Calcutta Killing."

Back at his flat, Sudhin destroyed a booklet he'd been writing arguing that his countrymen were allergic to violence. In an unsigned editorial he made the case that the Great Calcutta Killing, "a tragedy unparalleled in India's tragic communal history," called for a "special gesture." He begged Nehru to keep open the seats he'd offered to Jinnah in his provisional government in hopes of an eventual Congress–Muslim League rapprochement. The League, in turn, might thereby desist from its "demonstrably disastrous" obstructionist stance in fear of hardening communal tensions still further. When a week passed with no movement toward a compromise, Sudhin bitterly blamed the "orgy of death" on the "gross negligence" of Chief Minister Shaheed Suhrawardy's Home Ministry. Though Sudhin was never as close to Shaheed as he was to his brother, he had known him for twenty years. He imagined they were part of the same world and shared the same understandings. If this was true once, it was no longer.

Suhrawardy, who had stationed himself in the police control room at Lalbazar during the riots, blamed the commissioner of police for having lost control of the city. During the public inquiry that followed, a Congressman and political opponent in the Bengal Provincial Assembly stood up and denounced Shaheed, using Leo Amery's paraphrase of Cromwell: "Depart, I say, and let us have done with you. In the name of God, go!" Unlike Neville Chamberlain, Shaheed had chips to call in and soundly defeated a motion of no confidence.

"The devil was loose here for three days," John wrote Wystan after the worst was over. He spent a day helping bury five hundred corpses. With the August heat it wasn't long before the corpses were too putrid even for rats and vultures. They bloated into grotesque positions: legs splayed, buttocks thrust in the air, scrotums the size of footballs. The calloused soles of their feet, John couldn't help but notice, peeled off like old carpet slippers. Those that were a week old were already skeletons. The perpetrators, he told Wystan, claimed Europeans would be next. They weren't.

Flare-ups continued for months. Special Branch incident files described Muslim bustees set aflame, bodies pulled from manholes, found in gunnysacks, ponds, pumping stations, and slaughterhouses. During Diwali, a printed leaflet circulated. "The dark Diwali should be coloured with the blood of these Pakistani Muslims. In front of Mother

Kali Muslims in place of buffaloes should be sacrificed." Angry that
their chief minister had done nothing to protect them, convinced that
Hindus were arriving in the city by the trainload, Calcutta's Muslims
armed themselves with bombs, acid, and guns. An answering massacre of Hindus was orchestrated in Noakhali, in East Bengal. In an
effort to quell the violence, Gandhi walked all over the district.

Neither Jinnah nor Nehru went to Calcutta. Jinnah addressed the
riots from his home on Malabar Hill in Bombay and Nehru from his on
York Road in Delhi. This was the sort of treatment Muslims will receive
under a Hindu Raj, Jinnah declared. Nehru, adamant in his refusal to
consider a partitioning of India, insisted nothing had changed.

He was wrong. The Great Calcutta Killing changed everything.
Sudhin would cite the Muslim-Hindu riots of August 1946, the first of
their kind in India's history, as the ignominious end to Pax Britannica
in the very city where the British Empire had been born two centuries
before. "With [these riots] disappeared the unity of India that was considered the greatest achievement of British rule; and perhaps the special
destiny of Calcutta was thus fulfilled." For the next seven months, similar if less deadly riots broke out all over India. In Bihar Nehru encountered a Hindu mob intent on lynching Muslims. Shocked at its ferocity,
he had thrown its leader to the ground, nearly throttling him.

The last viceroy of India sensed what was coming. After six years
of war, Britain had neither the troops nor the will needed to assert
control over events. When Lord Mountbatten moved up the date of
the handover by ten months, to August 15, 1947, a caul of foreboding
settled over Calcutta.

17 Aurangzeb Road, New Delhi,
    August 15, 1947

"American business magnates in appalling ties are arriving in India
by the planeload," John wrote Wystan, "offering in the name of democracy to uplift the masses with enormous contracts." And not just India.
One hundred and ninety-eight Russians were assigned to the Soviet
embassy in Thailand, and the new maps of China included most of
Burma. John imagined Mr. Norris, a shady character from Christopher

Isherwood's Berlin stories, arriving from Ostend to sell explosives and trawl for boys.

Evidently assuming Louis MacNeice was a fellow oilman, a Standard Oil scout appalled him on his flight out to India by cracking one crude joke after another. On a refueling stop in Cairo, the man pointed out the remarkable resemblance between the fez and the Shriner hat. Some clever American must have sold them on it, he crowed. Stopping to refuel in Baghdad, he mistook it for Delhi. When Louis pointed out he was in Iraq, he observed, "Ah yes, yes, the New Britain."

The ink expended on English county cricket scores in the Delhi papers surprised Louis, but it was the letters to the editor urging that cow slaughter be made illegal that brought him to Aurangzeb Road. Ramkrishna Dalmia, the founder of the Anti–Cow Slaughter League, was known as the Henry Ford of India. Only Dalmia did not limit himself to one industry, but had holdings in alphabetized dozens, from aviation to biscuits to collieries. During the war U-boat attacks on shipping had effectively halted imports from England. The price of cloth quintupled, industrialization was kick-started, and vast fortunes were made. Dalmia was one of the victors. Many believed his cow crusade to be a stunt to divert attention from his sharp business deals.

"This campaign of yours for cow protection," Louis asked the small, wizened man with a knife-edged face in a Congress cap, "is it primarily religious or economic?"

Dalmia's blue silk suit matched his sofa. A steady stream of assistants filed in and out. Whenever Dalmia's attention was diverted, Louis took in a drawing room fitted with splashy gold moldings, a color scheme repeated throughout the mansion. Dalmia's nervous, flicking hand movements would pat his thigh to bring him back.

"My dear young man," Dalmia replied, "you cannot separate things like that. Everything is one. Cow is sacred because valuable like the mother but more so. What benefits humanity is sacred and vice versa."

Many of the Muslim senior bureaucrats Louis spoke to could trace their ancestral history in Delhi back centuries. "The Hindu abhors my insides," one said. They were under enormous pressure to leave. For them the upcoming partition was a Hindu victory. Yet while the road to the railway station was cluttered with bullock carts piled high with babies and old women heading for Pakistan, these men seemed in no great hurry to pack up. Rumors of disturbances in the Punjab were indistinct amid the fireworks and festivities in the capital. Even Jinnah was said to be holding on to his house on Malabar Hill. Dalmia was a fast friend of his. Indeed, the mansion Louis was sitting in had until recently belonged to Jinnah. It was very confusing. But Dalmia had already moved on to his next pet scheme—One-World Government overseen by a benevolent autocrat.

Himself? Louis scribbled. *Sincere? Probably. Megalom? Likely.*

Democracy was finished, Dalmia said; the West had proved it. They were still counting up the dead from the war. Sensing Louis's skepticism, he switched back to the subject of cow slaughter.

"The cow is like your mother, only more so; she goes on giving you milk. Tell me, would you kill your mother? And even when she's very old, she still pays her way with her dung. I have statistics to prove that."

Few telephones were working, so the BBC team was reduced to sending messages by tonga. That was how Louis got in touch with John Auden's friend Sinbad Sinclair. Sinclair had arranged the Dalmia interview and proved to be rather cultivated for an oilman and something of a dandy. He lived in a grand bungalow not far from Dalmia's mansion. His wife was in England with the children, Sinbad said; Louis was welcome to stay. Returning each evening, Louis would sit on a lawn the texture of velvet, drink Sinbad's whiskey, and try to make sense of it all.

In a frantic round of teas and lunches, he met colonels and commissioners, finance ministers, museum directors, and archaeologists with curly mustaches, even a former head prefect from Marlborough. The sheer variety of humanity overwhelmed him, though the incompetence of the local BBC office meant he missed half of the pre–Independence Day festivities he had tickets to. At a cocktail party at the viceregal residence, with "Old Man River" on the gramophone, the poet and Congress leader Sarojini Naidu told him she was disappointed that he didn't have a blue beard.

God only knew where she got that. John Auden?

He met a Congressman who told him he'd edited a highbrow literary quarterly with Aldous Huxley at Oxford. He was charming, spoke beautifully, and had been repeatedly imprisoned by the British. Executive types tended to spice their talk with "old chap" and "what the dickens," phrases he hadn't heard since Edward was king. Field Marshal Kodandera Cariappa, veteran of Waziristan border conflicts, was more Sandhurst than Sandhurst and was celebrated for having introduced the loudspeaker as a field tactic. He demonstrated for Louis by curling a loose fist around his mouth.

"*Salaams to you*, our brothers of the hills," he trumpeted, startling the assembled. "It has been reported to me that you have fired several shots at one of my pickets. This disturbs the peace of our camp and prevents us from sleeping. *Salaams to you.* If you continue to disturb us we shall have to kill you. We do not wish to do this. *Salaams to you.* I suggest therefore that you all go away and go to bed. If any of you has any complaints let him come and see me in the morning. Good night, our brothers of the hills. *Salaams to you.*" Cariappa now made a practice of using a mobile van and loudspeaker to drive about Delhi quoting a bit of the Koran, a bit of the Gita, to get the attention of mobs growing more restive by the minute. "Chaps will fall for it, you know," he said. "Jolly good show."

The number of servants running to attend to him left Louis in a constant state of embarrassment. Each morning a south Indian in a spotless turban jumped out of nowhere to put his socks on for him. Sinbad had his calves massaged and powder put between his toes every morning while he read the paper. And then there was the wee fellow from the *Hindustan Times* who asked Louis what might be done to solve India's problems. He made some vague noises only to have the man say mournfully, "I will come again in September when perhaps you will have more definite ideas." That about crushed him.

At the midnight session of the Constituent Assembly, India readied itself to declare its independence. From his seat in the high gallery, Louis looked down through a windy whir of ceiling fans into a sea of Congress caps and flapping homespun. The president came off like an old Labour MP and Nehru seemed exhausted. Sarvepalli Radhakrishnan, the new vice president, gave what Louis believed was the best speech. The one discordant note was the braying conch in the middle of bells chiming midnight.

In a beautifully lit garden at Government House the following evening, he was finally introduced to India's new prime minister. A number-one charmer, Louis thought, noting Jawaharlal Nehru's varsity English and parson-like bearing. An estimated half million people had been present that afternoon at India Gate for the ceremonial raising of the Indian flag. Nehru had nearly been stranded in a flood of excited humanity.

"You must be quite tired," Louis said.

"I'm quite fond of a crowd," Nehru said. "My first instinct is to pitch myself into it but sometimes I have to rush out and beat it." He had beaten a man with his own topee in that afternoon's crush, but Louis imagined instead a crowd in a worshipful frenzy trying to tear off his clothes. Nehru invited him for lunch two days hence, a Sunday. He wanted to talk about something other than politics.

Sunday was publication day of the map of all maps. An English barrister named Sir Cyril Radcliffe, knowing nothing of India, had reviewed censuses and land records wrapped in red cloth (Assistant District Officer Carritt's doubtless among them) to decide where the new borders would fall. Bengal was partitioned once again: Punjab for the first time. The map would outline a nation in two parts, East and West Pakistan, with the breadth of India between.

Perhaps in inviting Louis for Sunday lunch, Nehru believed that, having acceded to Jinnah's demand for Pakistan, India might be healed of its communal fever, like an abscess lanced by a knife. Perhaps this was how Nehru imagined he might turn away from politics for an hour, and speak of something else. But with the publication of the Radcliffe maps, violence on both sides of the line dividing the Punjab exploded. Hindus and Sikhs traveling east were set upon by Muslim mobs before they could reach the Indian border, sparking a chain reaction of revenge on the other side, as gangs of Sikhs armed with guns and spears lay in wait for trains filled with Muslims heading west. Lunch was canceled.

"Others were able to play on our weakness because we had them," Radhakrishnan had said at the midnight session. Decades of listening to high British officials use the Hindu-Muslim conflict as a stalking horse deepened this divide and blinded many to its growing strength.

Addressing the assembled lawmakers still mourning the loss of an undivided India, Radhakrishnan asked, "Were we not victims, *ready* victims, so to say, of the separatist tendencies foisted upon us?"

The violence reached Delhi after Louis left for Lahore in the Punjab. On the night of September 6, the Muslim neighborhoods of Old Delhi were set aflame. Crazed-looking Sikhs waving kirpans above their heads surrounded the bungalow Louis had only just vacated, demanding that the Muslim servants be sent outside. Armed with his prize niblick and mashie, Sinbad Sinclair faced them down.

Louis found Delhi a ghost town on his return. The beggars were gone; tongas and taxis nowhere to be found. The home of the Muslim secretary of the Constituent Assembly, where he had been served a sumptuous meal a month before, had been looted. At the fort where sixty thousand Muslims were corralled in the open air, he watched Pakistan's portly prime minister give a speech from a lorry, begging them to stay in India, promising the Hindus wouldn't kill them. Everywhere Louis looked children were squatting and shitting. From there he went to Gandhi's prayer meeting. Gandhi had just returned from Calcutta, where the papers were saying he had single-handedly stopped the violence. Louis was dubious.

That night, back at Sinbad Sinclair's bungalow, the skies opened with biblical ferocity while Louis lay awake thinking about the refugees and about Gandhi.

After reflecting on vanity, in the Ecclesiastical sense, Louis went to bed. And the next morning he caught a train for Calcutta.

Suite no. 6, 6 Russell Street, Calcutta,
      September 25, 1947

Despite his criminal handling of the Bengal famine and his evasion of blame for the Great Calcutta Killing, Shaheed Suhrawardy had remained royally ensconced as Bengal's premier de jure, the leader of over sixty million people. He had, nonetheless, gone into a complete panic upon hearing that Gandhi, rather than be party to Independence Day festivities in Delhi, was en route once more to the backwaters of Noakhali. Having failed to stop the partition of India, Gandhi thought he might at least sacrifice himself on behalf of those who would be in the crosshairs when East Bengal became East Pakistan.

Should Gandhi be murdered on his watch, Shaheed's political prospects would never recover. Even worse would be the bloodbath of Calcutta Muslims sure to follow. Shaheed sped to the Sodepur Ashram to beg the old man to remain in the city and help him maintain peace. When Shaheed personally guaranteed the safety of the Noakhali Hindus, Gandhi relented, but on one condition. Shaheed must share his lodgings. They moved to the ramshackle home of a Muslim trader in the mixed and restive neighborhood of Beliaghata. Shaheed went further, exchanging his bespoke suits for penitential khadi pyjamas.

Independence Day passed without incident. Hindus and Muslims fraternized openly on streets that had run with their blood exactly one year before. The boundary map had divided Bengal so that Calcutta had made it into India and this provided an occasion of joy for both communities. When attacks on Hindus were threatened in what was now East Pakistan, they were quelled. Shaheed shared Gandhi's vegetarian meals (though he was seen on occasion to slip away to a restaurant) and sat alongside him during prayer meetings. He even accepted responsibility for the Great Calcutta Killing of 1946. Tributes flowed in from the viceroy and the Muslim League. Gandhi had wrought a miracle in Calcutta, the newspapers said.

But the news from the Punjab was remorseless. In time rocks smashed through the windows. A Hindu mob broke in, demanding Suhrawardy be turned over. Gandhi offered himself, Sudhin noted, in place of their "execrable" chief minister. The police ejected them and used tear gas to disperse the crowds outside, but the next day the city erupted. Dozens were killed. Gandhi announced a fast unto death beginning at 8:15 p.m. September 1, 1947. The *Times of India* declared that the peace of all India was at stake. Shaheed and representatives of the Hindu right wing kept vigil on either side of his bed.

Seventy-three hours into the fast, envoys from both communities produced a signed undertaking attesting the city was quiet. They pledged their lives to maintaining the peace. The Mahatma took a little orange juice. In answer to the clamor for a statement, he wrote a sentence in Bengali on a slip of paper: *Amar jibanee amar bannee*, My life is my message.

Rabindranath Tagore had imagined himself as he imagined India, as a pivot point and bridge between Europe and Asia. *Parichay* and Sudhin's adda embodied a similar project. But for Gandhi, India was always the center of the universe. The West had more to learn from India, he held, than India could learn from the West. Having lived through bombardment, famine, massacre, and partition, Sudhin now grasped the breadth and depth of this vision. This peculiar, half-naked little man's dream of India would outlast them all, he wrote.

By the time Louis MacNeice arrived, Calcutta seemed leagues away from the horrors of the north. Sudhin Datta swiftly arranged for him to move into the guest bedroom of his rambling and airy flat on Russell Street, deep within a neighborhood formerly known as *sahib para*. With its wall-to-wall collection of Bengali paintings, Sudhin's flat was infinitely more agreeable than the Great Eastern Hotel, where every time Louis turned around a white-gloved hand appeared for a tip.

Louis and Sudhin discovered an immediate kinship. For one thing, Sudhin had more books in more languages than Louis had yet seen in any Indian home. And he was very sprightly for forty-six, with a disarmingly silly and sophisticated sense of humor. The dishes from his kitchen were exquisite and, just when Louis imagined the meal over, another course would appear. John Auden's sister-in-law, in town from Bombay with her husband, joined them one evening. She said she was the only Bonnerjee sister not to have married an Englishman. Though as her husband was a Parsee, she had come pretty near it, Louis thought.

Another point of sympathy was that Sudhin appeared to be the only intellectual in the city not in thrall to communism. Like Communists everywhere, Louis found Bengali ones magnificently impervious to reason. At a meeting with the Progressive Writers' Association, he was obliged to field some unexpectedly sharp inquiries about Auden and Spender. One Communist's eight-year-old daughter recited a poem dedicated to Winston Churchill. It concluded with the line, "You said you wouldn't leave India. Well! What now?"

"Which gives you an idea of their political precocity," Louis wrote his wife, Hedli.

It was true; India was now free of Winston Churchill. Yet though the English were finally leaving, they left their language behind. There was now an edge of restraint to the Bengali love for English letters; never again would English words and English writers be taken at face value. Bengalis would make the most of their independence. Stories would be told and histories written to unmask the lies, expose the trifling and breathtaking betrayals suffered at the hands of this language and those who ruled them with it. As Louis had foreseen, there was something to be learned from them. Exclaiming that India had conquered him, Louis left Calcutta with a painting by Jamini Roy, a saree for Hedli, and recordings of Indian classical music. Sudhin's charming and soft-spoken young wife had taken him shopping.

The Set had been scandalized when Chhabi was sent back to her family so that Sudhin Datta might marry a much younger woman. Most shocking of all was that Rajeswari wasn't even a Bengali but a Punjabi. She soon adapted herself to her husband's interests, learning to speak and read French, Italian, and Bengali all the while carrying on her career as a professional singer of Tagore songs. Sudhin's closest friends eventually drifted back, happy to discover that she had helped free him from the depression that had overtaken him in 1940.

Otherwise, freedom, both personal and political, hadn't really changed Sudhin. Exasperation over his godforsaken city continued to be a staple of his conversation. Bedeviled by writer's block, he remained unconvinced that the celebrated marriage of Bengal and England had been an altogether happy one. He still sparred with bhadralok Communists who took him to task for his lack of political engagement, still introduced visiting foreigners (Stephen Spender among them) to the work of young Bengali poets, painters, and intellectuals. And he still entertained all at his drink and stand-ups. Sudhin had once assured John Auden that age wouldn't dull the fineness of his feelings but simply make them more intelligible. Perhaps his own raging heart had at last become intelligible.

Like all poets, Sudhin wondered if he would be read and remembered. He often caricatured himself as a faded and tattered relic of another age. And there were days when he seemed to be waiting for the
moment when, like so much of the history he had witnessed, he joined
the dust. But then a friend would drop by to sit on the veranda and the
pure pleasure of talking for hours would revive and delight him.

Sudhin formed from his despair, it was said, a life that was itself a
work of art.

Sinclair Bungalow, 17 Aurangzeb Road, New Delhi,
     November 17, 1947

While Sheila and the girls traveled to the cottage in the Lake District,
where Dr. Auden spent his summers, John went to London to explore whether he should remain with the GSI in Calcutta or join its
sibling in Pakistan. Large as London was, John was always running
into Erica Spender. When Sheila and the girls joined him there they
met up with Elinor Sinclair and her children, as well as Nancy with
hers. It was Nancy who had found them a flat for their stay. She was
teaching art at a private school to support herself. Nancy and Sheila
talked painting.

It wasn't until the Audens returned to Calcutta and learned of the
butchery in the Punjab that the idea of relocating to Pakistan was
abandoned. Sudhin and Minnie, meanwhile, could talk of little but
Louis MacNeice. His visit had been a "crashing success," John reported
to Nancy. Arriving in Delhi five days after Louis returned to London,
John learned Louis had been a hit there, too. Even his bathwater was
still standing, John wrote from the Sinclair's guest bedroom.

Was it Sinbad's whiskey, he wondered, or the dithyrambs of Louis's
verses echoing off the walls that charged his sleep that night with
memories of 1938?

> *Who has left a scent on my life and left my walls*
> *Dancing over and over with her shadow,*
> *Whose hair is twined in all my waterfalls*
> *And all of London littered with remembered kisses.*

Geological Survey of India, 27 Chowringhee, Calcutta,
   May 29, 1953

In 1950, when Nepal's borders were finally opened, Bill Tilman invited John Auden on a mountain-climbing expedition. He declined. Just as India no longer offered a ready stage for Englishmen to perform their superior Englishness, so John's aspiration to climb Everest had been replaced in his mind with another, even more daunting, ambition.

He wanted to become a better man.

In March 1951 John traveled to a small hill station near Darjeeling to see a Jesuit and mountaineer named Anderson Bakewell. Father Bakewell had recently accompanied Tilman on an expedition to Solo Khumbu, the home of the Darjeeling Sherpas of the Himalayan expeditions of the 1930s. On the same trip Bakewell and Tilman did a quick reconnaissance of Everest from the south. Bakewell's 16 mm panoramic footage seemed to show a possible route to the summit from a valley south of the neighboring peaks of Makalu and Lhotse. Though it remained unclear whether this offered a path to the summit, the route they explored would be useful to Shipton when he returned for a more thorough reconnaissance in 1952. Under Father Bakewell's counsel, John Auden became a Catholic.

After his conversion, John offered to deliver Bakewell's Everest photos to the Jesuit College in Rome, en route to London. After six happy years in Calcutta it was time for Anita and Rita, now ten and nine, to acquire a proper English boarding school education. In what would be John's final leave before his retirement, he and Sheila planned a summer trip to England to settle the girls at a convent school in Birmingham. They planned a stopover in Italy to visit Wystan and Chester at their villa in Ischia. John also wanted to explore the possibility of a semiprivate audience with Pope Pius and to visit a Vatican confessional. By then John had learned grace worked slowly.

Sheila had also hoped for better results. While her husband was in Rome, she asked Wystan whether John had been unfaithful to her. Incapable of dissembling, Wystan dutifully confirmed her suspicions by providing chapter and verse. As India's freedom and independence unfolded four years before, John had renewed his affair with Nancy.

Since then he had been secretly sending her letters and gifts. Confronting John on his return from Rome, Sheila gave him an ultimatum: he must choose between his family and Nancy Spender. John vowed never to see or correspond with Nancy ever again. He traveled to England, settled his wife and daughters into their new lives, and returned to India without seeing her.

Back in Calcutta John reported on everything from well yields, irrigation, and the hydrogeology of the Indo-Gangetic Plain to hydropower. All kinds of engineering schemes were in the works; "Dams are to be built 100 feet higher than Boulder and in half the time for nothing is impossible to resurgent nationalism," John wrote his brother in exasperation. Industrial development, on an epic scale, was under way. Gandhi would have been appalled had an assassin's bullet in 1948 not found him first. His pastoral vision of India, one of small-scale cottage industries, a vision not that far from the Romantic poet's Lake District idyll, died with him. Sudhin had been so shattered by his death that for the first time in his life he contemplated leaving India.

"Apart from Nehru, Rajagopalachari and Sarojini Naidu, the country is being run by half-educated sycophants and time-servers," John complained. As the last Englishman standing at the GSI his position grew precarious. He watched *hypocrites lecteurs* dispatch the last director, another Englishman, while on leave. When he questioned the wisdom of building high dams in tectonically active areas of the Himalaya with heavy debris flows, there were insinuations about his true loyalties. Word had come back about his having considered pursuing a post in Pakistan; the English who ended up there were considered quislings. When John refused to take the directorship of the GSI without a salary increase, the central ministry threatened to withhold the release of his pension.

Without Sheila, John began to slip back into doom and gloom. In 1940 he had resigned from the Saturday and the Tollygunj Clubs, knowing Sheila wouldn't be welcomed. Now he couldn't afford membership. He gave up smoking and whiskey to save money. He railed, too, about Minnie's housekeeping, her rapacious cook, the loo that wouldn't flush, and the dog that relieved itself by the side of his bed where his foot would find it in the morning. But for Sudhin, he had scarcely any friends left to call on and when he did he feared he was making a nuisance of himself. Shahid Suhrawardy was in Pakistan. Susobhan Sarkar was busy teaching and working on behalf of the Communist Party. Minnie and Lindsay were out every night; he wasn't invited anywhere. He felt like a man out of his time, a fossil embedded in a catafalque of stone, never to be seen on earth again. He drove himself to exhaustion.

Toward the end of John's GSI tenure, Jawaharlal Nehru inquired about his departure. Men like Auden were needed in India, the prime minister said to the new GSI director, a man who had done his best to make John's life impossible. Indeed, John Auden's fieldwork would fuel countless World Bank projects in the decades to come. In his final weeks in Calcutta he was besieged by an eruption of boils and carbuncles brought on by stress and the worst hot season he could remember. On Hastings Street he saw a miserable-looking Sikh taxi driver wiping his brow and when the man saw him looking he raised his shirt to show the rash of prickly heat emblazoned on his chest. John raised his shirt to show him his.

As he was packing up his office, much of his life in India was thrown back in his face. He scarcely recognized himself as the author of such papers as "The Structure of the Himalaya in the Garhwal." Unable to sleep the night before he left Calcutta for the last time, he reread all Sheila's letters from Simla, Darjeeling, and London. Sheila had resumed the peripatetic existence she had known during the war, living in a boardinghouse during term and spending school holidays with Dr. Auden and the girls. Though John's affectionate letters appeared regularly, it was a lonely life.

When morning came, John sat down to acknowledge all she had endured in their thirteen-year marriage. All those cold nights in small rooms, telescoped into one, showed him once more how much he had failed her as a husband. To provide her a place to call her own was sufficient reason to leave India without regrets. In a separate message to his daughters he mentioned the new queen, but passed over the news that had been held back to coincide with her coronation. The summit of Everest had at last been reached.

Both Edmund Hillary and Tenzing Norgay were a far cry from Arthur Hinks's template of the ideal Englishman. Hilary was a New Zealander and Norgay, who had accompanied Michael Spender to Everest in 1935, a Nepal-born Tibetan and a citizen of India. Not that maps and their borders defined him: Tenzing reached the summit, not as a Tibetan, Indian, Nepali, or Darjeeling Sherpa, but as a mountaineer.

On his first leave home from a new position in Khartoum, John saw Nancy on a bus traveling between Harrods and St. James's Place. He did not speak to her.

"I am your wife," Sheila once wrote John, five months after Minnie's early death left her devastated. "I should try and comfort you and boost your morale—and not taunt you. I should remember that it is good not to be alone and that in sickness and sorrow you would look after me just as I would look after you." By then Sheila knew; her husband had broken the vow he had made to her in Ischia in 1951. Working for Burmah Shell in London, John had once more resumed his affair with Nancy. There were years of lunchtime assignations at the Barbican Hotel, whispered telephone conversations, and back-channel notes and gifts. A look from Sheila was all it took for his face to flush. When she wept, he remained dry eyed, astonished and appalled by his shallowness of feeling.

For a time Sheila became, in her words, a nasty person with a bad temper and a cruel tongue. It wasn't so much the years of physical frustration, she told him, but his ceaseless lies and protestations of innocence. That he would lie to her to "protect" her she found deeply insulting. Schooled in the talk of the "sacred trust" between England and India, of viceroys claiming to have India's best interests at heart, she heard only the familiar humbug. She told him his lies made it impossible to know what was true and what was a fraud about their lives, indeed about anything at all.

In this way a marriage John had once portrayed as "an island against the bitterness" that lay between India and England became, instead, a vessel of its long acrimony.

Highfield Residential Home,
      Marlborough, Wiltshire, 1999

Nancy never remarried. She kept her love letters like neatly folded maps of territories, once conquered and now lost. After the war she embarked on a long career as an art teacher, achieving the independence she had long sought. At the nursing home where she spent her last days, her unease among the other residents made her rude, particularly if she felt she was being given the cold shoulder. A few of the men showed interest but she soon quarreled with them. So she occupied herself painting a housecat that had come with her from London. When the cat was poisoned she behaved as if a lover had been murdered.

She once hoped she would discover serenity in her old age. She hadn't.

"*You* are one I always shall remember," Louis had written of her. Nancy thought his letters had been lost, forgotten in a desk Bill had taken with him when he left her just before the war. Or was it during the war? She couldn't remember.

After Michael, Louis was the first to go, then Wystan, Bill, and finally John. Except when biographers or the BBC showed up, a bottle of champagne in hand to loosen her tongue, this was not the past Nancy dwelled on. Her childhood memories prevailed. Her doctor had started her down this road before the war, but she had made it her own since, applying herself with a doggedness generally associated with criminal inquiries. These memories were the last to fade and long before they did she wrote them down.

What are the conditions for healing a tear in the known world? Can a sense of loss ever be redeemed? While some are content to let go of the past, there will always be those left staring into the distance, haunted by the fragments that survive and struggling to see how they fit together. Even the humblest relics—a scrap of parchment or a faded Georgette sari, an empty cigarette tin or a map of a country that no longer exists—can hold a full measure of pain and perplexity. A young man might be the one digging around in boxes, looking for the father he never knew in books about the war and the years leading up to it. A daughter might date the family photographs

or order the letters written during long separations, in search of
that moment when her mother first disappeared behind stylish dark
glasses. A scholar will sift through old land records in search of an
ancestral home known only from a grandmother's stories. Another
will work to place a number on a famine, lacking faces, names, or
any souvenir beyond bones and old censuses to commemorate an
absence.

Finally, there is that distinguished-looking gentleman sitting at a
desk in a city where he will never feel at home. He will work and re-
work a frayed chapter of his life so as to better grasp the hold a city
or a country, a woman or a mountain once had over him.

And, in his dreams, still does.

43 Thurloe Square, South Kensington, London,
        January 2002

Wystan Auden's one visit to India was not a success. He had sulked
over the lack of alcohol, the late nights, and indigestible food. During
an interminable dance performance hosted by Prime Minister Nehru
in his honor, he had walked out in a huff. Sheila didn't entirely blame
him for that. But once, over dinner, she accused her famous brother-
in-law of having an antipathy to all things Indian. She went on to pronounce all the Audens hypocrites.

The next day, over John's objections, Sheila wrote Wystan a note of
apology, admitting she'd had too much to drink. After Sheila's death
in January 2002, her daughter found Wystan's reply in her wallet.

"*In vino veritas* is not a proposition I believe—one knows and tells
a greater part of the truth when one is sober," Wystan's letter began,
with his customary portentousness. Resentments, however, particularly those regarding immediate family, were more likely to find an
outlet under the influence. To his mind, it was just as well they did.

As far as India was concerned Wystan frankly acknowledged he
was defensive. "The East is a whole world or several whole worlds, of
religion, art, thought, which must be taken seriously, not dabbled in."
Since he wasn't about to dedicate his all to a study of the East, "the
wisest and most respectful course is not to consider it at all." But he

agreed with her about the Audens' hypocrisy. His father had once ranted about Jews in front of Chester.

"It is not just the Audens, English society as a whole is an in-bred snooty family. Why do you think that I went to America? Try to be patient with us, though, my dear."

Sheila Bonnerjee Auden had done her best.

– CHAPTER 20 –

Night Falls

Night falls on Kipling's Grand Trunk Road and all the deserted cantonments.
Night falls on the Murree Hills and the rhododendrons of Simla
Night falls on temple and temple car, on Moghul garden and Moghul tomb,
On jute mill and ashram, on cross and lingam.
On the dreaming sleeper on the railway platform
On the crop watcher on the gimcrack perch,
On the man who has never left the forest
On the last Englishman to leave

LOUIS MACNEICE, "INDIA DIARY"

Tapovan, near Gaumukh, Garhwal District,
May 6, 2015

At the foot of Shivling, not far from the snout of the Gangotri Glacier in the Garhwal Himalaya, is the glacial valley of Tapovan. Tapovan has been home to generations of babas. They live in caves under boulders or in crude stone huts in Shivling's shadow. Even now three men share this valley. They are Shaivites, following the difficult path of the god Shiva. Each has taken a vow of silence and chastity. The pyramid of granite before them and the glacier beneath them bear witness to their austerities. One baba, a former accountant for a telecommunication firm, has lived there for three years, another for eleven.

Like the mountaineers who trek through here to climb Kedarnath or Kedarnath Dome, these babas are aware of their lineage. They know the names of the saints who preceded them, men who suffered greater privations than a snowbound winter brings for them. One of the saintly was the Nanga Baba. The babas keep his photograph among their few possessions. Just as Shipton and Tilman scaled great heights without nylon tents or Google Earth, the Nanga Baba did not have aviator sunglasses or a wardrobe of orange fleece. He was naked. The palms of his hands and the soles of his feet were as hard as stone. In search of a holy life, the Nanga Baba tested the limits of his body and mind. If asked about him, babas up and down the pilgrimage route speak of him with awe.

Yet despite the mystic powers acquired from self-denial, when a winter storm brought down a heavy snowfall the Nanga Baba was buried alive in his cave. Does the baba who now lives under his rock ever fear the same might happen to him? Does he not wonder about the Nanga Baba's last thoughts? Alas, he is in Uttarkashi seeing a doctor; there is a sign warning the curious not to enter. An intestinal problem, the former accountant explains, whispering so as not to betray his vow of silence.

Not far from Tapovan, a two-day walk at most, is the mouth of the Rudagaira Valley. After a four-day climb to the top of this valley, one reaches the treacherous pass that John Auden and Juin Singh crossed on June 29, 1939. Though it is higher than any mountain in the Alps, for the Himalaya an 18,000-foot pass is unremarkable. Crossing it involves a steep ascent from the valley floor and a roped descent to the heavily crevassed Khatling Glacier on the far side, in Bhilangna Valley. Nepali porters from Uttarkashi refer to this pass as Udan Col, which they translate as "so windy it will make you fly." Indian guides with maps know it as Auden's Col, named after some forgotten Englishman who once crossed it. It is one of the most dangerous passes in all the Garhwal.

In 1945 John Auden was sent to America to learn about hydroelectric projects as part of India's postwar industrialization. On his way home he passed through London, seeing Eric Shipton at the RGS and delivering a pair of stockings to Nancy. Michael had been dead for five months. Enraged at John's refusal to sleep with her, bitter that he was alive and Michael was not, Nancy taunted him. Here you are again, she said, standing witless and gutless at the gate of my nunnery. You only went to India because you couldn't make it in England.

She had used this before to wound him. It still found its mark.

For someone of her intelligence, he wrote her on board a troopship returning him to India, it was narrow-minded to think that England held the sole measure of success. "No country has a monopoly on the first rate," he said, pointing out that one aspect of Michael's greatness was the restlessness that took him to the Great Barrier Reef, East Greenland, and India. He admitted that all he could recall of his own youthful dreams was his unrealized desire to climb Everest and to know something of the forces that had raised it. He admitted he had failed in both.

Though he never succeeded in being the first to climb the highest peaks, no other explorer of his time looked as closely at the mountains of the Himalaya and the rocks they were made of as John Auden. Like the most faith-filled pilgrim, he had also walked up the trail to the sacred wellspring of the Ganges and the glacial valley of Tapovan. But it was on mile 158 of the pilgrimage trek to Badrinath that he noted how the appearance of highly metamorphosed and massively dislocated blocks of stone provided surface evidence of an underlying fault deep within the Himalayan crust. He had seen similar dislocations elsewhere along the Himalayan chain, with the same thrusts of high-grade crystalline rocks. While John Auden always resisted the theory of continental drift, he knew in his bones that this fault had something to do with how the Himalaya first arose.

It was an Indian geologist who noticed that though John Auden had focused his conclusions on a single district, he was the first to suggest that the dislocation he mapped and described in his beloved Garhwal arced from west to east down the entire fifteen-hundred-mile length of the Himalayan chain. As indeed it did.

This fault is now known as the Main Central Thrust.

POSTSCRIPT

After a dinner at Minnie and Lindsay Emmerson's in honor of a rare return of John Auden to Calcutta, Sudhin Datta died peacefully in his sleep on June 25, 1960.

Shaheed Suhrawardy, the "Butcher of Bengal," became the fifth prime minister of Pakistan, forging a close relationship with the United States before being tossed from office. Some ascribed his early death to poisoning. His brother Shahid wrote many books on art, founded Pakistan PEN, and was posted as Pakistan's ambassador to Spain, Morocco, Tunisia, and the Vatican. He became a close friend of Nehru.

As a professor of history at Presidency College and Jadavpur University, Susobhan Sarkar nurtured a slate of scholars and intellectuals, among them the future Nobel Prize winner in economics Amartya Sen. Hiren Mukherjee became a member of the Lok Sabha and to the day he died never ceased to admire Joseph Stalin. Apurba Chanda was last seen complaining about the dreadful people who managed to get elected as members to the Calcutta Club.

Noticing a pile of recently disturbed earth in the garden of the Carritt family home in Boars Hill, a vigilant Oxford constable unearthed a uniform case filled with official Government of India papers marked SECRET. In this way MI5 learned that Michael John Carritt, a high-ranking Indian Civil Service officer, had been a Communist spy. Carritt's ICS pension was promptly revoked. Humphry House dedicated his most celebrated work, *The Dickens World*, to Sudhin Datta. Reverend Scott eventually fell out with the leaders of the Indian Communist Party, went on to work on behalf of the tribals in Assam and labored to end apartheid in South Africa. At his death, he was known in Namibia as the British Gandhi.

At her death Nancy Sharp was memorialized as one of the most under-rated painters of her generation. Her portrait of Louis MacNeice hangs in the National Portrait Gallery. Bill Coldstream became director of the Slade. Sonia Brownell married George Orwell.

In 1949 Sir George Schuster heralded the British repayment of sterling balances as evidence of how much England was doing for India, "its own form of a Marshall Plan."

When the Everest Committee replaced him as leader of the 1953 expedition Eric Shipton had to convince Edmund Hillary not to quit in protest; he ended his life as a scout leader. Bill Tilman, along with the entire crew of his sailing vessel, was lost at sea en route to the Falklands. He was eighty.

Stephen Spender was knighted. Wystan Auden wasn't.

Winston Churchill may be living still.

NOTES

People

CRA – Constance Rosalie Auden
GAA – George Augustus Auden
JBA – John Bicknell Auden
HH – Humphry House
HM – Hedli MacNeice née Anderson
LM – Louis MacNeice
MC – Michael Carritt
MS – Michael Spender
NS – Nancy Sharp
SB – Sheila Bonnerjee
SD – Sudhindranath Datta
SS – Stephen Spender
WC – William Coldstream
WHA – Wystan Hugh Auden

Archives

PRIVATE ARCHIVES

AMA – Anita Money Archive
John Auden's daughter correspondence with Sheila Bonnerjee; his 1929 and
1938–1939 journals, the latter of which often contained drafts of letters and
cables to Wystan Auden and Sheila. Unpublished writings by Sheila Bonnerjee
and John Auden are quoted with the permission of Anita Money.

PSA – Philip Spender Archive
The papers of Michael Spender and Nancy Sharp, including letters, typescripts
of unpublished work, photographs, sketchbooks, dream journals, datebooks,
as well as Violet Spender's 1917 journal and a photocopy of Stephen Spender's
novel, "Miss Pangborne." Unpublished writings by Michael Spender are quoted
with the permission of the Estate of Michael Spender.

PUBLIC ARCHIVES

AHCUW *American Heritage Center University of Wyoming*
H. W. Tilman diaries 1934–1967

BERG *Henry W. and Albert A. Berg Collection of English and American Literature; the Research Libraries of the New York Public Library; Astor, Lenox, and Tilden Foundations.*
John Bicknell Auden's papers are part of W. H. Auden Collection. The Berg also has two volumes of Louis MacNeice's "1947 notes for radio programs about India," and mimeographed drafts of three radio plays from the BBC 3rd Programme series.

BL *British Library*

BLASR *British Library Archival Sound Recordings, National Life Stories Collection: Artists Lives.*
Humphrey Spender Interview.

BL: Mss Eu *British Library Private Papers*
Papers of John Bicknell Auden, Michael Carritt, George Schuster, Sir Arthur Dash, and Leonard George Pinnell.

BL: IOR *British Library, Indian Office Records*

IOR/L/PJ/12 *Indian Office Records, Public and Judicial Department (Separate) series*
Scotland Yard Reports on Michael John Carritt and Hassan Shahid Suhrawardy.

IOR/L/I *Indian Office Records Information Department*
Ministry of Information records on India and America.

IOR/L/PS *India Office Records: Political and Secret Department*
Records of frontier expeditions to Everest, Tibet, and Northern India.

IOR/V *Official Publications series*
The Geological Survey of India and the war.

BOD *Special Collections, Bodleian Libraries, University of Oxford*
Papers of Louis MacNeice, E. R. Dodds, and Sir Isaiah Berlin. Diaries of Erika Haarmann, Mrs. Michael Spender.

HL *Huntington Library, San Marino, California*
Christopher Isherwood Papers.

HRC *Harry Ransom Humanities Research Center, University of Texas at Austin*
The Diary of Kathleen Bradshaw Isherwood, Christopher Isherwood Collection.

LHAC *The Labour History Archive and Study Center, People's History Museum, Manchester*
Michael Carritt Papers and files relating to the Communist Party of India and the Indian National Congress.

MED *The Medmenham Collection Archive in Wyton*
Papers of Constance Babington Smith.

NLS *National Library of Scotland*
"Wings Over Everest: The Story of the Houston–Mt. Everest Flight," 1934.

PMROK *Police Museum and Record Office Kolkata*
Special Branch and Intelligence Branch files up to 1947.

PRO *Public Record Office at Kew*
William Townsend journals, vols. 1–15.

RAFL *Royal Air Force Museum, London*
Oral histories of the RAF.

TGA *Tate Gallery Archive*
Papers of William Coldstream and Claude Rogers.

UVASC *Special Collections, University of Virginia Library, Charlottesville, Virginia*
Papers of Louis Arthur Johnson.

Prologue

xix **Apart from what he'd read . . . teeth on edge.** MacNeice, "India at First Sight," 2. BERG.

xix **His one Indian . . . the man said.** MacNeice, *The Strings Are False*, 209.

xix **Even so, Louis . . . Our foe. Your friend.** MacNeice, "India and Pakistan," 6. BERG.

xx **Snowbound and . . . to join up.** Dodds, *Missing Persons*, 136.

xx **For his Cornell University . . . well informed.** LM to NS, March 26, 1940. BOD. MacNeice, *Selected Prose*, 95.

xx **Though he'd never . . . they were right.** MacNeice, *Letters of Louis MacNeice*, 366.

xx **Or was freedom simply . . . his own defeat.** MacNeice, *Autumn Journal*, 4.

xx **"If one's going to be . . . mind out of it."** MacNeice, *Letters of Louis MacNeice*, 319.

xxi **Finally, Louis tried . . . other half lives.** MacNeice, "India at First Sight," 3. BERG.

xxi **Perhaps, he thought . . . into them.** LM to NS, March, 13, 1940, MS. Eng. c. 7381. BOD.

xxi **He read translations . . . Muhammed Ali Jinnah.** MacNeice, "1947 Notes." BERG.

xxii **The first woman he saw . . . cut open with a penknife.** MacNeice, "India at First Sight," 29. BERG.

xxii **Twenty miles away . . . or set on fire.** *Times*, August 29, 1947.

xxii **They lay in a field hospital . . . wound in her side.** MacNeice, "India at First Sight," 29. BERG. And LM to HM, August 31, 1947. Box 64, BOD.

xxii   **The scene . . . miserably insufficient.** LM to HM, September 16, 1947. Box 64, BOD.

xxii   **From Lahore Louis . . . Protestants in Ireland.** LM to HM, September 6, 1947. Box 64, BOD.

xxiii   **On his arrival in Delhi . . . turn on each other.** LM to HM, August 16, 1947. Box 64, BOD.

xxiii   **The London papers . . . unfit for self-government.** LM to HM, September 16, 1947. Box 64, BOD.

xxiii   **But who were we . . . bore no responsibility for this?** MacNeice, *Selected Prose*, 195.

xxiii   **Traveling to Srinagar . . . given it a spine.** LM to HM, September 6 and 16, 1947. Box 64, BOD.

xxiv   **A fortune-teller . . . he most wanted.** Stallworthy, *Louis MacNeice*, 211.

xxiv   **It was Nancy who had once . . . poem about Gandhi.** LM to NS, January 20, 1940. PSA.

xxiv   **And was he now destined . . . Ecclesiastes "vanity of vanities" sense.** LM to HM, September 22, 1947. Box 64, BOD.

xxiv   **From Srinagar . . . "The Ascent of C3."** LM to HM, September 6, 1947. Box 64, BOD.

xxiv   **Once upon a time . . . once been England's.** Isserman, *Fallen Giants*, 148–49.

xxiv   **With its white mane . . . heaven and earth.** MacNeice, "India at First Sight," 44. BERG.

1. The Lakes

3   **The path . . . fell away into the valley.** Violet Spender, "1917 Diary," 2. PSA.

3   **On their arrival on August . . . would climb.** Stephen Spender, "Miss Pangborne," 196–98. PSA.

3   **"Daddy! What's that noise . . . was a war on.** Spender, "1917 Diary," 3. PSA.

4   **Not long after Violet's death . . . Skiddaw itself were reciting.** Spender, "Miss Pangborne," 196–98. PSA. *World within World*, 87.

5   **In the summer of 1917 . . . off to die in France.** Spender, "1917 Diary," 4. PSA.

5   **"Our laughing children . . . English blood are wet."** http://femalewarpoets .blogspot.com/2014/04/violet-spender-one-of-her-poems.html.

5   **Harold's engagement . . . their little duty.** Humphrey Spender interview, BLASR.

6   **One day before he left . . . out yourself?"** Spender, "Miss Pangborne," 196–98. PSA

6   **In the summer of 1917 . . . mail important letters.** Spender, *World within World*, 324.

6   **Michael was a demigod.** Sutherland, *Stephen Spender*, 23.

6   **When the sun returned . . . best corrective."** Spender, "1917 Diary," 25. PSA. The quotation is from Tagore's *Reminiscences*.

7   **She'd ruined her husband's . . . all this."** Spender, "Miss Pangborne," 196–98. PSA.

8   **The mist made it easier . . . distant prospect.** Spender, *World within World*, 5, 6–7.

9   **When war was . . . force of five thousand.** Harold Spender, *The Fire of Life*, 193–96.

9   **In weekly Downing Street . . . publish any of it.** Ibid., 207.

9   **Yet when Harold's idol . . . call that never came.** Ibid., 218.

9   **He would not have a good war.** Sutherland, *Stephen Spender*, 31.

9   **That fall every day . . . cuffs and collars.** Violet Spender, "1917 Diary," 22. PSA.

9   **Violet liked to dress . . . backs of their knees.** Humphrey Spender interview, BLASR.

10   **Sometime between . . . egged Harold on.** Stephen Spender, *The Backward Son*, 134–35. Humphrey Spender interview, BLASR.

10   **Wystan and Michael . . . to Oxford.** *Balliol Record*, 2008, 18–19.

11   **They explored . . . lead and gold.** Stephen Spender, *W. H. Auden*, 26.

2. *The Steamship and the Spinning Wheel*

12   **Before he knew . . . never would.** Townsend, "Journal," Vol. 5, July 2, 1929. PRO. This account of Auden's passage is put together from other, roughly contemporary, accounts of passages to India.

12   **The scene in the hallways . . . remarked upon at dinner.** J. A. Spender, *Indian Scene*, 5, 7, 14.

13   **At Port Said . . . Gulf of Suez.** Muggeridge, *Chronicles*, 95.

13   **All at once, a hundred . . . at nightfall.** Spender, "1935 Everest Journal," 4–5. PSA.

13   **The next morning . . . stentorian cry of "Boy!"** Muggeridge, *Chronicles*, 95.

14   **He always got . . . up Cader Idris.** John Auden, "1913 Journal of Family Holiday in Rhayader." BERG. Spender, *W. H. Auden*, 26.

15   **Egalitarian, they . . . and a cook.** Spender, *W. H. Auden*, 26.

15   **Stowed in a trunk . . . *Expedition of 1922.*** Papers of John Bicknell Auden. BL: Mss Eur D 843/12.

16   **Launches flying . . . British Empire.** Muggeridge, *Chronicles*, 96.

16   **The infernal hubbub . . . a curious face.** Spender, *Indian Scene*, 17–19.

17   **Between dawn . . . preposterous topee.** Auden, *Reminiscences of Retired Officers*, 41.

18   **Aunt May prided . . . Night Thoughts with her husband.** Spender, *World within World*, 86.

19   **His Harrow- and Cambridge . . . agreed.** Bose, *The Indian Struggle*, 210.

21   **Indeed, even Alfred despaired . . . minority Muslim community.** Spender, *Indian Scene*, 231.

21   **Even the Great War . . . inevitability of progress.** Ibid., 139. Spender, *World within World*, 77.

22   **Once a scrub forest . . . silhouetted against the sky.** Auden et al., *Centenary of the Geological Survey*, 6.

22   **Pit mines worked . . . of their caste.** Peterson, *Bengal District Gazetteers*, 173.

22   **As John sweated through . . . the Roman Wall.** J. B. Auden, "1929 Journal." AMA.

23   **When John confessed . . . in the library.** WHA to JBA [June or December 1927]. BERG.

23   **As for John's fears . . . would save him.** WHA to JBA [April and December 1927]. BERG. John Auden, "1929 Journal." AMA.

24   **Modeled on the *Alpine Journal* . . . literature, and sport."** Mason, *Abode of Snow*, 190.

24   **John's GSI supervisors . . . of the Himalaya?** Auden et al., *Reminiscences of Retired Officers*, 42.

24   **The highest point on a sixty-mile . . . the Krol Belt.** Valdiya, *The Making of India*, 344.

25   **John drew cross sections . . . How did this happen?** "The Geology of the Krol Belt," in Radhakrishna, *J. B. Auden*, 55, 121.

3. Bengali Baboo

27   **Following British traders . . . their English airs.** Datta, *World of Twilight*, 51–52, 58.

28   **They granted Bengalis . . . a ruling race.** Spender, *Indian Scene*, 220.

28   **"By his legs . . . always must be."** Steevens, *In India*, 73.

28   **A British Resident . . . demand a reckoning."** Sarkisyanz, *From Imperialism to Fascism*, 163–64, citing Al Carthill, *Verlorene Herrschaft*, 141–43. Carthill, whose real name was Bennet Christian Huntingdon Calcraft Kennedy, was the author of *Lost Dominion*, a handbook on racial imperialism later translated into German and taken up by Karl Haushofer, Rudolf Hess, and Adolf Hitler. Hannah Arendt also noted the widespread influence of Carthill's handbook on Nazi ideology.

29   **"What milk . . . polysyllabic baboo."** Aberigh-Mackay, *Twenty-One Days*, 51–52.

29   **"quick to discern the fire of ideas behind the smoke of guns."** Bose, *An Acre of Green Grass*, 70–71.

29   **A boycott was called . . . state of West Bengal.** Sarkar, *The Swadeshi Movement*, 18–20.

29   **That and other acts . . . a sense of honor.** Datta, *The World of Twilight*, 64.

30   **In 1901, this uncle . . . England unharmed.** Datta, *Art of the Intellect*, 230. Datta, *World of Twilight*, 73–76.

30   **When he sailed to England . . . by British troops.** King, *Partner in Empire*, 104.

31   **As guarantor of . . . sunrise to sunset.** Datta, *World of Twilight*, 7–9, 27–29.

32   **After Sudhin came of age . . . outside their bedroom.** Sinclair, "A Memoir," 54. PSA.

32 **Was it surprising ... own woolly minds?** Datta, *Art of the Intellect*, 18.

33 **In Germany he disarmed ... return their *Heils*.** Dev, *Sudhindranath Datta*, 24, citing Edward Shils, introduction to Datta, *World of Twilight*, xvi.

33 **The love poems ... bitterly controlled wrath.** Bose, *Acre of Green Grass*, 65.

33 **"A more ill-assorted ... you cannot imagine."** Datta, *Art of the Intellect*, 231.

34 **As a child ... greatest delights.** Datta, *World of Twilight*, 49–50.

34 **What gunfighters ... was to Calcutta.** Suraiya, *Rickshaw Ragtime*, 108–10.

34 **Among the subjects ... European literature.** Dev, *Sudhindranath Datta*, 28, 34–35.

34 **"Ask a Bengali ... his own eloquence."** Suraiya, *Rickshaw Ragtime*, 108–10.

34 **At the center of an adda ... members orbited.** Chakrabarty, *Provincializing Europe*, 208, citing *Nana katha* by Srikumar Chattopadhyay, 9, 16.

34 **In its first year the adda ... as a clerk.** Sarkar, *Essays in Honour*, 23.

34 **On the upper floors ... covered with sheets.** Muggeridge, *Like It Was*, 103.

35 **Two enormous bookshelves ... of course, Tagore.** Dev, *Sudhindranath Datta*, 36, citing *Amar Jauban*, by Buddhadeb Bose.

35 **A lamp of frosted glass ... they were good.** Reminiscences of Kanakendranath Datta (nephew), translated by Gouri Chatterjee.

35 **Even an Englishman ... unfailing courtesy.** Mukherji, "The Dickens World Revisted."

35 **At ease on any number ... swerve to a "yet."** Bose, *Acre of Green Grass*, 55.

35 **He would consider ... unassailable confidence.** Ghosh, *Parichay-er Adda*, August 27, 1937, 41. The secret diarist was Shyamal Krishna Ghosh. Though he did come to write in Bengali after his involvement with the Parichaya group, he wrote his diary in English. Unfortunately, the diary was lost, but not before parts of it had been translated into Bengali and published. Gouri Chatterjee retranslated them back into English for me, but I have edited her translations for style.

35 **The more aggressive nationalists ... nothing but Sanskrit.** Ghosh, *Parichay-er Adda*, September 16, 1932, 123.

35 **He took equally ... blindingly white dhotis.** Datta, *Art of the Intellect*, 230.

35 **And the Mahatma's constant resort ... unsettled Sudhin the most.** Ibid., 230.

36 **When he encountered ... on his tweeds.** Datta, *World of Twilight*, xviii.

36 **All assumed the ... business interests.** See Dasgupta, *English Poets on India*, 1–2.

36 **He took shelter ... come home.** Hassan Shahid Suhrawardy, BL: IOR/L/PJ/12/3, File 1256/17.

36 **On his reluctant return to ... wine, and food.** Muggeridge, *Like It Was*, 92, 95. Muggeridge, *Chronicles*, 28.

36 **Both Scotland Yard ... not a Bolshevik.** Hassan Shahid Suhrawardy, BL: IOR/L/PJ/12/3, File 1256/17.

37 **A former deputy mayor . . . disgraceful situations."** Dash Papers, BL: Mss Eur D1066/2.

37 **He had acquaintances . . . at the same time.** Leonard George Pinnell, "Pages relating to Bengal Famine." BL: Mss Eur D911/37.

37 **On his rare visits . . . local politics.** Sarkar, *Essays in Honour*, 32.

37 **The Suhrawardy brothers . . . Nothing.** Muggeridge, *Like It Was*, 100.

37 **A monologue on classical . . . the Himalayan foothills.** Ghosh, *Parichay-er Adda*, 118.

37 **While his interlocutor . . . appearance of cant.** Sarkar, *Essays in Honour*, 27, 29–31.

37 **After his father lost . . . warring intellects.** Mitra, *Three Score and Ten*, 82.

38 **Finally, there was . . . slightly exaggerated.** Sarkar, *Essays in Honour*, 23, 30–31.

38 **To some Sudhin was . . . nature of truth and reality.** Abu Sayeed Ayyub, "Sudhindranath Datta."

38 **Yet whatever face he turned . . . give up his own.** Datta, *World of Twilight*, 60.

4. *The Thrust Fault*

39 **The "fishing fleets" . . . a thousand pounds a year.** Sinclair, "A Memoir," 40. PSA.

40 **There were Sunday . . . the Bally, and the Slap.** Carritt, *Mole in the Crown*, 83–84.

40 **These establishments, too . . . Girls were extra.** Suraiya, *Rickshaw Ragtime*, 100–101.

40 **"Not just because of an *idea*?"** J. B. Auden, "1929 Journal," is the main source for this chapter. Direct quotations, except where otherwise indicated, are from this and have been lightly edited for clarity. AMA.

41 **It was Wystan who . . . see Margaret Marshall.** WHA to JBA [late July 1927]. BERG.

41 **Margaret had pronounced Wystan's libido perfectly normal.** WHA to Christopher Isherwood [March/April 1928]. HL.

43 **John could never bring . . . more fully expressed.** JBA to WHA [June or July 1927]. BERG.

45 **Petitioners found him . . . foremost in his mind: Capital.** Dash Papers, "A Bengal Diary 1910–1950." Box 2-5, BL: Mss Eur C188.

45 **No one needed to tell . . . peace was preserved.** Moon, *Strangers in India*, 14.

46 **If Gandhi followed through . . . English mill worker.** Muldoon, *Empire, Politics*, 14. *Straits Times*, September 1, 1930.

46 **"The British government in India . . . culturally, and spiritually."** Extract from the Independence Day Resolution passed by the INC in 1930. www .nationalarchives.gov.uk/education/empire/transcript/g3cs3s2t.htm.

5. Triangles

49　**While Alfred Spender . . . vote was reversed.** Sarkar, *Essays in Honour*, 18–20. Citing coverage in *Amrita Bazar Patrika*, February 14, 1926, 5; February 20, 1926, 10; and March 9, 1926, 4.

49　**At the war's end . . . were starving.** Townsend, journals, vol. 1, May 6–12, 1926. PRO.

49　**Though Michael Spender . . . for engine drivers.** Sutherland, *Stephen Spender*, 63.

50　**Driving a locomotive . . . friend from university.** MS to Anthony Bull, undated. PSA. Bull was a future president of the Institute of Transport.

50　**Michael's only concern . . . arrived at the station.** Philip Spender, interview, summer 2014.

50　**By the second . . . Canning Town.** Laybourn, *General Strike*; Townsend, journals, vol. 1, May 6–12, 1926. PRO.

50　**"Am not I a man of crisis?". . . of the moment.** MS to Anthony Bull, undated. PSA.

50　**By the fifth day . . . starve, he thundered.** Laybourn, *General Strike*, 16.

50　**By day eight . . . dockworkers.** Townsend, journals, vol. 1, May 6–12, 1926. PRO. Laybourn, *General Strike*, 62.

50　**Still dazed by the glow . . . now saw, outrageous.** MS to Anthony Bull, undated. PSA.

50　**Even the Conservative . . . been overdone.** MS to Anthony Bull, undated. PSA.

50　**Researching an article . . . nightly programming.** Chris Baraniuk to Philip Spender, January 6 and 10, 2010. PSA.

51　**When Alfred finally . . . the Indian Civil Service.** Spender, *The Changing East*, 153.

51　**Like the color bar . . . of the British Raj.** Ibid., 148–49.

51　***The Changing East* . . . were the remedy.** Ibid., 155–56.

51　**On the eve . . . choose someone else.** MS to Anthony Bull, February 18, 1927. PSA.

52　**Michael Spender was . . . terribly keen.** C. F. Jenkin to Arthur Hinks, February 20, 1928: RGS Archive Gt Barrier Reef CB, 1921–1928.

52　**On hearing the news . . . Harold had been.** Spender, *World within World*, 44.

52　**The four rugby-playing . . . best jobs going.** Carritt, *Mole in the Crown*, 7.

53　**Having spent more time . . . for a posting.** Ibid., 15–17.

53　**He foresaw sharing pegs . . . chukkers of polo.** Steevens, *In India*, 72.

53　**But to Carritt's bitter . . . of the ICS deck.** Carritt, *Mole in the Crown*, 14.

54　**Gandhi's volunteers had offered only . . . congratulation from prison.** www.midnapore.in/town_contai_freedom.html.

54　**If Carritt distinguished himself . . . inquiries were threatened.** Michael Carritt, "Tour Diary, Tangail." BL: Mss Eur D 1172/4.

55　**Yet Carritt did admit that . . . and no doctor.** Carritt, *Mole in the Crown*, 30–32.

55 **He died the next morning . . . two assailants.** Special Branch file no. 6234 Outrage—Midnapur shooting murder of Mr. Peddie, ICS Midnapur on April 7, 1931. PMROK.

55 **Peddie's assassins were . . . arrests of young men.** Battacharya, *Chittagong*, 147, 465. www.midnapore.in/town_contai_freedom.html.

55 **The Marquess of Willingdon . . . was kindness.** Muggeridge, *Chronicles*, 44.

55 **When another campaign . . . with sitting targets.** Dash Papers, "A Bengal Diary 1910–1950," Box 2-5. BL: Mss Eur C188.

56 **On his return he accepted a job . . . Then he resigned.** Philip Spender's notes on Nancy Sharp's memories of Michael Spender, January 9, 1967. PSA.

56 **To Arthur Hinks . . . felt futile.** MS to Arthur Hinks, January 8, 1931. RGS.

57 **In 1800 a sweet-tempered . . . it was begun.** Keay, *The Great Arc*, 9, 31, 80.

58 **A no less monumental . . . village in India.** Collier, "Impact on Topographic Mapping."

58 **Every ICS officer . . . seen and measured.** Carritt, *Mole in the Crown*, 42, 46.

59 **The maps of the southern . . . about that?** MS to Arthur Hinks, January 8, 1931. PSA.

59 **Hinks knew from the Everest Committee . . . stereographic surveying.** Arthur Hinks to Professor Carl Fridolin Baeschlin, December 1, 1930. PSA.

59 **Just beyond this contraption . . . here to work."** MS to Arthur Hinks, January 8, 1931. PSA.

59 **Switzerland's leading expert . . . proof of the rotation equation.** MS to Arthur Hinks, February 26, 1931. PSA.

60 **A map, however . . . fitted onto it.** Spender, "Geography at Work." PSA.

60 **The algorithms used . . . mountainous terrain.** Collier, "Impact on Topographic Mapping."

60 **This physiological phenomenon . . . and an early night.** Spender, "The New Photographic Survey."

62 **The Germans were so . . . mentioning the Wild.** MS to Arthur Hinks, February 26, 1931. PSA.

62 **For some time now . . . streets for the beggars.** Christopher Isherwood to Olive Mangeot, December 1931. Box 64, CI Papers, HL.

63 **Erica Haarmann.** Diary of Erika Haarmann MSS. German e. 16-19. BOD. Erica spelled her name Erika and Erica, Haarmann and Harman.

63 **"There isn't a girl . . . to commit suicide."** Spender, *World within World*, 47.

64 **"spiritual astigmatism."** Ibid., 46.

6. The School of Art

65 **Until she left for Cheltenham Ladies' . . . of her youth into Art.** Sharp, "Memoir and Chronology," PSA. Unless otherwise noted, various versions of Nancy Sharp's Memoir and Chronology form the basis of this chapter.

65   **An early self-portrait . . . at peace.** Spender, *Nancy Sharp (Nancy Spender)*, from
      the introduction.

66   **If she was going . . . hall of the Slade.** Devas, *Two Flamboyant Fathers*, 149–50.

66   **So Nancy's studio . . . became her stage.** Townsend, journals, vol. 7, July 1, 1930.
      PRO.

66   **Her parties and the wild revels . . . had possessed them.** Townsend, journals,
      vol. 7, June 18, 1930. PRO.

66   **Thin as a pencil . . . shrewd look about him.** Medley, *Drawn from Life*, 204. Pery,
      The Affectionate Eye, 26–27.

67   **Pictorial art . . . to be watched.** Townsend, journals, vol. 5. January 30, 1929. PRO.

67   **While his witty . . . that haunted him.** Pery, *The Affectionate Eye*, 26. Rogers
      Papers, 8121. TGA.

67   **The Slade Boys all agreed . . . holiday a year.** Townsend, journals, vol. 5,
      December 13, 1928. PRO.

67   **"Herd masturbation" one of them called it.** Townsend, journals, vol. 7,
      November 11, 1930. PRO.

67   **Mixed parties soon brought . . . drunken spectacle.** Townsend, journals, vol. 7,
      October 14, 1929, July 1, 1930. PRO.

67   **The Boys blamed the arrival . . . detestable creature.** Townsend, journals, vol. 7,
      December 9, 1929. PRO.

68   **Money, and the lack . . . and Ben Nicolson.** Townsend, journals, vol. 10, January 12,
      1936. PRO

68   **They looked to Bill . . . but to show them.** Townsend, journals, vol. 9, August 5
      and 9, 1934. PRO.

68   **But Bill's paintings . . . had been disturbed.** Coldstream Papers, 8922/1. TGA.

68   **He couldn't draw . . . out his brushes.** Graham Bell to Ann Bell, April 27 and 29,
      1938. Coldstream Papers, 8922/4. TGA.

68   **"Just what does Bill think he's up to?"** Rogers Papers, 8121/9. TGA. Moynihan,
      Restless Lives, 30.

68   **Whatever happened . . . feel of his studio.** Devas, *Two Flamboyant Fathers*, 175.
      Moynihan, *Restless Lives*, 27.

68   **Flowers withered before she could paint them.** Graham Bell, Coldstream Papers,
      8922/4. TGA.

69   **"I can do nothing with your father . . . very sorry, sir."** Laughton, *William
      Coldstream*, 25. Laughton cites Townsend's journal for this but the date 1928 is
      wrong. They were married in 1932. Doubtless, many versions circulated.

69   **Seeing Bill emerge . . . like a corpse.** Moynihan, *Restless Lives*, 34–35.

69   **With her frantic . . . life out of him.** NS to JBA, May 17, 1938. MSS Auden. BERG.

70   **Where they had . . . eyeing Bill for answers.** Townsend, journals, vol. 7, May 10,
      1930.

70   **Bill told the Boys . . . newly impressed.** Townsend, journals, vol. 9, August 5 and 9, 1934. PRO.

70   **While Bill was out and about . . . to be an only."** Pery, *The Affectionate Eye*, 40. Rogers Papers, 8121/9. TGA.

70   **Cadging a shilling . . . for the baby.** Rogers Papers, 8121/9. TGA. Moynihan, *Restless Lives*, 27.

71   **"We'll just leave Juliet . . . that she's all right."** Rogers Papers, 8121/9. TGA.

71   **"veteran enemy of compulsory hygiene,"** Auden and Isherwood, *Journey to a War*, 59.

71   **When Nancy went . . . thick as thieves.** Interviews with Philip Spender, summer 2014.

71   **Wystan had arrived . . . his father's library.** George Augustus Auden to NS, May 4, 1946. PSA.

71   **In Berlin Wystan had . . . love of men?** W. H. Auden, "1929 Berlin Journal." BERG.

72   **When Wystan wrote . . . Bill was jealous.** NS to LM, July 12, 1937. BOD.

72   **If Bill was unable to be faithful . . . have affairs.** Sharp, memoir chronology, PSA. Carpenter, *W. H. Auden*, 26.

72 .   **One afternoon . . . in the lock.** Interviews with Philip Spender, summer 2014.

72   **Yet when Wystan . . . didn't think she'd mind.** NS to JBA, May 25, 1938. PSA.

7. Perfect Monsters

77   **Then, on Sunday, January . . . indigestible scraps.** Andrews, *The Indian Earthquake*, 34.

78   **In Calcutta . . . masonry and timber.** Ibid., 22.

78   **In Kathmandu . . . the air unbreathable.** Brett, "A Report on the Bihar Earthquake."

78   **By the time the earth . . . made homeless.** Andrews, *Indian Earthquake*, 15–17.

79   **The king of Nepal . . . collapse of his palace.** Prashad, *The Life and Times of Maharaja Juddha*, 66.

79   **John Auden was invited . . . had to withdraw.** J. B. Auden, "Traverses in Nepal."

81   **In the future . . . precedence over American.** Coll 37/11 (1) Northern India: Mount Everest; British Expeditions 1933–1936. BL: IOR/PS/12/4242.

81   **"Almost every nation . . . they have failed."** Unsworth, *Everest*, 111.

81   **The British had obliged . . . Everest via Tibet in return.** Hansen, "The Dancing Lamas of Everest."

82   **"The first, most anxious . . . depend upon him."** *London Times*, September 3, 1932.

82   **The flight over Everest's . . . thirty miles square.** Fellowes et al., *First over Everest*, v–vi.

82   "The chief aim of the Marquis . . . TO HELL WITH RAMSAY MACDONALD." Pugh, *Hurrah for the Blackshirts*, 190, 188.

83   In the opening montage . . . their astonishment. *Wings over Everest*, NLS.

84   Climbing to 19,000 . . . summit from Makalu's. Blacker, "The Mount Everest Flights."

84   The altimeter showed . . . handshakes, and backslapping. "Wings Over Everest," NLS.

84   A spokesman for . . . last penetralia." Isserman, *Fallen Giants*, 160, citing the *Times*, April 4, 1933.

85   He'd also done . . . simultaneous intrusions. Radhakrishna, *J. B. Auden*, 55, 121.

85   The talk was all . . . swagger. L. R. Wager to JBA, April 25, 1933. BERG.

85   Bill Wager fit Hinks's . . . East Greenland coast. *Biographical Memoirs of the Fellows of the Royal Society*, Laurence Rickard Wager (1940–1965), 358–85. rsbm.royalsocietypublishing.org/content/13/358.

86   Until the final roster . . . this tactless. Shipton, *Six Mountain Travel Books*, 395–96.

86   But for his triumphant . . . to the newspapers. Isserman, *Fallen Giants*, 151–58.

86   "We must have a leader . . . to the nails of his toes." Ibid., 157. Citing Francis Younghusband's letter to William Goodenough, August 10, 1932, in Mount Everest expedition archives. RGS.

87   There were striking . . . kill something. Ruttledge, *Everest*, 6.

87   This debate began . . . go over well. L. R. Wager to JBA [May 1933]. BERG.

88   Eric Shipton joked . . . getting bedsores. Shipton, *That Untravelled World*, 77.

88   Only Bill Wager . . . salt in his wounds. L. R. Wager to JBA, April 25, 1933. BERG.

88   A fully recovered Bill Wager . . . Mallory's ice ax. Ruttledge, *Everest, 1933*, 138.

88   In winter, high winds . . . monsoon conditions. L. R. Wager, "Mount Everest's Weather in 1933."

89   Down on the East . . . like a shroud. Ruttledge, "The Mount Everest Expedition, 1933."

89   During the night . . . to Smythe. Shipton, *Six Mountain Travel Books*, 390–91.

89   Smythe might have . . . descended on him. Shipton, *That Untravelled World*, 173.

89   Two weeks earlier . . . in an hour. Mason, "The Problem of Mount Everest." Ruttledge, *Everest, 1933*, 160.

89   The Dalai Lama . . . guardian deities. Coll 37/11 (1) Northern India: Mount Everest; British expeditions 1933–36. BL: IOR/PS/12/4242.

89   But Eric Shipton . . . get a foothold. Shipton, *Six Mountain Travel Books*, 377, 395–97.

89   Meanwhile the air . . . prevailed elsewhere. Fellowes et al., *First over Everest*, 143.

90   Around Everest . . . note of triumph. Michael Spender, review of *The Pilot's Book of Everest*. PSA.

90   **Bill Wager blamed Ruttledge . . . he'd known him.** L. R. Wager to JBA, April 25, 1933. BERG.

8. Goddess Mother of the World

91   **While in Calcutta . . . 1936 summit attempt.** "Announcements," *Science*, 81, (1935).

91   **Two years after . . . taken a shine.** Perrin, *Shipton and Tilman*, 245.

92   **He found Bengalis insufferable.** H. W. Tilman, "Diaries 1934–1967." Collection Number 02456, AHCUW.

92   **Where Tilman was . . . splayed stance like a penguin.** Philip Spender's notes on meeting Eric Shipton, October 23, 1967. PSA.

92   **Tilman was the son . . . easy affability.** Perrin, *Shipton and Tilman*, 247.

92   **(Tilman called her "The Holy").** Tilman, "Diaries 1934–1967." Collection Number 02456. AHCUW.

92   **On Shipton's return . . . he countered.** Shipton, *Six Mountain Travel Books*, 401.

93   **Shipton was thereby . . . on Everest.** Ibid., 403–4.

93   **Wager advised Shipton . . . close companionship."** Shipton, *That Untravelled World*, 95.

93   **His wife, Erica, hadn't taken . . . he was away.** Spender, "1935 Everest Journal." PSA. Except where otherwise noted, this is the main source for my narrative of the expedition, but I have only cited page numbers for direct quotes. Michael's recollections would make their way into Auden and Isherwood's play, *The Ascent of F6*.

94   **"the top" . . . "No controversy for me."** Spender, "1935 Everest Journal," 7. PSA.

94   **"The less said about to-day the better."** Ibid., 14. PSA.

95   **Even Tilman declared . . . ever experienced.** Tilman, "Diaries 1934–1967." Collection Number 02456. AHCUW.

95   **"Dear, dear E, if only one could meet you at the end of a day's march."** Spender, "1935 Everest Journal," 14. PSA.

96   **Many of the Sherpas . . . of the World."** Norgay, *Tiger of the Snows*, 20.

97   **At their good-bye meal . . . New Zealander's legs.** Astill, *Mount Everest*, 130–31.

97   **"Western ways leave behind nothing but unhappiness."** Perrin, *Shipton and Tilman*, 251.

97   **"silly medievalism."** Ibid., 253.

98   **What will I do . . . into our lives.** Spender, "1935 Everest Journal," 7. PSA. Spender, "Mount Everest, 1938."

98   **The shepherd's wife . . . points awaited.** Spender, "Tibetan Tent." In Michael's diary account, he writes that he shared their meal. In the *Spectator*, he says he made excuses and left.

102 **"O Gawd! O Gawd!"** Spender, "1935 Everest Journal," 59. PSA.

105 **Dawa Tendrup . . . Everest in 1933.** Mason, "Notes." *HJ* 8 (1935).

105   **After a two-day trek . . . another glacial valley.** J. B. Auden, "An Excursion to Gangotri." This is the principal source for this section.

106   **The Boys waited patiently . . . the director.** Elsie Few's account of WHA's filming of the New Year's party at 38 Upper Park Road in Rogers Papers, 8121/10. TGA.

106   **The GPO left him . . . interested in making.** WHA to JBA, February 24, 1936. BERG.

106   **He did enjoy . . . a lyricist.** Pery, *The Affectionate Eye*, 66.

107   **There would also be . . . while at Oxford?** WHA to JBA, February 24, 1936. BERG.

107   **Wystan had complained . . . heard of.** Carpenter, *W. H. Auden*, 78. Spender, *W. H. Auden*, 48.

107   **"We are beginning to make ourselves look very ridiculous"** and subsequent quotes from the *Morning Post*, London, October 17, 1936.

108   **The decision to limit . . . chauvinism.** Ruttledge, *Everest*, 11–12.

9. I Spy

110   **According to the book . . . was its flower.** Aberigh-Mackay, *Twenty-One Days*, 4–5.

110   **At six feet four the 2nd Marquess . . . was a very tall flower.** Snow, *People on Our Side*, 40.

110   **The *Daily Mail* . . . regional autonomy.** Birla, *In the Shadow of the Mahatma*, 161, 163.

111   **As before . . . over to baboos.** Glendevon, *Viceroy at Bay*, 109.

111   **Secretly, Linlithgow . . . painted lilac.** Muggeridge, *Chronicles*, 44.

111   **The Calcutta residence . . . neglect of duties.** Glendevon, *Viceroy at Bay*, 92.

112   **The king found his letters . . . tiresome.** Wavell, *Wavell: The Viceroy's Journal*, 11.

112   **To arrange a meeting . . . could do.** Scott, *Time to Speak*, 69, 75, 76.

114   **Periodically, the strain . . . they had.** Ibid., 82. See also Yates and Chester, *The Troublemaker*.

114   **It was during his . . . of the British Empire.** Michael Carritt, "Tour Diary, Tangail," BL: Mss Eur D 1172/4. Michael Carritt (former ICS), BL: IOR/L/PJ/12/618, File 1209/38. Michael Carritt, Indian Civil Service, Bengal 1930–1939, Communist underground worker, notebooks containing notes on CP organization in India (1936–37); twelve page memo, "Notes on Selected Carritt Documents," Inventory no. 111.58, Report no. 8. CP/IND/CP/INC/MONT/7/4. LHASC.

116   **If Carritt dismissed . . . in the first place.** Spender, *World within World*, 77.

116   **Every once in a while . . . decency sustained.** Carritt, *Mole in the Crown*, 80.

116   **A police officer had once . . . inflicted upon him.** Scotland Yard Report of Meeting of Indian League, Holborn Hall, Easter Sunday, April 13, 1941. "[Michael John Carritt] discussed the treatment of prisoners and torture of those sentenced to death by police intent on obtaining the names of accomplices. Carritt said he had obtained these facts from the police officer himself, who described with

considerable gusto the psychological reaction of the condemned man. [T]he speaker was extremely calm and he made his points in a very matter of fact way. Whether [Carritt] intended to do so or not he conveyed the impression that he was making one or two disclosures in sorrow rather than in anger and suggesting that he could disclose much more if he wanted. Michael John Carritt former ICS.: association with Communist Party of Great Britain. BL: IOR/L/PJ/12/618, File 1209/38; Apr. 1940–Nov. 1948.

117 **How many spies . . . to sign it.** Humphry House, *I Spy with My Little Eye*, 8. Self-published.

117 **Carritt's superiors . . . seized for study.** Opinion of the Public Prosecutor Calcutta regarding the mode of disposal of properties seized and classified under the following heads: a. literature which are proscribed, b. literature not proscribed but objectionable, c. literature which are innocuous. Special Branch file no. 12885. PMROC.

118 **Carritt was meant . . . they'd been sent.** Scott, *Time to Speak*, 67.

119 **The Comintern had previously . . . represent the masses.** Overstreet and Windmiller, *Communism in India*, 514.

119 **Carritt had hoped . . . "put into the picture."** Carritt, *Mole in the Crown*, 130–33.

119 **Susobhan was just as steeped . . . eagerly discussed.** Sarkar, *Essays in Honour*, 22.

119 **On this particular . . . Gandhi simultaneously.** Ghosh, *Parichay-er Adda*, March 27, 1936, 129. Sarkar, *Essays in Honour*, 32.

120 **There followed a lot of pointless . . . Eritrea!** Sarkar, *Essays in Honour*, 30.

120 **But Susobhan . . . England desired it.** Ghosh, *Parichay-er Adda*, March 27, 1936, 128.

120 **The adda diarist . . . Communism does."** Ghosh, *Parichay-er Adda*, April 17, 1936, 129.

121 **Chief Secretary P. C. Joshi . . . envelopes of money.** Sarkar, *Essays in Honour*, 6.

121 **Susobhan and Hiren-da . . . Soviet Russia's.** Ghosh, *Parichay-er Adda*, April 17, 1936, 129.

121 **Sudhin Datta and . . . Bourgeois Party.** Ghosh, *Parichay-er Adda*, April 23, 1937, 294.

121 **Sudhin said he fully . . . communism arrived.** SD to JBA, March 19, 1937. BERG.

121 **When the Comintern . . . about Stalin.** Sarkar, *Essays in Honour*, 32.

121 **That evening all the . . . talking at once.** Ghosh, *Parichay-er Adda*, April 17, 1936, 128.

122 **Otherwise Apurba liked to . . . Writers' Building.** Sinclair, "A Memoir," 54. PSA.

122 **His department head . . . he went out.** Scott, *Time to Speak*, 76.

123 **Humphry's watchers . . . about many things."** House, *I Spy with My Little Eye*, 5.

123 **Clearing his throat . . . their way home.** Ghosh, *Parichay-er Adda*, April 17, 1936, 129.

124 **One of Michael John Carritt's first . . . passed along.** Carritt, *Mole in the Crown*, 141–42.

124 **Though John's voice . . . a different cloth.** MC to JBA [March 1940]. BERG.

125 **He saw nothing funny . . . Union Jack.** Scott, *Time to Speak*, 66.

125 **They had an easier . . . endure forever.** Carritt, *Mole in the Crown*, 85.

125 **But then he would . . . mango and neem.** Ibid., 85–86.

126 **Would Gandhi sign . . . with gold buttons.** Aberigh-Mackay, *Twenty-One Days*, 13.

126 **The throne room . . . two Oval Offices.** Snow, *People on Our Side*, 40.

126 **A formal application . . . make it easy.** Rao, *India's Freedom Movement*, 64.

10. *The Moscow Agent*

127 **Wystan quipped he was . . . dining at the Ritz.** Spender, *W. H. Auden*, 63.

127 **Stephen Spender had been quick to . . . insufficiently dramatized.** Parker, *Isherwood*, 334.

128 **John, to whom . . . into a monastery.** WHA to JBA, October 4 or 11, 1936; he uses the expression *sans feu et sans reproche*. BERG.

128 **In London . . . eager-to-please court poet.** Carpenter, *W. H. Auden*, 195. Spender, *W. H. Auden*, 28.

128 **Wystan would either . . . a terrible driver.** WHA to E. R. Dodds. MSS. Eng. c. 6766, e. 3302. BOD.

128 **When Wystan left . . . saw him off at Victoria.** Laughton, *William Coldstream*, 40.

129 **Later, Louis would say . . . had been color blind.** Stallworthy, *Louis MacNeice*, 214; MacNeice, *The Strings Are False*, 171.

129 **On their return to London . . . through with it.** Sharp, memoir chronology, PSA.

129 **Louis returned . . . into a troubled sleep.** MacNeice, *I Crossed the Minch*, 21.

129 **"He simply mustn't risk himself,"** HH to JBA, February 26, 1937. BERG.

129 **It was only on . . . revelation to him.** JBA to SD [November 1936]. BERG.

129 **Calcutta might appear . . . usurp its own.** JBA to SD [November 1936]. BERG.

130 **It was indeed wicked . . . he was a coward.** WHA to JBA, January 1932 as cited in Davenport-Hines, *Auden*, 157.

130 **And however much bile . . . remind them of those.** JBA to SD [November 1936]. BERG.

130 **Sudhin had long been schooled . . . inner turmoil the more turbulent."** SD to JBA, November 20, 1936. BERG.

132 **He admitted he was . . . to be forgiven.** JBA to HH, March 7, 1937. BERG.

132 **Like Sudhin, Humphry didn't . . . Europe or America would.** HH to JBA, March 20, 1937. BERG.

133   **It would be a terrible pity . . . start on his book?** SD to JBA, March 19, 1937. BERG.

133   **Finally, it was a grave mistake . . . moment's consideration?"** SD to JBA, March 29, 1937. BERG.

133   **While John was off . . . argue about politics.** HH to JBA, February 26, 1937. BERG.

134   **When Humphry told Hiren-da . . . got very excited.** HH to JBA, January 7, 1937. BERG.

134   **We'll hear how . . . holy chaps.** JBA to HH, March 7, 1937. BERG. Slightly edited for clarity and sense.

135   **Soon after Humphry . . . Humphry an idea.** Mukherji, "The Dickens World Revisited."

135   **He would immortalize . . . John and Sudhin.** HH to JBA, February 26, 1937. BERG.

135   **Humphry's new . . . "Jesus what a town!"** HH to JBA, March 20, 1937. BERG.

135   **With the grim news . . . know any better.** MC to JBA [early March], 1937. BERG.

135   **"Carritt, old boy . . . they are saying."** Carritt, *Mole in the Crown*, 174–76; see also Carritt, "India Before the Storm."

135   **"Carritt, old boy . . . Don't worry."** Carritt, *Mole in the Crown*, 174–76.

136   **Carritt had once feared . . . a "babu raj."** MC to JBA [early March 1937]. BERG.

136   **Instead, the movement . . . workers and peasants.** MC to JBA [early March], 1937. BERG.

136   **Glassblowers, tea workers . . . salary increase.** Special Branch files (one for each union). PMROK.

136   **"For weeks we haven't . . . named Humphry House.** Carritt, *Mole in the Crown*, 175–77.

137   **"What does a Moscow . . . international status."** Ibid., 177–78.

138   **"You are a literary man . . . Police (IB) Calcutta."** Ibid., 184–87.

139   **"I tremble to think . . . Mulk Anands."** Berlin, *Flourishing*, 186, 262.

139   **Carritt had first visited . . . Kanchenjunga.** Carritt, *Mole in the Crown*, 39.

139   **His landlady had greeted . . . diagnosed them both.** MC to JBA [July 1937]. BERG.

140   **"The Lakes are a training . . . pukka sahibs instead.** "The Lakes are a training ground for ambition; they breed ideals. He came to Bengal to realise them. The future held his liberalism's death, a large car, a thousand rupees a month saved, itch of inquisitiveness, gloating over secret documents by a policeman's lamplight." House, *I Spy with My Little Eye*, 2.

140   **Maybe his own work . . . very *very* bourgeois."** MC to JBA [July 1937]. BERG.

141   **Carritt's elation . . . settle in the dunes.** Carritt, *Mole in the Crown*, 189.

142   **The tall chap was . . . to propaganda work.** Kutsobin, *Ajoy Kumar Ghosh*, 18–19.

142   **Come meet *Our Friend* here.** Carritt, *Mole in the Crown*, 189.

142   **He took notes . . . than a Popular one.** Michael Carritt Papers, CP/IND/MISC/3/2. LHASC; Carritt, *Mole in the Crown*, 188–92.

142   **Events in Europe . . . could protect them.** Michael John Carritt (former ICS), BL: IOR/L/PJ/12/618.

143   **For this reason alone, Bose . . . he to play?** Carritt, *Mole in the Crown*, 192.

143   **Neither man . . . where was it?** Howe, *Anticolonialism in British Politics*, 71–77. Carritt never did learn what this mysterious man's real name was or who he later became. He never saw either man ever again. By the end of 1937, riven by sectarian squabbles within the Communist Party and distracted by events in Europe, Bradley's League Against Imperialism was disbanded.

11. In the Ice Mountains

144   **The sound of . . . in a few days.** Spender, "1937 Karakoram Journal," 2 vols. PSA. Unless otherwise indicated, this is the main source for this chapter; only direct quotations are cited.

144   **Somewhere along the . . . in the field.** Isserman, *Fallen Giants*, 148–49.

144   **As with Germany's . . . Hitler happy.** Ibid., 135.

145   **Baltoro Glacier in short pants.** Shipton, *Six Mountain Travel Books*, 176.

145   **A letter from Granny . . . to Nanga Parbat.** Granny Schuster to MS [1937]. PSA.

146   **At the point of . . . a moment of panic.** Michael Spender, "The End of an Expedition." *The Spectator*, December 10, 1937. PSA.

146   **In the course of . . . was the Aghil Range.** Shipton, *Six Mountain Travel Books*, 249, 162.

147   **The exact location . . . conceivably take place.** Younghusband, "The Problem of the Shaksgam Valley."

147   **After fixing the position . . . might be dangerous.** Shipton, *Six Mountain Travel Books*, 164.

147   **The chief bogey . . . no-man's-land.** Shipton, Tilman, Spender, and Auden, "The Shaksgam Expedition, 1937."

148   **In Shipton and Tilman's . . . geological equipment.** Auden, *Reminiscences*, 42.

148   **The Darjeeling Sherpas took pride . . . large, heavy boots.** Norgay, *Tiger of the Snows*, 21–22, and interview with Dhamey Norgay in Bhutan, 2016.

149   **Sherpas never grew . . . often a target.** Shipton, *Six Mountain Travel Books*, 171.

149   **There was no mention . . . any further concern.** When Stephen asked him if he didn't find it dreadful leaving his son, Michael said, "Oh I knew I'd have to do this, so I had not been paying any attention to him for some time." Babington Smith interview with Rose Macaulay DFG 5783, May 1956/7. MED.

150   **"Such fun to go exploring!"** Spender, "1937 Karakoram Journal," vol 1, 30. PSA.

151   **"like a cathedral spire above the roofs of a provincial town."** Shipton, Tilman, Spender, and Auden, "The Shaksgam Expedition, 1937," 332.

152   **"There arranged before me . . . ever reached before."** French, *Younghusband*, 55.

152   *"Na jaayega"* . . . *"Ham jaenge."* Spender, "1937 Karakoram Journal," vol. 1, 45. PSA.

153   **"If we go up . . . Going on."** Spender, "1937 Karakoram Journal," vol. 1, 50. PSA.

156   **Tilman had no patience for Michael's carping.** Perrin, *Shipton and Tilman*, 330.

156   **"not too patient uncle . . . expecting his lunch."** Tilman, *Men and Mountains*, 7.

156   **"If everyone was carrying . . . instead of treble."** Spender, "1937 Karakoram Journal," vol. 1, 67–68. PSA.

157   **When Shipton got . . . strain on a party.** Shipton, *Six Mountain Travel Books*, 242.

157   **He later claimed it was . . . was disingenuous.** Ibid., 446.

157   **While he admired . . . best Alpine guides.** Ibid., 407.

157   **The following year . . . reach safety.** Norgay, *Tiger of the Snows*, 57.

157   **More to the point, topographical maps . . . Burma's border with China.** Michael Spender, "Trans-Himalayan Coronation." PSA.

157   **In his grant application . . . Chinese Turkestan.** Coll 37/90 Northern Frontier and Tibet: Mr. Eric Shipton IOR/L/PS/12/4324; 25 Mar. 1933–Nov. 1936. BL.

158   **With so much of . . . modern superiority!"** Shipton, *Six Mountain Travel Books*, 168.

158   **On the 1935 Everest reconnaissance . . . wisdom of the Tibetans.** Tilman, *Seven Mountain Travel Books*, 746.

158   **"Can you ever . . . lures you on."** Steevens, *In India*, 230.

159   **"The further we go . . . There is no retreat."** Spender, "1937 Karakoram Journal," vol. 1, 68. PSA.

160   **Instead, John's last view . . . plentiful in Skoro La.** Shipton, Tilman, Spender, and Auden, "The Shaksgam Expedition, 1937," 332.

161   **Despite Congress's . . . viceroy could remedy that.** Chanda, *India's Struggle*, 325.

162   **"Whatever that means."** Spender, "1937 Karakoram Journal," vol. 2, 6. PSA.

163   **In Christianity asceticism . . . one thing: death.** Spender, "End of an Expedition." PSA.

163   **The only evidence . . . should anyone?** Spender, "Trans-Himalayan Coronation." PSA.

163   **It was at a Copenhagen . . . British Empire.** Spender, "Address on Greenland." PSA.

164   **"Even a philosophy of Empire could be worked out on the basis of personal relationships."** Spender, "1937 Karakoram Journal," vol. 2, 18. PSA.

164   **Shipton felt Michael . . . hold very firmly.** See Warren, "Eric Shipton," and Shipton, "Michael Spender."

164   **Christopher Isherwood's mother . . . "Poor Mrs. Auden."** Diary of Kathleen Bradshaw Isherwood, February 26, 1937, Box 4. HRC.

165   **William Butler Yeats . . . good theatre."** Medley, *Drawn from Life*, 139.

165 **Wystan promised . . . "connubial requests."** NS to LM, July 12, 1937. PSA.

165 **"Up the Old Flag."** WHA to NS, July 10, 1937. PSA.

165 **"That was cheering."** NS to LM, July 12, 1937. PSA.

12. *Taking a Hat off a Mouse*

166 **Driving to Zurich from London . . . unsettling signs.** Spender, "Guns and Carbohydrates."

166 **Six days after . . . same stark choice.** Townsend, journals, vol. 12, March 18, 1938. PRO.

167 **He ascribed the rise of . . . of German trains.** Spender, "Guns and Carbohydrates."

167 **The annual spring festival . . . distance themselves.** Michael Spender, unpublished essay, ca. April 1938. PSA.

167 **Michael had argued . . . take charge.** Spender, "New Maps for Britain."

167 **She had had enough . . . they once had.** Diary of Erika Haarmann MSS. German e. 16–19. BOD.

168 **The director of . . . excellent work on Dorset.** E. B. Bailey to JBA, February 2, 1938. BERG.

168 **Nancy Coldstream . . . Wystan's brother.** Interview with Miranda Coldstream, summer 2014.

168 **Nancy had finally . . . with Lady Chatterley.** NS to JBA, May 25, 1938. BERG.

169 **"Any other man . . . knocked her flat.** Interview with Philip Spender, summer 2014.

169 **Her affair with Louis . . . rage at his presumption.** Stallworthy, *Louis MacNeice*, 203.

169 **"I do feel your . . . interfere with Bill."** NS to JBA [May 17, 1938?]. BERG.

169 **She went so far . . . feverish declarations.** NS to JBA [June 1938]. BERG.

170 **In Bude he carried Miranda . . . do over again.** NS to JBA [May 1938]. BERG.

170 **"The thing to be aimed at was independence" . . . happiness possible.** NS to JBA [May 17, 1938?]. BERG.

170 **Perhaps this was what true . . . soup in one's face?** J. B. Auden, "1939 Journal." AMA.

170 **He planned another . . . Tuesday, May 31?** JBA to NS [June 1938]. PSA.

171 **"So my puss . . . very warm."** NS to JBA, May 25, 1938. BERG.

171 **He'd been invited . . . Everest expeditions, was presiding.** Tilman, "The Himalayan Club Dinner."

171 **Though his May visit . . . Michael Spender instead.** Interviews with Philip Spender, summer 2014.

172 **On his return . . . whenever he liked.** Erica Spender to JBA, July 5, 1938. BERG.

172 **But John already knew . . . spiritual between them.** Draft letter, Auden, "1938–1939 Journal." AMA.

172 **John found her consumed . . . last time before he left.** JBA to NS [July 1938]. PSA.

173 **"And tomorrow, dearest . . . it to herself.** LM to NS, May 8, 1938, MS. Eng. c. 7381. BOD.

173 **Fantasies of violence . . . feet at the door.** LM to NS December 9, 1939, MS. Eng. c. 7381. BOD.

174 **He hated rows . . . to be daring him to.** LM to NS, January 20, 1940, MS. Eng. c. 7381. BOD. See "Trilogy for X," lines beginning "And love still as crystal over the bed," in MacNeice, *Collected Poems*, 89.

174 **Even Wystan . . . flowers in hand.** Interviews with Philip Spender, summer 2014.

174 **But then there was . . . When will it begin?** MacNeice, *Strings Are False*, 172.

174 **Louis would have told him . . . on another rendezvous."** MacNeice, *Autumn Journal*, 18.

175 **When Eric Shipton rang . . . Michael Spender instead.** NS to MS, September 27, 1938. PSA.

175 **"I am so glad I'm here . . . give up painting."** Rogers Papers, 8121. TGA.

175 **There . . . to send Nancy.** WHA to JBA [received October 1938]. BERG.

175 **He phoned her in Cornwall instead . . . Cornflower's arrival.** NS to MS, September 29, 1938. PSA.

176 **Protesters were just then . . . Chamberlain Must Go!"** Townsend, journals, vol. 13, September 25, 1938. PRO.

176 **Had Chamberlain . . . they all were, really.** Townsend, journals, vol. 13, September 21 and 28, 1938. PRO.

176 **Christine lit into . . . Granny and Chamberlain.** NS to LM, September 25, 1938. PSA.

176 **Though Michael sat . . . Granny against him.** NS to MS, September 29, 1938. PSA.

176 **Tea ended . . . in tears.** NS to LM, September 25, 1938. PSA.

176 **Nancy, stewing in . . . and told Erica.** NS to MS, September 29, 1938. PSA. The neighbor was John Layard and his common-law wife, Doris. NS to JBA [May 17, 1938?]. BERG.

176 **Despite Wystan's betrayal . . . bridge-playing relations.** NS to MS, September 25 and 29, 1938. PSA.

177 **Then, on the morning of . . . STOP MICHAEL.** NS to LM, September 28, 1938. PSA.

177 **For the past month . . . run in any direction.** Isherwood, "Diary," September 14, 1938. Christopher Isherwood Papers, HL.

177 **As the two o'clock deadline . . . bought another paper.** Isherwood, "Diary," September 28, 1938. Christopher Isherwood Papers, HL. Isherwood, *Christopher and His Kind*, 323–24.

177 **At the end . . . once more to Germany.** Townsend, journals, vol. 13, September 28, 1938. PRO.

177 **She hoped he . . . she had long sought.** NS to JBA, September 28, 1938. BERG.

177 **Of course her mother . . . after her children.** NS to MS, September 29, 1938. PSA.

177 **But if she had to . . . hopelessly tied up.** NS to JBA, September 28, 1938. PSA.

178 **When she pressed him . . . there wouldn't be a war.** NS to JBA, September 28, 1938. BERG.

178 **War would come when . . . be proved wrong.** LM to NS, April 20, 1939. MS. Eng. c. 7381. BOD.

178 **In the silences . . . calmed her.** NS to LM, September 28, 1938. PSA.

178 **Even before Chamberlain . . . to leave London.** NS to MS, September 28, 1938. PSA.

178 **"turned forests into lies."** Auden and Isherwood, *Journey to a War*, 270–71.

178 **Not while there is either a virgin or a rupee left.** Christopher Isherwood Papers, Box 42, Diary of a Trip to Asia May–June 1938. HL.

178 **Bishop Foss Wescott . . . write his Sunday sermon.** Scott, *Time to Speak*, 77, 81–82.

179 **He broke the steering . . . everything to the old man.** Scott, *Time to Speak*, 81–82.

179 **At the Parichay adda . . . say Aldous Huxley."** Ghosh, *Parichay-er Adda*, March 5, 1937, 132.

180 **In keeping with . . . imperialist mind-set?** Ibid. House arranged permission from Forster to have an excerpt published in *Parichay*, but the war intervened; it was believed that the novel would never have seen the light of day in England had not Krishna Menon tricked his partner at the new Penguin imprint, Allen Lane, into thinking it was a travel book. *Telegraph*, October 14, 2007.

180 **Auden and Isherwood's play had been recently staged at Calcutta University.** Michael Carritt to JBA, February 24, 1939. SD to JBA, January 11, 1937. BERG.

180 **Though W. H. Auden . . . name of British rule.** Mulgan, *Poems of Freedom*, 7–8.

180 **For all the left's . . . Indian dividends.** Dasgupta, *English Poets on India*, 1–2.

180 **Mulk Raj Anand . . . agreed.** Ghosh, *Parichay-er Adda*, March 5, 1937, 132.

180 **Anand was a small . . . scarlet shirts.** MacNeice, *Strings Are False*, 209.

180 **Anand had also crossed . . . ready for independence.** Anand, *Author to Critic*, 83.

180 **Though Stephen seemed to . . . political aspirations.** Spender, *Forward from Liberalism*, 138.

181 **Orwell was just beginning . . . British proletariat.** Orwell, *Collected Essays*, 397.

181 **Yet while Orwell had none . . . for being silly.** Anand, *Author to Critic*, 83.

181 **Mill was a . . . imperial rocking-chair.** House, *I Spy with My Little Eye*, 12.

13. The Truth about Love

182 **He promised Nancy . . . if war broke out.** NS to JBA, December 18, 1941. PSA. Coldstream, "Journal," undated. Coldstream Papers. TGA 8922/1.

182 **At the farewell party . . . in hostile territory.** Coldstream, "Journal." TGA 8922/1.

182   **Stephen was too soft . . . a real man.** NS to JBA, December 7, 1940. PSA.

183   **Michael would write . . . dinner by seven?** NS to MS, September 30, 1938. PSA.

183   **"Why are you behaving . . . than she could.** WHA to JBA [October 1938]. BERG.

183   **Hedli Anderson, a late . . . Bill tottered off.** Coldstream, "Journal," TGA 8922/1.

183   **"O Tell Me the Truth about Love."** in Auden, *Tell Me the Truth about Love: Ten Poems*, unpaginated.

183   **He'd been trying to convince . . . him out of it.** SD to JBA, August 9, 1939. BERG.

184   **The one time . . . frozen to death.** Ghosh, *Parichay-er Adda*, January 10, 1936, 235.

184   **The beau monde . . . Italian as well.** Suraiya, *Rickshaw Ragtime*, 97.

184   **. . . shabby suits and carrying rolled-up.** Interview with Sunanda K. Datta-Ray, March 2014, Kolkata.

184   **"Yes, of course I've heard . . . like his father, Ratna, Auden thought.** J. B. Auden, "1938–1939 Journal." AMA.

185   **W. C. had been . . . coach and four.** Burton, *Family History*, 60.

185   **Once, in a righteous . . . on its head.** Anita Money, "Sheila." AMA.

185   **Ratna's four formidable . . . oldest friends.** Author interview with Sunanda K. Datta-Ray, March 2014, Kolkata.

186   **Ratna spoiled his . . . relieved themselves of them.** SB to JBA, August 30, 1942. AMA.

186   **He raised them on . . . and Hindu mythology.** Sinclair, "A Memoir," 55. PSA.

186   **They threw extravagant . . . to Rabindranath.** Datta, *The World of Twilight*, 72.

186   **"grace and favor."** Interview with Sunanda K. Datta-Ray, March 2014, Kolkata.

186   **The rumor was . . . had been kind.** Auden, "1938–1939 Journal." AMA.

187   **Perhaps if Sudhin . . . invite her instead.** Ibid.

187   **When Betty Boggins . . . to the mountains.** SD to JBA, August 9, 1939. BERG.

187   **On New Year's Day . . . with Margaret.** Auden, "1938–1939 Journal." AMA.

187   **Two weeks later . . . in the next room.** Ibid.

187   **When he fell ill . . . eau de cologne.** JBA to NS, April 16, 1939. PSA.

188   **He studied the blueprints . . . Nelong-Gangotri region.** Auden, "1938–1939 Journal." AMA.

188   **The day after Betty . . . open the festivities.** JBA to NS, April 16, 1939. PSA.

188   **By custom men . . . stalked off, insulted.** Sharma, *Through the Valley of the Gods*, 40–41.

188   **A letter from Eric Shipton . . . was in London.** Eric Shipton to JBA, January 20, 1939. BERG.

188   **There was also . . . perpetual devotion.** JBA to NS, April 16, 1939. PSA.

188   **Christ, he thought.** Auden, "1938–1939 Journal." AMA.

189   **After declining Shipton's . . . was off again.** Ibid., April 30, 1939.

189 **Michael Spender could . . . second-rate device.** MS to Anthony Bull, undated. PSA.

189 **Hard work, accurate . . . quite readily.** MS to NS, March 3, 1939. PSA.

189 **He called this capacity . . . unfathomable.** Spender, "The Elusive Element." Spender, "The Gentle Savage."

189 **His analyst had advised . . . placid nature.** MS to NS, March 3, 1939. PSA.

189 **The Wild A5 was . . . dust at the RGS.** F. L. Wills (AOC) to Philip Spender, November 8, 1966. PSA.

189 **Combined with . . . Everest's *Felszeichnung*.** Spender, "The Photo-Surveyed Maps of the Mount Everest Region and Nyonno Ri."

189 **Sitting beneath the A5's . . . the North Face himself.** Eric Shipton to JBA, January 20, 1939. BERG. I am grateful to the *Britain from Above* exhibition featuring the Wild cartographic plotting machine at the RAF Museum at Wembley. The flying altitude and the focal length of the camera determined the final map's scale; the longer the focal length, the larger the image caught on film. A five-by-five-inch square print would capture eight square miles. The final North Face map was 1:50,000 with contour lines at 250-foot intervals. Another map of the entire Everest region was mislaid within the RGS for many years. Michael and Shipton also worked on a second map covering 450 square kilometers of the region around the Tibetan village of Sar, including Nyonno Ri.

190 **He saw his prospects for happiness . . . thought of losing him.** MS to NS, April 14, 1939. PSA.

190 **. . . aerial survey of the Iraq oil fields.** Courtauld, "Michael Spender."

190 **Shipton left for the Karakoram without him.** Katy Whitaker, email to Philip Spender, February 10, 2014. PSA.

190 **On his arrival in Harsil . . . fallen through.** Auden, "1938–1939 Journal." AMA.

191 **The Jadh Ganga Valley . . . coexisted peacefully.** Sharma, *Through the Valley*, 197.

191 **The new maps . . . a rotten slagheap.** Auden, "A Season's Work."

192 **His efforts seemed preposterous . . . and defenseless.** Auden, "1938–1939 Journal." AMA.

192 **They finally made camp . . . triumph, was all his.** Auden, "A Season's Work." Auden, "1938–1939 Journal." AMA.

194 **For three months . . . more desperate.** JBA to WHA, July 7, 1939. BERG.

194 **Amid the Savoy's shabby . . . accompanied by Jimsie.** Auden, *Reminiscences*, 42.

195 **Juin Singh had once asked . . . John the sahib.** Auden, "A Season's Work."

195 **In London the previous . . . he was unlovable.** Parker, *Isherwood*, 383.

195 **Bitter heartache was . . . all the luck.** JBA to WHA, July 7, 1939. BERG.

195 **Now, from the Mussoorie . . . in New Orleans.** WHA to JBA, June 27, 1939. BERG.

195 **In his reply . . . brother every happiness.** JBA to WBA, draft of letter, July 11, 1939, in Auden, "1938–1939 Journal." AMA.

195 **Near about the time . . . ward off the chill.** Ghosh, *Paricha-yer Adda*, May 12, 1939, 130.

196 **Gandhi was warmer . . . laugh as she was.** Singh, *Sahibs Who Loved India*, 47.

196 **While Sarojini told a . . . smoldering Pink.** Sarkar, *Essays in Honour*, 29.

196 **Slim and sharp . . . incarnation of Vishnu.** Sinclair, "A Memoir," 56. PSA.

196 **After the death of . . . unattractive ones.** Ghosh, *Parichay-er Adda*, July 15, 1938, 94.

196 **But what Minnie lacked . . . House had adored her.** Sinclair, "A Memoir," 55. PSA.

196 **Sheila, both the prettiest . . . shift to London.** Special Branch file: Records of Indians travelling abroad, 1936. PMROK.

196 **Recently returned to Calcutta . . . all just attended.** Ghosh, *Parichay-er Adda*, May 12, 1939, 130. LM to HM, September 25, 1947. BOD. Jamini Roy's paintings took their subjects from Hindu and Christian mythology and used a limited palette of seven colors that he mixed himself from rock dust, mud, chalk, tamarind seed, and indigo, with lampblack for his lines. His canvases were made from homespun, cardboard, or plywood, coated with cow dung and whitewash.

197 **Had he not needed . . . too westernized.** Ghosh, *Parichay-er Adda*, February 24, 1939, and May 12, 1939, 127, 130.

197 **"John Auden sounds like a . . . pained look.** SB to JBA August 30, 1942. AMA.

197 **Sheila had been fifteen . . . were all dispersed.** Money, "Sheila." AMA.

198 **De Sahib, the Special Branch . . . he pointed out.** Ghosh, *Parichay-er Adda*, August 19, 1938, 218.

198 **Still, en route to . . . whispered to Anila.** SB to JBA, August 30, 1942. AMA.

198 **Sheila was struck first . . . across the room.** SB to JBA August 30, 1942. AMA.

199 **At Cathay, in Chinatown . . . with Sudhin.** Auden, "1938–1939 Journal." AMA.

199 **The previous night's adda . . . lapsing into silence.** Ghosh, *Parichay-er Adda*, August 25, 1939, 218.

200 **At Firpo's the next day . . . safe as houses."** Auden, "1938–1939 Journal." AMA.

14. Somewhere a Strange and Shrewd Tomorrow

203 **For nearly six months . . . on other people?"** NS to JBA, September 15, 1939. AMA.

203 **Michael said it . . . return to Cornwall.** Sharp, memoir chronology, 1939. PSA.

204 **Though Sonia Brownell . . . she added, shrewdly.** Spurling, *The Girl from the Fiction Department*, 34.

204 **Was he really coming back? . . . a bloody hypocrite.** NS to JBA, September 15, 1939. AMA.

204 **When Nancy made . . . being called up.** Moynihan, *Restless Lives*, 51.

204 **Nancy suspected . . . her off to Bill.** Spurling, *The Girl from the Fiction Department*, 36–7.

204   **Had Louis MacNeice not left London . . . so trapped.** Townsend, journals, vol. 14, September 8, 1939. PRO.

204   **Wystan had got Bill . . . return to painting.** Rogers Papers, 8121/10. TGA.

204   **Nancy tried to brazen . . . listened politely.** Townsend, journals, vol. 14, September 8, 1939. PRO.

204   **Louis wrote her a stream . . . under a bomb.** MacNeice, *Letters*, 373–74. NS to LM, February 10, 1940, MS. Eng. c. 7381. BOD.

204   **Nancy assumed that . . . been beastly.** LM to NS, January 20, 1940, MS. Eng. c. 7381. BOD.

205   **"Do go on painting . . . away from London."** LM to NS, Sunday [January 7, 1940], MS. Eng. c. 7381. BOD.

205   **A fortnight after . . . front of the Boys.** Sharp, memoir chronology. PSA. Townsend, journals, vol. 15, February 7, 1940. PRO.

205   **They got her . . . Baker Street hotel.** Rogers Papers, 8121. TGA. Sharp, memoir chronology. PSA.

205   **It would take a bomb . . . the Boys remarked.** Townsend, journals, vol. 15, December 6, 1939, and February 7, 1939. PRO.

205   **In twice-weekly . . . a long way.** NS to LM, February 10, 1940. MS. Eng. c. 7381. BOD.

205   **Having heard from . . . before signing up.** WHA to JBA [September 1939]. BERG.

205   **"make action urgent and its nature clear."** Auden and Garrett, *The Poet's Tongue*, ix.

206   **Point 1. If John . . . one's public life.** WHA to JBA [September 1939]. BERG.

206   **He didn't see . . . Spain and Munich.** MacNeice, *Letters*, 319.

207   **John had just been . . . he would give his life.** JBA, draft of letter to WHA, November 11, 1939, in Auden, "1938–1939 Journal." AMA.

207   **He hoped his ability . . . would prove useful.** JBA, draft of letter to NS, dated September 29, 1939, in Auden, "1938–1939 Journal." AMA. JBA to NS, October 14, 1941. PSA.

207   **Sudhin knew that he and . . . asleep on his desk.** Auden, "1938–1939 Journal." AMA.

207   **The late nights . . . chance to be happy.** JBA, draft of letter to Sheila Bonnerjee, September 2, 1939, in Auden, "1938–1939 Journal." AMA.

208   **And he'd rather die . . . the same revulsion as the Nazis.** Auden, "1938–1939 Journal." AMA.

208   **Sheila would soon . . . into the mire.** JBA, draft of letter to NS, September 29, 1939, in Auden, "1938–1939 Journal." AMA.

208   **Sheila had the right . . . nothing really mattered.** JBA, draft of letter to Sheila Bonnerjee, September 2, 1939, in Auden, "1938–1939 Journal." AMA.

208   **Stay in America . . . wouldn't judge him.** JBA, draft of letter to WHA, July 9, 1939, in Auden, "1938–1939 Journal." AMA.

209   **The viceroy and the . . . the subject with him.** Glendevon, *The Viceroy at Bay*, 103–4.

209   **To Linlithgow's surprise . . . had upset him.** Glendevon, *Viceroy at Bay*, 136.

209   **"I was greatly struck . . . to continue."** French, *Liberty or Death*, 120.

209   **What sort of ultimatum . . . had thundered.** Roy, *India and War*, 4–5.

210   **Roy had pressed . . . war was declared.** Roy, *M. N. Roy and Mahatma Gandhi*, 47.

210   **"Winston rejoiced . . . firm as a rock."** Colville, *Fringes of Power*, 79.

211   **Whatever the reason . . . distress did not go unnoted.** Datta, *The World of Twilight*, 6–7.

211   **The adda regulars . . . reluctantly.** Ghosh, *Parichay-er Adda*, March 18, 1940, 198.

211   **Sudhin furnished . . . remained the same.** Ghosh, *Parichay-er Adda*, May 10, 1940, 204.

211   **Since the outbreak of war . . . in the East."** Roy, *M. N. Roy's Memoirs*, vi–vii.

211   **"Manabendra can speak . . . say anything.** Ghosh, *Parichay-er Adda*, April 12, 1940, 201.

212   **The diarist had recently . . . women smoking.** Ghosh, *Parichay-er Adda*, June 30, 1939, 208.

212   **On Fridays the fireworks . . . down the street.** Ghosh, *Parichay-er Adda*, July 5, 1940, 210.

212   **Sudhin, whom they all . . . unaccountably irritable.** Ghosh, *Parichay-er Adda*, April 19, 1940, 201.

212   **But it was not until . . . defend Europe.** Ghosh, *Parichay-er Adda*, April 12, 1940, 201.

212   **Even an atrocious . . . ignite his exasperation.** Ghosh, *Parichay-er Adda*, May 10, 1940, 204.

213   **When the talk turned . . . gifted talker.** Ghosh, *Parichay-er Adda*, June 14, 1940, 206.

213   **His wife, Elinor . . . had excellent legs.** Sinclair, "A Memoir," 54. PSA.

213   **"Never before in . . . absolute success."** Ghosh, *Parichay-er Adda*, June 14, 1940, 206.

214   **"Are you happy . . . eventually triumph."** Ghosh, *Parichay-er Adda*, June 28, 1940, 207.

214   **Hiren doubtless knew . . . with war material.** Intelligence Branch, Home Department, New Delhi. May 17, 1940, CPI Secret Mtg. PMROK.

214   **"The west has yet . . . end of Communism."** Ghosh, *Parichay-er Adda*, June 28, 1940, 207.

214   **Sudhin's coeditor . . . death of Christ.** Sanyal, *Twenty Years*, September 16, 1932, 6.

214   **But that evening . . . another sun's orbit.** Ghosh, *Parichay-er Adda*, June 28, 1940, 208.

215   **Susobhan, who'd said little . . . making a profit."** Ghosh, *Parichay-er Adda*, July 5, 1940, 210–11.

216   **"There is scarcely . . . conclusion of the war."** Amery, *Empire at Bay*, 606–7.

216   **Bypassing Amery . . . being invaded?** Moore, *Churchill, Cripps and India*, 34–35.

216   **Churchill regarded . . . on their mettle.** Colville, *The Fringes of Power*, 159.

216   **Accordingly, the Viceroy folded . . . sent in installments.** Amery, *Empire at Bay*, 634.

216   **"A piece of hypocrisy from beginning to end."** Colville, *The Fringes of Power*, 166.

15. The Magnified Earth

217   **Michael Spender's expertise . . . would be back.** F. L. Wills to Philip Spender, November 8, 1966. PSA.

217   **In February 1940 . . . survey and mapmaking firm.** Michael felt the Ordnance Survey was cramped by a military outlook and thereby failed to grasp the potential of the Wild A5. MS to Sir Harold Hartley, July 16, 1938. PSA.

217   **He'd written a . . . civil mapmaking.** "To the Editor of the Spectator." *Spectator*, December 9, 1938, 1006.

217   **Though Hemming hadn't been . . . "Come and see."** Babington Smith, *Evidence in Camera*, 36–37. Constance Babington Smith was in charge of the aircraft section and wrote the first book on wartime photographic intelligence. Of Michael she wrote, "He was to become one of the greatest influences on the development of interpretation in the early part of the war."

218   **When war was declared . . . in dry dock.** Beesley, *Very Special Intelligence*, 74.

218   **He photographed all of it.** Barker, *Aviator Extraordinary*, 138–39.

218   **Michael was so intent . . . nine times magnification."** Babington Smith, *Evidence in Camera*, 38.

218   **Yet to maintain . . . suicidal for pilots.** Millar, *The Bruneval Raid*, 131. Beesley, Very Special Intelligence, 127.

218   **"Don't worry about . . . something better."** Babington Smith, *Evidence in Camera*, 36–38.

218   **Cotton had managed . . . identify ships.** Ibid., 38.

219   **To increase flying . . . Wilhelmshaven.** Ibid., 45.

219   **By the time . . . identified in this way.** Halsall, "Historical Record, Squadron Leader Michael Spender."

219   **The Air Ministry refused . . . to Naval Intelligence.** Millar, *Bruneval Raid*, 29.

220   **The chief of naval . . . miracle machine.** Babington Smith, *Evidence in Camera*, 49.

220 **Only then did he realize . . . interpretation, or PI.** Babington Smith interview with FO Eve Holiday, DFG 5690, May 1956. MED. Holiday credits MS for this insight, as did Sidney Cotton. Also Babington Smith interview with Air Vice Marshal Sir Geoffrey Tuttle, DFG 5791, May 1956/7. MED. After Cotton's dismissal Tuttle took over command and was responsible for establishing PI on a regular RAF footing.

220 **Antoine Saint-Exupéry . . . which devours."** As cited in Babington Smith, *Evidence in Camera*, 246.

221 **He developed a . . . top of his head.** Babington Smith interview with FO Eve Holiday, DGF 5690, May 1956. MED.

221 **A number of possibilities . . . should consider it.** Fleming, *Invasion 1940*, 172.

221 **One-eyed Hemming . . . for civilian officers.** *London Gazette*, July 23, 1940.

221 **When the king . . . those, would you?"** Babington Smith, *Evidence in Camera*, 79–80.

222 **By the summer of 1940 . . . once been typists.** Mrs. Doreen Mackie oral history, Article ID: A4587645, July 28, 2005. RAFL.

222 **Cotton believed women . . . radar installations.** Babington Smith, *Evidence in Camera*, 73–74.

222 **A female aircraft . . . swelled the PI ranks.** Daniel, *Some Small Harvest*, 132.

222 **When Stephen heard . . . that is, America.** SS to MS, February 14, 194[1?]. PSA.

223 **Michael noticed . . . tanks and troops.** Daniel, *Some Small Harvest*, 112.

223 **Intelligence maps . . . in London's docklands.** Idle, *War over West Ham*, 113.

223 **After crossing the . . . engines reached them.** FitzGibbon, *Winter of the Bombs*, 42.

224 **"Is this right for Oriental Road?". . . "Oriental Road's in Silvertown."** Nancy Coldstream's account of the evening of September 7, 1940, is taken from letters written to her mother in the immediate wake of that night, another written two months later to John Auden, and also a taped account at the Imperial War Museum. The latter is the same account she gave to Constantine FitzGibbon for his book *The Winter of the Bombs*, 67–70. Nancy had written it up in December and, after Louis MacNeice edited it, sent it to *Horizon*. PSA.

226 **Stacks of Canadian . . . showering sparks.** FitzGibbon, *Winter of the Bombs*, 49.

226 **Barrels of West Indian . . . burning ground.** Ministry of Home Security, *Front Line*, 26.

227 **The barges of Burma teak . . . prayer was called.** Fleming, *Invasion 1940*, 283.

227 **The civil authorities . . . Gandhi, who had.** Scott, *Time to Speak*, 91–92.

227 **Three weeks later . . . were still there.** Ministry of Home Security, *Front Line*, 73.

228 **By then the press . . . than the living.** Calder, *The Lesson of London*, 23–24.

228 **He called Anderson Jehovah.** Amery, *Empire at Bay*, 699, 834.

228 **By the time . . . she was homeless.** NS to JBA, December 7, 1940. PSA.

228 **The editor . . . "not literature."** NS to MS, January 17, 1941. PSA. Sharp, "Memoir and Chronology." PSA. Moynihan, *Restless Lives*, 75.

228   **That December, en route . . . They wept.** NS to JBA, December 7, 1940. BERG.

228   **Sonia had dumped him.** Moynihan, *Restless Lives*, 75.

228   **In the coming months . . . fiery heart.** NS to JB, December 7, 1940. PSA.

228   **When Michael arrived at midnight . . . trained in PI.** Babington Smith interview with Harry Dawe, DFG 5673 [April 1956], 2. MED.

229   **"Haven't you had . . . drive to Dover."** Daniel, *Some Small Harvest*, 112.

229   **By the time . . . had declined.** Babington Smith, *Evidence in Camera*, 79.

229   **When Michael came on duty . . . French ports?"** Daniel, *Some Small Harvest*, 129.

16. A Representative Indian

230   **The secret diarist . . . sea from torpedoes.** Ghosh, *Parichay-er Adda*, August 9, 1940, 216.

230   **It was well-nigh . . . looking at Hiren-da.** Ibid., September 1, 1939.

230   **"England will surrender . . . 'August Proposals?'"** Ibid., August 9, 1940, 216.

231   **Linlithgow was as dim-witted . . . self-awareness.** Nehru, *The Discovery of India*, 414.

231   **Apurba paused long enough . . . to the natives.'"** Ghosh, *Parichay-er Adda*, August 9, 1940, 216.

231   **When the wireless began . . . not to gloat.** Ibid., September 13, 1940, 220.

232   **At the end of September . . . store window displays.** Ibid., September 27, 1940, 225.

232   **The adda diarist had heard . . . pass through cleanly.** Ibid., July 12, 1940, 211.

233   **When someone ventured . . . enlighten us?"** Ibid., November 22, 1940, 229.

233   **Where Susobhan argued . . . India her natural ally.** Ibid., November 15, 1940, 227.

233   **If Stalin hadn't . . . they are Jews?"** Ibid., November 22, 1940, 230.

233   **Boatloads of Jews . . . worn with exhaustion.** Sinclair, "A Memoir," 52.

233   **"I will take you . . . homeland."** Ghosh, *Parichay-er Adda*, November 15, 1940, 228.

234   **"Muslims in Madras . . . Hiren-da predicted.** Ibid., November 22, 1940, 229.

234   **A number of his . . . nonviolent strategy as toothless.** Intelligence Branch, Home Department, New Delhi, May 17, 1940, CPI Secret Mtg. PMROK.

234   **Sudhin had it . . . into the Blitz.** Ghosh, *Parichay-er Adda*, November 22, 1940, 230.

235   **For the Ministry of Information . . . a night of bombing.** January 18, 1944. "Since Walter White has been in London White has heard two Air Raid alerts, accompanied by a very moderate amount of gun fire, but this has impressed him quite beyond expectation. "Ah" said he, shaking his silver head, "that brings home the terrible terrible reality of war in a way you could never know in New York." I think this is a key to the solving of the White problem here: he is an imaginative and impressionable character and if our people can show him stirring and remarkable things as he goes about the Empire it will do much more good than arguing over his race theories. AF Morley File 462/32BB Proposed

visit of Walter White, secretary, National Association for the Advancement of Coloured People, to UK and India, BL: IOR/L/I/1/830 1943–1945.

235 **Upon his appointment . . . "distressing and repugnant in the last degree."** Gilbert, *Winston S. Churchill*, vol. 5 companion, part 3, 827. Cited in Mukerjee, *Churchill's Secret War*, 10.

236 **"As you have laid it . . . hold the line.** AMEL 1/6/21, India Office to PM, April 8, 1941. Cited in Mukerjee, *Churchill's Secret War*, 13.

236 **Where was India . . . of Nations"?** Raghavan, *India's War*, 214–215. Sarila, *The Shadow of the Great Game*, 112.

236 **"What a story that might be!"** Schuster, "The Deadlock in India."

236 **Uncle George had this from Leo Amery.** Amery, *Empire at Bay*, 758. "Incidentally I think I have done a good bit indirectly through Wint and Schuster's book which I largely influenced. . . . The expansion of the Indian Army and of India's munitions production during the year has been a very considerable thing."

236 **Blessed with . . . to be imported.** Snow, *People on Our Side*, 20.

236 **"Can anyone be satisfied . . . the full scale?"** Schuster, "The Deadlock in India."

237 **The GSI director . . . even more cheaply.** Cyril S. Fox, "The GSI and War, Confidential memo." BL: IOR/V/27/610/4 1940 and BL: IOR/V/27/410/13B 1943.

237 **The tycoon in . . . "Baboo" aeroplanes.** Amery, *Empire at Bay*, 675.

237 **"He need only tell the truth . . . war is over."** Schuster, "The Deadlock in India."

237 **Sudhin was in . . . and his wife.** Ghosh, *Parichay-er Adda*, January 10, 1941, 220.

237 **After the fall . . . for a year.** Raghavan, *India's War*, 59, citing various sources.

238 **"How do I become . . . never survive.** Roy, *In Freedom's Quest*, vol. 1, ix–xi.

238 **Sudhin asked Roy . . . a good likeness.** Ghosh, *Parichay-er Adda*, January 10, 1941, 235.

238 **Roy's foreign . . . he thought, grumpily.** Ibid., January 10, 1941, 235.

239 **Lindsay Emmerson . . . "Who *is* this?"** Interview with Datta-Ray, March 2014, Kolkata.

239 **"I quite realized that Sheila is an Indian."** CRA to JBA, April 12, 1940, May 15, 1940. BERG.

239 **"Since I began coming . . . gallantly.** Ghosh, *Parichay-er Adda*, February 14, 1941, 240.

239 **Sudhin was preparing . . . Hiren-da ignored him.** Ibid., March 21, 1941, 242.

240 **The times seemed . . . the geological record.** SD to JBA, January 11, 1937. BERG.

240 **He had shared . . . it was thought.** Ghosh, *Parichay-er Adda*, June 14, 1940, 205.

240 **Sudhin blamed Shaheed . . . were among his patrons.** Sinclair, "A Memoir," 54. PSA.

240 **No one needed . . . loan of one hundred thousand pounds.** Tharoor, *An Era of Darkness*, 138.

240   **Jinnah's dream . . . feel inevitable.** Ghosh, *Parichay-er Adda*, March 14, 1941, 241.

240   **It's not as if . . . iron to Japan."** Ibid., March 18, 1941, 244.

241   **Japan was believed . . . Japan was up to.** Ibid., June 21, 1940, 206.

242   **"I had hoped . . . realization each day."** Datta and Robinson, *Selected Letters of Rabindranath Tagore*, 525.

242   **Twenty light bombers . . . tons of merchant shipping.** Amery, *Empire at Bay*, 725.

242   **"[Should India] be . . . fire the wrong way?"** Mukerjee, *Churchill's Secret War*, 57. Citing Connell, *Wavell: Supreme Commander*, 31, 19.

242   **FDR and Churchill . . . familiar to Leo Amery.** Raghavan, *India's War*, 216–18.

243   **"really not quite normal."** Amery, *Empire at Bay*, 750.

243   **The following morning . . . to the Germans."** Ibid., 841.

243   **Even in happier . . . set him apart.** Kanakendranath Datta, memoir of his uncle.

243   **While Wystan . . . the Blitz began.** Spender, "Letter to a Colleague in America."

243   **"We are where we are, because we believe what we believe."** Spender, *Citizens in War, and After*, 12.

243   **Yet when Michael . . . "mass life outside?"** SS to MS, February 14, 194[1]. PSA.

244   **Stephen eventually . . . BBC Light Programme.** Spender, *World within World*, 270.

244   **Wystan accused him . . . version of his uncle.** WHA to SS, March 13, 1941. BERG.

244   **As India would doubtless . . . found this fatuous.** BL: IOR/I/1506.

244   **"I think it's too late . . . talk like that."** Schuster, *India and Democracy*, 441–42.

245   **His once elliptical . . . or third language.** Bose, *An Acre of Green Grass*, 66, 77–78.

245   **He abandoned his father's . . . East and West.** Datta, *World of Twilight*, 52.

245   **And therein lay . . . wholeheartedly of it.** Shils, *The Culture of the Indian Intellectual*, 21. Originally published in *Quest* and *Sewanee Review* (1958). Though Datta is unnamed, it seems clear from the context that Shils was describing the man for whom he arranged a fellowship at the University of Chicago.

17. An Infinite Ocean of Sorrow

246   **During the Great War . . . into the 1930s.** Raghavan, *India's War*, 35.

246   **"the shoulders of our small island."** Churchill, *The Second World War*, vol. 4, 181. "No great portion of the world population was so effectively protected from the horrors and perils of the World War as were the peoples of Hindustan. They were carried through the struggle on the shoulders of our small island."

246   **At the war's peak . . . every month.** Raghavan, *India's War*, 68–71.

246   **"largest volunteer force in history."** Kamtekar, "A Different War Dance."

247   **With the sudden . . . Bengal and Bihar.** Khan, *The Raj at War*, 162–63, 170.

247   **While Nehru . . . money to be made.** Roy, *In Freedom's Quest*, vol. 1, ix–xi.

247   **Even so there . . . after the war.** Voigt, *India in the Second World War*, 170–71.

247   **Since the viceroy . . . twenty-two billion.** Bose and Jayal, *Modern South Asia*, 131.

247   **"A new station . . . Azad Hind could be attained."** Special Branch file, March 1942. PMROK.

248   **Who would get . . . Japanese Zeros?** Curie, *Journey among Warriors*, 401.

248   **India was wide open . . . pigeons than warships.** Newell, *Burma: 1942*, 36.

248   **Everyone was . . . from Delhi.** SB to JBA, March 31, 1942. BERG.

248   **The first thing the foreign press . . . journalist said.** Weigold, *Churchill, Roosevelt and India*, 101. Curie, *Journey among Warriors*, 448.

248   **Roosevelt's envoy . . . had played him.** The Papers of Colonel Louis B. Johnson, UVASC: "To my amazement, when a satisfactory solution seemed certain with an unimportant concession, Cripps with embarrassment told me that he could not change the original draft declaration without Churchill's approval."

248   **"Everyone was frightfully . . . was even possible.** SB to JBA, March 31, 1942. AMA.

248   **The cost of living was up 400 percent.** LM to HM, September 25, 1947, Box 64. BOD.

248   **Minnie was dead broke . . . humiliated in return.** SB to JBA, March 31, 1942. AMA.

249   **Sheila had met Elinor and Sinbad . . . Simla was revolting.** Sinclair, "A Memoir," 49, 54–56, 64, 66. PSA.

249   **Whenever Sheila heard . . . increasingly frantic.** SB to JBA, August 30, 1942. AMA.

250   **By way of a reply . . . now be crushed.** Snow, *People on Our Side*, 42.

250   **A mob descended . . . pillar boxes."** *Statesman*, August 14, 1942, 1, 5; August 16, 1942, 1.

250   **Referencing "secret evidence" . . . All-India Radio.** Orwell, *Diaries*, 359.

250   **Viceroy Linlithgow . . . acts of terrorism."** Mansergh and Lumby, *Transfer of Power*, vol. 3, 661.

250   **Calcutta's Special Branch . . . went with it.** Informer Report of Fifth Column activity, July 1942. Special Branch file. PMROK.

250   **One of Subhas Bose's broadcasts . . . BBC Eastern Service.** *The Argus* (Melbourne), February 24, 1943, citing Lionel Felden in the *Evening Standard*.

250   **"A few blows . . . can sink a ship."** West, *Orwell*, 78.

251   **Sheila couldn't bear Lila . . . in Burmese jungles.** SB to JBA, April 4, 1942, and August 31, 1942. AMA.

251   **Sheila confessed a . . . done too badly.** SB to JBA, May 19, 1942. AMA.

251   **When he finally received . . . vengeful Anglo-Saxons.** JBA to NS, July 16, 1944. PSA.

252   **Sheila liked to relive . . . in her life.** SB to JBA, December 2, 1943. BERG.

252   **"The whole world now sees . . . not meant for India."** Bose, *Azad Hind*, 8.

253   **"Letters by soldiers . . . become an American."** Special Branch file no. 757. PMROK. These rumors, translated from Bengali, have been edited for readability.

253   **Referencing the central . . . protect their crops.** Mitra, *Towards Independence*, 113.

254   **The fall of Burma . . . the Bay of Bengal.** Mitra, *Towards Independence*, 104. Special Branch file no. 803. PMROK.

254   **All forms of local . . . were taken up.** Ray, *My Reminiscences*, 107.

254   **Oxcarts were broken . . . were destroyed.** Mitra, *Towards Independence*, 105.

254   **The following month . . . not be spared.** Mukerjee, *Churchill's Secret War*, 122.

254   **"This is our hour . . . did it matter?** Mansergh and Lumby, *The Transfer of Power*, 632. Amery, *Empire at Bay*, 872.

255   **The week Gandhi's . . . Amery's denial.** "India: Death by Hunger," *Time*, February 8, 1943.

255   **An autopsy on . . . stuffed with grass.** Moorhouse, *Calcutta*, 121.

255   **"It is difficult . . . professional techniques."** Special Branch file. Report Re: Importation of rice and paddy. April 27, 1943. 01522/105 1943. PMROK.

255   **That same month . . . indeed, with anyone.** Amery, *Empire at Bay*, 887–89. Mansergh and Lumby, *Transfer of Power*, vol. 3, 953, 995.

256   **Roosevelt's newest envoy . . . all parties incommunicado.** Phillips, *Ventures in Diplomacy*, 353.

256   **Six weeks later Linlithgow . . . risen 600 percent.** Mansergh and Lumby, *Transfer of Power*, 1052.

256   **When a relief worker . . . League government.** Ray, *My Reminiscences*, 108.

257   **Everywhere Shaheed went . . . quite vindictive.** Roy, *My People Uprooted*.

257   **That same month . . . nearly twice that.** Venkataramani, *Bengal Famine of 1943*, 38.

257   **Linlithgow, still toiling . . . now upon him.** Ministry of Transport Papers, Government of India to Secretary of State for India, July 21, 1943, as quoted in Mukerjee, *Churchill's Secret War*, 130. Mansergh and Lumby, *Transfer of Power*, vol. 4, 169.

257   **Reports of rural . . . cholera epidemic.** Special Branch file. Report Re: Importation of rice and paddy. 01522/105 1943. PMROK.

257   **On Cornwallis Street . . . eaten by dogs.** Moorhouse, *Calcutta*, 123.

257   **Vultures lined . . . less patient.** Burchett, *Democracy with a Tommygun*, 145–46.

257   **The burning ghats . . . death was everywhere.** Das, *Bengal Famine*, 5.

257   **The photographs, of skeletal . . . at the U.S. State Department.** Venkataramani, *Bengal Famine of 1943*, 31.

258   **In early October . . . eighteen hundred per week.** Calcutta *Statesman*, October 19, 1943, 1.

258   **The *Statesman* . . . on the paper's front pages.** "Mr. Amery on Food Crisis," Calcutta *Statesman*, October 13, 1943, 1. Calcutta *Statesman*, October 24, 1943, 8.

258   **Following Amery's lead . . . of their own people.** Branson, *British Soldier in India*, 103.

258 **It was also said ... civic nuisance.** Das, *Bengal Famine*, 7.

258 **And the British governor ... officers and soldiers.** Mukerjee, *Churchill's Secret War*, 100.

258 **Such moves had cynically ... consolidate his power.** Branson, *British Soldier in India*, 98, 103–4.

258 **"This knocks ... Punch and Judy show was ended?"** Moorhouse, *Calcutta*, 126–27.

258 **When the famine was ... to stay alive."** Fast, *Departure and Other Stories*, 130–42.

259 **On the insistence of ... hiding in stairwells.** Branson, *British Soldier in India*, 111.

259 **After the war Sudhin ... had a new flat.** Datta, *World of Twilight*, xix–xxi, 85.

260 **Sudhin would tell ... from their doorsteps.** LM India Diary: Ms Res. C. 1059 Box 44. BOD. Burchett, *Democracy with a Tommygun*, 153.

260 **Shipments of grain ... the starving.** Ray, *My Reminiscences*, 108.

260 **A bumper ... Mymensingh districts.** Bayley and Harper, *Forgotten Armies*, 296.

260 **The new viceroy ... and the Yugoslavs.** Wavell deemed the Bengal famine "one of the greatest disasters that has befallen any people under British rule." Wavell, *Wavell: The Viceroy's Journal*, 54. Mukerjee, *Churchill's Secret War*, 207.

260 **Until mid-1943 ... debt exploded.** de Paiva Abreu, "India as Creditor: Sterling Balances." Website.

260 **Churchill demanded ... violently policed).** Wavell, *Wavell: The Viceroy's Journal*, 12–13.

260 **But India paid ... breaking point.** Voigt, *India in the Second World War*, 170–171. Amery, *Empire at Bay*, 836, 948.

260 **While J. M. Keynes ... the final bill.** Amery, *Empire at Bay*, 899. Mansergh and Lumby, *The Transfer of Power*, vol. 4, 129.

261 **Instead, in one of his ... population still more."** Mukerjee, *Churchill's Secret War*, 203.

261 **"They breed like rabbits ... done to Hamburg.** Amery, *Empire at Bay*, 950. Colville, *The Fringes of Power*, 534.

261 **Meanwhile, the British ... would be cut.** Panter-Downes, *London War Notes*, 288.

18. A Boy Falling Out of the Sky

262 **He stayed up ... during the Great War.** NS to JBA, December 7, 1940. PSA.

262 **By studying the wake ... find it again.** Babington Smith, *Evidence in Camera*, 145.

263 **"permanent super-flap."** MS to NS [end of March 1941]. PSA.

263 **There had been a panic ... *Gneisenau* had.** Beesley, *Very Special Intelligence*, 79.

263 **Michael didn't always bathe.** Babington Smith interview with Quentin Craig, DFG 5670 [April 1956]. MED.

263 **His imperious voice carried over everyone's desks.** Babington Smith, interview with Peter Riddell, DFG 5764 [May 1957]. MED.

263   **. . . treating them like pieces of luggage.** Babington Smith interview with
       Geoff Dimbleby, September 1956. **. . . half of the unit's personnel were useless.**
       Babington Smith interview with Rose Macaulay, DFG 5783, May 1956/7. MED.

263   **He kept three kittens . . . rolled-up newspaper.** Babington Smith interview with
       Ann Rendell [May 1957], 2. MED.

263   **He was often caught out.** MS to NS, June 7, 1942. PSA.

263   **But the man understood . . . write reports.** MS to JA Spender, August 15, 1941. PSA.

263   **Michael railed at . . . large RAF contracts.** Spender, *World within World*, 282.

263   **Though their unit . . . "for disposal."** MS to JA Spender, August 15, 1941. PSA.

263   **After that, Michael . . . went on there.** MS to NS, March 9, 1941. PSA.

263   **From the cockpit . . . Louis's book.** MS to NS, February 21 [1941]. PSA.

264   **These machines were . . . acting up.** Spender, *World within World*, 282. Also
       Babington Smith interview with Rose Macaulay, DFG 5783, May 1956/7. MED.

264   **They shared the Eskimo's . . . talk of the dead.** MS to NS, January 13, 1943. PSA.

264   **And when, three hours . . . entirely forgotten.** MS to NS, April 15, 1941. PSA.

264   **Four nights later . . . went missing.** MS to NS, April 19, 1941. PSA.

264   **She had rung him . . . in his parked car.** NS to LM, May 7, 1940.

265   **Were the pipes . . . took my pajamas."** MS to NS, February 17, 1941. PSA.

265   **That first winter she . . . patience and domesticity.** NS to MS, March 12, 1941. PSA.

265   **If, on the phone . . . with her coat on.** NS to MS, January 17, 1941. PSA.

265   **It was up to . . . be a treat?** NS to MS, January 1, 1941. PSA.

266   **The talk at RAF Medmenham . . . monumental tactlessness.** NS to MS,
       February 21, 1943. PSA.

266   **In August 1941 he was stripped . . . card in his face.** MS to J. A. Spender, August 15,
       1941. MS to G. E. Schuster [September 1941]. PSA. Babington Smith interview
       with Humphrey Spender, DFG 5782, June 1957, 1. MED.

266   **"slap in the face with a wet fish."** H. Hemming to MS, June 6, 1941. PSA.

266   **He wrote outraged . . . Elizabethan proportions.** MS to J. A. Spender, August 15,
       1941. PSA.

266   **Part of him hoped . . . anywhere else.** MS to NS, July 26, 1943. PSA.

266   **People he had barely . . . dismay and support.** MS to J. A. Spender, August 15, 1941.
       PSA.

267   **Uncle Alfred warned . . . written off.** J. A. Spender to MS [March 1942]. PSA.

267   **"For people like us . . . doubt him.** MS to NS, September 9, 1942. PSA.

267   **On the understanding . . . photo intelligence.** MS to NS, September 12, 1942. PSA.

267   **And when Bill . . . said nothing.** MS to NS, September 9, 1942. PSA.

267   **Instead, while sitting . . . with a ring.** MS to NS, January 1, 1945. NS to JBA,
       December 18, 1941. PSA.

267   He followed up . . . tinker with it. MS to NS, February 20, 1943. PSA.

268   "Juliet and Miranda . . . threatened to drown it). NS to JBA, March 4, 1944. PSA.

268   It wasn't long . . . overanxious nanny. MS to NS, February 26, 1945. PSA.

268   When Michael arrived . . . was to be human. Babington Smith interview with
       Humphrey Spender, DFG 5782 [June 1957], 1. MED.

268   Then, just after . . . Second Tactical Air Force. Michael Alfred Spender RAF
       Service Record. PSA.

269   He had to travel . . . German occupation. MS to NS, September 26, October 2
       and 5, 1944. PSA.

269   "I have to use all my . . . and get killed for." MS to NS, October 25, 1944. PSA.

269   Against such . . . lived through, he wrote. MS to NS, December 1, 1944. PSA.

270   He took responsibility . . . to keep hope. MS to NS, February 1, 1945. PSA.

270   On the night of . . . at ninety miles an hour. Sebald, *On the Natural History of
       Destruction*, 27.

271   Within minutes . . . sizzling tar. Grayling, *Among the Dead Cities*, 89.

271   "The bombing of Hamburg . . . part of Europe." Spender, *World within World*, 282.
       Babington Smith interview with Rose Macaulay, DFG 5783, May 1956/7. MED.

271   One and a quarter . . . dumb with shock. Sebald, *A Natural History of
       Destruction*, 29.

271   In the course of . . . London alone. Grayling, *Among the Dead Cities*, 20.

271   What he'd seen . . . resistance by force. MS to NS, November 17, 1944. PSA.

271   Churchill's speech . . . English morality." MS to NS, December 9, 1944. PSA.

271   When, long after . . . before the war. Wing Commander Edward Gordon Hughes
       DSO, DFC, "Appreciation of Michael Spender." PSA.

271   Propaganda programs . . . casualties now." MS to NS, February 12, 1945. PSA.

272   Reading between the lines . . . "This is the end!" MS to NS, April 26, 1945. PSA.

272   Michael liked to say . . . be safe. Wing Commander Edward Gordon Hughes
       DSO, DFC, "Appreciation of Michael Spender." PSA.

272   But when he left . . . against him. Babington Smith interview with Humphrey
       Spender, DFG 5782, June 1957, 2. MED.

272   There had been scares . . . he was fine. MS to NS, January 22, 1941. PSA.

272   Two months later . . . forest in Germany. Wing Commander Edward Gordon
       Hughes DSO, DFC, "Appreciation of Michael Spender." PSA. Hughes, the pilot,
       was grievously injured but survived. He felt it possible that the plane was
       shot down. There were "unsurrendered" German outposts around many air-
       fields. The Ministry of Defence records concluded the cause of the crash was
       obscure.

272   Early the next morning . . . RAF Northolt. Email, Philip Spender to author,
       July 13, 2016.

272   **Late in the war . . . to Nancy.** MS to NS, December 23, 1944. PSA. The poem had appeared in a French publication.

273   **Though he was often . . . in thirty minutes.** Stern, *The Hidden Damage*, 126.

273   **In Brueghel's *Icarus*, for instance . . .** "Musée des Beaux Arts," in Auden, *Collected Poems*, 143.

19. Incompatible Gods, Irreconcilable Differences

274   **"I read the papers . . . to the B.E."** WHA to JBA, February 27, 1946. BERG.

274   **Shaheed Suhrawardy . . . citywide holiday.** Dalton, *Mahatma Gandhi*, 145.

274   **Moreover, he threatened . . . office in Delhi.** Talbot, *An American Witness*, 188.

274   **"Bloodshed and disorder . . . a noble cause."** Mosley, *The Last Days of the British Raj*, 31–32, as quoted in Hajari, *Midnight's Furies*, 13.

275   **"It is not a ridiculous assumption . . . in advance."** *Sunday Statesman*, August 18, 1946, 4.

275   **For forty-eight hours the police were nowhere to be seen.** *Sunday Statesman*, September 1, 1946, 1.

275   **Over four days . . . majority of them were Muslims.** Special Branch file. Incident Reports, August–November 1946. PMROK.

275   **Shops and tenements . . . bodies were everywhere.** Talbot, *An American Witness*, 191–92. Talbot estimated the number of dead at 4,000 but cites military estimates of 7,000 to 10,000.

275   **"Those in possession . . . of rotting carcasses."** Datta, *World of Twilight*, 85.

275   **Great Calcutta Killing . . . "gross negligence."** *Sunday Statesman*, August 25, 1946, 4, and September 4, 1946, 4. LM to HM, September 25, 1947, Box 64. BOD.

276   **During the public inquiry . . . name of God, go!"** *Statesman*, September 20, 1946, 8.

276   **"The devil was loose here for three days."** JBA to WHA, August 30, 1946. BERG.

276   **With the August heat . . . rats and vultures.** Datta, *World of Twilight*, 85.

276   **They bloated into grotesque . . . would be next.** JBA to WHA, August 30, 1946. BERG. Datta, *World of Twilight*, 85.

276   **Flare-ups continued . . . and slaughterhouses.** *Bharat*, October 8, 1946. Special Branch Incident files, August–November 1946. PMROK.

276   **During Diwali . . . should be sacrificed."** Special Branch Incident files, August–November 1946. PMROK.

277   **Neither Jinnah nor Nehru . . . nothing had changed.** Hajari, *Midnight's Furies*, 18, citing Ispahani, *Quaid-e-Azam as I Knew Him*, 234, and "Mr. Nehru on Riots," *Times of India*, August 19, 1946, 7.

277   **Sudhin would cite . . . was thus fulfilled."** Datta, *World of Twilight*, 85–86.

277   **"American business magnates . . . trawl for boys.** JBA to WHA, January 17, 1948, draft of letter in Auden, "1938–1939 Journal." AMA.

278   Evidently assuming . . . the New Britain." LM to HM, August 10, 1947. Box 64. BOD.

278   "This campaign of yours . . . and vice versa." MacNeice, "1947 Notes." BERG. LM to HM, August 16, 1947. Box 64. BOD.

278   Many of the . . . hurry to pack up. LM to HM, August 16, 1947. Box 64. BOD.

279   But Dalmia had already . . . to prove that." MacNeice, "1947 Notes." BERG. LM to HM, August 10, 1947. Box 64. BOD.

279   Few telephones were . . . John Auden? LM to HM, August 10, 1947. Box 64. BOD.

279   He met a Congressman . . . "what the dickens." LM to HM, August 19 and 28, 1947. Box 64. BOD.

280   "Salaams to you . . . Jolly good show." LM to HM, August 28, 1947. Box 64. BOD.

280   Sinbad had his calves . . . read the paper. Sinclair, "A Memoir," 45. PSA.

280   And then there . . . crushed him. LM to HM, August 28, 1947. Box 64. BOD.

280   At the midnight session . . . chiming midnight. MacNeice, "1947 Notes." MSS MacNeice. BERG.

281   In a beautifully lit . . . other than politics. Ibid.

281   "Others were able to play . . . foisted upon us?" http://parliamentofindia.nic .in/ls/debates/vol5p1.html. Indian Parliament website.

282   The violence reached . . . were set aflame. Hajari, *Midnight's Furies*, 153.

282   Crazed-looking Sikhs . . . faced them down. Sinclair, "A Memoir," 89–90. PSA.

282   Louis found Delhi . . . train for Calcutta. LM to HM, September 21 and 22, 1947. Box 64. BOD.

283   Shaheed sped to the Sodepur . . . prayer meetings. Dalton, *Mahatma Gandhi*, 153.

283   He even . . . Great Calcutta Killing of 1946. Ray, *My Reminiscences*, 126. Chadha, *Gandhi*, 440.

283   Gandhi offered . . . "execrable" chief minister. Datta, *World of Twilight*, 86.

283   Shaheed and representatives . . . side of his bed. Dalton, *Mahatma Gandhi*, 155.

283   Seventy-three hours . . . is my message. Ray, *My Reminiscences*, 127–129.

284   This peculiar . . . he wrote. All else will crumble into dust; but, should / His name be uttered at the zero hour, The dream of independence would survive / The ruin of aggressive opulence. Datta, *Art of the Intellect*, xiv. Datta, *World of Twilight*, 87.

284   By the time . . . for a tip. LM to HM, September 25, 1947. Box 64. BOD.

284   Louis and Sudhin . . . immediate kinship. LM to HM, September 16 and 20, 1947. Box 64. BOD.

284   For one thing . . . Louis thought. LM to HM, September 26, 1947. Box 64. BOD.

284   At a meeting with . . . Auden and Spender. MacNeice, "1947 Notes." BERG.

284   One Communist's eight-year-old . . . his wife, Hedli." LM to HM, September 29, 1947. Box 64. BOD. The poet was Sushin Dey.

285 **Exclaiming that India . . . him shopping.** LM to HM, September 29, 1947. Box 64. BOD.

285 **The Set had been . . . but a Punjabi.** Sinclair, "A Memoir," 66–67. PSA.

285 **Sudhin had once . . . become intelligible.** SD to JBA, March 19, 1937. BERG.

286 **Sudhin formed from . . . work of art.** Datta, *World of Twilight*, xxiv.

286 **Large as London . . . into Erica Spender.** JBA to NS, August 27, 1947. PSA.

286 **His visit had been . . . memories of 1938?** JBA to NS, November 17, 1947; July 22, 1948; and July 9, 1949. PSA.

286 **Who has left a scent on my life . . .** MacNeice, *Autumn Journal*, 5.

287 **In 1950, when . . . reconnaissance in 1952.** Horrell, "Tilman's Everest Southside Reconnaisance." www.markhorrell.com/blog/2015/tilmans-everest-south -side-reconnaissance. Father Bakewell was a friend of Charles Houston, one of the American undergraduates who, with his father, had asked Tilman to guide them up Nanda Devi in 1936. The Houstons were also on this reconnaissance.

287 **John also wanted to . . . grace worked slowly.** JBA to WHA, March 15, 1951. BERG.

287 **While her husband was in Rome . . . chapter and verse.** JBA to WHA, June 3, 1951. BERG. JBA to NS, July 15, 1951; JBA to NS, September 20, 1956. PSA.

287 **As India's freedom . . . letters and gifts.** JBA to NS, July 22, 1948. PSA.

288 **Confronting John on his return . . . ever again.** JBA to NS, July 19, 1951. PSA.

288 **"Dams are to be built . . . resurgent nationalism."** JBA to WHA, January 17, 1948, BERG.

288 **Sudhin had been so . . . contemplated leaving India.** Datta, *World of Twilight*, xx.

288 **As the last Englishman standing . . . while on leave.** JBA to WHA, September 10, 1946. BERG. JBA to NS, July 21, 1949. PSA.

288 **When he questioned . . . considered quislings.** JBA to WHA, September 10, 1945, BERG. JBA to SB, March 25, 1952. AMA. See also J. B. Auden, "The Bearing of Geology on Multipurpose Projects," in Radhakrishna, *J. B. Auden*, 221.

288 **When John refused . . . release of his pension.** GAA to SB, February 19, 1951. BERG.

288 **Without Sheila . . . in the morning.** JBA to SB, July 2, 1952, and April 3, 1953. AMA.

289 **But for Sudhin . . . invited anywhere.** JBA to SB, April 3 and 11, 1953. AMA.

289 **Toward the end . . . John's life impossible.** JBA to SB, May 19, 1953. AMA.

289 **Indeed John Auden's . . . decades to come.** Jeremy Berkoff to SB after JBA's death on January 21, 1991.

289 **In his final weeks . . . show him his.** JBA to SB, May 28, 1953. AMA.

289 **As he was packing up . . . in the Garhwal."** JBA to WHA, September 19, 1946. BERG.

289 **When morning came . . . without regrets.** JBA to SB, May 27, 1953. AMA.

290 **On his first leave . . . speak to her.** JBA to NS, October 17, 1956. PSA.

290   "I am your wife . . . look after you." SB to JBA, August 20, 1968. AMA.

290   When she wept . . . shallowness of feeling. Auden, "1938–1939 Journal." AMA.

290   For a time . . . cruel tongue. Radhakrishna, *J. B. Auden*, 14.

290   It wasn't so much . . . deeply insulting. SB to JBA, August 20, 1968. AMA.

290   She told him his lies . . . anything at all. JBA to SB, October 23, 1955. AMA.

290   "an island against the bitterness." JBA to NS, October 17, 1945. PSA.

291   At the nursing home . . . wrote them down. Philip Spender, emails and interviews, and introduction in *Nancy Sharp (Nancy Spender) 1909-2001*. PSA.

292   *"In vino veritas . . . patient with us, though, my dear."* WHA to SB, undated. AMA.

20. Night Falls

294   Night falls on . . . the last Englishman to leave. MacNeice, "India Diary." BOD. See also MacNeice, "India at First Sight," 42–43. BERG.

295   Enraged at John's . . . failed in both. JBA to NS, October 17, 1945, May 16, 1947. PSA.

296   It was an Indian geologist . . . of the Himalayan chain. Radhakrishna, *J. B. Auden*, comment by S. V. Srikantia, 222. In August Gansser's 1991 obituary of Auden, he wrote: "Many of the problems which still occupy Himalayan geologists of today were already realized through Auden's careful field observations and critical deductions." Gansser, a legendary Swiss geologist, regarded John Auden, "one of the greatest Himalayan geologists," as his personal hero.

BIBLIOGRAPHY

Unpublished Primary Sources

Auden, J. B. "1929 Journal" and "1938–39 Journal." Unpublished notebooks.

Halsall, Christine. "Historical Record, Squadron Leader Michael Spender at the Air Operating Company." Personal email, September 5, 2013.

Money, Anita. "Sheila." Unpublished Word document, July 24, 2015.

Mukherji, Sajni. "The Dickens World Revisited: Humphry House in 1930s Calcutta." Unpublished typescript. Courtesy of the author.

Sinclair, Elinor. "A Memoir." Unpublished Word document. Courtesy of Margaret Sinclair.

Spender, Michael. "Address on Greenland." Delivered at the Rembrandt Hotel on behalf of the Danish Council in 1942. Unpublished typescript.

———. "The End of an Expedition." [1937]. Unpublished typescript.

———. "Geography at Work." Unpublished typescript.

———. "Mediaeval Incident." December 13, 1936. Unpublished typescript.

———. "1935 Everest Journal" and "1937 Karakoram Journal." 2 vols. Unpublished notebooks.

———. Review of *The Pilot's Book of Everest*. [1936]. Unpublished typescript.

———. "Trans-Himalayan Coronation." [1937]. Unpublished typescript.

Spender, Nancy. "Memoir and Chronology." Various versions, unpublished MSS.

Spender, Stephen. "Miss Pangborne." Unpublished typescript.

Spender, Violet. "1917 Diary."

Books and Journal Articles

Aberigh-Mackay, George R. *Twenty-One Days in India: Being the Tour of Sir Ali Baba, K.C.B.* London: W. H. Allen, 1896.

Amery, Leopold. *The Empire at Bay: The Leo Amery Diaries, 1929–1945.* Edited by John Barnes and David Nicholson. Foreword by Lord Stockton. London: Hutchinson, 1988.

Anand, Mulk Raj. *Author to Critic: The Letters of Mulk Raj Anand to Saros Cowasjee.* Calcutta: A Writer's Workshop Production, 1973.

Andrews, C. F. *The Indian Earthquake*. London: Allen and Unwin, 1935.

Astill, Tony. *Everest: The Reconnaissance 1935; The Forgotten Adventure*. Southampton: privately printed, 2005.

Auden, J. B. *Centenary of the Geological Survey of India 1851–1951: A Short History of the First Hundred Years*. Calcutta: GSI, 1951.

———. "An Excursion to Gangotri." *Himalayan Journal* 8 (1936).

———. *Reminiscences of Retired Officers and Staff of the Geological Survey of India and Eminent Geoscientists from the Country and Abroad*. Calcutta: GSI, 1964.

———. "A Season's Work in the Central Himalaya." *Himalayan Journal* 12 (1940).

———. "The Structure of the Himalaya in Garhwal." *Records of the Geological Survey of India* 7 (1937): 407–33.

———. "Traverses in Nepal." *Himalayan Journal* 7 (1935).

Auden, W. H., and Christopher Isherwood. *The Ascent of F6* and *On the Frontier*. New York: Random House, 1986.

———. *Collected Poems*. Edward Mendelson, ed. London: Faber and Faber, 1991.

———, and Christopher Isherwood. *Journey to a War*. London: Faber, 1939.

———. *Juvenilia: Poems 1922–1928*. Edited by Katherine Bucknell. London: Faber and Faber, 1994.

———, and Louis MacNeice. *Letters from Iceland*. New York: Faber and Faber, 1937.

———, and John Garrett, eds. *The Poet's Tongue: An Anthology*. London: G. Bell, 1957.

———. *Selected Poems*. Edited by Edward Mendelson. New York: Vintage, 2007.

———. *Tell Me the Truth about Love: Ten Poems*. New York: Vintage, 1994.

Ayyub, Abu Sayeed. "Sudhindranath Datta." *Quest* (Fall 1960).

Babington Smith, Constance. *Evidence in Camera: The Story of Photographic Intelligence in World War II*. With a foreword by Marshal of the Royal Air Force, the Lord Tedder G.C.B. London: Chatto & Windus, 1958.

Battacharya, Manoshi. *Chittagong: Eye of the Tiger*. Noida, UP: HarperCollins, 2014.

Bayley, C. A., and T. N. Harper. *Forgotten Armies: The Fall of British Asia*. Cambridge, MA: Belknap Press, 2005.

Beesley, Patrick. *Very Special Intelligence: The Story of the Admiralty's Operational Intelligence Centre 1939–1945*. London: Hamilton, 1977.

Bell, Kathleen. "Nancy Spender's Recollections of Wystan Auden." *W. H. Auden Society Newsletter*, nos. 10 and 11 (September, 1993): 1–3.

Berlin, Isaiah. *Flourishing: Letters 1928–1946*. Edited by Henry Hardy. London: Chatto & Windus, 2004.

Birla, G. D. *In the Shadow of the Mahatma: A Personal Memoir*. Bombay: Orient Longmans, 1953.

Blacker, L. V. Stewart. "The Mount Everest Flights." *Himalayan Journal* 6 (1934).

Bose, Buddhadeva. *An Acre of Green Grass: A Review of Modern Bengali Literature*. Calcutta: Orient Longmans, 1948.

Bose, Subhas Chandra. *Azad Hind: Writings and Speeches 1941–1943*. Delhi: Permanent Black, 2002.

———. *The Indian Struggle 1929–1934*. London: Wishart, 1935.

Bose, Subrato, and Ayesha Jalal. *Modern South Asia: History, Culture, Political Economy*. London: Routledge, 1998.

Branson, Clive. *British Soldier in India: The Letters of Clive Branson*. London: Communist Party, 1944.

Brett, William Bailie. *A Report on the Bihar Earthquake and the Measures Taken in Consequence Thereof*. Bihar: Government Printing, 1935.

Burchett, Wilfred. "Life and Death in India." From *Democracy with a Tommygun*, 145–46. www.marxists.org/archive/burchett/1946/democracy-with-a-tommygun/ch08.htm.

Burton, Antoinette, ed. *Family History: Janaki Agnes Penelope Majumdar*. New Delhi: Oxford University Press, 2003.

Calder, Ritchie. *The Lesson of London*. London: Secker & Warburg, 1941.

Carpenter, Humphrey. *W. H. Auden: A Biography*. Boston: Houghton Mifflin, 1981.

Carritt, Michael. "India before the Storm." *Labour Monthly* 22, no. 5 (May 1940): 294.

———. *A Mole in the Crown: Memoires of a British Official in India Who Worked with the Communist Underground in the 1930s*. New Delhi: Rupa, 1986.

Chadha, Yogesh. *Gandhi*. New York: John Wiley and Sons, 1997.

Chakrabarty, Dipesh. *Provincializing Europe: Postcolonial Thought and Historical Difference*. Princeton, NJ: Princeton University Press, 2000.

Chandra, Bipan, et al. *India's Struggle for Independence 1857–1947*. London: Penguin, 1987.

Churchill, Winston S. *The Second World War*, vol. 4, *The Hinge of Fate*. Boston: Houghton Mifflin, 1950.

Collier, Peter. "The Impact on Topographic Mapping of Developments in Land and Air Survey 1900–1939." *Cartography and Geographic Information Science* 29, no. 3 (2002): 155–74.

Colville, John. *The Fringes of Power: Downing Street Diaries 1939–1955*. Rev. ed. London: Weidenfeld & Nicolson, 2004.

Cotton, Sidney, with Ralph Barker. *Aviator Extraordinary: The Sidney Cotton Story.* London: Chatto & Windus, 1969.

Courtauld, Augustine. "Michael Spender." *Polar Record* 4, no. 31 (1945): 352–53.

Curie, Eve. *Journey among Warriors.* Garden City, NY: Doubleday, Doran, 1943.

Curtis Brown, Beatrice, ed. *Women of Britain: Letters from England.* New York: Harcourt, Brace, 1941.

Dalton, Dennis. *Mahatma Gandhi: Non-violent Power in Action.* New York: Columbia University Press, 1993.

Daniel, Glyn Edmund. *Some Small Harvest.* London: Thames & Hudson, 1986.

Das, Tarak Chandra. *Bengal Famine 1943: As Revealed in a Survey of the Destitutes in Calcutta.* Calcutta: University of Calcutta Press, 1949.

Dasgupta, R. K. *English Poets on India and Other Essays.* Calcutta: Calcutta Book House, 1945.

Datta, Sudhindranath. *Art of the Intellect: Uncollected English Writings of Sudhindranath Datta.* Edited by Sukanta Chaudhuri. Introduction by Amiya Deb. New Delhi: Chronicle Books, 2008.

——. *The World of Twilight: Essays and Poems.* Bombay: Oxford University Press, 1970.

Davenport-Hines, Richard. *Auden.* New York: Random House, 1995.

Dev, Amiya. *Sudhindranath Datta.* New Delhi: Sahitya Akademi, 1982.

Devas, Nicolette. *Two Flamboyant Fathers.* London: Collins, 1966.

Dodds, W. E. *Missing Persons: An Autobiography.* Oxford: Clarendon Press, 1977.

Fast, Howard. *Departure and Other Stories.* New York: Little, Brown, 1949.

Fellowes, P. F. M., L. V. Stewart Blacker, P. T. Etherton, and Squadron Leader the Marquess of Douglas and Clydesdale. *First over Everest: The Houston-Mount Everest Expedition, 1933.* With a foreword by John Buchan and an account of the filming of the flight by Geoffrey Barkas. London: John Lane The Bodley Head, 1933.

FitzGibbon, Constantine. *The Winter of the Bombs; The Story of the Blitz of London.* London: Norton, 1958.

Fleming, Peter. *Invasion 1940: An Account of the German Preparations and the British Counter-Measures.* London: R. Hart-Davis, 1957.

French, Patrick. *Younghusband: The Last Great Imperial Adventurer.* London: HarperCollins, 1994.

——. *Liberty or Death: India's Journey to Independence and Division.* London: HarperCollins, 1997.

Ghosh, Shyamalkrishna. *Parichay-er Adda.* Calcutta: K. P. Bagchi, 1990.

Gilbert, Martin. *Winston S. Churchill,* vol. 5 companion, part 3, documents, *The Coming of War 1936–1939.* London: Heinemann, 1982.

Glendevon, John. *The Viceroy at Bay: Lord Linlithgow in India*. London: Collins, 1971.

Grayling, A. C. *Among the Dead Cities: The History and Moral Legacy of the WWII Bombing of Civilians in Germany and Japan*. New York: Walker, 2006.

Hajari, Nisid. *Midnight's Furies: The Deadly Legacy of India's Partition*. Boston: Houghton Mifflin Harcourt, 2015.

Hansen, Peter H. "The Dancing Lamas of Everest." *American Historical Review* 101, no. 3 (June 1996): 712–47.

House, Humphry. *I Spy with My Little Eye*. Calcutta: Bharati Bhavan, 1937.

Howe, Stephen. *Anticolonialism in British Politics: The Left and the End of Empire, 1918–1964*. New York: Oxford University Press, 1993.

Idle, E. Doreen. *War over West Ham: A Study of Community Adjustment; A Report Prepared for the Fabian Society and the Ethical Union*. London: Faber & Faber, 1943.

Isherwood, Christopher. *Christopher and His Kind 1929–1939*. New York: Farrar, Straus & Giroux, 1976.

Ishwari, Prasad. *The Life and Times of Maharaja Juddha Shumsher Jung Bahadur Rana of Nepal*. New Delhi: Ashish Publishing House, 1975.

Isserman, Maurice. *Fallen Giants: A History of Himalayan Mountaineering*. New Haven, CT: Yale University Press, 2008.

Kamtekar, Indivar. "A Different War Dance: State and Class in India 1939–1945." *Past and Present*, no. 176 (2002): 187–221.

Keay, John. *The Great Arc: The Dramatic Tale of How India Was Mapped and Everest Was Named*. New York: HarperCollins, 2000.

Khan, Yasmin. *The Raj at War: A People's History of India's Second World War*. Delhi: Penguin Random House, 2015.

Kling, Blair B. *Partner in Empire: Dwarkanath Tagore and the Age of Enterprise in Eastern India*. Berkeley: University of California Press, 1976.

Kutsobin, Pyotr. *Ajoy Kumar Ghosh and Communist Movement in India*. New Delhi: Sterling Publishers, 1987.

Laughton, Bruce. *William Coldstream*. New Haven, CT: Yale University Press, 2004.

Laybourn, Keith. *The General Strike Day by Day*. Stroud: Alan Sutton Publishing, 1996.

MacNeice, Louis. *Autumn Journal: A Poem*. New York: Random House, 1939.

———. *Collected Poems*. New York: Oxford University Press, 1967.

———. *I Crossed the Minch*. With eight drawings by Nancy Sharp. London: Longmans Green, 1938.

———. *Selected Letters of Louis MacNeice*. Edited by Jonathan Allison. London: Faber & Faber, 2010.

———. *Selected Prose of Louis MacNeice.* Oxford: Clarendon Press; New York: Oxford University Press, 1990.

———. *The Strings Are False: An Unfinished Autobiography.* London: Faber & Faber, 1982.

Mansergh, Nicholas, and E. W. R. Lumby, eds. *The Transfer of Power 1942–7.* London: Her Majesty's Stationery Office, 1971.

Mason, Kenneth. *Abode of Snow.* Foreword by Doug Scott. Seattle: Mountaineers Books; London: Diadem Books, 1987.

———. "Notes." *Himalayan Journal* 8 (1935).

———. "The Problem of Mount Everest." *Himalayan Journal* 9 (1937).

Medley, Robert. *Drawn from Life.* Boston: Faber & Faber, 1983.

Mendelson, Edward, ed. *Early Auden.* New York: Viking Press, 1981.

Millar, George. *The Bruneval Raid: Flashpoint of the Radar War.* London: Bodley Head, 1974.

Ministry of Home Security by the Ministry of Information. *Front Line, 1940–41: The Official Story of the Civil Defence of Britain.* London: His Majesty's Stationery Office, 1942.

Mitra, Asok. *Three Score and Ten*, vol. 1. Calcutta: Mandira, 1987.

———. *Towards Independence 1940–1947: Memoirs of an Indian Civil Servant.* Bombay: Popular Prakashan, 1991.

Moon, Penderel. *Strangers in India.* New York: Reynal & Hitchcock, 1945.

Moore, R. J. *Churchill, Cripps and India.* Oxford: Clarendon; New York: Oxford University Press, 1979.

Moorhouse, Geoffrey. *Calcutta.* London: Weidenfeld, 1972.

Mosley, Leonard. *The Last Days of the British Raj.* London: Weidenfeld & Nicolson, 1964.

Moynihan, John. *Restless Lives.* Bristol: Sansom, 2002.

Muggeridge, Malcolm. *Chronicles of Wasted Time*, vols. 1 and 2. London: Collins, 1972–73.

———. *Like It Was; The Diaries of Malcolm Muggeridge.* Selected and edited by John Bright-Holmes. London: Collins, 1981.

Mukerjee, Madhusree. *Churchill's Secret War: The British Empire and the Ravaging of India during World War II.* New York: Basic Books, 2010.

Muldoon, Andrew. *Empire, Politics and the Creation of the 1935 India Act: Last Act of the Raj.* London: Ashgate, 2013.

Mulgan, John, ed. *Poems of Freedom.* Introduction by W. H. Auden. London: Victor Gollancz, 1938.

Nehru, Jawaharlal. *The Discovery of India.* New York: John Day, 1946.

Newell, Clayton R. *Burma, 1942.* Washington, DC: US Government Printing Office, 1995.

Norgay, Tenzing, with James Ramsey Ullman. *Tiger of the Snows: The Autobiography of Tenzing of Everest*. New York: G. P. Putnam's Sons, 1955.

Orwell, George. *The Collected Essays, Journalism, and Letters of George Orwell*. 4 vols. New York: Harcourt Brace and World, 1968.

———. *Diaries*. Edited by Peter Davison. London: Penguin, 2010.

Overstreet, Gene D., and Marshall Windmiller. *Communism in India*. Berkeley: University of California Press, 1959.

Panter-Downes, Mollie. *London War Notes, 1939–1945*. New York: Farrar, Straus & Giroux, 1971.

Parker, Peter. *Isherwood: A Life*. New York: Random House, 2004.

Perrin, Jim. *Shipton and Tilman: The Great Decade of Himalayan Exploration*. London: Hutchinson, 2013.

Pery, Jenny. *The Affectionate Eye: The Life of Claude Rogers*. Bristol: Sansom, 1995.

Peterson, J. C. K. *Bengal District Gazetteers: Burdwan*. Calcutta: Bengal Secretariat Book Depot, 1910.

Phillips, William. *Ventures in Diplomacy*. Boston: Beacon Press, 1953.

Powys-Lybbe, Ursula. *The Eye of Intelligence*. London: W. Kimber, 1983.

Prashad, I. *The Life and Times of Maharaja Juddha Shumsher Jung Bahadur Rana of Nepal*. New Delhi: Ashish Publishing House, 1996.

Pugh, Martin. *Hurrah for the Blackshirts: Fascists and Fascism in Britain between the Wars*. London: Jonathan Cape, 2005.

Radhakrishna, B. P., ed. *J. B. Auden: A Centenary Tribute*. Bangalore: Geological Society of India, 2003.

Raghaven, Srinath. *India's War: The Making of Modern South Asia 1939–1945*. London: Allen Lane, 2016.

Rao, B. Shiva. *India's Freedom Movement: Some Notable Figures*. New Delhi: Orient Longman, 1972.

Ray, Renuka. *My Reminiscences: Social Development during the Gandhian Era and After*. New Delhi: Allied, 1982.

Roy, M. N. *India and War*. Lucknow: Radical Democratic Party, 1942.

———. *M. N. Roy's Memoirs*. Bombay: Allied Publishers, 1964.

Roy, Samaren. *In Freedom's Quest: A Study of the Life and Works of M. N. Roy*. Calcutta: Minerva Associates, 1998.

———. *M. N. Roy and Mahatma Gandhi*. Calcutta: Minerva Associates, 1987.

Roy, Tathagata, *My People Uprooted*. Kolkata: Ratna Prakashan, 2001.

Ruttledge, Hugh. *Everest, 1933*. London: Hodder & Stoughton, 1934.

———. *Everest: The Unfinished Adventure*. London: Hodder & Stoughton, 1937.

Sanyal, Hirankumar, ed. *Twenty Years of Parichay and Other Memories* [*Paricha-yer Kudi Bacchar o onyano smritichia*]. Calcutta: Papyrus, 1978.

Sarila, Narendra Singh. *The Shadow of the Great Game*. New Delhi: HarperCollins India, 2005.

Sarkar, Sumit. *The Swadeshi Movement in Bengal 1903–1908*. New Delhi: Peoples Publishing House, 1973.

Sarkar, Susobhan Chandra. *Essays in Honour of Professor S. C. Sarkar*. New Delhi: Peoples Publishing House, 1976.

Sarkisyanz, Manuel. *From Imperialism to Fascism: Why Hitler's "India" Was to Be Russia*. New Delhi: Deep & Deep, 2003.

Schuster, George. "The Deadlock in India." *Spectator*, May 15, 1941, 7.

——, and Guy Wint. *India and Democracy*. London: Macmillan, 1941.

Science, "Announcements." Vol. 81, no. 2106 (May 10, 1935): 443–70.

Scott, Michael. *A Time to Speak*. Garden City, NY: Doubleday, 1958.

Sebald, W. G. *On the Natural History of Destruction*. New York: Random House, 2003.

Sharma, Man Mohan. *Through the Valley of Gods: Travels in the Central Himalayas*. New Delhi: Vision Books, 1978.

Shils, Edward. *The Culture of the Indian Intellectual*. Chicago: University of Chicago, Committee on South Asian Studies, 1959.

Shipton, Eric. "Michael Spender." Obituary. *Geographical Journal* 106, no. 5/6 (1945): 238–39.

—— with H. W. Tilman, Michael Spender, and J. B. Auden. "The Shaksgam Expedition." *Geographical Journal* 91, no. 4 (1938): 313–39.

——. *The Six Mountain Travel Books: Nanda Devi, Blank on the Map, Upon That Mountain, Mountains of Tartary, Mount Everest Reconnaissance Expedition 1951, Land of Tempest*. With an introduction by Jim Perrin. Seattle: The Mountaineers, 1985.

——. *That Untravelled World: An Autobiography*. New York: Scribner, 1969.

——, and R. Scott Russell. "Karakoram, 1939." *Geographical Journal* 95, no. 6 (1940): 409–24.

Singh, Kushwant. *Sahibs Who Loved India*. New Delhi: Viking, 2008.

Snow, Edgar. *People on Our Side*. New York: Random House, 1944.

Spender, Harold. *The Fire of Life: A Book of Memories*. Foreword by F. S. Marvin. London: Hodder & Stoughton, 1926.

Spender, J. A. *The Changing East*. London: Cassell, 1926.

——. *The Indian Scene*. London: Methuen, 1912.

Spender, Michael. "The Elusive Element." *Spectator*, June 19, 1938, 30.

——. "The Gentle Savage." *Spectator*, October 14, 1938, 30.

——. "Guns and Carbohydrates." *Spectator*, April 9, 1937, 657–58.

——. "Mount Everest, 1938." *Spectator*, March 11, 1938, 9.

———. "New Maps for Britain." *Spectator*, November 18, 1938, 11.

———. "The New Photographic Survey of Switzerland." *Geographical Journal* 79, no. 5 (1932): 383–97.

———. "The Photo-Surveyed Maps of the Mount Everest Region and Nyonno Ri." *Himalayan Journal* 11 (1939): 176–79.

———. "Tibetan Tent." *Spectator*, October 16, 1936, 9.

Spender, Philip. *Nancy Sharp (Nancy Spender) 1909–2001: Paintings and Works on Paper*. London: The Gallery, 2002. Exhibition catalog.

Spender, Stephen. *The Backward Son*. London: Hogarth Press, 1940.

———. *Citizens in War, and After*. Foreword by Herbert Morrison. Photography by John Hinde. London: G. G. Harrap, 1945.

———. *Forward from Liberalism*. London: Victor Gollancz, 1937.

———. "Letter to a Colleague in America." *New Statesman and Nation*, November 16, 1940, 490.

———. *World within World*. New York: St. Martin's Press, 1994.

———, ed. *W. H. Auden: A Tribute*. London: Weidenfeld & Nicholson, 1975.

Spurling, Hilary. *The Girl from the Fiction Department: A Portrait of Sonia Orwell*. London: Hamish Hamilton, 2002.

Stallworthy, Jon. *Louis MacNeice*. New York: Norton, 1995.

Steevens, G. W. *In India*. New York: Dodd, Mead, 1899.

Stern, Jacques. *The Hidden Damage*. New York: Harcourt Brace, 1947.

Suraiya, Jug. *Rickshaw Ragtime: Calcutta Remembered*. New York: Penguin Books, 1993.

Sutherland, John. *Stephen Spender: The Authorized Biography*. New York: Penguin Books, 2004.

Tagore, Rabindranath. *Selected Letters of Rabindranath Tagore*. Edited by Andrew Robinson and Krishna Datta. Cambridge: Cambridge University Press, 1997.

Talbot, Philips. *An American Witness to India's Partition*. Foreword by B. R. Nanda. New Delhi: Sage, 2007.

Tharoor, Shashi. *An Era of Darkness: The British Empire in India*. New Delhi: Aleph, 2016.

Tilman, H. W. "The Himalayan Club Dinner." *Himalayan Journal* 11 (1939): 176–79.

———. *When Men and Mountains Meet*. Cambridge: Cambridge University Press, 1946.

Unsworth, Walt. *Everest: The Mountaineering History*. 3rd ed. Seattle: Mountaineers, 2000.

Valdiya, K. S. *The Making of India: Geodynamic Evolution*. Chennai: Springer, 2015.

Venkataramani, M. S. *Bengal Famine of 1943: The American Response*. Delhi: Vikas, 1973.

Voigt, Johannes H. *India in the Second World War*. New Delhi: Arnold-Heinemann, 1987.

Wager, L. R. "Mount Everest's Weather in 1933." *Himalayan Journal* 6 (1934).

Warren, Charles. "Eric Shipton." Obituary. *Alpine Journal* 83, no. 327 (1978).

Wavell, Archibald Perceval. *Wavell: The Viceroy's Journal*. Edited by Penderel Moon. London: Oxford University Press, 1973.

Weigold, Auriol. *Churchill, Roosevelt and India: Propaganda during WWII*. New York: Routledge, 2008.

West, W. J., ed. *Orwell: The War Broadcasts*. London: Duckworth BBC, 1985.

Yates, Anne, and Lewis Chester. *The Troublemaker: Michael Scott and His Lonely Struggle against Injustice*. London: Aurum Press, 2006.

Younghusband, Francis. "The Problem of the Shaksgam Valley." *Geographical Journal* 68, no. 3 (1926): 225–30.

Science, "Announcements." Vol. 81, no. 2106 (May 10, 1935): 443–70.

Websites

Biographical Memoirs of Fellows of the Royal Society
rsbm.royalsocietypublishing.org/content/13/358

Female Poets of the First World War
http://femalewarpoets.blogspot.com/2014/04/violet-spender-one-of-her-poems.html

Marcela de Paiva Abreu, "India as Creditor: Sterling Balances"
http://nehrumemorial.nic.in/en/news/368-india-as-a-creditor-sterling-balances-1940-1956-22nd-january-2015.html

Independence Day Resolution passed by the Indian National Congress in 1930
www.nationalarchives.gov.uk/education/empire/transcript/g3cs3s2t.htm

Legacy of Midnapore: Freedom Movements at Contai
www.midnapore.in/town_contai_freedom.html

Indian Parliament: Constituent Debates (Proceedings)
http://parliamentofindia.nic.in/ls/debates/vol5p1.htm

Wings over Everest
www.youtube.com/results?search_query=wings+over+everest

Tilman's Everest Southside Reconnaissance, by Mark Horrell
www.markhorrell.com/blog/2015/tilmans-everest-south-side-reconnaissance

INDEX

DEBORAH BAKER is the author of *Making a Farm*; *In Extremis*, which was shortlisted for the Pulitzer Prize for Biography; *A Blue Hand*; and *The Convert*, which was a finalist for the National Book Award. She lives in India and New York.

The text of *The Last Englishmen* is set in Kepler Std. Kepler is a Modern serif designed by Robert Slimbach. Kepler is named after German astronomer Johannes Kepler and was inspired by classic Modern eighteenth-century typefaces. Book design by Ann Sudmeier. Composition by Bookmobile Design & Digital Publisher Services, Minneapolis, Minnesota. Manufactured by Friesens on acid-free, 100 percent postconsumer wastepaper.